Wealth Management

Wealth Management

**Private Banking, Investment Decisions
and Structured Financial Products**

Dimitris N. Chorafas

AMSTERDAM • BOSTON • HEIDELBERG • LONDON
NEW YORK • OXFORD • PARIS • SAN DIEGO
SAN FRANCISCO • SINGAPORE • SYDNEY • TOKYO

Butterworth-Heinemann is an imprint of Elsevier

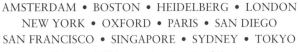

Butterworth-Heinemann is an imprint of Elsevier
Linacre House, Jordan Hill, Oxford OX2 8DP, UK
30 Corporate Drive, Suite 400, Burlington, MA 01803, USA

First edition 2006
Reprinted 2007 (twice)

Notice
No responsibility is assumed by the publisher for any injury and/or damage to persons
or property as a matter of products liability, negligence or otherwise, or from any use
or operation of any methods, products, instructions or ideas contained in the material
herein. Because of rapid advances in the medical sciences, in particular, independent
verification of diagnoses and drug dosages should be made

British Library Cataloguing in Publication Data
A catalogue record for this book is available from the British Library

Library of Congress Cataloging-in-Publication Data
A catalog record for this book is available from the Library of Congress

ISBN: 978-0-7506-6855-2

For information on all Butterworth-Heinemann publications
visit our website at books.elsevier.com

Printed and bound in *Great Britain*

07 08 09 10 10 9 8 7 6 5 4 3

Working together to grow
libraries in developing countries

www.elsevier.com | www.bookaid.org | www.sabre.org

ELSEVIER   BOOK AID
International   Sabre Foundation

Contents

Preface

An investment is a voyage with a purpose, and therefore investors must navigate in charted waters. Whether a person or a legal entity, an investor who starts nowhere generally gets there. Few people truly appreciate that wealth management is a process that never succeeds if it has not been calculated and planned in advance.

What's more, while the management of wealth seems to be a process simple enough in its conception, in the general case this is not true. In addition, even if a certain investment seems to be rather simple, chances are that it will be fairly complicated in its execution and in its monitoring, particularly when:

- The market is nervous,
- Volatility is rather high, and
- The investor cannot see clearly the aftermath of his or her moves and commitments.

Just as an airline pilot readies himself to act with cool precision in an emergency, by continually posing to himself problems that could arise at any moment, the investor should get ready for different market scenarios, including panic. He or she can do so by examining several alternative courses of action even if one knows in advance that they have a low probability of materializing. A thorough examination of alternative plans and market scenarios helps in:

- Seeing more clearly, and
- Getting ready to act.

Plans made for wealth management must be factual and documented, which is not always the case. Because of wanting analysis, many investment plans are substandard, distinguished for nothing else than their confusion. 'Everything that can be thought at all, can be thought clearly. Everything that can be said, can be said clearly', said Dr Ludwig Wittgenstein. This is precisely the attitude that should characterize the investor.

Addressed to private investors, a growing breed, as well as institutional investors, this book has two themes: *Private banking* and investment decisions regarding *Structured financial products*. In meeting this second goal, the text examines in a rigorous way whether structured financial products are advisable investments for retail and institutional investors and, if yes, which risks they entail.

The link between private banking and structured products is strong because, since the early twenty-first century, banks have offered a whole array of structured financial instruments to clients whose wealth they manage,. Then, time and again, they come back to their clients with new structured products that involve many unknowns.

During the past few years, private bankers have made plenty of effort to convince investors that their portfolio should feature a whole array of structured products, up to 5, 10 or 20 per cent of its worth. There is nothing rational about this and, in fact, the exact percentage depends on the bank's strategy. The large majority of these clients do not know enough about derivative instruments to evaluate risk and return. The present book provides such knowledge, and that is why it is so important to put in the same cover:

- Structured products, and
- Private banking.

The chapters pertaining to *Private Banking* have been written mainly, but not exclusively, for high net worth individuals and people on their way to becoming financially independent. In the background lies the fact that the wealth characteristics of our society are changing. Just after World War II the Probate Court Records in New York showed that 85 per cent of people left nothing at all after death; and only 3.3 per cent left over $40 000.

Happily we are no longer there. Astute individuals realize that on a rainy day they can depend only on themselves and, therefore, they have to be wealth managers. This is a fast growing population. In June 2005, the Merrill Lynch/Cap Gemini world wealth report said that 8.3 million people around the globe have more than $1 million each.

On the institutional side, the typical audience of this book comprises practitioners and professionals, from treasurers to operations executives, investment officers, risk management officers and their staff, as well as auditors and financial analysts. On the retail side, the readership is the educated person in the street, who has become an investor and cares about his or her nest-egg.

Other populations of readership include investment consultancies, accountancies, auditing firms, independent rating agencies and, evidently, central bankers, as well as college and university students. The text has been designed to lead the reader through ways and means permitting them to capitalize from experience that has been so far acquired in:

- Institutional investment projects, and
- Individual investment practices.

As our society becomes increasingly affluent, and state-supported pension and health-care schemes find it difficult to survive, a growing number of individuals and families have become retail or private investors. In so doing, they are looking for ways and means to optimize the management of their wealth. Private banking and asset management or the main issues addressed by Parts 1 and 2.

The approach that has been chosen deliberately confronts both institutional investor and private investor requirements. This has been done for three reasons. First, in many cases, it is difficult to state the difference between an institutional investor and a high net worth individual, because the latter sets up a company to manage his or her wealth.

Second, all organizations are made of people. The institutional investors, who are pension funds, mutual funds and insurance companies, have very similar wealth management goals to those of private individuals. What both populations are after is to safeguard their capital and gain a decent return, or a much larger return by assuming, unwisely but quite often, an inordinate amount of risk.

The third reason for the synergy existing between the aforementioned two populations is that both institutional and retail investors are being offered structured financial products by the banks managing their account. Typically, these are securities that provide them with a redemption amount, featuring either full or partial capital protection and some sort of usually unsecured return. Parts 3 and 4 address structured financial products,

- Their polyvalent nature, and
- Risk and return that could be expected from them.

Return on structured instruments, which are essentially derivatives, is paid in function of a specific investment strategy on selected underlying asset(s). This practically means that a great deal depends on the performance of underlyings. There is no assurance that expected performance will be obtained. This is one of the risks.

Down to basics, with all structured products, risk and return to be expected from structured products are related to the volatility of future value of an underlying, therefore of an a priori investment or trade. Results are based a great deal on market changes, largely conditioned by the unpredictability of future events. The keywords are:

- Volatility
- Uncertainty
- Exposure.

There are many reasons behind these three keywords and the forces propelling them; for instance, general and specific leverage. Both general market leverage and the specific gearing of the structured product magnify the risk(s) confronting the investor. Other reasons are market psychology and possible market illiquidity. Both can lead to conditions of growing exposure. Moreover, all financial instruments have embedded in them the credit risk of their issuer.

Because this book has been written for investors and not for speculators, another deliberate decision has been to focus on the more common structured instruments sold as packaged products. In this sense, the more basic characteristics of credit default swaps, collateralized debt obligations, credit-linked notes and mortgage-backed securities have not been included in this text. They will be the subject of another volume.

Examples of structured instruments that are covered are interest rate notes, such as step-ups and products following different interest rate scenarios, and equity-type structured instruments linked to a basket of stocks or an equity index. The latter offer exposure to equity markets, and usually feature different maturities, currencies and participation levels.

Still other case studies focus on foreign exchange structured products, which often come in currency pairs and are usually characterized by a strategy that can act on both the downside and upside of an underlying. Structured notes in connection to commodities such as currencies, equities and debt are conceived to generate opportunistic returns according to prevailing macroeconomic or other conditions.

Some banks offer their clients structured products linked to selected hedge funds, which typically feature highly risky mechanisms in order to yield theoretically attractive returns of the underlying funds. With the exception of the occasional reference, hedge funds and funds of funds are not part of this text.

Instead of spreading itself too thin on the myriad of market players, the book pays significant attention to risk management and damage control. Every type of investment is subject to market forces, and the more leveraged a portfolio, the greater the risk assumed in expectation of reward. The fact that structured financial products appeal, or at least are being marketed, to both retail investors and institutional investors, calls for a dual approach to risk control.

In a nutshell, the best advice that can be given to individual investors, personal bankers and institutional assets managers on risk control is the way in which Andrew Carnegie, the great Scottish American industrialist, instructed the directors of his factories: 'You have only to rise to the occasion, but no half-way measures. If you are not going to cross the stream, do not enter at all and be content to dwindle into second place.'[1]

In conclusion, the key elements of both institutional and private investments are linked to the role of the banking industry in our modern economic and social fabric. Investing for the future is a necessary precondition for better living, as well as for many other activities that could not take place without the availability of capital in the name of private individuals.

At a fundamental level, investing is a peculiar business where the saver pays, often during many years and well in advance of a potential event, for the coverage of later years in his or her life. This coverage may then help him to bear the consequences of adversity. In this sense, investing is an insurance and a trust requiring good governance.

If the trust is shattered even by a small group of individuals or entities in the investment business, and regardless of whether these individuals violated express company policy or not, such breach of confidence has repercussions for the banking industry as a whole, as well as for its clients. This is why wealth management should be treated boldly as a whole, going to the root of problems and setting it upon sound foundations.

My thanks go to a long list of knowledgeable people and their organizations, who contributed to the research that led to this text. Without their contributions this book would not have been possible. I am also indebted to several senior executives of financial institutions and securities experts for constructive criticism during the preparation of the manuscript.

Let me take this opportunity to thank Karen Maloney for suggesting this project, Fran Ford for her hand-holding, Melissa Read for seeing it all the way to publication, Charlotte Pover and Anne Powell for the editorial work, and Eva-Maria Binder for compiling the research results, typing the text, and preparing the camera-ready artwork and index.

Valmer and Vitznau   *Dimitris N. Chorafas*
                                                                                                  May 2005

Note

1 P. Krass, *Carnegie*, Wiley, New York, 2002.

Part 1
Private banking

1 Private banking defined

1.1 Introduction

Switzerland's strength has traditionally been, and remains, in private banking. This is a business greatly enhanced by globalization. In today's world, there are sixty to seventy countries whose citizens have surplus money and want to invest in a safer place than their own, while there are six or seven centres with expertise in *wealth management*, and with the necessary infrastructure. Swiss banks lead in the lucrative business of private banking, but they are followed closely by challengers.

Private banking is an assets gathering and managing business, which has helped many credit institutions to turn in their best performance year after year. Switzerland's UBS, for example, controls the world's biggest private bank, and its profitability has been consistently helped by good results from its private banking unit, a reward for the attention that it brings to its private clients. Investors are the people who today constitute the new global *ownership society*.

As this and subsequent chapters demonstrate, closely connected to the private banking business are an entity's asset management operations addressed to institutional investors, which can bring to the bank's treasury a stream of net new money. Up to a point, private banking and asset management for institutional investors tend to merge. As briefly stated in the Preface, this happens for three reasons:

- The more clear-eyed high net worth individuals set up a company and manage their investment through that firm, which may outsource some or all of its asset management duties (see Chapter 7).
- As investors, organizations and private people have fairly similar goals, the most important being protecting their capital and earning good interest (see section 1.8).
- Banks and other institutions have acquired the habit of offering fairly similar instruments to both institutional and private investors, an example being structured products (see Chapters 9 and 10).

Today, an overriding issue for private investors is that restructuring of the social security net is raising two problems: an urgency in taking one's own future in one's own hands, and the need to understand fully the mechanics of wealth management. Private investing will partly complement and partly overlap with the now classical social security system and existing pension fund entities. The latter are institutional investors.

To appreciate the torrent of funds that may run along the private investing frame of reference, it is wise to recall that in just one country, the USA, the social security system receives $500 billion a year in employees' payroll contributions. With partial privatization of social security, a good chunk of this cash flow, probably one-third of it, will be turned into private accounts.

A different way of looking into this subject is that individuals who contribute to the new and the old pension structures want to see them survive in a way such that they will be able to take good care of them. To survive and grow, social security, institutional investment business and private banking require able management that extends its expertise:

- From efficient customer handholding,
- To the preservation of assets in which investments are made, and their profitability.

In private banking, handholding is often custom-made for the clientele to which it appeals. Its upper end is for high net worth individuals, not for the merely comfortably off. Today in the USA, for instance, the richest 1 per cent of the population owns 41 per cent of the country's wealth, which people invest, to a significant extent, through asset managers.[1] In Europe, on average, the richest 1 per cent of the population owns about 35 per cent of their country's wealth.

As far as investment skills and the customer contact are concerned, some private banks are better equipped than others. What's more, success breeds success. Switzerland is a good example because it knows how to attract a huge share of international wealth. According to some estimates, Swiss banks look after about one-third of all private financial assets invested across borders, much more than any other banks anywhere. This:

- Contributes about one-third of Switzerland's consistently large current account surplus, and
- Generates significant tax revenues, which help to keep down taxation elsewhere in the economy.

Successful private banking operations need to understand the goals and needs of affluent investors, and they are judged by their ability to meet those needs within the framework of a financial advisor relationship. This requires that the bank is distinguished by its personal approach to client relationships, placing the financial advisor at the forefront of its interactions with clientele. Equally vital is a commitment to, and understanding of, the benefits for personal banking clients of a truly open selection and management of the best financial products available in the market.

1.2 Private banking clients

There is a French saying: 'L'argent n'a pas de sexe, mais cela ne doit pas l'empecher de se reproduire.' (Money has no sex, but this should not inhibit its reproduction.) That's exactly what private banking and asset management at large are all about: Money's reproduction through the four phases of the economic cycle shown in Figure 1.1.

Part of the wealth effect of the early years of the twenty-first century has been created by what is known as the *global saving glut*, created largely by emerging economies. In 1996, the developing world was a net borrower, running a joint

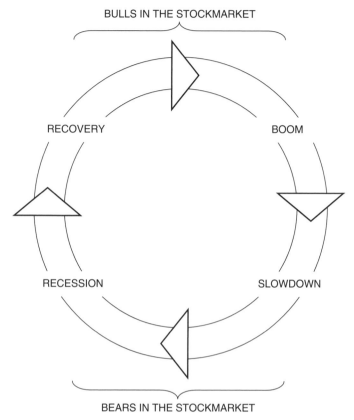

Figure 1.1 The four phases of the economic cycle to which all
investors are exposed

current account deficit of over $87 billion. After a string of financial crises,
developing countries became a big net lender, running a surplus of $205 billion
by 2003.[2]

This glut of saving, economists point out, is either invested or offset by a dearth
elsewhere. Down to the bottom line, this means that the developing world's determination to live well within its means has enabled other countries to live well beyond
their own. The USA, with its huge current account deficits, is one example. Japan and
most European countries are other cases in point.

Money that has been saved must be invested, in a more profitable way than
through a low-interest-bearing bank account. Whether the investor's goals are short
or long term, successful wealth management depends both on know-how and on
timely and accurate information that affects the portfolio's performance. Investing in
equities, bonds, precious metals, other commodities or derivative financial instruments
can be successful only if executed with:

■ Precision, and
■ Professional skill.

A successful wealth management organization is able to provide its clients with quick access to all of the world's financial markets, supplying them with the same kind of information available to its own specialists. Much of this information is supplied by the bank's financial analysts working in a global research network. Indeed, in today's financial arena private banking's *global network*, and strong commitment to *research and analysis*, are at the foundations of its expertise in professional asset management.

■ If these two factors are wanting,
■ Then the service private banks offer their clients will be substandard.

A full-service private banking operation will support not only first class investment advice and day-to-day wealth management, but also facilities for money market transactions, foreign currency trading and other activities that private clients want and need. The private banker must be able to assist his or her customers in all aspects of the investment business:

■ Helping to safeguard assets through secure investments, and
■ Advising on how to acquire and build up greater wealth.

Private bankers must also assure their clients, through practical evidence, that all investment-related areas are properly covered. One way of doing so is by making available in-house professional advice on tax and legal matters, as well as on issues associated to settling an estate, establishing a foundation or trust, making inheritance provisions, and so on.

Expert advice along the aforementioned frame of reference is one of the reasons why private banking is a business appealing to high net worth individuals. Although the threshold characterizing 'higher net worth' changes over time, in 2005 such individuals are generally considered to be people with more than US $1 million in assets that can be invested. This threshold is raised over time:

■ Partly because of inflation, and
■ Mainly because rapid economic expansion continues creating wealth.

The dual impact of greater wealth and of worry about having enough means for comfortable retirement ensures that plenty of money comes into the orbit of professional fund managers. Moreover, as the better-off people diversify from real estate property and gold into bonds, equities, and maybe alternative investments offered by banks and hedge funds,[3] the range of investment possibilities increases.

Because a person with a positive cash flow, for which he or she must look for a secure and rewarding home, is in all likelihood a professional or manager, he or she demands high standards with regard to personal investment advisory and wealth management services; average will not do. Affluent, self-made people know and appreciate the value of money. Therefore, they desire comprehensive financial advice as well as a significant amount of documentation. They also expect specially tailored financial solutions, including the bank's ability to address in an able manner questions regarding:

■ Investments,
■ Financing,

- Taxes,
- Pensions, and
- Inheritance law.

As far as his or her own responsibilities in wealth management are concerned, the modern investor should ask himself or herself the question: 'When was the last time I took a closer look at my securities account?' The success of any account depends primarily on its structure. Private bankers may be pleased to assist their client in checking the structure of his securities account to see whether it still suits personal investment goals. This, however, does not mean that the client should abdicate his or her responsibilities.

Part and parcel of an individual investor's responsibilities is the decision about what to do with money, beyond the immediate goal of a more comfortable life. In a memo to himself, Andrew Carnegie wrote: 'The amassing of wealth is one of the worst species of idolatry. To continue much longer overwhelmed by business cares and with most of my thoughts wholly upon the way to make more money in the shortest time, must degrade me beyond hope of permanent recovery.'

1.3 Organizational challenges in private banking

Even the best intentions by a private banking entity will not be able to deliver without the appropriate organization and a first class staff. Organization-wise, there are three fundamental issues involved in the assignment of activities related to investment counselling and asset management. In a nutshell, these are:

- The need to recognize each advisory function,
- The process of combining functions, to provide a well-rounded service, and
- The required principles of association, to ensure that the asset management organization is able to deliver.

In a structural sense, the bank must be able to incorporate the consulting process with that of trading and of fiduciary duties, into a single, comprehensive service. This service should include access to hundreds of instruments, including funds managed by some of the world's leading investment companies. The client must be guided through a personal evaluation of investment needs (see Chapter 2) to determine the desired:

- Risk profile, and
- Investment mix.

In terms of able management, the things that come first are objectives be realized and activities necessary for facilitating their achievement. Concomitant to this is the ability of the organization to endure by keeping step with:

- Customer demands,
- Market trends,
- Social goals,
- Technological developments,
- Economic and political changes.

Other organizational qualities of a private banking enterprise include flexibility, innovation, global presence and leadership in financial information. The latter can be obtained through a worldwide network tapping the best services and products of the world's most serious financial institutions, and fashioning them into solutions that fit the clients' distinctive goals.

Following its 2001 acquisition of PaineWebber in the USA, the Private Clients unit of UBS became the fourth largest private client business in America, with an affluent client base representing $254 billion in invested assets. This business unit employed 8870 financial advisors providing a full range of wealth management services to some 2.5 million affluent households, including:

- Financial planning and asset management consulting,
- Transaction-based services, such as securities brokerage,
- Asset-based and advisory services, such as discretionary portfolio management, money market accounts, loans and fiduciary services.

These activities covered a range of products available to private clients, including purchase and sale of securities, option contracts, commodity and financial futures, fixed income instruments, mutual funds, trusts, wrap-fee products, alternative investments and selected insurance services. In this and many other cases, client support has been backed up by on-line capabilities providing information and analysis to each client, about:

- His/her account(s),
- The markets and stocks they may want to invest in, and
- A range of trading, bill payment and other transactional tools.

It should, however, be appreciated that the search for excellence by private bankers has its cost. It needs no explaining that major investments are necessary for providing the infrastructure needed for effective tailormade private banking services. This activity is expensive and labour intensive in terms of advisory and management skills, but when it is done properly it allows a sound return (see Chapter 3).

The competition in the personal banking market is so tough that second rate outfits will sink and disappear. Credit institutions, investment banks, brokers, asset managers and other financial organizations targeting private banking should appreciate that, to a fairly substantial extent, private clients are discriminating individuals, and rightly so. Their professional instincts tell them that they should choose their bank with care.

- They expect personal service from first rate advisors, and
- They demand complete solutions that answer all their wealth-related needs.

In their effort to protect and build up their assets, a fairly significant number of affluent individuals, particularly in Western countries, want to have round-the-clock access to markets and instruments. They also look for clarity in the flood of available information. Yet, sometimes, they fall with a *trend*, as attested by the fact that roughly half the money that is managed by hedge funds comes from high net worth people. One of the reasons is that in the first years of the twenty-first century:

■ The stock market has been in the doldrums,
■ Interest rates are the lowest in nearly fifty years,
■ But inflation is always present, even though it has kept a relatively low (but steady) profile, as shown in Figure 1.2.

For financial institutions who know how to manage private banking activities, this product line represents a lucrative business because of fees and commissions. Through a constant organizational effort, these institutions strive to provide sophisticated banking services concentrating on:

■ New financial products, and
■ Knowledgeable investment advisors.

As underlined in section 1.2, high net worth individuals want to deal with learned private bankers, able to collaborate with them in developing tailored financial strategies that are actively reviewed and re-evaluated to comply with the client's risk appetite. Private banking advisors must be on call, and should exhibit comprehensive knowledge of investment matters, including domestic and foreign products. This requires as interfaces relationship managers who are dependable, highly educated, easy to work with, sensitive to clients' needs, readily accessible, highly competent, and aware of the need for secrecy and security.

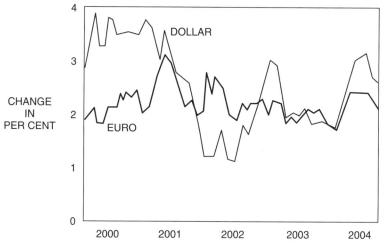

Figure 1.2 Percentage changes in inflation rate for the US dollar and euro
(2000–2004)

1.4   Security and secrecy requirements

Beyond the organizational factors mentioned in section 1.3 as poles of attraction for high net worth individuals, comes *safety* of the money entrusted for management, and *secrecy* related to all matters concerning the client's account and his or her business with the bank. This is the theme of the present section.

In respect to safety of capital, in America, private accounts can be protected up to $150 million per customer. This sum incorporates up to $1 million for cash. The first $500 000 of protection, including up to $100 000 for cash, is provided by the Securities Investor Protection Corporation (SIPC). For customers who have reached the full SIPC limits, several asset managers provide further protection up to $149.5 million, including up to $900 000 cash, through an insurance policy to which they subscribe, subject to an aggregate limit of $600 million.

Notice, however, that this coverage targets credit risk related to the asset manager as an entity; it does not address market risk. Hence, it does not protect against loss of market value of securities in the investor's portfolio.

Cash held in bank deposits is insured by the Federal Deposit Insurance Corporation (FDIC), subject to FDIC limits. Regulatory safeguards mandated by the Securities and Exchange Commission's (SEC) Customer Protection Rule, combined with employment of safe securities holding practices by the credit institution, investment bank or assets manager, the protection of SIPC and appropriate insurance, tend to assure the investor that his or her private banking customer's assets are safe, at least to a reasonable extent.

Such a comprehensive safety net is not available in all jurisdictions. In Europe, the limits mandated by deposit insurance are much lower and they vary from one country to the next, although the dozen European Union (EU) countries that have adopted the euro have a common upper limit of €20 000 ($26 000 under the current exchange rate). This is way below the limit in the USA.

Regarding account secrecy, private banking clients want the protection benefiting their personal privacy to be extended to their financial privacy. For this reason, banks are fundamentally obliged not to pass on client information to unauthorized third parties, although recent international accords targeting whitewashing of money and financing of terrorist activities, as well as laws resulting from them, tend to move in the opposite direction.

High-technology crime and identity theft are other risks. In March 2005 a high-tech crime ring tried to steal £220 million ($400 million) from the London offices of Sumitomo, the Japanese banking group. This was one of the most audacious attempts in the City of London.

Lower profile but higher frequency security breaches concern identity theft. Banks and information brokers have the responsibility of protecting the financial data of individuals, but sometimes this work is sloppy. According to the Federal Trade Commission (FTC),

- In 2004 there were 246 570 US complaints of identity theft, against 1380 in 1999, and
- In 2003 the FTC estimated that annual losses from such fraud stood at about $47.6 billion.[4]

Bank client secrecy, as well as protection from high-tech and other types of fraud, have the purpose of assuring the respect of the rights of individuals to have their banking records kept secret within legal and contractual margins. In Switzerland, for example, bank client secrecy is based on Article 47 of the Federal Law on Banks and Savings Banks (BankG), whereby all members of a bank's governing bodies, employees and representatives are obligated to keep client information secret. This professional duty of confidentiality also continues after bank personnel leave the credit institution.

With the exception of cash flows financing terrorism or whitewashing money, bank client secrecy should apply to all information elements arising from business relationships between banks and their customers. In principle, subject to the aforementioned exceptions, business relationships must be kept confidential in terms of:

- Their exact nature,
- Transactions being performed, and
- Data about clients' financial and personal situation.

Moreover, it is not permissible for banks to respond to negatively formulated queries; for example, confirming that a certain person does not have any connection to a particular bank. Bank client secrecy also applies to former business relationships, even if they no longer exist at the time of asking. In addition, under Swiss law, customers who merely enter negotiations with a bank are protected, even if there is no contractual agreement.

In Switzerland, one consequence of breaching bank client secrecy regulations is prosecution under Article 47 BankG. This provision penalizes the violation of bank client secrecy as well as solicitation to breach confidentiality regulations. In case of (criminal) intent, the penalty is imprisonment for up to six months or a fine of up to CHF 50 000 ($40 000). In case of simple negligence, the penalty is up to CHF 30 000.

There are limits to bank client secrecy, as this process cannot be unconditional. One of the limits is consent of clients. For instance, the client can authorize his or her bank to disclose information as a general rule or in special cases. Another, more important limit, is criminal proceedings.

Further on in this case study of Swiss bank secrecy laws, where required by the courts in conjunction with criminal proceedings, such as the case of tax fraud, banks are obligated to disclose the necessary information about their clients. In the case of prosecution abroad, under certain circumstances banks are obligated to co-operate in matters of legal assistance.

It is interesting to note, however, that in Switzerland misdemeanour tax evasion is not an indictable offence. Tax evasion is considered fraudulent when documents are falsified, as in the case of double bookkeeping, unreliable annual reports or other records, with the intention of deceiving the tax authorities and the public. Tax fraud also includes wilful deception by means of special manoeuvrings or fabrications. Bank client secrecy may as well be lifted in cases of international tax fraud.

Civil law proceedings is another example where rules regarding secrecy can be breached. Bank secrecy must be lifted if required by the courts. A specific case is that of legal heirs and executors who, under provision of a court order, can claim information about deceased persons from the bank(s) concerned (see also Chapter 8 on legal risk).

1.5   A private banking roadmap

At the service provider's side, private banking is not a market that a bank can attack without a roadmap. The ownership society has prerequisites. Once the institution has clearly stated its private banking objectives and management set the guidelines of a business plan, a factual and documented study is necessary to decide whether:

- It should be executed *as is*, or
- It is necessary to revamp it, integrating it with other service channels.

For a credit institution, the infrastructure for private banking is an investment requiring a sound business plan. This plan should be factual and documented, but also complete and detailed, taking into account both past performance and projected improvements, including their reasons, likelihood and timing. Most importantly, any valid private banking plan must be capable of being executed, which poses significant requirements on the institution's:

- Financial resources,
- Human capital, and
- Technological infrastructure.

The reason for paying attention to the institution's financial resources is that a successful private banking product line requires significant investments. Not all banks can afford them, particularly when they are experiencing a loss of intermediation that has in its background several reasons, the top three being that:

- Globalization has created a huge capital market,
- Institutional investors have taken control of money flows, and
- At about 200 basis points (bp), banking costs for lending are four times higher than the capital market's.

In the post-World War II years, intermediation was a credit institution's bread and butter business. However, since the late 1980s, the loss of intermediation in deposits and loans has meant that net interest income for banks is declining, as Figure 1.3 demonstrates. To compensate, commercial banks became increasingly involved in:

- Trading, particularly in derivative financial instruments,
- Personal banking and the management of assets.

Other reasons for loss of intermediation is that, with globalization, banks do not know their clients as well as they used to. This means depending more and more on credit risk rating by independent agencies. Such credit ratings are also available to the capital market, which is a tough competitor to the banking industry.

As a product line, private banking is evidence that strategic priorities change over time. In past years, large market segments in order of importance to the banking

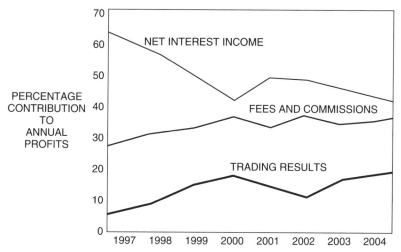

Figure 1.3 General trend lines in the three main income channels of internationally active European banks, over eight years

industry have been corporate, institutional and retail. Within this framework, corporate and institutional banking activities have opposite aims regarding the goals they are after:

■ Corporate clients search for competitively priced funding, and
■ Institutional investors look for best value.

The behaviour of personal banking clients integrates both patterns, and it is influenced by a combination of shifting demographics, changes in returns in equities and bonds, and technological advances allowing on-line deals. This produces a much larger investing universe but, as explained in section 1.2, leadership in private banking also poses significant requirements.

The processes characterizing a bank's most profitable product lines have gone through plenty of innovation and restructuring. Take Swiss banks as an example of evolution in the personal banking roadmap. As an article in the *Economist* put it, historically, Swiss banking's success was based on a few simple principles:

■ No turmoil,
■ No talk, and
■ No taxes.[5]

In terms of the first ingredient, which is to a large extent political, Switzerland remains a very stable country. But no talk and no taxes are no longer guaranteed. Banking secrecy has been bent, because of international (read US) pressures connected to tracking money from terrorists, organized crime and hideaways by autocratic, repressive governments.

Moreover, neutral Switzerland is no longer a safe tax haven. Not only as a concession to the EU, but also as its neighbours have instituted a policy for tax amnesties, the Swiss government is considering imposing a withholding tax at source on interest, as the price for keeping confidential the identities of EU citizens depositing their wealth in Swiss banks.

Under this policy, tax-dodging citizens who bring home money that had been salted away abroad are not prosecuted. Italian amnesties resulted in some €50 billion ($65 billion) owned by Italian high net worth individuals, who classically brought their money to Switzerland, being returned to Italy. This is not good news for small and medium-size Swiss private banks. While UBS and Crédit Suisse, Switzerland's largest and second largest bank, have deep enough pockets to finance international expansion, this is difficult for the smaller private banks, which:

- Are typically partnerships, and
- Lack the capital to fund a rapid expansion.

A two-speed private banking roadmap has an evident impact on some of the banks' profitability, all the way to credit rating. A recent financial analysis newsletter stated that Moody's downgraded a known credit institution to Aa2, from Aa1, reflecting the challenges that it is facing in its private banking business.

Another challenge confronting credit institutions that want to strengthen their private banking presence is that today's rich are more demanding than the monied of old, who were more interested in preserving wealth than in boosting it. To respond to their customers' new drive, banks must provide a broader range of sophisticated investments. One of the better known global banks offers wealthy clients advice on the art market.

As these examples demonstrate, there is a great deal behind the statement that to be competitive, and attract high net worth individuals, a private banking organization should offer comprehensive wealth management services. These must not only be centred on investment advice, but also expand both geographically and in terms of investment domains. High technology is a contributor, but it is no substitute for commitment to:

- Long-term personal relationships, and
- Provision of a full range of products and services, specifically designed for 'this' and 'that' target audience.

Successful personal banking entities use high technology not only to help them focus on customer service excellence, profitability and growth of the investment, but also to control their exposure. Another reason is that higher net worth individuals are becoming younger, and they are high-tech orientated. Based on statistics by Swiss Re, Figure 1.4 shows a distribution of financial assets by American families whose primary earner is thirty-five to forty-four years old.

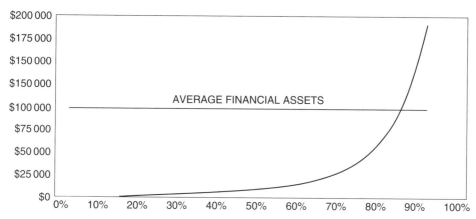

Figure 1.4 Distribution of financial assets held by US families whose primary earner is thirty-five to forty-four years old. (Statistics by Swiss Re Economic Research & Consulting)

1.6 Household debt and private banking

The strategy and methods of private banking should reflect the changing profile of the ownership society, as well as the fact of increasing living in a debt-dominated world. Despite their modern incarnation as investors, few people and even fewer companies appreciate the wisdom of Dr Marriner Eccles, chairman of the Federal Reserve in the 1930s, who said: 'A business, like an individual, could remain free only if it kept out of debt.'[6] One of the ironies of the leveraged world is that two things happen simultaneously:

- People and companies are at the same time savers and borrowers, and
- They find no difficulty in accepting as part of their assets the securitized debt of other people and companies.

Another fact of strategic importance in private banking is that many of its clients are taking an active role in managing their wealth. They are also demanding more sophisticated products as well as a broader geographical range of services, and they accept investing and trading in debt instruments rather than real assets. These debt instruments are financial paper that represents liabilities of individuals and legal entities. For instance:

- Commercial paper,
- Securitized business loans,
- Securitized house mortgages,
- Securitized auto loans, and
- Securitized credit card receivables.

To appreciate better this statement about liabilities turned into assets, we should take a look at consumer debt and the shifting ground on which rest the main pillars of a modern economy. This is an ongoing change that alters the nature and composition of forces supporting future economic growth.

Going back to the basics, economic and financial history teaches that, in the post-World War II years, the first major switch in factors that make the economy tick took place in the early 1950s. This postwar repositioning was most significant because, with it, the drivers of the economy changed:

- From the industrial/military complex financed through government deficits,
- To a wide range of consumer spending, largely done through personal debt.

First the American consumers, then consumers of other nations, most particularly in Western Europe, became the new growth engine that propelled the financial market and the economy at large. This consumer-based model worked well for nearly half a century, but overleveraging through inordinate consumer debt meant that by 2000 it was showing signs of strain.

It is interesting to observe that two new forces have entered the personal debt arena, joining the classical mature households in this process: the young and the elderly. The debt of elderly US households is climbing dramatically. In 1992, just 34.5 per cent of households of people aged sixty-five or older had debt obligations. In 2001, 58.8 per cent did so.[7] During the 1990s up to 2001, in the USA:

- The average amount of personal debt owed by an individual nearly tripled from $8000 to $23 000, and
- Bankruptcies among the elderly increased from 23 890 in 1991 to 82 200 in 2001.

As for the young, particularly US college students, their spending spree is demonstrated by the histogram in Figure 1.5. This covers the four years of college studies. As the reader can easily see, debt in year 1 (freshman) to year 4 (senior) is characterized by a step function, with young students accumulating a (so far) unprecedented amount of liabilities.

One cause for concern about mounting college student debt is that it creates structural imbalances that have not yet been sufficiently studied as to how and when they may be corrected. For instance, what happens in case of unemployment after graduation? What if real wages are unsupportive of expected level of living, leading to greater personal debt? The facts are that:

- Real wages have fallen at the end of every previous recession, and
- The service economy with its part-time work lowers the cost of labour and, therefore, take-home pay.

Far from being theoretical, these are very practical issues because they set the pattern of the evolving ownership society, where people are debtors and savers at the same time. They also challenge different notions about restructuring social security, such as the one advanced by Paul O'Neil, the former Treasury Secretary: endowing every newborn with a $2000 savings account, and adding $2000 on his or her birthday. Who will put up that money? The already leveraged parents?

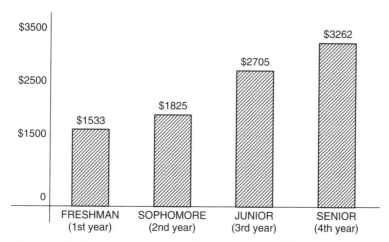

Figure 1.5 The growing amount of college debt in 2002. (Statistics by
USA Today.)

Beyond the growing debt of private individuals, and the new miracle of turning
personal liabilities into assets, comes the corporate debt that is securitized and sold
to investors. By January 2002 net debt for American firms became twice as high as
the country's gross domestic product (GDP). Analysts noted that at the end of the last
recession in 1992, debt was only 1.4 times as high as GDP. A similar statement about
galloping indebtedness applies to private households, which contributed largely to the
economic growth of the 1990s through debt-financed consumption.

The USA is by no means alone in this private spending spree financed by a growing
amount of debt. Based on Australian statistics, Figure 1.6 provides an image of the

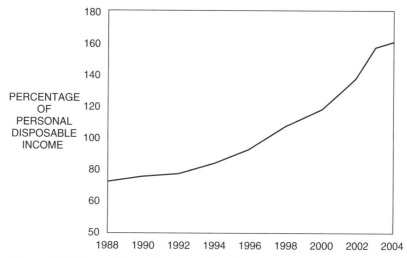

Figure 1.6 The rapid growth in Australia's household debt as percentage of
personal disposable income

extent of consumer leveraging. In Australia, as a percentage of personal disposable income household debt has gone:

- From slightly over 70 per cent in 1988
- To well past the 160 per cent mark in 2004.

In the EU, too, there is a huge switch in the pattern of spending, savings and investments of households and non-financial corporations. Overall, households have a growing amount of accumulated debt: from mortgages, to credit card purchases, cars and other borrowing. Yet, because households buy the securitized liabilities of other households as investments, they end up having a net lending position, while non-financial corporations maintain a net borrowing position. This curious twist is the effect of securitization. In the EU in 1995 the ratio of debt to disposable income of households was about 65 per cent; in 2004 this figure had reached nearly 90 per cent.[8] (See also the shift of risk to households in section A.5 of the Appendix.)

1.7   The ownership society's recycling pattern

In classical economics, the zooming debt, documented through statistics presented in section 1.6, would have been very bad news. But with the new economics of the ownership society, because the asset base has also grown, with much of the growth being securities based on the liabilities of other people, the debt to financial assets ratio has grown only a little, from about 27 per cent to 30 per cent.

Another piece of good news for the economy is that even this increase corresponds to the level of acquisition of housing property and gross capital expenditures, in relation to GDP. Taken together, these references bring in perspective two new signs of our time:

- On the one hand, households continue increasing their demand for loans to finance housing acquisitions, causing their debt as a ratio to disposable income to rise steadily,
- On the other, the indebtedness of households is compensated by the fact that people and companies, particularly institutional investors, accept liabilities created in this way as assets.

Still another fact is the changing pattern of compensation, which has an after-effect. As a percentage of disposable income, in Euroland debt has actually fallen from 5.3 per cent in 1995 to 4.7 in 2003, because income levels have been on the rise (European Central Bank statistics).

The fact that income levels are on the rise is a boon to private banking operations. Recycling is the keyword. As long as consumers are accepting and buying the securitized debt of other consumers, and using it as part of their assets, the economy maintains a sense of balance. In major financial institutions, private banking specialists help families to preserve that balance.

This is the way that debt recycling works. Once the principle of securitization of other people's (and companies') liabilities is accepted, the exact nature of services provided by the banks' family advisory teams can vary from client to client. For instance, investments advisory may:

- Focus only on an upgrading of savings accounts, or
- Cover institutional-style strategic asset allocation and portfolio risk analysis.

In either case private banking investment advisors can help the client to build up a portfolio from scratch or, alternatively, to restructure thoroughly an existing portfolio. In so doing, the specialist role is to identify and analyse the client's unique needs, and then to tailor investment products and services to meet those needs in an efficient manner. For technology-savvy clients, network-based portfolio analysis:

- Provides an on-line view of the client's assets and liabilities,
- Supports clients in self-evaluation of their financial situation, and
- Ensures a direct communications link for clients, routing messages automatically to their investment advisor and back.

As these references document, top-tier financial institutions are in the process of turning private banking into a finely tuned mechanism, which profits both their clients and themselves. The risk connected to this recycling comes from the fact that even with securitization an inordinate growth in consumer debt cannot continue forever, particularly if:

- There is loss of confidence to the creditworthiness of debtors, or
- Adverse economic conditions mean that income levels start to fall significantly.

The hope is that the economy will be able to restructure itself in time. Indeed, there are reasons to believe that, starting in the American economy, there may be a shift from a base that is almost entirely consumer led, to one that is more evenly balanced between consumers and capital spending by the government. In other terms, a shift back to the industrial/military complex is seen on the horizon, a model close to Keynesian economics:

- The military again becomes the flywheel of the economy, and
- Governments may well forget about balanced budgets.

In the USA, total government spending grew by 33 per cent in George W. Bush's first term, in the opening years of the new century. The Republican Party, once a brake on spending, has become an accelerator.

- The US Congress trimmed Clinton's budgets by $57 billion in 1996–2001,
- But in Bush's term it added an extra $91 billion of domestic spending.[9]

Not to be outdone, consumers continued their leveraging, creating a housing market bubble. Fannie Mae and Freddie Mac, the US Government-sponsored enterprises that recycle mortgage money by securitizing it, have in their portfolio 47 per cent of mortgages on American homes. This portfolio stood at $132 billion at the end of the 1990s; it zoomed to $1.5 trillion (a 1136 per cent increase) in 2005.[10]

In the junction between the reborn economic role of the industrial/military complex and the consumer-propelled market are corporate drivers. This duality in market dependence, however, poses a challenge with respect to investments because few companies appeal to both the military and consumer markets, and those on the consumer side currently face the problem of:

■ Trimming down their inventories, and
■ Rightsizing their production capacity.

One of the links between these two markets, industrial/military and consumer, can be found in the fact that, as a number of precedents suggest, geopolitical turmoil stimulates massive innovation, with subsequent adaptation of new technology to wider commercial use. In addition, requirements of sustained overseas military campaigns, such as in Afghanistan and Iraq, revive demand for industrial materials and equipment, at a time when the consumer is taking time out to:

■ Rethink his or her priorities, and
■ Find ways and means for the servicing of debts.

Some experts believe that this rethinking can easily affect private banking, particularly so as the social security system crumbles and consumers look at personal investments not only as their cover for old age, but also for spikes in health-care costs. Social and health-care costs have a nasty habit of increasing rapidly, as our society is greying and its retiree population is growing quickly. The forecast is that by 2050,

■ The USA will have 34 retirees for every 100 working-age people, compared with 21 now.[11]
■ Japan will have about 78 retirees for every 100 20–64-year-olds, and
■ Europe, on average, will be faring better than Japan, with 60 retirees for every 100 people working, but less well than the USA.

A growing opinion among experts is that in the coming years private banking clients will be focused not only on levels of assets and their proper allocation, coupled with transparency and accuracy of information on the performance of portfolio positions, but also on investment advice on how the gaps in the social net can best be filled, from health insurance to retirement. This will require a functional view with health-care and other social costs.

1.8   Synergy of private banking and institutional investments

The European Central Bank recently reported that, for the second quarter of 2004, data on financial investments by investment funds, insurance companies and pensions funds suggest that the portfolio allocation behaviour of institutional investors has continued to shift towards riskier assets.[12] This increases the need for both investment research and damage control.

The assumption of greater exposure cannot be confronted with the worn-out tools of the past. Investors need to understand and appreciate the exposure that they are assuming with their assets. Part of this issue is the concentration of risk. In the UK, pension funds, insurance companies, unit trusts and investment trusts currently command some 90 per cent of British funds under management.

■ About fifty firms account for more than three-quarters of this total, and
■ The share of the ten largest entities is 32 per cent.

This high concentration provides a basis for herd-like movements in the markets, and it also places enormous power in the hands of a very small group of people. The problem is that accountability and transparency are not as high as they should be, while fees are usually heavy and structured in a way that often rewards failure in wealth management.

The strategy followed by banks to face up to the challenge posed by institutional investors is that of strengthening their investment banking, as well as equity research and fixed income research arms. Faced with mounting costs and the assumption of great exposure, however, some credit institutions have shed their investment banking activities. This policy has backfired.

A study in the UK in 1999 demonstrated that British banks, such as NatWest and Barclays, that dropped their investment banking arms (NatWest Markets and BZW, respectively) in the mid- to late 1990s, suffered an attrition of their private banking activities. This became particularly acute at the high net worth individuals' end.

The major reason for such attrition, this study has suggested, is that by eliminating their investment banking activities the credit institutions deprived themselves of the skills of rocket scientists and other professionals who designed and marketed new products for the area of overlap between investment banking and personal banking (see Figure 1.7).

Classically, investment banking research has been considered to be a 'must' in attracting and retaining a clientele of institutional investors. But as affluent individuals become more sophisticated in their market evaluation and investment decisions, private banking clients are increasingly acquiring an institutional investor's business philosophy, characterized by:

■ Advice-led but self-made investment decisions (see Chapter 7), and
■ A relationship based on quality of investment advisors and account managers.

Therefore, credit institutions, investment banks and other fund managers must offer their private banking clients first class research services to cement their relationships, and continue being ahead of the curve. As shown in preceding sections, this policy has associated with it major expenses, including systems, procedures and technology that should be used with the objectives of:

■ Improving performance,
■ Contributing to cost reduction, and
■ Promoting earnings enhancement initiatives.

In the background of all three bullet points should lie a policy able to maintain high private banking and institutional banking standards. On the one hand, funds

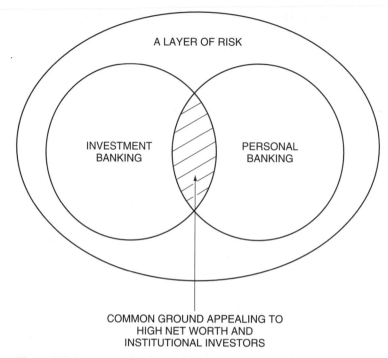

Figure 1.7 Investment banking and private banking correlate, as proven
by a study in the UK

managers must keep their cost/income ratio to a level that compares positively with
best-in-class competitors. On the other, they should strive to achieve a competitive
edge over these corporate opponents.

My personal experience, spanning nearly six decades, tells me that this dual objective is obtainable. The reward is that of achieving growth in net new money in the private client and institutional investor business. The better managed investment banks
and commercial banks know by experience that, to retain and expand their market
share, they must have a policy of:

- Unrelenting product innovation,
- Top-quality research,
- Factual and documented investment advice,
- Complete access to the world's capital markets, and
- Round-the-clock rigorous risk management.

The financial industry's leaders appreciate that they have to provide a complete set
of banking and securities services focused on customer-perceived excellence. They also
understand that the synergy between private banking and the institutional investors'
market permits learning from the latter to benefit the former, and vice versa.

Such duality is most crucial to *asset management* as a unified discipline. Seen from
a narrower viewpoint, this term usually refers to institutional business such as the

administration of pension fund assets. But there is no reason why a narrow viewpoint should prevail. The broader perspective incorporates investment strategies tailored to affluent individuals.

Investment risk analysis and optimization should address this broader perspective, and also actively search for alternative investment vehicles. As an example, one of the best known banks was mentioning its acquisition, in the USA, of an asset management company specializing in forestry investments. Because of their low volatility and stable earnings, forestry investments provide a means of balancing exposure in other investment categories.

Moreover, sound investment proposals must be backed up by a macroanalysis focusing on all issues that could affect the level of credit risk and market risk, increasing by so much the visibility of the investments' future behaviour. Good visibility should include prevailing laws in terms of ownership, investor rights and asset protection, which can be a daunting task when investments are made cross-border. Whether national or global, well-documented equities investments require:

■ Research about companies, industry sectors, geographical markets and macro-economic trends, and
■ Structuring, originating, distributing and trading newly issued equity, equity-linked and equity derivative products, as well as fixed income structured products.

In the fixed income domain, the top banks' research activities and business operations address a broad spectrum of products and markets; for example, government and corporate bonds, fixed income derivatives, mortgage-backed securities, foreign exchange, cash and collateral trading, principal finance and credit derivatives.

To help themselves in providing investment advice to their clients, top-tier banks have developed and operate a multilocal model, with membership on eighty or more different stock exchanges in a two-digit number of countries. This allows them to offer 'local presence globally'. Both their office network and high technology are designed to give them access to 90 per cent or more of market capitalization.

Notes

1 *BusinessWeek*, 29 November 2004.
2 *The Economist*, 19 March 2005.
3 D.N. Chorafas, *Alternative Investments and the Mismanagement of Risk*, Macmillan/Palgrave, London, 2003.
4 *BusinessWeek*, 28 March 2005.
5 *Economist*, 15 November 2003.
6 W. Greider, *Secrets of the Temple*, Touchstone/Simon & Schuster, New York, 1987.
7 *EIR*, 18 January 2002.
8 European Central Bank, *Monthly Bulletin*, December 2004.
9 *Economist*, 14 May 2005.
10 *La Republica*, 20 May 2005.
11 *BusinessWeek*, 28 March 2005.
12 European Central Bank, *Monthly Bulletin*, December 2004.

2 Know your customer and his or her profile

2.1 Introduction

Good investments are never made on the spur of the moment. One of the best ways to lose money is by following a market trend, or buying a security favoured by other investors. Not only are the customer's requirements precise goals, and his or her risk and reward profile a must for factual and documented asset allocation, but this profile also:

- Has to be positioned against market forces that constantly change, and
- Should be subject to intensive research regarding its feasibility, accompanied by a focused risk management effort.

The *know your customer* (KYC) principle underpins all professional investment services (see section 2.2). KYC is a principle that can be applied at different levels of reference. One, the most effective, is that of elaborating the investor's profile on the basis on self-evaluation (see section 2.3) and interview(s) preferably assisted through an expert system (see section 2.4).

The investment advisor's assistance is precious in establishing a priori a realistic estimate of risk and reward because, in the majority of cases, investors are not forthcoming with crisp criteria that can be used effectively in choosing and managing assets. One of the reasons is that although many private banking clients are professionals in other channels of activity, few have a clear idea of what is involved behind financial risk and return. Therefore, it is the duty of the personal banker to help them in sorting out their priorities, and this must be done at two levels of reference:

- The establishment of an effective banking relationship characterized by mutual trust (see Chapter 8), and
- Steady management of the client's assets, including a cost-effective execution of transactions involving buying and selling of financial products.

What should exist in connection to the first bullet point has been defined in Chapter 1. Regarding the second point, steady asset management involves research and analysis for asset allocation and reallocation, which is a steady process because of changing market conditions. For instance, one of the basic rules in asset allocation is that returns on capital are:

■ Higher where capital is scarce, and
■ Lower, indeed much lower, when capital is abundant.

This is a rule that applies with any commodity. In the 2002–2004 time-frame, for example, no asset class has been starved for cash. This reason has been given by experts to explain why beneficial returns in bonds and stocks were small, both in absolute terms and in comparison to other classes of investments such as real estate.

Over the aforementioned period not only has return on investment been low, because of plenty of money searching for a home, but also the risks have been heightened. For instance, credit risk grew rapidly as counterparties became unable to settle an obligation in full, either when due or at any time thereafter, while the market did not factor this likelihood into the financial products' price.

Foreign exchange risk, a market risk that is faced by all global investors, also grew as the volatility in currency exchange markets increased and the dollar hit an all-time low against the euro and pound sterling. (Currency risk with structured products is discussed in Chapter 16.) Moreover, the Basel Committee on Banking Supervision brought into focus *operational risk*, essentially the risk of human error, including:

■ System management failures,
■ Deficiencies in information systems,
■ Fraud and other misbehaviour, and
■ Failure of internal controls, the presence of which is crucial to every banking operation including payments and settlement.

Credit risk, market risk and operational risk make respositioning the investor's portfolio a demanding task, which is aided significantly through the KYC principle. Responsibilities associated with the process of KYC go further than establishing an initial risk and return profile, because they have become an essential element of the new regulations connected to Basel II.[1]

2.2 The sense of 'know your customer'

Know your customer is a sound principle, particularly in a globalized financial environment that has decoupled bankers and asset managers from their clients, where long-term relationships that existed in the past are no longer the order of the day. Although through the internet the average investor has easy access to a world of financial information and the ability to trade stocks on-line,

■ A growing number of high net worth individuals are turning to professional investment advisors.
■ The internet is a great communications medium, but security is substandard and the human touch has been lost.

According to surveys, about 80 per cent of Americans are now interested in working with a professional investment advisor, compared with only 55 per cent in the mid-1990s. Money lost in the stockmarket crash of 2000 evidently has something to do with this change in hearts and numbers. Another factor is that financial instruments have become more complex:

■ To understand, and
■ To manage in terms of exposure.

Even people who see themselves as sophisticated investors are increasingly inclined to seek professional advice, underscoring the difficulties in making investment decisions in today's sophisticated and volatile markets.

There are further reasons why people are retaining professional investment advisors. High net worth individuals are mostly busy professionals who prefer to spend as little time as possible in managing their money in capricious markets, and the rules are enacted after successive scams that oblige regulators to get tougher and legislators to change the letter of the law. Typically, but not always, these new rules revolve around the dual concept that transparency in financial reporting should be king, and that customer exposure must be managed in an integrative way, regardless of whether his or her accounts are held:

■ On-balance sheet,
■ Off-balance sheet,
■ As assets under management, or
■ On a fiduciary trust basis (see Chapter 8).

Both human skill and technology are at the kernel of a rigorous solution to KYC. Not only investments advised by the bank but also customer-assumed exposures must be monitored through the use of databases of account balances, account activity, payments and settlements, and so on. The solution to be chosen should permit local and centralized monitoring across accounts. It should also facilitate monitoring of interoffice activity of customers with accounts in more than one of the credit institution's offices.

Moreover, because many jurisdictions do not permit the routine transmission of customer data outside their perimeter, an approach should be chosen that makes it possible to integrate global client information while accounting for privacy laws and other constraints. Local monitoring should be complemented by a robust process of information sharing between the head office, its branches and subsidiaries regarding account activity that represents heightened risk. The Basel Committee correctly insists that such information should flow both ways.[2]

Precisely for this reason, private banking outfits must be technology leaders. Having investment and trust professionals ready to assist their clients in their financial planning needs is necessary, but not enough. The contribution that skilled people can make is so much greater if they use knowledge artefacts to flash interesting aspects of the client profile. The private banking outfit's investment advisors and asset management professionals should also use expert systems when they work with the client to develop:[3]

■ A list of investment priorities,
■ Appropriate objectives,

- A plan to achieve them, and
- Ways and means to co-ordinate investment and tax planning.

In performing these activities, investment advisors and account managers draw upon the expertise of in-house staff, including financial analysts, estate planning experts and tax professionals, as well as cost analysts and management accounting specialists. A team approach enables better understanding of how to respond to clients' needs and goals, while ensuring that fees and commissions cover costs and leave a profit for the bank. By co-ordinating estate and tax planning with investment decisions, it becomes possible to ensure that investment recommendations:

- Are designed to carry out the overall estate plan, and
- Are consistent with the business purpose that the institution targets in its private banking activities.

The *customer mirror* is instrumental in reaching the objectives outlined by these two bullet points, which at first sight may seem contradictory. Figure 2.1 explains this concept in a nutshell. Customer-by-customer, the first row addresses business costs, and the second, business income.

Steady risk evaluation is crucial because all transactions involve greater or lesser exposure to the bank, particularly when it is inventorying some of the products itself. The risk being assumed should be monetized and subtracted from the theoretical profit and loss estimate, to produce a pragmatic profit estimate for each client.

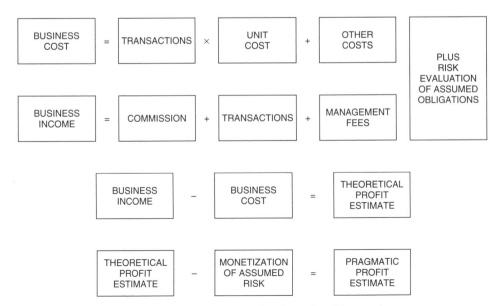

Figure 2.1 Customer mirror by channel and integration

Such integration of goals and means, of costs and risks is very important for good governance reasons. This is true whether the client is interested in establishing strategies for the protection of his or her accumulated wealth, is planning for the children's college education, reserves assets to fill gaps in state-sponsored health care, develops an alternative plan for retirement, wants a customized portfolio for pension plan rollovers or aims to fulfil any other purpose.

Notice that rigorous in-person due diligence and ability to reposition the investor's portfolio against market forces require that both the private banker and the investor are alert to identification and monitoring of market changes. To gain from professional advice, each private and each institutional investor must provide information that allows the portfolio structure to be rethought and revamped.

Not only is the preservation of capital and returns commensurate with the best market results important, but also a portfolio's liquidity must be looked after. To enhance a portfolio's liquidity, some experts suggest that its contents should be polyvalent, involving shares, both ordinary and preferred; treasury bonds and treasury notes; corporate bonds, of a range of credit ratings and maturities; certificates of deposit; warrants; traded options; mutual funds; and other instruments.

Other experts, however, believe that a better investment policy would seek to include in the portfolio fewer instruments, which have been selected with great care. Less diversity is easier to evaluate in terms of exposure, as well as to gain insight on each position, which permits one to be ahead of market forces. This approach requires that the investor clearly states whether his or her objective is:

- *Income*, obtaining a continuing stream of cash flow from bonds and other instruments,
- *Growth*, accumulating wealth over time through price appreciation rather than current income, or
- *Total return*, striking a balance, for example, between fixed income instruments for current income and equities for growth.

Meeting any of these goals presents risks. For instance, to satisfy the aim of current yield the investor may be willing to accept more credit risk, which can result in principal loss. Regarding growth, assumed exposure is a function of price volatility and this, too, may result in principal loss. In spite of targeting a relatively balanced investment approach with a total return strategy, all of the above exposures from credit risk, price volatility and principal loss are present.

2.3   A system approach to wealth management

Whether it concerns private banking clients or institutional investors, a system approach to wealth management is, by definition, holistic. In its construction, it is conceptual, covering nearly all investment domains. However, many of its component parts are analytical, studying, examining and documenting expected risk and return, as well as providing accurate feedback for corrective action.

Because the goals are challenging, and risk associated with investments can be heavy, in many cases, the private banking and institutional banking departments of a bank have to co-operate extensively to exploit the synergy of investments that are of interest to both populations, as well as to keep exposure under lock and key. The aim is to ensure that while each individual client receives a tailored set of investment to suit his or her

- Objectives and
- Risk appetite,

in the background exists a unified research and quality control effort, which can be focused as the situation demands. This is a different way of saying that client advisory services must be able to draw on research sources within the bank and from third parties, formulating an independent and consistent investment policy tailored to the needs of each client, while keeping a close eye on exposure.

Unrelenting risk control is an integral, indeed a vital, part of a system approach to wealth management. This is particularly true today as banks provide access to a wide range of cash and derivative products covering foreign exchange, equities, bonds and other fixed income products. Investors must know the risks they take. This is a basic private and investment banking responsibility, which cannot be delegated to a third party.

Investors must appreciate that conflicting viewpoints, if not conflicts of interest, may exist between them and the wealth manager to whom they outsource the handling of their assets. Where there is potential for risk-adjusted returns, conflicts are almost inevitable. Exposure can often only be controlled at the expense of returns and commissions.

Whether investors like it or not, it is a business principle that asset managers focus on earning higher margins in specialized products, where they can develop a position as a dominant global intermediary. The problem is that whereas in the past these activities were particularly intended to address the requirements of institutional investors and wholesale corporate clients, they are now increasingly being used to answer the investment needs of private clients. For this, and several other reasons, sound controls are of crucial importance to both parties:

- The investor, and
- The wealth manager.

A system approach will also care about the communications means, which themselves are evolving, and ensure that a direct client contact is complemented by leading-edge technology. Whether the target is private banking clients or institutional investors, technology allows the intensification of business relationships:

- Automating routine tasks, and
- Providing individualized content.

Automating trivial and administrative chores makes it possible, for the asset manager and his staff, to concentrate on providing value-added advice, while the investor benefits from ready access to databases containing research results, investment highlights and possible warnings. Learned investors appreciate that interactive access to the pulse of the market helps to secure the antibodies necessary to fight market blues.

There are also the effects of globalization. Whereas in the past a great deal of wealth was managed within the confines of the domestic markets where personal banking clients were domiciled, today wealth management addresses clients in the four corners of the globe. Moreover, whereas in the past the more popular forms of investments were equity and bonds, as capital markets become more globalized and securitized debt received the investors' approval, the content of portfolios became polyvalent.

Because of this a unique mix of businesses intelligence and well-documented investment position is necessary to maintain customer loyalty, in a situation that is never static. New developments and changes are always on the horizon. Therefore, private bankers must keep themselves, their products and approaches to their clients dynamic and flexible.

To a large measure, flexibility means moving away from rigid client segmentation, towards clients self-segmenting themselves based on the different levels of services that the bank provides at different costs. An integral part of this process is brand strength. Brand recognition is a key success factor in the private banking industry, helping to create a situation in which clients trust the institution to provide them with products and services within the realm of security, secrecy and trust discussed in Chapter 1.

Based on this background, Figure 2.2 presents in a snapshot a system for risk and return evaluation that reflects investor profile, incorporates input by the private bank's research department and integrates the investment advisor's expertise. The portfolio's composition should be most sensitive to the investor's goals, which may change over time for personal or other reasons; for instance, because of market transition:

- From low interest rates to higher interest rates,
- From deflation to inflation, and greater inflation, or
- Changes in the stock market happening in an exaggerated way.

Within this holistic approach, the investment policy being chosen may be conservative, moderate or aggressive. The goal of a conservative approach is preservation. The downside is that adjusted for inflation, investment returns may be very low, and in some years the real interest may even be negative. In the background of an aggressive investment strategy, investors accept possible loss of capital. There is plenty of investment risk incurred in the pursuit of higher total return. While theoretically the degree of risk can be reduced through:

- Diversification, and
- Periodic revisions to rebalance any excesses that develop,

practically, exposure to credit risk and market risk is always real and present. Therefore, investors choosing an aggressive investment strategy must be able and willing to sustain a good deal in the way of losses, in expectation that overall portfolio results will produce above-average returns.

All of these factors, and decisions associated with them, enter into the making of the investor's profile, the accuracy of which is a cornerstone to proper management of the client's private banking account. The same prevails with institutional investors. Therefore, investment advisors should spend time getting to know their customers.

This is not always the case, and there are inadequacies in private banking. In June 2003, a study by the consultancy Booz Allen Hamilton and the Reuters information group concluded that private bankers spend too much time on internal administration

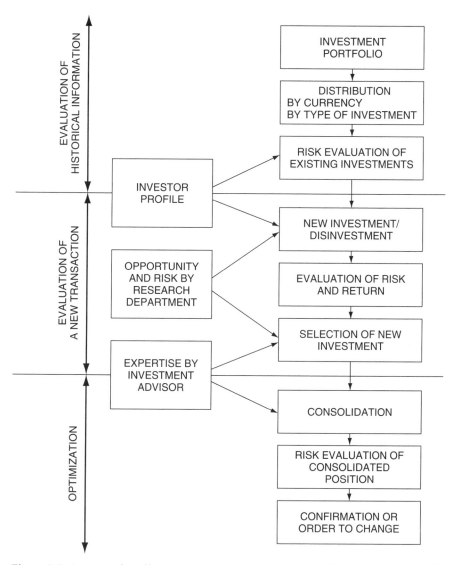

Figure 2.2 A system for effective portfolio management, according to investor profile and research results

and not enough on clients. Their survey found that, on average, private bankers spend just five to ten hours a year with each client.

These statistics are based on interviews with sixty advisers from twenty-seven private banks in the UK, Germany and Switzerland, plus sixty clients of private banks from the same countries with an average wealth of €4.7 million. The message delivered by this study has been that private clients:

■ Are not satisfied with the service they are receiving, and
■ Are beginning to reconsider their options.

Not every negative response, however, is due to defective handholding. The private clients' disaffection with their banks increased after many suffered severe losses on their investments as stock markets collapsed in 2000. As highlighted by private banking clients, areas for improvement include a competent and reliable point of contact, 100 per cent correct transactions (an operational risk), easily understandable financial reports, and more effective data capture to avoid frequent repetition of basic information such as contact details. All of these elements must be accounted for in a system approach.

2.4   Wealth management according to client profile

Because fee income from private banking and asset management activities is considered to be fairly stable (see Chapter 3), and carries with it less risk than either trading or loans, these two product lines are being sought out by banks that wish to diversify from other, more traditional or more risky, business channels. The profitability of private banking is further increased by the fact that, initial entry costs aside,

- It has lower capital requirements than, say, trading, and
- Its activities generally show on-balance sheet, while most trading is conducted off-balance sheet.

However, both private banking and trading are wide open to innovation, which is not true of most traditional banking channels. Up to a point, these two product lines have a synergy that several banks try to exploit by means of convincing their clients that it is good for them to put up to 20 per cent of their assets in alternative investments or, more precisely, derivative financial instruments, which they may not quite understand.[4] (More on this issue in Parts 3 and 4.)

The downside of this policy followed by many private bankers is that of *reputational risk*, which is higher in wealth management than in classical banking. It is therefore a wise strategy for credit institutions, brokers, investment banks and other entities engaged in fund management to pay considerable attention to the proper evaluation of:

- Investor profile, and
- The investor's risk appetite.

Every new private banking customer should be asked to define in simple but crisp terms the aim of the investment that he or she contemplates. A similar statement is valid in regard to periodic re-examination of investment goals. The relatively simple three-way split briefly discussed in section 2.2 should be brought to a further level of detail. For example:

- Preserving the value by minimizing the risk(s),
- Targeting current income while still going after relative safety,
- Placing equal weight on current income and growth, without inordinate risk,
- Having the value of the investment grow more rapidly, but also be exposed to a fair level of risk, to be quantified to the client,

■ Following an aggressive strategy, with the investment growing substantially over time, at the cost of a higher level of risk.

Although more than five options could be established, these points are enough to frame a general guideline, which leads to the next major query about investor profile. This concerns the acceptable degree to which the value of an investment moves up and down, and therefore its *volatility* (see also Chapter 4).

In principle, more volatile investments offer greater growth potential in the longer term, but they may also produce greater losses. Even the so-called capital-protected products may produce zero returns. Structured instruments fall into this class (see Part 3), because although they guarantee the invested capital at maturity, some six or seven years down the line, investors assume over that period:

■ Credit risk, that the instrument's issuer and/or guarantor may go bust, and
■ Market risk, that at maturity the investor receives only his initial capital, forgoing the interest that a credit risk-free, secure investment (for instance, government bonds) would have produced.

Capital protection some six or seven years later means little, because over that time inflation has eroded the originally invested capital. Private bankers are very thrifty in their words when it comes to explaining the effects of inflation and volatility. Wealth management in accordance with the client's profile should ask investors to make basic choices regarding volatility and its impact on their portfolio. For example:

■ As little as possible volatility, accepting the fact that total returns will be relatively small,
■ Some volatility, hence occasional losses in value, as long as the investment has potential for growth,
■ A considerable amount of volatility, which means taking substantial risk in the pursuit of higher total returns.

It is part of the private banker's mission to explain to each client that investments in which the principal is very safe may at times earn less than the rate of inflation. This results in a loss of purchasing power. Therefore, a most pertinent question is whether the customer opts for safety of the nominal capital amount, even if this means that returns do not keep up with inflation.

The customer must know the facts that come with the alternative strategy that the investment will grow more quickly than inflation, accepting risk while trying to achieve this goal. The best way to avoid ambiguity is for the customer to express quantitatively the amount of risk that he or she is willing to assume, relative to the investment's nominal value:

■ Less than 5 per cent
■ 5–9 per cent
■ 10–14 per cent
■ 15–19 per cent
■ 20 per cent or more.

Some private bankers have the policy of presenting clients with two or three portfolio options. For instance, investment A may offer a real interest rate of about 2 per cent (above inflation) at small risk. Investment B may provide an average annual real return of 5 per cent, at higher level of risk in loss of value, and investment C an average annual return of 10 per cent, but a potential loss of 20 per cent or more in capital value in any year. Then, the customer is asked how would he would divide the investment:

- 100 per cent in investment A
- 60 per cent in investment A, 30 per cent in investment B, 10 per cent in investment C
- 30 per cent in investment A, 50 per cent in investment B, 20 per cent in investment C
- 0 per cent in investment A, 60 per cent in investment B, 40 per cent in investment C
- 100 per cent in investment C, or other mix.

Another critical question posed to the investor is the earliest time at which he or she anticipates needing all or a substantial portion of investable assets. Usually three time-frames are proposed from which to choose: reasonably short term, meaning between now and two years; medium term, more than two but less than five years; and long term, five years or more; but there may also be a finer division of time-frames.

Last but not least is a question relating to the private banking client's total investable assets. A classic query is whether the amount is less than $1 million. If the answer is 'more', then the investment advisor asks whether the amount the client is now investing is less than 10 per cent of his or her investable assets.

Opinions differ as to the reason why this question is so often the last to be posed. One of the relevant answers is that by the time the investment advisor comes to it, the relationship with the client has warmed up, and the client has let down some of his defences. This makes it easier to obtain a larger amount for investment than might otherwise be the case.

2.5   Why knowledge engineering can assist the investor

As already explained, the client's choices that determine his or her investment profile must be ascertained through a personal interview. Alternatively, for lower net worth clients, they can be expressed by means of self-evaluation, in answer to a list of queries, or elicited through an expert system, which is the better solution. A personal interview can also benefit from the use of expert systems, as assistants to the investment advisor.

This section focuses on the use of knowledge artefacts that may be used interactively on-line by the client, or used as assistants to an investment professionals and asset managers. In either case, based on rules representing embedded knowledge, the expert system will more or less follow the path described in section 2.4, but with some added value.[5] A valid approach integrates different modules, the functionality of which is not always covered by an investment interview, and even less so by a self-scoring worksheet.

A holistic view of a knowledge artefact designed to address private banking requirements is shown in Figure 2.3. This section does not aim to discuss all of the modules that compose it but, rather, aims to deal with its dynamics, including the

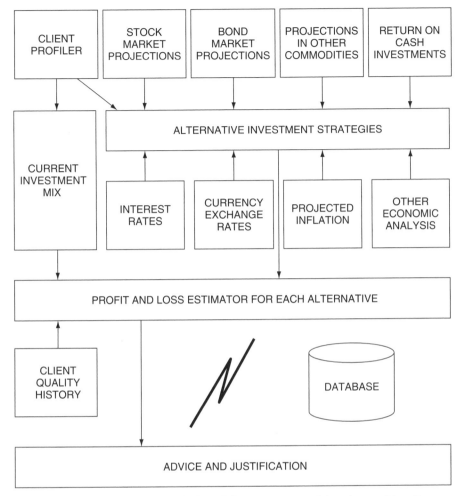

Figure 2.3 A knowledge-enriched modular investment advisor for wealthy clients

benefits that it presents as an interactive client profiler. In the background of the knowledge affecting the artefact's functionality lies the fact that:

■ The client's profile can be mapped into an investment template,
■ The rules underpinning the expert system ensure that securities are selected based on this template,
■ Information volatility and projected trends come from the bank's research department, and
■ The search is helped by up-to-date market input.

Recommendations made by the expert system are guided by the client's definition of his or her investment policy, whether this is income orientated or capital gains orientated. Graduations in each of these classes can be finer and more accurate than those achieved by a manual method, increasing by so much knowledge engineering's contribution to the investment process.

In addition, the range of factors being taken into account is more polyvalent and wider, with knowledge artefacts, than through legacy IT. Figure 2.3 shows a module that handles currency exchange risk. This is a vital component when the investor's preferred currency is explicitly stated and, therefore, there is a need to measure likely profits and losses from investments in different currencies. Overall, the expert system integrates domain knowledge of:

- Shares, bonds and other instruments, including their market(s) and price(s),
- Foreign currency markets, exchange rates and associated country risk.

Based on such inputs, including market values, the inference engine of the expert system will provide investment recommendations, capitalizing on the opinion of experts to enrich its domain knowledge. It will also document the opinion that it gives. For instance, given projections on market developments: 'Be as defensive as possible', 'Beware of the long-term bear market that commenced in 2000; it is still in force', 'Eliminate overweight positions in emerging-market stocks', 'Liquidate high-yield "junk" debt', and so on.

Based on its profiling module of an investor, and on market data fed into the bank's database by information providers, the expert system frames the advice that it gives by backtracking and identifying those of its rules that 'fired' during the computational process. An example from a real-life mid-2004 application is the advice given by an expert system: 'Neutralize equity allocations by reducing previously bullish ratings for the US market'.

Because knowledge artefacts are designed by people, and the rules in their knowledge bank reflect the opinion of expert investment advisors, expert systems are not free from human error. Expert artefacts are essentially a means for industrialization of knowledge. Reduced to nuts and bolts, Figure 2.4 presents the main modules of an expert system developed by the author for a commercial bank several years ago, which

- Is based on a non-procedural methodology,
- Includes an inference mechanism,
- Provides justification for its investment advice, and
- Features a learning facility, which helps to improve its accuracy over time.

After some years of implementation and experience, a well-made expert system becomes a knowledge refinery, through an integrated suite of modules for deriving, measuring and testing investment advice for a range of client profiles. The expert system to which the previous paragraph made reference has been subjected to post-mortem walkthroughs:

- Post-mortems documented that the reference rules were valid.
- Walkthroughs are important in ensuring that the rules are a properly understood part of the knowledge bank.

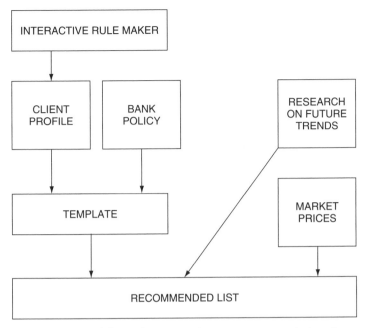

Figure 2.4 Modular architecture of an expert system designed to provide investment advice

Typically, expert systems designed as investment advisors have a significant number of rules to produce a small number of answers. They are also designed to act in the way a human investment advisor would behave. As they become more sophisticated, they are able to address fairly complex investment decisions that:

- Involve different types of assets,
- Integrate financial analysis of a growing range of securities,
- Handle edge cases of capital financing, and
- Evaluate tax consequences of the proposed investment.

All four bullet points are knowledge domains requiring expertise. By posing queries and receiving answers, the expert system leads itself towards *knowing the investor*, analysing his or her risk profile, helping to elicit specific answers, evaluating different types of investments, appreciating changes in the capital markets, and giving advice that may involve investment alternatives for a private banking client.

2.6 A financial advisory expert system for currency exchange

Investment advisory services are not the only beneficiaries from knowledge engineering artefacts. Through expert systems, foreign exchange trades can be handled in a more sophisticated manner than through classical computer support. The best implementations work interactively in real time and act as expert advisors to traders. The case study in this section brings into perspective the possibilities and limits of knowledge engineering.

The sophistication of foreign exchange applications varies (see also Chapter 16) with the goal to be served by the expert system. As shown in Figure 2.3, the investment advisory artefact designed for private banking included a module that addressed currency exchange rates. This was a relatively simple knowledge artefact mainly aimed at assisting clients with a globalized securities portfolio, therefore one including currencies other than their preferred reference currency.

By contrast, advanced currency exchange applications designed for forex traders map the global market into the machine. They also ensure that every time a forex deal is done there is an updated profit and loss statement to guide the dealer's hand, by currency and (when applicable) correspondent bank, client firm, day of trade, value date and other references.

- A cross-rate screen gives both raw data and evaluations, based on rules reflecting expert opinions, related to key decision factors.
- An arbitrage screen permits a review of different scenarios for changing, say, pounds into dollars, including special deals and other agreements if asked for.

The money market implementation of one of the artefacts has feature analysis permitting a comparison of what the cash market is doing against the futures market. Another forex system, designed along similar lines of reasoning, evaluates what the futures price should be, based on spot interest rates and expectations. One of its knowledge engineering modules predicts which position to take to offset any movement between, say,

- Buying January pounds, and
- Selling July dollars.

The expert system in reference knows a lot about the business in which it is operating; that is, the trader's business. It understands what the corporate policy is, who are its main users, what kinds of trade each person is allowed to do, and other most critical issues. It also has expertise on the return required on forex projects to be undertaken in order to break even and make a profit.

Expert systems designed along these briefly described principles usually feature a wealth of information, because they are networked to rich databases. They have plenty of expert rules, reflecting the fact that several domain experts have been interviewed by knowledge engineers. The latter learned the art of the domain experts in foreign exchange, and tailored the system to the needs of sophisticated forex operations, including:

- Business assumptions,
- Types of corporate client,
- Users' options and privileges,
- The forex market's status, trend and mood.

The business assumptions customize the calculations that take place as news and prices come in. Another expert system module, designed for internal accounting management information reasons, identifies traders and managers who have failed to correct their positions, sending them an alert signal. Other features include analysis of all of the day's transactions, cancelled deals and exceeded deals.

These and similar applications are dynamic, and their continuing success depends on both the skill of domain experts and that of knowledge engineers who design the artefacts, as well as the tools at their disposal. But at the same time, expert systems are not a sort of penicillin to financial troubles, or an all-weather answer to challenges in currency exchange. There are limits to their performance.

To ensure that an expert system will be able to continue to deliver, a great deal has to be done through direct application of human skill. Even the best experts may fail in their estimates of trends and future events. A good example is provided by predictions on the exchange rate of US dollars, with main variables: budget deficits, imbalance in the US current account and market psychology shaped by these events.

In early September 2004, no less an authority than Dr Paul Volcker, the former chairman of the Federal Reserve, predicted with 75 per cent probability a sharp fall in the dollar within five years. In the background of this and similar predictions on the dollar's fate lies the fact that official projections score the fiscal imbalance at a cumulative $5 trillion over the decade 2004–2014, while they exclude probable:

- Increases in overseas military and homeland-security expenditures,
- Extension, or at least non-reversal, of the 2003 tax cuts, and
- New entitlement increases proposed by politicians without due consideration on currency value and financial stability.

These are complex economic and financial issues that are not, and cannot, be addressed through knowledge artefacts. Key questions, such as what is the market's response to current account deficit and unbalanced budgets, are not linear and not answerable in advance. Therefore, they cannot be mapped into rules.

Experience teaches that events depend on many variables and political decisions, such as the destruction of the European Union's stability, according to expert prediction. For example, in the second week of December 2004 both sterling and the Australian dollar fell on soft trade data, with the Canadian dollar following suit. But as far as the greenback is concerned, when news came thereafter that the American trade gap had widened to a record level, the US dollar promptly rose.

The market's move ran contrary to the experts' predictions, a fact that all investors should always keep in sight. The US dollar rose while the country's October 2004 deficit soared to $55.5 billion, worse than forecast. Logically these financial data should have heightened fears over the ability of the USA to fund its external deficit, thus putting pressure on the dollar. But instead the dollar strengthened by 0.2 per cent to $1.3271 against the euro, 0.1 per cent to $1.9230 against sterling and 0.9 per cent to 105.73 against the yen.

Some experts labelled the move the start of the 'silly season', which essentially means, 'We don't know what happens next'. Others spoke of short-covering, with speculators closing short-dollar positions ahead of Japan's Tankan business confidence survey. More credible were the opinions that:

- We are seeing signs of short-term market players cutting back positions, and
- It is difficult to have confidence that the dollar move is still a one-way street, in spite of the ever growing US budget and current account deficits.

If there are no rules on which decisions can depend, then there are no expert systems. Logically, but only logically, while the budget and current account deficits are not the same subject, they do impact upon one another and they are fed by the same lukewarm policies.

- Increased fiscal shortfalls intensify the need for foreign capital, and
- External deficits almost certainly rise further in the aftermath of lack of budget discipline.

Algorithmic solutions underpinning expert systems can reflect these trends, but they fall short in mapping the changing mood of market psychology and the whims of politicians. Only personal flair can guess the psychological importance for financial markets of expectations, whether these concern political turmoil, current accounts or budget position. Knowledge engineering can be of great help to traders and investors but, like everything else, it has its limits. This should be kept in mind when we talk about currency exchange structured products for retail investors in Chapter 16, and about caveat emptor in the following sections.

2.7 Caveat emptor and reputational risk

Personal banking has its risks, and one of the key questions when things go wrong with investments is: Who is responsible? Logically both the investor and the private bank, as well as its agents, share the responsibility. Few things are, however, logical or linear in business. Therefore, accountability connected to personal banking is a theme worth examining (see also Chapter 8 on legal risk).

Caveat emptor is a clause from Roman law frequently referred to in commercial and financial transactions. It means 'let the buyer beware'. This is generally considered to be a good method of operating a market, not only because it has survived for so many centuries, but also for practical reasons. Caveat emptor's downside is that with today's complex financial instruments,

- The small investor does not have much of an understanding of the risks being involved and assumed,
- Many of the high net worth individuals assume exposures with only a meagre return, and
- Even institutional investors confront situations in which they have had no experience, while lacking the necessary risk management skills.

It follows that many investors, including people who could be considered professionals, do not stand a chance in a sophisticated market where innovation in financial instruments often means higher risk. The proof is that a great number of investors, particularly smaller ones, have time and again been taken to the cleaners.

In consequence, despite being one of the oldest rules of the marketplace, caveat emptor has been challenged in court. An recent example is the US Supreme Court ruling of 3 June 2002, in favour of a Securities and Exchange Commission action against a broker. The Supreme Court stated that the securities markets' regulations introduced in the 1930s 'sought to substitute a philosophy of full disclosure for the philosophy of caveat emptor, and this to achieve a high standard of business ethics in the securities industry'.

Therefore, private banks, investment banks and their analysts may have a legal duty of care for their retail customers. For example, this means offering them only such advice as they would give to themselves. On this ground, even before the Supreme Court decision, countless private lawsuits have been pending against financial services firms:

- Many among them seem likely to drag on for years, and
- According to the experts, some of them will result in huge payouts.

Among the twenty-first century public lawsuits is one by the New York Attorney General against Merrill Lynch. It focused on internal e-mails of the late 1990s, in which the broker's analysts abused internet firms as 'crap' and 'shit', while simultaneously issuing research reports that urged investors to buy their stock. Merrill Lynch paid $100 million to settle this case, although it did not admit any wrongdoing and was never charged with any specific offence. After the settlement, it was rumoured in New York that the Attorney General hoped to repeat that challenge by obtaining e-mails from Morgan Stanley and Citigroup.

Europe's largest financial scandal so far, Parmalat, came only eight months after J.P. Morgan Chase, Citigroup and Merrill Lynch coughed up $135 million, $101 million and $80 million, respectively, to settle charges over their role in Enron's fraud, albeit without admitting guilt. Scandals such as Enron's, Adelphia, Global Crossing, WorldCom, Parmalat and a myriad of others document how easily banks:

- Succumb to the temptation of fat fees taken out of transactions, and
- Leave the most important questions of exposure and reputational risk for later on.

Senior management seems to forget that *reputational risk* can be devastating (see also the discussion on business risk in Chapter 3). This is what Italian banks have found out the hard way in connection to the Parmalat scam. In its aftermath, they have been targeted by public opinion, the judiciary and even by parliament because, in spite of caveat emptor, they are considered responsible for the malfeasance that took place in the financial market.

- These cases have created a dramatic crisis of confidence in the banking system, and
- They have led to a mountain of legal risk that keeps the courts busy and pays for mink coats for the lawyers' wives.

American examples are provided by Citigroup in May 2004 and J.P. Morgan Chase in July 2004. In mid-July 2004, J.P. Morgan Chase, the second biggest bank in the USA, set aside $2.3 billion to cover the possible costs of litigation arising from the Enron and WorldCom affairs. A month or so earlier, in May, Citigroup paid $2.7 billion to settle a class-action lawsuit related to WorldCom's troubles, and put aside nearly $5 billion provisions for Enron-related and other court actions.

Less than a year later, in mid-March 2005, J.P. Morgan Chase said that it would pay $2 billion to settle a class-action suit by WorldCom shareholders. Several other banks had already settled, and Morgan's payment is the second largest. A couple of billion dollars here, a couple of billion dollars there, and pretty soon we talk of real money.

A tandem of financial scandals, investments that misfired, and their after-effect in defrauding investors, also risks killing the goose that lays the golden egg. It takes a lifetime to build a reputation, and it can be destroyed through some wrong steps. The Italian population, for instance, will not easily forget that hundreds of thousands of Italian families lost their savings in the Parmalat, Cirio and Argentinian debt scandals.[6]

Along with all of the largest Italian banks, and many minor banks, prosecutors in Milan and Parma have been investigating Bank of America, J.P. Morgan Chase, Morgan Stanley and Citicorp, from the USA; ABN-Amro, from the Netherlands; Banco Santander, from Spain; Deutsche Bank, from Germany, and more. Capitalia, Monte dei Paschi, Banca Intesa BCI, San Paolo IMI, Unicredito (the former Credito Italiano), Banca Nazionale di Lavoro, Casa di Risparmio di Parma, and many more were those who:

- Lent to Parmalat,
- Traded in derivatives,
- Underwrote its bonds, and
- Sold them to small investors.

Neither is Parmalat the only scam to hit Italian savers hard. According to estimates, 400 000 Italians, mostly retail clients of local banks, had been holding €14.7 billion ($19.6 billion) of Argentina's bonds when that country defaulted in December 2001. These unlucky people, and their families, were sold the toxic waste in the vaults of their banks, through their friendly bankers.

All these are incidents of the inappropriate sale of highly risky debt instruments to small savers. In Italy alone, nearly $25 billion in individual savings went up in smoke in the first year of the twenty-first century. At San Paolo IMI, one-third of the 4000 customers who were Cirio bondholders and 10 per cent of the 20 000 Parmalat bondholders have decided to seek compensation through legal means.

Evidently this did not please the bank's top brass. It has been reported that Alfonso Iozzo, San Paolo IMI's managing director, saw a risk of moral hazard if customers were given blanket reimbursement. 'People must learn to assess investments', he said. Technically, Iozzo is right: that's what caveat emptor is all about. But he forgets that:

- These clients should not have been sold toxic waste in the first place, and
- Small savers do not have the skill to recognize a rotten asset, and therefore they are easy prey to malpractice.

Capitalia, Italy's fourth biggest banking group, has chosen the opposite strategy. Almost all of its 3800 customers who bought bonds in Cirio, Parmalat and Giacomelli, another distressed and disgraced Italian company, have been reimbursed, either fully or at 50 per cent, depending on whether or not the bank played a part in placing the bonds. 'Reputation is a bank's most important value. We wanted to settle quickly to keep our customers' trust', said Matteo Arpe, Capitalia's managing director.[7]

2.8 Who is accountable for failures in fund management?

Section 2.7 presented the reader with American and Italian case studies where investors got burned, while bankers as well as fund managers have taken diametrically opposed attitudes in terms of compensation: some stuck to caveat emptor, others felt that covering part of the investors' losses is a better alternative to wholesale assumption of reputational risk. Because responsibility is always commensurate with the authority that an institution is assuming, before discussing accountability it is wise to have a functional view of what is involved in the management of funds.

Within the context of professional investment services described in the preceding sections, the functions of wealth management have been given different definitions by different experts and their institutions. Part of the reason for such discrepancies is that banks are not the only players in the field under discussion. For instance, many fund managers in the UK are owned by life insurance companies, and the institutional objectives differ. What many of these efforts, however, have in common is that, as underlined in the Introduction, at different degrees wealth management comprises both:

- Services addressed to private individuals, and
- Asset management services targeting institutional investors.

According to some of the experts, taken together the notions behind these two bullets constitute the broader domain of *fund management*, a definition deliberately adopted in this text, in the absence of a universal terminology. Notice, however, that this is not a generally accepted way of looking at fund management in contrast to asset management and other professional investment services.

Nothing is really totally new in an overall fund management sense. For many years banks have played a significant role in advising their clients about investments. Added value comes from the fact that with private banking not only has their involvement increased, but also the instruments and methods being used have changed. They became more sophisticated for three main reasons:

- Market forces propelled by customer demands,
- The growing competition because of new entrants, and
- The competitive role being played by cutting-edge technology.

The greater the potential for profits perceived by different institutions in the broader field of fund management, the greater the number of players entering this field. In its earlier, more limited form, private banking (also known as personal banking) used to be considered a specialist business, but in recent years it has seen a significant number of new entrants, including many of the larger universal banks, investment banks and hedge funds.

While the domain of investment services should be and remain open, in order to be vibrant, investors are well advised to monitor and keep track of the quality history of fund managers with whom they deal or plan to associate. Policies for car insurance provide an example. In terms of premium, a new driver without a previous quality record is treated as a drunk driver, until such a record is established and the company issuing the policy is comfortable with it.

Investors should do the same, otherwise they can be subject to surprises. In mid-March 2005 German authorities were trying to piece together the accounts of Phoenix Kapitaldienst GmbH, a brokerage firm in Frankfurt. According to the authorities, Phoenix may have misstated assets by as much as €800 million ($1.4 billion) in what could be one of the biggest ever cases of fraud in Europe involving an investment fund.

Bafin, the German markets regulator, prosecutors in Frankfurt and an insolvency administrator have been working to determine how much money may actually be missing from Phoenix. The firm offered a product that tried to predict trends in financial markets using derivatives contracts (see Parts 3 and 4). This gamble had attracted about 30 000 investors from Germany and Scandinavian countries.

'We are investigating Phoenix for fraud and breach of fiduciary duty spanning a number of years', said Thomas Bechtel, a spokesman for the Frankfurt prosecutor's office.[8] Managers at Phoenix uncovered the potential fraud after discovering that a purported trading account said to contain about €600 million did not exist.

Apart from in Germany and Sweden, Phoenix sold its products, known as managed futures, through a marketing company based in Denmark. Even with this interface, clients invested money directly with the German parent company which, for regulatory purposes, was treated as a credit institution that sold savings products, as if this could ever be the case with derivatives. This is one way of taking investors for a ride.

Reinhold Keitel, a spokesperson for SdK, the German Association for Investor Protection, said Phoenix's activities also aroused suspicion within that entity. 'We keep a register of companies that are known for suspicious practices', she said. 'Phoenix has been on this register several times over the past years, going back as far as the 1990s'. This is what I have been suggesting, in the opening paragraphs of this section, that investors should do.

One of the curiosities of the Phoenix fraud, which parallels that of Parmalat, is that it is not clear whether the money is missing or was never there. The company's trading account said to contain €600 million was supposedly held with Man Financial, the brokerage arm of London's Man Group, the world's largest publicly traded hedge-fund company. In Parmalat's case several billion were supposedly held in Parmalat's name by the Bank of America.

In a statement reported in the *Wall Street Journal*, Man said: 'It appears that certain accounts in the books of Phoenix do not exist at any company at the Man Group. We have undertaken a detailed review of our own records, and are satisfied that there are no irregularities of any kind at any Man Group company'. The statement added that Man had not incurred any losses due to Phoenix, and that it had no financial exposure to the firm.

With these references in the background, who is accountable for the small fortunes lost by 30 000 people? The investors themselves because of caveat emptor? Phoenix, where allegedly the money has sunk? The regulators who took apparently no pro-active action? Or somebody else?

The investors are basically left with two options: get depressed, or start to rebuild with whatever money they are able to recover. Small investors in Phoenix from countries in the European Union will probably be entitled to some compensation since Bafin said that the case was serious enough to warrant a referral to the German investor-compensation scheme for securities companies. Under that scheme, creditors can get back as much as 90 per cent of their claims up to €20 000.

If caveat emptor is not the best guide in private banking and asset management, what then? Religious teachings have different versions. The Christian version is: 'Treat others as you would like them to treat you' (Luke 6, v. 31) and 'Love your neighbour as yourself' (Matthew 22, v. 39). The Muslim version is: 'No man is a true believer unless he desires for his brother that which he desires for himself' (Hadith Muslim, imam 71-2), and the Jewish says: 'What is hateful to yourself do not do to your fellow man. This is the Torah Law' (Babylonian Talmud, Shabbath 31a). Try to teach this to fund managers.

The Hindu version is: 'Let not any man do unto another any act that he wisheth not done to himself by others, knowing it to be painful to himself' (Mahabharata, Shanti Parva). The Buddhist version states: 'hurt not others with that which pains yourself' (Udanavarga, v. 18), and Confucius said 'Do not do to others what you would not want them to do to you' (Analects, Book xii # 2). Religious and philosophical teaching does not talk of caveat emptor, but neither is it clear about who is accountable for failures in fund management.

Notes

1 D.N. Chorafas, *Economic Capital Allocation with Basle II. Cost and Benefit Analysis*, Butterworth-Heinemann, London, 2004.
2 Basle Committee, *Consultative Document. Consolidated KYC Risk Management*, BIS, August 2003.
3 D.N. Chorafas and H. Steinmann, *Expert Systems in Banking*, Macmillan, London, 1991.
4 D.N. Chorafas, *Alternative Investments and the Mismanagement of Risk*, Macmillan/Palgrave, London, 2003.
5 D.N. Chorafas and H. Steinmann, *Expert Systems in Banking*, Macmillan, London, 1991.
6 D.N. Chorafas, *The Management of Equity Investments*, Butterworth-Heinemann, London, 2005.
7 *Economist*, 24 July 2004.
8 *Wall Street Journal*, 17 March 2005.

3 Business opportunity, fees and commissions from private banking

3.1 Introduction

'One does not plan and then try to make the circumstances fit those plans', said General George Patton. 'One tries to make plans fit the circumstances. I think *the difference between success and failure* in high command depends on the ability, or lack of it, to do just that'. Patton's words are a golden rule for all financial institutions and for all investors.

Markets are the driving force of the twenty-first century. To be ahead of the curve, however, a financial institution needs a sound business strategy and plans that are never fixed over the longer term. Flexibility in planning, and in the execution of business plans, is never more important than in an age where research and development is king, and innovation can turn existing instruments, tools and concepts on their head at a moment's notice.

The exploitation of business opportunity needs conceptual skills and an agile mind. Stereotypes can be deadly. Sam Walton, one of the most successful businessmen of the post-World War II years, described in the following manner how his mind worked: 'When I decide that I am wrong, I am ready to move to something else'. A project or process may prove unable to deliver what was promised, because some of the contributors did not do their job. And as Walton aptly remarked on another occasion: 'One should never underwrite somebody else's inefficiencies'.[1]

These references to business opportunity, dynamic planning, innovation and flexibility in decision making are most relevant to private banking and its future. As described in Chapters 1 and 2, over the past two decades banking has undergone a very significant evolution. Globality, technology and market developments have altered the *design* and *marketing* priorities of financial activities.

- New financial instruments are being researched and applied to sustain competitiveness.
- Entities active in private banking are eager to develop and maintain a global delivery system, customized by area.
- Fees have become of prime importance to compensate for loss of intermediation and lack of pricing power in trading channels.

Figure 3.1 provides in a snapshot the major market trends affecting financial institutions. The fact that financial assets are increasing overall is good news for private

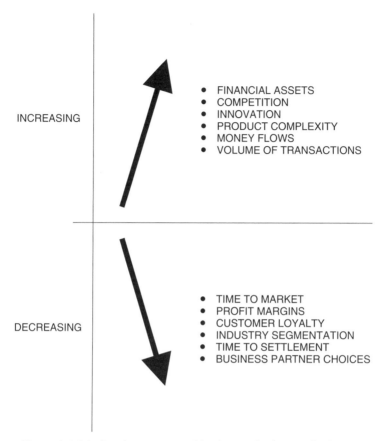

INCREASING

- FINANCIAL ASSETS
- COMPETITION
- INNOVATION
- PRODUCT COMPLEXITY
- MONEY FLOWS
- VOLUME OF TRANSACTIONS

DECREASING

- TIME TO MARKET
- PROFIT MARGINS
- CUSTOMER LOYALTY
- INDUSTRY SEGMENTATION
- TIME TO SETTLEMENT
- BUSINESS PARTNER CHOICES

Figure 3.1 Market dynamics steadily change the frame of reference
affecting financial institutions

banking. The challenge comes from heightened competition, the shrinking time
to market, decreasing customer loyalty and, in several cases, reduced profit margins.
All of these are reasons necessitating strategic plan revisions.

Moreover, as we will see in this chapter, the formerly fat fees from private banking
are coming under pressure. Major changes are foreseen in the coming years in wealth
management, as entry barriers are falling owing to the internet which, by many
accounts, increases the influx of new service providers. In addition, cross-border
mergers and acquisitions (M&As) are expected to become an increasingly important
factor behind the process of globalization in fund management. Other things being
equal, this will mean greater competition.

As far as private banking and assets management are concerned, integrated financial markets have positive and negative effects at the same time. Financial markets are
thought to be integrated if there are no obstacles to capital movements, and transaction costs of moving capital from one country to another, in their broad sense, are the
same as those for capital movements within one country. An additional criterion of
fully integrated financial markets is that same types of securities are traded at the

same prices, irrespective of where the transactions take place, who is trading in these securities and how much is being traded (see section 3.3 on the law of one price).

3.2   Trades, investments and private banking customers

The last paragraph of the Introduction presented to the reader criteria that allow one to say whether financial markets are integrated. Beyond the lack of obstacles to capital movements, there should be no obstacles to investments and trades. For clarity of definition, to qualify as a *trade* a deal must be a transaction designed and executed using financial instruments. The goal of a trade is to profit from insight into a market opportunity.

- A trade cannot be something that happened by accident or sheer luck, and
- It cannot be a deal such as a merger or takeover, even if it is clever and lucrative.

In a similar manner, the word *investment* is frequently confused because it is used to mean different things, an example being the use made of this term in preceding chapters. Classically, 'investment' has meant purchasing real production facilities such as factories and machine tools. More recently, it has been connected to financial transactions, such as buying stocks and bonds, and in this sense it is used in private banking as well as, to a significant extent, in connection to institutional investments.

The two notions are not disconnected. Buying stocks and bonds can have implications for real investments, but at the same time these two definitions identify different things. According to Caouette et al., money managers can invest in a wide range of instruments, from equities to real estate, but basically they have two ways to make profits:

- To the extent that they are able to lend money at a reasonable rental, they gain by taking credit risk.
- To the extent that they are able to buy low and sell high, they defy market risk and earn money through price appreciation.[2]

It is precisely in their approach in handling credit risk and market risk that professional asset managers differ dramatically from less skilled investors and savers, as well as cottage industry players in the investment arena. As long as the management of investors' and savers' accounts was free of cost, banks could afford to employ less skilled individuals, but fees and commissions have changed that leisurely perspective.

Chapters 1 and 2 presented the sort of knowledge required today by investment advisors and asset managers, and the high-technology support they should have at their disposal. Moreover, their skills need to keep on being updated and to expand because global portfolio management requires extensive knowledge of the world's financial markets, as well as the expertise of:

- Economists,
- Equity analysts,

- Debt instrument experts, and
- Currency exchange specialists.

All these people cost money, but also make money for the companies for which they work, through trades and investment management fees. That is why they are so much in demand, albeit at greater or lesser level depending on the jurisdiction, sophistication of the bank's clients and maturity of the market in which they work.

Cross-border comparison between private banking outfits and asset management units is not easy because before yields on securities, or fees on services, denominated in different currencies and countries can be compared, these need to be converted into a reference currency at forward exchange rate. This being said, as far as the profitability of private banking and asset management is concerned, there are differences that may be attributable to:

- Prevailing local market conditions,
- Credit rating of private banking institutions,
- Strategic moves by a bank's competitors, or
- What local investors can afford to pay for fees.

The message to retain from these references is that while financial markets are becoming increasingly integrated, this does not rule out a certain amount of segmentation. There are, and probably will always be, differences in cross-border valuation of common factors, and this is true even within different segments of one and the same market.

Where there seems to be little difference among private banking institutions that operate in different countries is that (with few exceptions)[3] they target the top of the pyramid in net worth. This is hardly surprising. One of the credit institutions participating in the research that led to this book suggested that:

- The top 20 per cent of a bank's customers generate up to six times as much revenue as they cost.
- By contrast, the bottom 20 per cent cost three to four times more than their contribution to the bank's income.

This is an excellent example of Pareto's law, named after the Swiss–Italian economist and mathematician of the late nineteenth century. As Figure 3.2 suggests, fat profits but also greater risks are found at the peak of the pyramid of clients and other counterparties, with the top 2 per cent bringing in roughly half of the year's profits.

Because these statistics are fairly well known in the banking industry, for more than two decades credit institutions have been increasingly segmenting their customers into profitability tranches. But tiering has also drawbacks, particularly for marketing, as:

- Most classical sales programmes fail to measure the *potential* value of a customer, and
- Evaluating a tranche's profit and loss (P&L) may be biased, because most institutions typically measure only past transactions.

POPULATION OF CLIENTS   SUM OF PROFITS
IN %   IN %

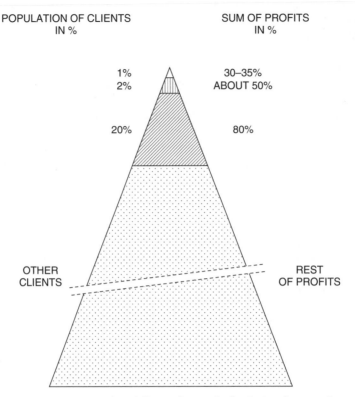

1%	30–35%
2%	ABOUT 50%
20%	80%

OTHER   REST
CLIENTS   OF PROFITS

Figure 3.2 Pareto's law fully applies to the bank, its clients and
its profits

Moreover, investment patterns change and this impacts not only on customer profiling (discussed in Chapter 2), but also on the profitability of clients to the institution.
What a person invests today is not always a good predictor of what he or she will
invest tomorrow, as employment patterns, family life and spending habits evolve over
time. A similar statement is valid with regard to institutional investors.

To be able to follow these changes in a factual manner, as well as for effective
implementation of the know your customer (KYC) principle, which was discussed in
Chapter 2, it is wise to develop an internal control system that provides the bank with
business-orientated information about:

■ Each customer relationship, and
■ The resulting P&L to the firm.

The careful reader will recall the reference made in Chapter 2 to the customer mirror, which should display all transactions done, by channel; the cost of these transactions to the bank; the risk assumed by the bank, by type of transaction; monetization
of the risk the bank has taken with these transactions, and so on. At the same time,
on the income side, should be written all fees and commissions,

- Portfolio management and safekeeping,
- Investment advice, if unbundled from portfolio fees,
- Volume and amount of cross-sales through relationship banking,
- The benefit to the bank, or asset manager, by having the client's shares and other assets 'at street level'.[4]

The P&L with *each* customer, taken as profit centre, would be derived from these two sets of data. Notice that some judgements may be subjective.

For instance, the reference to cross-selling banking products has no standard measure of success. A usual statistic is average number of products bought by each customer.

- Some experts say that an American household buys 16 different financial products.
- However, on average, a bank supplies just 4.3 products to its typical customer.

One major US bancassurance suggests that only 11 per cent of its clients buy insurance and only 16 per cent have a mortgage with the bank. Still, as far as this institution is concerned, 80 per cent of its growth comes from selling additional products to existing customers, and personal banking accounts are a good basis for doing so.

It is no less true, however, that Pareto's law should be paid full attention when targeting the customer population. As the statistics in Figure 3.2 show, 20 per cent of clients contribute roughly 80 per cent of each financial institution's profits. These, it should be noted, are very demanding clients with plenty of requirements for custom-made financial instruments, and for solutions characterized by properly studied risk and return.

3.3 Establishing a strategy for fees and commissions

With the stockmarket crash of year 2000, and associated collapse of mergers and acquisitions, the banking industry lost a great deal of its income stream. The better managed credit institutions and investment banks, however, had prepared themselves for the market change by taking greater advantage of income generated from fees and commissions business.

Institutions that knew how to position themselves against market forces made sure that their fees and commissions strategy was able to offset declining income from loans, M&As and other business lines. At the same time, the topmost private bankers made splendid earnings from commissions. Among the stronger players in the personal banking domain, fees received from this line of activity accounted for:

- About 60 per cent of the aggregate net commissions received, and
- Nearly 70 per cent of their increase in earnings in 2001, the year after the stockmarket crash.

Innovation in financial instruments has been instrumental in promoting this strategy. Using derivatives and rapidly packaging loans, selling them to hedge funds, institutional investors and even retail investors, credit institutions earn good fees while reducing their credit risk. In fact, beyond the statistics on top players in the preceding bullet points, on average major financial companies now receive:

- 42 per cent of their revenues from fees, compared with 20 per cent in 1980, and
- 58 per cent from interest, compared with 80 per cent in 1980.

Behind this reversal in the profitability of product lines in banking lies the fact that derivatives markets are continuing to grow at a rapid rate, according to the latest survey by the International Securities Dealers Association (ISDA). The notional principal amount of outstanding credit derivatives rose by nearly 55 per cent in the last six months of 2004, compared with the first six months, and year-on-year the increase in credit derivatives was 123 per cent.

- A big chunk of the market for these products comprises institutional investors and high net worth individuals.
- Retail investors, too, have become part of the structured products market, and this brings to the foreground the need for them to understand risk management (see Chapter 4).

At the same time, while fees from personal banking, commissions from institutional investors and profits from structured products are good, rising interest rates hurt financial companies because the risk of bad loans increases. Lenders are especially vulnerable to defaults as they have become a lot less choosy about who they lend to, in the aftermath of tough competition for loans.

At the end of the first quarter of 2005, credit analysts were predicting an increase in defaults of junk bonds to 3.2 per cent of issuers over 2006 from 2.5 per cent as of February 2005. Some reports spoke of a significant risk that companies will not be able to refinance junk bonds maturing over the next three years, when a glut of exceptionally low-quality debt comes due.

These woes in traditional banking lines underline the strategic importance of the fees and commission business, enhanced by a strong market position among the better tooled private banks. Operating banking income received a boost from both securities commission and the safe custody business.

In several Western countries, securities deposits statistics show that the number of safe custody accounts at credit institutions, including investment trusts, continues to rise. This is largely due to households' efforts to build additional private capital-covered pensions. However, the margins are narrowing as a result of competition between similar facilities offered by all categories of banks and brokers. (The nature of the trust function and risks associated with it are discussed in Chapter 8.)

What about the pricing of services? The answer is that there is nothing resembling a universal price list in private banking, neither are the rules characterizing price setting cast in stone (more on this subject in sections 3.4 and 3.5). This contradicts the rule stated in the Introduction that, according to prevailing economic theory, a basic criterion of integrated financial markets is that the law of one price should prevail.

The *law of one price* has an evident impact on every entity's bottom line. Therefore, it is not surprising that deviations from it happen frequently, a fact that sheds light on obstacles to the creation of a level field cross-border. The relative wealth of banking public and P&L considerations impact private banking's fee structure, which might have been thought of as being universal.

In the majority of cases, individual price lists offered to private banking clients are just indicative and open for negotiation. Moreover, the growing competition for private banking business and fund management at large has led many financial institutions to re-examine both their:

■ Trading fee, and
■ Management fee.

Banks are much more willing than before to negotiate both of them with their most important clients. The trading fee is calculated on the basis of trading activity. By contrast, management fee is a percentage on net worth of the private banking client's account, and it is charged on a yearly or quarterly basis depending on the policy adopted by the bank. (More on this in section 3.4.)

Beyond the law of one price, effective convergence in the globalized economy must be characterized by other factors that help to eliminate asymmetries and imbalances. According to Malcolm Knight, general manager of the Bank for International Settlements (BIS), effective convergence must be obtained across a three-dimensional frame of reference. This is shown in Figure 3.3.

Another challenge to private banking's profitability comes from the fact that financial conglomerates, defined as groups of companies operating in different sectors of the financial industry, have entered the fee-producing service lines. The increasing relevance of deals involving large financial institutions appears to be related to the transformation of money and capital market activity as a result of globalization,

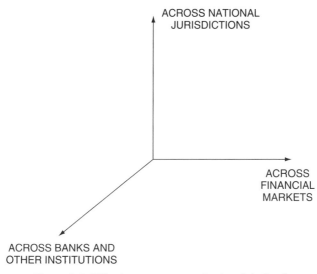

Figure 3.3 Effective convergence in the globalized economy must be obtained across a three-dimensional frame of reference

deregulation and technology. The trend towards bank consolidation, particularly in the USA, signals that some factors at play are in full evolution.

This process, sometimes called *conglomeration*, is today mainly bank driven, as credit institutions and investment banks have been actively expanding into fund management. They are doing so by using both their international presence and their technology as competitive factors against their local, smaller opponents. They are also capitalizing on their brand name, which they promote worldwide, in a way not too different to other multinational companies such as Microsoft and Coca-Cola.

3.4 Unbundling the management fee

Section 3.3 made reference to the private banker's management fee. The fee is supposed to cover services to the client associated with handholding, investment counselling and administration of the account, including collection of fees and dividends, as well as refunds. Not all banks, however, have a standard cost system that allows them to track the expenses incurred by customer account, and some do not even know their expenses associated with private banking as a whole. Under these conditions:

- It is not possible to establish the customer mirror discussed in Chapter 2 and section 3.2.
- Profitability from customer banking, in contrast to cash flow from fees and commissions, largely becomes a hit-and-run affair.

Moreover, what exactly comes into account management varies from one bank to the next. Some differentiate between *management fees*, which are proportional to type of mandate, and *administrative fees*, which are flat. Others adjust the level of administrative fee according to the services the customer buys. For instance, Swiss banks price their services based, among other things, on whether the client has a numbered account or wishes his or her mail to be held at the bank.

A more or less universal practice is that charges connected to private banking apply to the entire portfolio value, with the fee schedule forming an integral part of the management mandate to which the client subscribes. Typically, credit institutions also assess individual surcharges on especially labour-intensive work to be done to fulfil a mandate; less typically, they unbundle the overall management fee into constituent parts.

The fee structure changes over time. In the 1980s and the first half of the 1990s, for instance, Swiss banks were applying a charge for coupon collection associated with bonds in their custody. Intensive competition meant that this went out of the window, or has been bundled in with an overall administrative fee. In other countries, however, banks still apply the coupon collection or even dividend collection charge.

Table 3.1 presents, as an example, the portfolio management charges at a Swiss credit institution. A distinction is made between discretionary account management (full powers are given to the bank) and an all-inclusive administrative fee for non-discretionary accounts. The latter include in-house safekeeping, external safekeeping (usually billed to the bank in reference by correspondent banks), and charges

Table 3.1 Transaction fees, portfolio management and administration fees per year by a Swiss bank[a]

Transaction brokerage fees	Transactions in Switzerland	Transactions abroad
Equities, options, warrants		
Up to $40 000	1.10%	1.90%
This is reduced by thresholds, down to:		
For over $800 000	0.20%	0.20% + foreign commission
Bonds, notes		
Up to $40 000	0.90%	1.50%
This is reduced by thresholds, down to:		
For over $800 000	0.20%	0.20% + foreign commission

Administrative fees, non-discretionary mandates[b]	% of housekeeping value
Named accounts	0.15 per year
Numbered accounts	0.20 per year

Portfolio management fees, discretionary mandates	Fixed income portfolios	Equity portfolios	Mixed portfolios
Up to $800 000	0.75%	1.25%	1.00%
This is reduced by thresholds, down to:			
For over $40 million	0.20%	0.55%	0.30%

[a] Amounts and costs converted to US dollars as common reference.
[b] For fund units of the bank's own issuance, and that of its affiliates, there is a fee reduction of 30%. No administrative fee is applied for investments in the bank's own shares.

for securities administration, account maintenance, reports on balances, postage, and so on.

There are also charges for payment transactions, foreign exchange commissions, commissions for money transfers, commissions for bill collection, credit card(s) issued to the private banking customer, including commissions for credit-card guarantees, issuance of traveller's cheques and so on. These are examples of cross-selling banking products to private banking customers, mentioned in section 3.2.

Table 3.2 presents transaction fees and management fees of a German financial institution. To these percentages is added value added tax (VAT). Notice, as another example of cross-selling, that this particular institution has on the side a major firm whose insurance business it promotes among private banking clients, and it also gains a cash flow from other ancillary services.

As would be expected, different rates are followed by American funds management and trust services entities. These are shown in Table 3.3. The financial institution to which these fee scales pertain notes in its communication that accounts beyond a certain level of wealth management would be given special consideration as far as

Table 3.2 Transaction fees and management fees charged by a German bank

Transaction fees	
For equities	0.55%
For bonds	0.28%
Management fees (perceived every semester)	
Bundled management and administration fee	0.18%
Charges for other administration services	
Debit in account: overnight charges (EONIA)	+6%
Money withdrawn from account, other than euro	0.50% (minimum $28)
Payment order in euro	0.10% (minimum $28, maximum $280)
Credit card	$160 per year
Closing of account	$160

charges are concerned. The downsizing of charges is fairly similar to that of the German bank in the previous example.

In connection to transaction fees, practically all banks pass on to the client third party charges, such as commission, brokerages and stamp duties. Physical deliveries from portfolio are also charged per security position. The charge for non-physical deliveries from portfolio, also per security position, are lower, but they are present, although in terms of non-physical deliveries there is usually a ceiling.

Many private banking entities have an all-inclusive fee per year per position charged for the safe custody of special assets such as envelopes, documents and non-valuables, but they unbundle the cost of portfolio positions outside their mainstream business.

Table 3.3 An American financial institution's annual fee summary for investment management, advisory and trustee services

	Individual securities portfolio		100% Own funds or approved mutual funds[a]	
Account value[b]	Management account	Trustee or advisory account	Managed account	Trustee or advisory account
First $1 000 000	0.95%	1.00%	0.60%	0.65%
$1 000 000–2 000 000	0.80%	0.85%	0.50%	0.55%
$2 000 000–4 000 000	0.65%	0.60%	0.30%	0.35%
Over $4 000 000	0.55%	0.60%	0.30%	0.35%
Minimum annual fee	$5000	$5000	$3000	$3000

For accounts that require a fiduciary income tax return, there is a minimum annual tax preparation fee of $325, which includes the first three hours of preparation time.
Co-trustee fees will be in addition to the trust company fees and will be equal to one-quarter of the trust company's fee unless otherwise specified by state law or in the trust instrument.
[a] Mutual fund expenses will be in addition to the trust company's fee.
[b] Each account.

An American broker operating in Europe charges a (fairly low) annual flat fee for safekeeping American securities, but it applies an extra quarterly fee for each position in the client's portfolio that is in euros.

Applicable taxes pertaining to a client's portfolio are billed to its owner. In practically all countries with VAT the management fee is subject to VAT, although for clients domiciled abroad the portfolio management charges tend to be free of VAT (depending on the country and institution).

There are also other different rules, including exceptions affecting fee schedules. These concern minimum brokerage fees, transactions made in other exchanges than that of the bank's home country, whether or not positions concern the bank's own investment funds, fiduciary type investments and so on, as well as investments in the money market.

For example, in the case of Swiss banks the minimum brokerage fee for transactions in Switzerland or primary stock markets abroad tends to be $180 per transaction, while for transactions on other stockmarkets abroad it is double that amount (also per transaction). The fee schedule for transactions in Switzerland and abroad is 0.10–0.40 per cent for bonds and 0.20–0.70 per cent for equities and external investment funds. Here again, third party charges and fees are passed on to the client.

Charges for money market paper vary according to maturity and type of transaction from 0.125 to 0.5 per cent of the invested amount, with a minimum commission of $180. This minimum amount usually depends on currency and investment instrument, but also on the policy of the institution and certain criteria that go with it.

Banks also offer other services for which they feature a fee schedule. Examples are safe-deposit box rental, securities tax statement, tax refunds, special reporting agreements, short-term investments, legal counselling, estate planning, trust services, and securities lending and borrowing. All of these are income sources and their proceeds should be reflected in the customer mirror discussed in section 3.2.

3.5 Different companies have different private banking aims

Brokerages and commercial banks have traditionally followed different guidelines in managing their clients' private accounts, as well as in regard to fees they receive for their services. Banks have primarily focused on gaining control of their clients' asset base, with their income policy turned in this direction. Brokers have been particularly interested in trading fees, this being strategically more important than direct commission-generating business. Within this perspective, a key question facing brokerages concerns market opportunity for:

- Advice dispensing, and
- More trading in the aftermath of such advice.

Funds run by stockbrokers usually have much higher turnover than funds run by professional investment advisors on a flat-fee basis. The difference in policy can be explained in one word: commissions, which leads to some investment banks waiving their annual management fees (see also the reaction of a broker in one of the case studies in Chapter 8).

Financial analysts who participated in this research, however, think that fee-waiving for private accounts is why portfolios run by brokers return about 1 per cent a year less than those that charge fees. By contrast, fees are charged by brokers in connection with discretionary asset management accounts that are often connected to an annual performance target: a double-edged sword. Fund managers following this strategy say that one of the questions that requires a significant amount of focus is how to find out about the client's:

- Tolerance to increasing risk, and
- Underlying factors affecting the asset base.

Institutional investors who go for performance-type contracts, when they outsource asset management, are not always forthcoming with information that would answer these queries in a factual and documented manner. Banks face similar challenges when they are refocusing private banking clients' asset base, or try to achieve a better hold on it.

Behind many refocusing efforts is the realization that better control of the clients' assets is a good way to improve overall profitability, since there are fees associated with managed assets and commissions associated with transactions. This policy is particularly followed with accounts where the bank has discretionary powers, but it is controversial and may lead to business risk (see section 3.8).

As far as a commercial bank's or investment bank's profitability is concerned, senior management should never lose sight of the fact that income from fees is by no means synonymous with net profit. There used to be a time when costs associated with asset management and trust activity were primarily salary costs, of which a large portion was officer administration time. This is no longer true because other costs have come into the picture:

- Information technology,
- Communications,
- Fees paid to information providers, and
- Overheads.

Although salaries are still a large expense associated with private banking and asset management, these other expenses are not trivial. That is precisely why time and again I press the need for instituting a *customer mirror*, both for directly allocated human time per account and for indirect time, including the cost of supporting services.

No matter which specific strategy is followed by an asset manager, when the amount of time spent on each particular customer account, and associated supporting services, is recorded, it is not unusual to find out that for some accounts the fees do not cover all incurred expenses. This is the downside of fee schedules based on asset valuation.

- Different accounts with similar or the same assets may incur different costs because of different activity levels and customer contact needs.
- There is an underlying reason why some brokers say that commissions based on transactions are a better revenue-generating basis than flat fees.

Fundamentally, assuming that activity costs have been determined and that each private banking account has had its total activity costs properly assigned to it, the institution's management is well placed to be in charge of P&L, by client profit centre and in this line of business as a whole. Client accounts can be further ranked for evaluating their contribution to the private banking entity's bottom line, according to:

- Amount of funds
- Type of portfolio
- Activity of portfolio
- Prevailing asset mix, and
- Amount of responsibility assumed by the bank or broker.

These factors can lead to a better documented and flexible fee structure, and at the same time provide a sound basis for comparisons among clients, and between areas of operations. Moreover, there should be an internal schedule of special pricing considerations accounting for events such as an unusually high amount of senior management time that is not reflected in time records, and business risk, such as likely damage to the asset manager's brand name (see section 3.8).

As a concluding remark on the making of fee schedules, take the example provided by George Anders in connection with Kohlberg, Kravis, Roberts (KKR). The company assured itself of three types of management fees, and beyond that a sizeable cut of profits that clients made on KKR investments. First, it charged passive investors an annual management fee of 1.5 per cent of funds committed, for the privilege of having KKR handle their cash and look for deals. Then there was a 1 per cent commission on each acquisition's price. This is money that KKR collected for itself. Once KKR acquired a company, it also charged either a monitoring fee or annual directors fees.[5]

Furthermore, as in all hedge funds, KKR laid claim to 20 per cent of any investment gains ultimately achieved from buyouts. This 20 per cent cut on gain is generally known as *carried interests*, and it has become standard for hedge funds, venture capital outfits, and oil and gas pools. For entities with steadily growing buyout funds, the 20 per cent share on investors' profits has become a major source of income, based on risks taken with other people's money rather than risking one's own.

3.6 Performance and remuneration of investment managers

Most financial institutions keep a tight rein on the performance of their investment advisors, traders and managers, whose results are appraised, on average, once every three months. Appraisal is done in the light of changes in value of the investment portfolios entrusted to them. The three-month average, however, can be misleading.

- Fund managers of well-established ability are appraised on the basis of their performance once a year.
- Those who are starting their career, or faced problems in the past, are subject to a monthly appraisal.

Benchmark indices are the preferred means of comparing the performance of a fund, and of the person(s) who run it. A strategy based on benchmarks aims to take explicit account of price risks and obtained growth in investment. The results of these appraisals have longer term career impact, as well as short-term effects. Salaries of almost all fund managers include performance-based components.

As would be expected, the structure of salary and bonuses varies from one firm to the next, although there is a general trend. Barring exceptions, as a general rule the majority of fund managers can make up to 60 per cent of their gross basic annual salary through bonuses, with 30 per cent being the median. Numbers, however, vary by country and by company.

In the USA, roughly one-quarter of investment advisors work solely for client fees. Another quarter work on commission only, and roughly 40 per cent combine fees and commissions. Of the remainder, 5 per cent draw a salary and the rest receive a combination of salary and commissions. Bonus awards include one of more of the following primary criteria:

- Relative fund performance, compared with a benchmark
- Absolute fund performance, in terms of net returns
- Internal appraisal by colleagues and superiors
- Overall profitability of the investment company, and
- Inflowing of new financial resources from satisfied clients.

Associated with the latter reference are marketing aspects such as explicit customer satisfaction that can be used to acquire new clients. This is particularly important to a fee structure, sometimes used by brokerages and insurance companies in compensating investment advisors for selling policies. It is also a practice that may eventually lead to conflicts of interest.

The ideal is a performance evaluation and compensation set-up which, while rewarding good results, eliminates the likelihood of conflicts of interest. Also ideal is a compensation system leaving investment advisors free to concentrate on consulting and managing assets, instead of pushing products with sales charges. These are the *loads*, or front money paid by the customer for subscribing to an investment fund.

The amounts earned by investment advisors and managers from performing different tasks and selling different products can vary greatly with the method of payment. Moreover, there is considerable evidence that remuneration incentives and other control measures applied by investment companies influence the fund managers' investment decisions to a fairly large extent. Such influence involves:

- Business risk (see section 3.8) and
- Eventually legal risk (see Chapter 8).

In practically all countries, the law prescribes that investment managers 'administer the private banking accounts and trusts with the caution of a responsible business person'. But when it comes to investments, and fees and commissions derived from them, it is not easy to leave human nature aside.

- Fund managers have preferences, and
- Compensation schemes affect the investment choices being made.

Nor are there universal rules addressing all investors, all investment advisors and all fund managers. Institutional investors tend to have other objectives and preferences to private investors who bet their own money. Furthermore, unlike advisors who occupy themselves with private investors, asset managers in charge of institutional accounts have to provide justification for their decisions, as part of an internal control and evaluation process.

Sometimes, to attract talent in investment management and therefore clients, credit institutions, investment banks and other fund managers overpay their advisors and end up overcharging the investors. Based on a thorough investigation of industry practices, in September 2000, a spokesman for the Financial Services Authority (FSA) said: 'People are paying about twice as much as they realize. For every £2 of investment growth produced by one of these schemes, the industry takes £1'.[6]

By and large, these charges, which amount to £3 billion a year in the UK's unit trust industry alone, are hidden by City firms in undisclosed stockmarket dealing fees. Some experts estimate that a further £7 billion is taken by fund managers in the life insurance and pension funds industry, adding up to a very significant amount of money indeed.

In the USA, the fees of traders and investment managers have skyrocketed in line with the pay of chief executive officers (CEOs). The average CEO's pay has increased from 42 times in 1982, to 411 times that of the average production worker in 2001.[7] Responding to that sort of eye-opening statistics, William J. McDonough, then New York Fed President, acknowledged that a market economy requires that some people will be rewarded more than others, but asked: 'Should there not be both economic and moral limitations on the gap created by the market-driven reward system?'

McDonough answered his own query by stating: 'I can find nothing in economic theory that justifies this development'. Other cognizant people, including Dr Peter Drucker, had a similar response. Their point is that such huge, × 411 gap between top-brass salaries and wages of production workers has no ground whatsoever and is counterproductive.

According to *The Wall Street Journal*, McDonough cited the biblical admonition to 'love thy neighbour as thyself' as justification for voluntary CEO pay cuts, beginning with the strongest companies. He said: 'CEOs and their boards should simply reach the conclusion that executive pay is excessive and adjust it to more reasonable and justifiable levels'.[8]

Affirming McDonough's comments, the *Milwaukee Journal-Sentinel* editorialized that regulating executive compensation is the business of corporate boards, or should be. Unfortunately, too many corporate directors on company compensation committees simply rubber-stamp decisions made by the CEO, and this leads to:

- Runaway top salaries, and
- Outrageous stock options.[9]

While the reasons for going well beyond a fair and reasonable pay package for traders and investment managers are different to those impacting the CEOs' pay, the effect is very similar. Because the costs have to be covered, a spike in compensation packages invariably leads to client overcharging. This is not without consequences.

A similar statement is valid regarding procedures followed by different entities in selectively applying discounts. In the last week of August 2003 the National Association of Securities Dealers (NASD) ordered brokerage firms to reimburse mutual fund investors millions of dollars in overlooked discounts on sales commission to buy mutual fund shares. The order involved *breakpoint discounts* for large investments.

For example, a fund might charge a 5.75 per cent sales commission on a $10 000 investment, but just 4 per cent if the investment is $100 000. Breakpoint discounts typically apply to investments of $50 000 or more, while some kick in at just $25 000. But regulators say the breakpoint system is unfair because its criteria have broken down. An investigation in early 2003 found that brokers failed to give investors discounts in about one-third of all transactions. This confirms the thesis presented in Chapters 1 and 2, that investors should be proactive in managing their money.

3.7 Simulation of portfolio performance

Section 3.6 has pressed the point that the performance of investment advisors and investment managers is regularly evaluated and their bonuses, and sometimes most of their pay, are based on the results of performance tests. Two methods are mainly used to this end: *benchmarking*, often resting on an index, and *absolute performance*.

There is also a third method that should be paid attention because it makes feasible periodic pre-evaluation of investment results, and therefore it can be instrumental in promoting sound portfolio management. This method is simulation, and it can also be used to complement real-life tests, which are evidently post-mortem.

Simulation is a working analogy. When we find or develop systems, processes or products that behave in an analogous way, experimentation on one of them can lead to the study of the other. This concept was originally elaborated in the 1930s in the context of *analogue* simulation; an example being the wind tunnel. Another example of simulation is the digital differential analyser widely used in the post-World War II years by the electricity production and distribution industry.

An alternative is mathematical simulation through algorithmic and/or heuristic approaches. In the eighteenth century, in Baghdad, Muhammed Ben Musa, called *Alkhawarizmi*, wrote the first book on algebra. Later on, in a Dutch translation of his book his name was latinized to *Algorithmus*. At present, the word 'algorithm' is used to designate a process of calculation that leads:

■ From variable input data,
■ To results determined by a mathematically described step-by-step procedure.

Heuristic approaches are also used in simulation, and they rest on a different basis. An easy way to describe them is that they are characterized by trial and error, thereby following the way the human mind often works in difficult investigations, as well as in making decisions. Hence, heuristics are particularly useful in:

■ Relatively diffuse, and
■ Fuzzy problem areas.[10]

Whether the chosen solution is algorithmic, heuristic or a combination of the two, the process of simulation requires abstraction from the real world. This is necessary because many of the problems with which we are confronted are too complex to be effectively handled. The fact of leaving many of the variables out of the system, and of simplifying others, evidently introduces a certain amount of error. The conceptual process behind modelling and simulation is described in Figure 3.4.

Simulation based on mathematical modelling is a fast growing discipline in finance, but not all models are properly used, let alone accurate. As an adage has it, 'All models are wrong. But some are useful'. When developing and using simulators, private bankers, institutional investors and all other parties should remember that:

- Accuracy is more important than precision, and
- 80 per cent of the challenge is connected to the database; only 20 per cent lies with the model.

With these basic notions in mind, it should be appreciated that whether we talk of simulating portfolio performance, or of any other applications domain, rich databases are a major 'plus'. The opposite is also true. Even if the model is fine, missing or (even worse) erroneous data lead to substandard results.

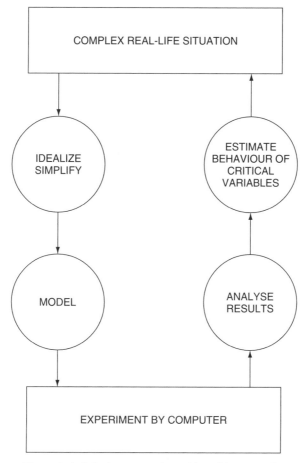

Figure 3.4 Solutions to real-world problems can be helped through simulation

Supposing the information elements (IEs) in the database are properly updated and dependable, a basic decision to be made when experimenting on the performance of investments is whether historical IEs should be given equal weight, or new ones be weighted more than the old. This can be done by reducing the relative importance of past IEs, so that:

- The most recent ones have a greater weight.
- But at the same time past data are still in the picture.

Working with a database spanning ten years or more, some analysts use a decay factor of 0.9841 for past IEs, which corresponds to the most recent monthly returns being ten times more likely to appear in the sample than the oldest monthly returns. This helps in the capture of some of the more recent market trends, while also paying attention to longer term developments.

Evidently, statistics should not be the only input to a simulation of portfolio performance. Another major component is qualitative, based on the most recent opinions of financial analysts and their projections. The '2005 – The Year Ahead' report by Merrill Lynch stated: 'Corporate bonds appear overpriced . . . (and) it now makes poor economic sense for a company to buy back debt rather than undertake more shareholder friendly actions such as share buybacks . . .'.[11]

Still another valuable input to simulation of portfolio performance is port-mortem walkthroughs of projections that have been made. The aim of post-mortems is to confront prognostications with real-life events. This helps in judging the accuracy of people's judgement, as well as improving the forecasting process.

Dr Harold D. Koontz, my professor of Business Strategy at UCLA, taught his students that the risk taken with prognostications is the cost of reading tomorrow's newspaper today. The reader should appreciate that prognostications are based on hypotheses, and these are nearly 100 per cent judgemental. Even the most elaborate hypotheses made by experts may not hold because the market is not efficient, as some economists believe it to be.[12] The most dangerous way of making forecasts is to base one's work on hypotheses supported by the leading theory at the time.

In principle, the accuracy of portfolio simulation can be improved by a holistic approach that is state of the art, modular and regularly updated. A template for such a strategy is shown in Figure 3.5. Notice the attention paid by the suggested approach to risk management (more on this in Chapter 4).

Lehman Brothers, the investment bank, developed a model that projects portfolio risk over the following month by means of values for a large number of observable risk sensitivities. The latter are taken as basic portfolio characteristics. It then maps these sensitivities into an estimated *return volatility*. Observable characteristics relate to 100 factors and include:

- Distribution of interest rate exposures along the yield curve,
- Portfolio allocation to industry sectors and credit qualities, and
- A range of variables concerning mortgages, and callable or putable securities.

Among the model's advantages is the fact that risk sensitivities are defined exogenously; therefore, they correspond to the parameters used by managers to make

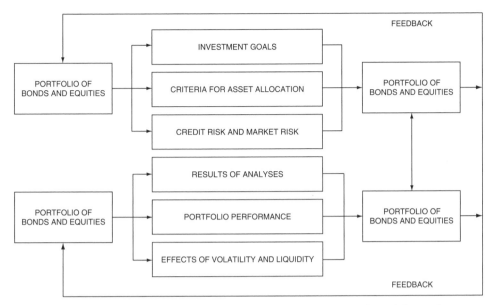

Figure 3.5 A modular, flexible and holistic approach to simulation of portfolio performance

portfolio allocations. In addition, credit risk is measured by spread durations, one for each credit tier. The model is calibrated to individual bond returns, while unexplained residuals are used to estimate security-specific risk, which may lead to firm-specific idiosyncratic sources, such as those characterized by Parmalat and other types of irregularities.

3.8   The impact of business risk

Financial institutions and other companies have different ways of defining business risk. Most of these, however, evolve around brand-name risk, events caused by uncertainty in profits, the effect of internal factors such as product obsolescence, system inefficiencies, shortfalls and price changes, external factors, such as changes in the competitive environment, and the after-effects of legal risk (see Chapter 8).

Brand name risk is particularly important in connection with private banking and asset management. It is essentially reputational risk (see Chapters 1 and 2) that comes from the fact that somebody knowingly, or by mistake, is abusing the regulation. For instance, the executive responsible for the operations in India of Crédit Suisse sold short securities. In the USA, and most of Europe, there is nothing illegal in selling short, but it is punishable in India. As this example demonstrates:

■ Globalization brings to the foreground huge differences in cultures and in regulations.
■ In turn, these legal, regulatory and cultural differences prevailing in financial markets make compliance much more complex.

Business risk may come from external or internal sources. Few companies pay the due amount of attention to product obsolescence as a major internal business risk. Yet, Henry Ford was 100 per cent on the right track when he said that a company's product is by far the number one reason for its business success or failure. Investors should always consider a company's product line, its market appeal and its evolution before buying its equity. The same principle applies to the products and services offered by private banks and asset managers.

Some experts believe that another major internal business risk factor is that of succession in a largely family businesses. Management succession is by no means linear. Henry Ford bullied his son Edsel for years and never gave him the reins of power. Thomas Watson Sr, the founder of IBM, refused to pass on the reins to Thomas Jr until he was eighty-two. Serge Dassault, of Dassault Enterprises, was sixty-one years old before his father gave him the chairmanship of the family's aircraft and electronics business.

There is also the case where the family retreats mainly to an ownership role. When this happens, one of the key decisions that impacts on business risk is how to constitute the board. Next to it comes another vital decision: the circumstances in which family members can join the company, and at which position. In connection to private banking, asset management and elsewhere, the best policy is to insist that:

■ Family members work successfully elsewhere before they apply, and
■ They face an evaluation as rigorous as any outsider before being taken on, along the lines described in section 3.6.

A case on the borderline between business risk and legal risk is the examination of Citigroup by Bafin, the German banking regulator. Towards the end of 2004, Bafin was investigating Citigroup for possible market manipulation in the Eurozone government bond futures market. This inquiry looked into whether the bank's bond traders manipulated the Bund futures market on the Eurex exchange in the summer of 2004.[13]

Experts suggest that Bafin's investigation may have a wider impact because it is being co-ordinated with a separate inquiry by the FSA of the UK. The FSA's investigation, too, is looking into Citigroup's bond trades in the cash market. If the regulators find evidence of market manipulation in either the British or the German case, Citigroup could face business risk along two lines:

■ The aftermath of a lawsuit, and
■ The ire of European governments.

According to market watchers, in August 2004 Citigroup took advantage of a quirk of the EuroMTS platform for trading cash government bonds (which requires all market-makers to provide continuous price quotes), flooding the cash market with €11 billion sell orders and causing rivals to rush to hedge their exposure in the Eurex market for German government bonds, by selling the futures. About half an hour later, Citigroup bought back €4 billion of the bonds at a lower price, and this evidently raised suspicions and allegations of market manipulation.

There are many other sources of business risk that may hit a commercial bank, investment bank, or any other company. For instance, one external factor is *rating risk*, because of market grading through the proxy of independent rating agencies. One of the results of downgrading is the higher cost of lending. To overcome the strategic gap that affects business risk, Jos Wieleman of ABN-Amro advises:

- Taking the proverbial long, hard look in business strategy, and
- Going beyond the classical, short one-year planning period.

According to ABN-Amro, business losses can be directly traced to unexpected changes due to failed strategic decisions; events that damage the bank's franchise; mismatch in pricing of products and services; adverse conditions in revenue, from changes in the banking environment; and internal shortfalls in human resources, sales effort, outsourcing and other factors.

To be in charge of business risk, Wieleman suggests the *corporate performance management* (CPM) system, an umbrella term describing the methodologies, metrics, processes and technology necessary to monitor and manage business performance. A methodology for measurement and evaluation of business risk is crucial because, quite often, the best way to secure agreement in an important problem is to treat it boldly, provide documented evidence, go to the root of the problem and settle it upon sound foundations. This is excellent advice to private bankers and asset managers, complementing what was said in section 3.6 about evaluation of performance.

Notes

1 S. Walton, *Made in America*, Bantam, New York, 1993.
2 J.B. Caouette, E.I. Alyman and P. Narayanan, *Managing Credit Risk*, John Wiley, New York, 1998.
3 See the case of Citigroup's German affiliate Kundenkredit Bank (KKB), in D.N. Chorafas and H. Steinmann, *Expert Systems in Banking*, Macmillan, London, 1991.
4 Voting rights, power these bring to the institution, and so on. See D.N. Chorafas, *The Management of Equity Investments*, Butterworth-Heinemann, London, 2005.
5 G. Anders, *Merchants of Debt*, Basic Books, New York, 1992.
6 *Sunday Times*, 1 October 2000.
7 *BusinessWeek On-line*, 5 June 2002.
8 *Wall Street Journal*, 9 December 2002.
9 D.N. Chorafas, *Management Risk. The Bottleneck is at the Top of the Bottle*, Macmillan/Palgrave, London, 2004.
10 D.N. Chorafas, *Chaos Theory in the Financial Markets*, Probus, Chicago, 1994.
11 Merrill Lynch, *2005 – The Year Ahead*, 14 December 2004.
12 D.N. Chorafas, *The Management of Equity Investments*, Butterworth-Heinemann, London, 2005.
13 *Financial Times*, 15 December 2004.

4 Risk and return with investments

4.1 Introduction

Every investment has associated with it a type of exposure. As far as *market risk* is concerned, exposure is related to the volatility of market prices, and therefore of future value of the investment. The market changes steadily and uncertainty characterizes all future events.

Uncertainty affects both risk and return, and basically there is nothing wrong with uncertainty. As Francis Bacon put it, 'If a man will begin with certainties, he shall end in doubts. But if he will be content to begin in doubts, he will end in certainties.' No better dictum describes the work involved in *risk management*. The keywords are:

- Volatility,
- Uncertainty, and
- Exposure.

Many reasons exist in the background of these three keywords, and the forces propelling them; for instance *leverage*, which magnifies the risk(s) embedded in financial instruments, and market psychology and illiquidity, leading to conditions of growing exposure. Large market events are typically followed by periods of illiquidity, and this can have a significant aftermath on exposure assumed by the investor; hence the need for managing risk.

Risk management is really a process about the management of change, and of the exposure associated with the explosion of opportunities in the financial market. It is also a term sounding a warning that while the control of risk is every investor's business, this will be impossible without steady monitoring, quantitative measurements and accounting for qualitative factors that impact on exposure.

Not only investors but also institutions have to take risks. Notwithstanding the myriad of regulations and social responsibilities to which the banking industry is subject, a credit institution or asset management entity is, after all, a business that has to take risks in order to:

- Widen its opportunities, and
- Make profits for its stakeholders.

Risk-taking, however, has an evident impact on the bank's clients on the credit risk side, because the institution can go bankrupt (see section 4.2); hence the different safety nets provided by regulators and legislators for the bank's depositors, covered in

Chapter 1. Moreover, practically all of a bank's activities are subject to legal risk (see Chapter 8).

Indeed, as a profession the risk management was established in response to the growing importance of proactive action in regard to assumed exposure, as well as the need for damage control. Risks are never static. They evolve over time as new financial instruments develop and the market changes. The methods, tools and overall approach to risk control must be revised and renewed. In recent years traditional risk management functions are being challenged as:

- New types of exposure dominate the financial landscape, and
- The breadth and scope of existing risks has been amplified.

Investors, bankers and fund managers should appreciate that as the speed of change accelerates, and a networked global economy creates opportunities of unprecedented scale, the assumed exposure(s) also increase(s), while new factors come into play. A greater exposure is also assumed as new competitors are challenging mainline business,

- Making existing risk control systems obsolete, and
- Overpowering policies and procedures previously put in place to reduce risk.

One of the criteria of good governance is that an organization does not delay in adopting much more rigorous approaches in judging risk and return than those it used previously. Delays are unwanted because the competitive landscape is changing quickly. Dr Lev Borodovsky, the chief risk manager of Crédit Suisse First Boston, aptly comments that: 'The financial institution of the new economy is an advisor, an opportunistic broker, a research company, an asset manager, and most of all, an information technology firm'; also, most evidently, a risk manager.

4.2   Basic notions of risk assessment

Every investor's, private banker's or fund manager's business activities expose him or her to different types of risks. Many find it difficult to control exposure because they do not know where to start. This is a problem with which I am often confronted in my seminars. The answer is simple. As an old adage has it: Defining what the problem is, is half way to its solution.

People with experience in risk control appreciate that proper identification and assessment of every exposure that confronts us is essential to the success and financial soundness of any type of business operation. Figure 4.1 summarizes a methodology leading from risk and return objectives to problem solution. The problem, in this case, is that of being in charge of risks.

Managing risk begins with the conception of the basic nature of exposure(s) being assumed by an investor, or an entity. This definition must be enriched with expertise and experience resulting from sound risk management. A financial institution's

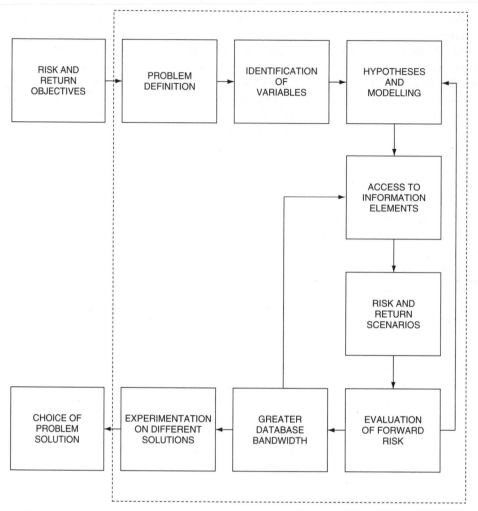

Figure 4.1 Problem definition is only the starting point to a solution on risk and return

assets manager's senior executives should take an active role in overseeing various risk categories,

■ Reviewing past and present exposures,
■ Prognosticating likely future developments,
■ Improving upon risk control practices, and
■ Analysing risk-related developments due to market moves, credit risk trends and changing regulations.

The volatility of market risk is the theme of section 4.6, but credit risk, too, is volatile. The likelihood that a counterparty will not be fulfilling its contractual obligations is by no means steady. There is a potential for loss due to this failure to perform, because of inability or unwillingness to do so.

As a term, credit risk is also used in connection with the value of collateral held to secure the counterparty's obligations, when this collateral is proving to be inadequate. In the general case, direct exposure to credit risk may result from:

■ Lending activities,
■ Investment decisions,
■ Trading operations,
■ The role of intermediary in financial contracts, and
■ All other types of portfolio positions being held.

For adequate protection from credit risk, particular attention has to be paid to credit concentrations in regard to a counterparty, or groups of counterparties when they have similar economic characteristics, as well as to conditions that would cause their ability to meet obligations to be similarly affected by economic, industrial or geographical factors.

Counterparties to proprietary trading, hedging and financing activities may be individuals or financial institutions, including brokers and dealers, banks, asset managers and other companies. Credit losses could arise if these other parties fail to perform under the terms of the contract. The theoretical way of managing credit risk is by dealing with creditworthy counterparties. Nobody would argue with that, except that it is not a practical proposition. The practical approach is:

■ Monitoring net exposure to individual counterparties,
■ Complying with established credit limits on a daily basis,
■ Obtaining collateral where appropriate, and steadily evaluating this collateral's value.

There is no way to ensure that one deals only with creditworthy counterparties, because creditworthiness itself is volatile. In the post-World War II years, and nearly until the end of the twentieth century, General Motors (GM) was considered to be the biggest company in the world, solid as the rock of Gibraltar. The same was true of its wholly owned financial subsidiary General Motors Acceptance Corporation (GMAC), one of the largest non-bank credit institutions.

However, on 16 March 2005, shares and bonds in GM, as well as bonds in GMAC, slid sharply after the world's biggest car-maker, and one of the heaviest corporate borrowers, warned that it would miss its profit targets. This announcement made investors nervous, because it narrowed the odds that GM's credit would soon be reduced to junk status.

Blaming tough competition in the North American car and truck market, GM said that it expected a first-quarter 2005 loss of about $850 million, or $1.50 a share, excluding special items. It had previously forecast that it would break even. The rating agency Standard & Poor's revised its outlook for GM's credit from stable to negative, and said that the present BBB– rating was 'tenuous'.

For the financial markets the credit risk problem is much wider than these numbers show. GM has outstanding debt of more than $300 billion. Not only did spreads on its bonds widen markedly following the announcement, but there was also the risk of a financial earthquake in the debt instruments market, if the rating agencies lowered GM's rating to junk status. Crucial considerations include:

- Whether the company's cash flow improved, and
- Whether the profit margins on its new line of trucks and sport-utility vehicles improved over the current margin.

Two large credit-rating providers, Moody's Investors Service and Standard & Poor's, placed GM's outstanding debt on watch for a possible downgrade, while Fitch lowered its rating to BBB– from BBB. All three events increased the likelihood that the company's bonds might go below investment grade, with the aftermath that many institutional investors holding these bonds would have to unload them, because their statutes do not allow them to have junk bonds in their portfolio.

In synergy to these events, GM's troubles fuelled concerns that the finances of other US companies might not be healthy enough to justify the low interest rates they have been paying on their debt. As a result, credit spreads for junk bonds started to widen, after they had been hovering at around three percentage points, the lowest level in more than two years. At GM, the CEO outlined a three-pronged approach to correcting the company's problems, comprising:

- Production cuts,
- A cost-reduction drive, and
- Efforts to improve demand through new models and more carefully targeted sales incentives.

The market was not impressed by these pronouncements, and it posed the most crucial question, 'Is GM a company-specific problem or a market problem?' Market participants remarked that GM is one of the biggest corporate bond issuers in the world, through its parent company and GMAC, its financing arm. A large amount of GM and GMAC paper has been in investment grade bonds. If it reaches junk status, it will hit like a hammer the junk bond market, which has limited capacity to absorb the sheer volume of GM/GMAC paper.

4.3   Mitigating the risk of losses

As the case study in section 4.2 demonstrated, risks are omnipresent and volatile. To mitigate the risk of losses, companies establish policies and procedures, which include elaborating and reviewing credit limits, monitoring the quality of counterparties, and increasing margin requirements for certain securities, counterparties or whole industries.

Arrangements concerning the control of credit risk should always be subject to requirements to provide additional collateral, in the event of market volatility resulting in declines in the value of collateral received. Part and parcel of steady vigilance is periodic assessment of the validity of credit ratings, reflecting the credit quality of a counterparty.[1] This is an integral part of the credit management process conducted with risk in mind. The bank's or asset manager's executives should regularly review asset quality, including:

- Concentrations,
- Delinquencies,
- Non-performing loans,
- Loan losses and recoveries.

Transaction management is another major area crying out for risk control. Every organization, and not only financial entities, depends on the type and object of transactions it is executing. In trading, client transactions are entered into on either a cash or a margin basis. In a margin transaction, the company extends credit to a client, which is collateralized by cash and securities in the client's account. While amounts loaned are limited by margin regulations by the authorities, margins always involve counterparty risk.

In manufacturing and merchandising, too, there is counterparty risk. The credit exposure is that counterparties will be financially unable to proceed with payments according to terms of agreement, making necessary a repossession of the goods. Manufacturing companies often use credit ratings by independent rating agencies in their decision to extend credit. An example reflecting the policy followed by General Electric has been published in its annual report, and is presented in Table 4.1.

Moreover, all financial and industrial operations are exposed to *market risk*, which (as we briefly saw in the Introduction) is the potential change in value of financial instruments. This is caused by unfavourable changes (to the investor) in interest rates, equity prices, other commodity prices, foreign currency exchange rates and other market variables. Companies have a variety of methods to monitor their market risk profile, which invariably involve reviewing their:

- Positions,
- Exposures,
- Investments, and
- Trading strategies.

Table 4.1 General Electric's counterparty credit criteria[a]

	Credit rating	
	Moody's	Standard & Poor's
Term of transaction		
Between one and five years	Aa3	AA−
Greater than five years	Aaa	AAA
Credit exposure limits		
Up to $50 million	Aa3	AA−
Up to $75 million	Aaa	AAA

[a] From the Annual Report 2000.

Some companies calculate market risk by means of modelling, based on estimating loss exposure through sensitivity testing. These results are compared to established limits, with exceptions subject to review and approval by senior management. Other market risk-control procedures include:

- Monitoring inventory ageings,
- Reviewing traders' positions, and
- Re-evaluating current risk management solutions.

Investors are exposed to interest rate risk primarily from changes in rates affecting their interest-earning assets. The values of debt instruments, all the way from government bonds, securitized corporate loans, mortgage-backed securities, and so on, is sensitive to changes in interest rates. The same is true of exposure to funding sources, particularly loans with floating interest rates.

Interest rate risk management programmes must focus on minimizing exposure to interest rate movements, setting an optimal mixture of floating- and fixed-rate debt, and following a strategy that is swamping liquidity risk. Tier-one companies use simulation (see Chapter 3) to assess their interest rate exposure and establish the desired ratio of floating- and fixed-rate debt. As far as possible, they:

- Manage interest rate exposure and the floating-to-fixed ratio through borrowings, or
- Use interest rate swaps and caps to adjust their interest rate risk profile.

Foreign exchange risk management programmes usually focus on hedging transaction exposure to optimize consolidated cash flow. Companies are mainly exposed to currency risk because of net payments made by international customers, as a result of their import of raw materials and semi-manufactured goods, and in the case of future export activities. Companies enter into forward contracts and options in foreign currencies, to reduce the impact of changes in currency exchange rates.

Because risks change over time, quoting a level of exposure by means of a methodology established years ago may become inaccurate. The obsolete exposure numbers given by the value at risk (VAR) model, advanced by the 1996 Market Risk Amendment, provide an example.[2] Another example from life insurance industry is that, in Western countries, insurers are exposed to *longevity risk* (of insured persons), which is of a systematic type and cannot be minimized.

Because the nature, type and amplitude of exposure change, investors, banks and assets managers are confronted with the challenge of developing new methods and models to manage risk properly. Moreover, the auditing department should have the skills needed to audit those methods and models, instead of simply questioning some difficult to deal with hypotheses.

The new capital adequacy framework by the Basel Committee on Banking Supervision (Basel II) has brought into view the fact that all entities and, by consequence, investors too, are exposed to *operational risk*.[3] Many reasons can be found in its origin, ranging from plain fraud to execution error, improper or inadequate business conduct, and lack of appropriate internal control. Figure 4.2 gives a birdseye view

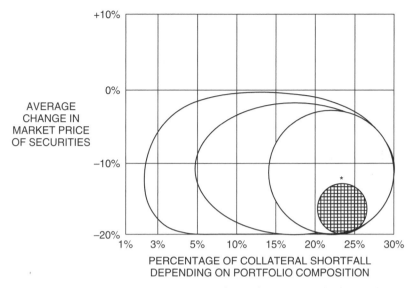

Figure 4.2 Operational risk because of shortfall due to volatility in the price of securities given as collateral. *High-risk area that significantly exceeds the typical haircut. (Based on an original concept by Donna Howe)

of operational risks because of shortfall due to volatility in the price of securities given as collateral.

Banks that have studied the origins of operational risk appreciate that it is causal and event orientated. Invariably, its aftermath is financial loss and damage, all the way to reputational risk (see Chapter 2). The Basle Committee has advanced different ways of accounting for operational risk in terms of needed financial resources. These range:

■ From the standardized method,
■ To a loss distribution approach, which is practically bottom–up,
■ And the scoreboard, which is top–down.

All of these risks are important references for individual investors, institutional investors and the industry at large. Increasingly, independent rating agencies rerate financial institutions and other organizations, on the basis of their *risk management solutions*. This is done on the understanding that the control of mounting on-balance sheet and off-balance sheet risks (the latter resulting from derivatives transactions) is one of the crucial tests for a company's survival.

4.4 Prerequisites for rigorous risk control

Nobody in any business can or should be under the illusion that investments are hazard free. The risks discussed in sections 4.2 and 4.3 exist in all investments and in all business partnerships. While many banks, fund managers and other entities, think that they have put their exposure under lock and key, this is never really proven.

Moreover, risk means opportunity. As the physicist Max Planck said, 'Without occasional venture or risk, no genuine invention can be accomplished, even in the most exact sciences.'

Max Planck's dictum applies 100 per cent in finance under any market conditions, including those of the most tightly controlled economy. This dictum is even more true when instruments are new and markets are nervous. The reader should also appreciate that past knowledge about risk events is not synonymous with the appropriate management of exposure, although it is one of its basic ingredients.

Risk and the methods for controlling it should be subject to steady research and analysis. Without steady vigilance, we will not find a solution in identifying the exposure that we are assuming, unless we stumble upon it. But this knowledge should be supplemented by means of experimentation that accounts for:

- Rising uncertainty,
- The likelihood that 'this' or 'that' risk may become a big force, and
- Re-evaluation of risk and reward associated with a changing market environment or investment strategy.

A disciplined approach in one's investment decisions, enhanced through internal control, is much more advisable today than in the past. International integration of securities markets has opened up new investment perspectives for both institutional and private investors which include new opportunities and novel risks.

- On the one hand, globalization is enabling investors to pursue their yield targets more efficiently.
- On the other hand, the variables surrounding investment decisions have increased significantly, making solutions to investment problems much more complex.

Investment analysts and advisors, rocket scientists and other experts, assisted by world-class technology, can effectively help investors, private bankers and asset managers. Sometimes, however, what they contribute does not quite compensate for the increase in the problem's challenges. Targeting portfolio combinations, which correspond to an enlarged scale of investors' requirements, introduces new risks.

The message to retain from these references is that good news and bad news go in tandem. As the number of investors increases, liquidity also seems to grow. However, *liquidity* is an expression of investors' confidence in their ability to adjust the securities portfolio promptly in the light of new information. Therefore, when the market grows nervous, liquidity among typical investors disappears, and it is reintroduced by contrarians, a role played by some hedge funds.

At the same time, the ability to draw in liquidity depends, to a significant degree, on the pricing of securities being transparent for buyers and sellers. Electronic trading platforms are helping in this role. They are also a useful means of grouping together investors' purchase requirements, regardless of their location. Properly used, technology can both:

- Promote price transparency, and
- Increase the speed at which orders are executed.

Technology helps in amplifying the advantages gained from capital market integration. Without high technology it is not possible to meet the requirements posed by large institutional investors. A global financial network enhances one's ability to be in control of global risk. Major investors choose their counterparties in the banking industry for:

- The solutions they provide to their problems,
- The contribution they make in handling a growing range of investment risks.

As Figure 4.3 suggests, technology provides an infrastructure that can be used effectively in controlling the investor's exposure; but while technology is important, it is not enough in assuming a rigorous risk control solution. The most important ingredient is management's awareness that:

- Risks must be controlled proactively, and
- Their identification and management should be done by a unit totally independent of risk-taking.

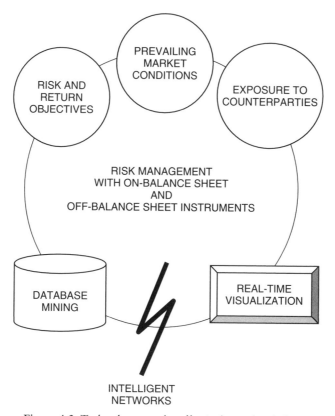

Figure 4.3 Technology can be effectively used to help in controlling the investor's exposure, but solutions are not fail-safe

A rigorous risk control plan would steadily track the nature, as well as magnitude, of risks being taken. Much of the uncertainty associated with the value of securities is due to the fact that while markets become more and more integrated, there is still a lack of international balance sheet standards and supervisory structures, although the International Financial Reporting Standard (IFRS) developed by London-based International Accounting Standards Board (IASB), applicable in the European Union and some other countries since January 2005, may improve this situation. A standard and transparent financial reporting format:

■ Reduces information asymmetries between investors and issuers, and
■ Leads to better understanding of risks, while also downsizing capital costs.

Greater investor confidence in issuers and issues raises market liquidity, through reduced bid-ask spreads, lower price volatility, larger trade volumes and other factors. The transition to internationally applicable disclosure regulations also helps to intensify a global competition for capital and to attract foreign investments.

The impact of reliable and easily understood information about the value of assets, and therefore their risk and return, should never be underestimated. Capital market prices have a key role in allocating an economy's resources. When the prices of assets actually reflect all relevant information known to market participants, capital is channelled to more efficient use. Examples of crucial information that should be produced on a universal standard are:

■ *Leverage*, that is total liabilities over total assets,
■ *Profitability*, net income over total assets,
■ *Acid test*, current assets over current liabilities,
■ *Cash velocity*, sales over cash and cash equivalents,
■ *Cash flow*, in its different forms and metrics,
■ *Fixed assets turnover*, sales over fixed assets,
■ *Interest earned*, earnings before interest and taxes (EBIT) over interest charges.

Other information important to financial transparency and, by extension, risk control, includes inventory turnover (sales/inventory marked-to-market) and inventory to net working capital (with net working capital taken as the difference between current assets and current liabilities).

In conclusion, a conscious approach to risk handling is dependent both on the financial market players being accountable for their own mistakes, and on the reliability of the methods and metrics they are using, as well as on their transparency both inside and outside the organization. Internal transparency is promoted by an effective and punctual internal control system.[4]

4.5 Fine-tuning the philosophy of investments

Thomas Clausen, the former CEO of Bank of America and the World Bank, used to say: 'We have to take risks. That is our business. But if we analyse them properly and price them right, our banks will remain sound.' Risk-based pricing is also a basic requirement with Basel II. However, properly analysing the risks being taken, and pricing them correctly, is a hugely demanding task at a time of:

- Fierce competition
- Hot new businesses, and
- Erratically behaving markets.

What makes the fine-tuning through risk-based pricing so much more challenging is the fact that fierce competition ends by bending the pricing rules. At the same time, hot new businesses that 'everyone has to be in' blur the judgement being made about an investment's or a transaction's risk and return.

Adding to the risks being taken even under normal business conditions is management's distaste for rigorous internal control. Following Clausen's dictum, the most important mission is not to micromanage risk, while losing contact with the big picture of exposure, but to detect the changes taking place and make sure that the amount of risk is within *tolerances* established by:

- Private investors,
- Institutional investors, and
- The bank as a whole.

In the background of this statement lies the fact that the management of a portfolio is not a simple matter of procedural approaches and mathematical modelling, although both these elements are important. Able solutions must reflect the *philosophy of investments*, for instance whether or not there should be international diversification that aims to spread risk among different:

- Markets
- Instruments, and
- Currencies.

A philosophy of investments will attempt to elaborate a *hedging strategy*, to be implemented by means of financial engineering. Such a strategy can be more effective when the investor's profile is defined in terms of risk and return, as discussed in Chapter 2; therefore, when we know the investor's risk appetite, which defines the level of exposure that could be taken in regard to investments.

Quite often, bankers, investment advisors and asset managers use the concept of 'minimum risk'. This is a coarse definition, which is not enough to identify applicable tolerances, and in cases it may even be counterproductive. Much more needs to be defined, in qualitative and in quantitative terms, in terms of investment guidelines and exposure limits, along the frame of reference shown in Figure 4.4.

Associated with every investment philosophy are important issues connected to risk measurement and monitoring. Any sound solution would provide investors with the ability both to quantify risks, and to qualify risks and return tradeoffs. Clear

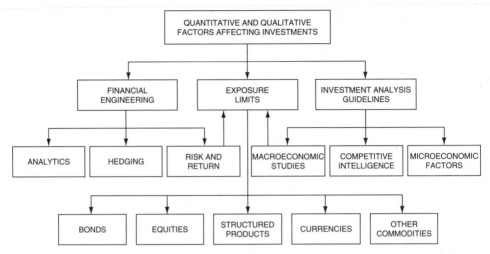

Figure 4.4 A philosophy of investments needs to be documented by decisions that help in screening assets and in setting levels of exposure

measurements encourage sound management practices connected to the control of exposure, but at the same time investors need to:

- Understand the limitations present in all methodologies, and
- Appreciate when it is necessary to supplement normal testing with stress testing (see section 4.8).

As people and companies become active participants in new instruments and new markets, taking on types of risks with which they are not familiar, they should develop the capability to assess these exposures in a dependable way. To do so, they must be aware of relevant innovations in risk management practices, and how these can be applied to their case. A sound stratagem is that of learning from the leaders in the field.

The Basel Committee on Banking Supervision advises that fully consolidated risk measurement and risk management systems and procedures should be the ultimate objective for all firms with activities that span multiple risk categories and business lines.[5] Hence, there is a need for continued effort to develop further a rigorous internal control methodology, in spite of the difficulties associated with the frequently negative organizational reaction to internal control.

The Basel Committee also brings attention to the potential for excessive optimism when making simplifying assumptions in the calculation of risk. For instance, it is tempting for firms to assume a significant amount of diversification benefits, rather than take a conservative approach. One example that comes to mind is that of a major financial institution, which

- First, quite objectively computed its economic capital requirements,
- Then reduced them by 20 per cent because of 'beneficial diversification effects'.

Supervisors also stress the point that emphasis on risk management within entities should ideally be complemented by a focus on the quality of the company's risk management process, including the way in which this is evaluated by market analysts, rating agencies and counterparties. This is part of market discipline, and market discipline plays a key role in helping to assure that:

■ Emerging risks are promptly identified and addressed, and
■ Banks and fund managers devote appropriate resources to risk control.

Moreover, an integral part of an investment philosophy is the evaluation of *management risk* associated with companies whose equity or debt one buys.[6] To make the quantitative and qualitative aspects of management risk more transparent, the US Congress passed the Sarbanes–Oxley Act in 2002, in the wake of the accounting scandals at Enron, WorldCom and many other mismanaged companies.

Critics of Sarbanes–Oxley point to the cost of compliance with the new law. The most effective, as well as the more onerous, part of the Act is section 404, which started to be applied on 15 November 2002. It requires the chief executives and chief financial officers of public companies, and their external auditors, to:

■ Appraise internal controls over financial transactions, and
■ Report any weaknesses within seventy-five days of the end of a company's fiscal year.

Classically, auditors have addressed quantitative information. The evaluation of internal control is of qualitative type, and it is practically being done for the first time. Some of America's large public companies estimate that they would devote more than 100 000 person-hours to compliance with section 404 in its first year.[7] Although the load should ease thereafter, if this is the price to pay for dependability of financial statements, then so be it.

4.6   Risk and return with implied volatility

The concept of volatility was introduced in Chapter 1. As a reminder, market volatility is a measure of variability in the price of a commodity or other asset. It is usually defined as the annualized standard deviation of natural logarithm of asset prices, but other metrics are also used. The distribution of prices of a certain commodity over a longer period is usually taken as being normal (bell-shaped), but in reality the normal distribution is only an approximation of real-life events, whether these are market prices or any other variable.

In any market and for any commodity, volatility is a statistic based on past experience, specifically the time series that it has produced. Although this information is most relevant, much more important than past volatility is future, or *implied volatility*, which is essentially an estimate. When available, measures of implied volatility provide valuable information on the uncertainty prevailing in the market. This is true of all commodities, including:

- Equities,
- Interest rates, and
- Currency exchange rates.

Estimates of implied volatility, which increases day to day, week to week, or month to month, create a certain level of anxiety among market players. Implied volatility is normally calculated on the basis of option pricing models, to obtain an estimate of expected dispersion of future percentage changes.

In terms of debt instruments, an implied bond market volatility represents the implied volatility of the near-contract future rolled over twenty days prior to expiry (as defined by Bloomberg). Therefore, twenty days before expiry of contracts, a change is made in the choice of contracts used to compute implied volatility:

- From the contract closer to maturity,
- To the next contract in the pool.

Regarding equity investments, implied volatility reflects the expected standard deviation of percentage stock price changes. Taken over a period of up to three months, this is considered as implied in prices of options on stock price indices, such as:

- S&P 500, for the USA
- Dow Jones Euro Stoxx 50, for Europe
- Nikkei 225, for Japan.

In all the aforementioned cases, implied volatility is an indicator of uncertainty as to future price movements. For instance, the implied volatility of the NASDAQ 100 index increased from an average value of 36 per cent in 1999 to 51 per cent in 2000. By contrast, the implied volatility of Standard & Poor's 500 index stood at 21 per cent in both 1999 and 2000. The difference reflected the fact that over the aforementioned period, technology stocks were highly volatile.

As a rule, a significant degree of co-movement between historical and implied volatility suggests that the more uncertain market players become about future stock prices, the higher their sensitivity to incoming news with regard to earnings, or other fundamental factors. This is reflected in large price fluctuations such as those of the NASDAQ index. The volatility of Brent crude oil price from its peak in 1979 to its new peak in 2004 provides another example.

Not only is the volatility of prices in the background of risk and reward faced by investors, but it can also provide useful information on trends in the value of assets. For instance, among other things, stock prices reflect the expectations of market players regarding future dividends as well as the upside in the equity's price. These are linked, in turn, to expected developments in demand by consumers and other companies. Therefore, they are mapped in corporate profits and eventually dividends.

Corporate profits are generally related to the anticipated pace of economic activity and internal company efficiency; for instance, cost control. Because equity price movements can be indicative of changes in market expectations with regard to economic growth, stock price developments complement information drawn from other asset prices, such as:

- Nominal bond yields, and
- Real yields on inflation-index-linked bonds.

Central banks monitor the evolution in stock prices to assess the wealth and confidence effects that may arise from equity price movements. From the viewpoint of monetary policy, high stock price volatility, together with the possibility of misalignments between stock prices and their fundamentals, makes the assessment of stock price developments for future economic conditions most important.

From time to time, there is a global rise in volatility of stock price indices, covering a broad range of industry sectors. Debt policies (and therefore the management of liabilities)[8] and equity prices tend to correlate, as shown in section 4.3 in connection with GM. Usually, rising markets keep this correlation on the backburner. However, in March 2000, when the stockmarket bubble burst, the different players appreciated that we had reached the point where:

- The outstanding financial debt of the world could never be paid, and
- The global economy was attempting to meet demands for payments that are fast multiplying: a nearly impossible task.

One day, economic historians will probably say that we began to enter the stage of global market instability not with the downturn of East Asia's 'tigers' in 1997 and other earthquakes such as the Russian meltdown, but in September 1998, with the collapse of Long Term Capital Management (LTCM).[9]

To appreciate the risk associated with the LTCM event, it is proper to recall that in the 1990s we entered a zone of economic activity based on liabilities. This means a mounting amount of debt (see Chapter 1) and the process of rolling over debt requires monetary and financial aggregates greater than the amount that is becoming due over a given course of time:

- The policy of bailout of entities too big to fail creates, in the long run, a greater problem than it is solving.
- Eventually, a flood of debt leads to financial crisis, as market players lose confidence in the system they themselves helped to create.

Under these conditions, both risk and return become very difficult to estimate, because nobody is truly certain which way the chips will fall, or for how long a downturn market psychology might prevail. Market psychology is often framed through analogical reasoning, and this gives another boost to volatility. For instance, in the first six months of 2000, in Japan, bankruptcies and bad debts reached record heights in spite of bailouts amounting to over $1 trillion.

In the first three months of 2000, in the USA and Europe, investors had become increasingly optimistic about the long-term profit perspectives of high technology. By contrast, after the high-tech bubble had burst, once again following a herd effect, they became pessimistic and uncertain about the stock markets prospects, which led to a depressed high-tech company market lasting for over five years.

4.7   Risk-adjusted pricing: an example with credit risk

Since the mid-1990s rigorous mathematical analysis has had a significant impact on the management of market risk. With Basel II it has become fashionable, and in cases necessary, to model credit risk, capitalizing on the market risk experience. This comes at the right time, as the use of credit derivatives leads to reshaping the lending culture.

Promoted by Basel II, good governance means that banks are becoming increasingly preoccupied with *risk-adjusted earnings* and with a more rigorous study of single transaction exposure than ever before. Associated with this new culture is *risk-adjusted pricing* of loans and bonds, which aims to reshape the:

- Concepts, and
- Algorithms

used in connection with the supply and demand of financial instruments, with their embedded but volatile risk and return. Restructuring the pricing equation can be helped by procedures substituting a price formation process that accounts for exposure. An example is pricing credit risk through default swaps.

The 'plain vanilla' version of credit derivative instruments is a credit swap where the protection buyer pays the protection seller a fixed recurring amount in exchange for a payment contingent upon a future credit event; for instance, bankruptcy. If that event takes place, then the protection seller must pay the agreed compensation to the protection buyer. Depending on the amount involved in the credit swap, this helps to cover part or all of credit loss pursuant to default.

By transferring credit risk from the protection buyer to the protection seller, credit default swaps have opened up new business opportunities. Previously, it was not possible to short a loan. Moreover, these instruments, which involve their own credit risk, help in price discovery. Many analysts believe that the pricing of default swaps is in a position to reveal a great deal of market information about expected credit risk. This is most important at a time when the market is thirsty for discovery about credit exposure.

- Because of being constrained by both hedging and arbitrage profits, default swaps pricing usually adjusts more quickly than cash market pricing, and
- Credit default swaps tend to widen before cash spreads, given that the demand to buy protection causes premiums to rise to a level wide enough to attract protection sellers.

This is important in risk-adjusted pricing. The relative value of a default swap can be measured by the spread to the asset swap level, with an indicator being the repurchase agreement (repo) premium. The market's funding benchmark is assuming a flat London interbank offered rate (Libor; the rate at which one bank lends to another). High implied repo premiums may signal high levels of potential stress in a given credit, since the market is willing to borrow it at more expensive levels.

Notice, however, that the correct pricing of default swaps, as well as of other credit derivatives, depends on the distribution of the future credit quality of the reference asset; for example, an underlying pool of corporate debt issues. What this means for the fixed income investor is that:

- The movement and co-movement of credit qualities is of critical importance, and
- The study of such movement requires the understanding of credit risk characteristics.

Such understanding can be helped through credit ratings, which have become a fundamental requirement with Basle II. Indeed, the more finely grained the credit rating scale, for instance, at the level of 20 thresholds practised by the leading independent rating agencies, such as Standard & Poor's and Moody's, the better the risk-adjusted pricing procedure established by the bank.

As the research conducted for this book in the USA, the UK and Continental Europe demonstrates, financial institutions that are best positioned to face the counterparty's risk whims and other market challenges have two common characteristics that correlate with what was stated in the preceding paragraph:

- They have in-house the skills needed for credit rating and rigorous management of credit risk, and
- They are prepared to confront exposure assumed with derivative instruments, but also use such instruments for risk-based pricing.

The answer to the question of why the outlined approach is not very widely used today is that companies often miss appropriate guidelines and have scant knowledge of what the new financial instruments can provide. Therefore, they keep on the beaten path. In order to be in charge of exposures assumed with investments, one should go well beyond the fundamental concepts, methods and tools of risk management. Having appreciated the importance of risk control, as well as how and why its exercise must relate to clearly defined objectives, one should capitalize on:

- The experience acquired so far in risk management projects, and
- Advanced tools which, while originally designed for trading, can provide effective support on risk-based price discovery.

An effort aimed at improving the pricing of financial products, so that it fully accounts for current and *implicit exposure*, should also pay attention to the relationship between financial market integration and the stability of the financial system. This is a very complex relationship. While an integrated financial market tends to cushion local shocks better than segmented markets, international risk-sharing has its downside.

In an integrated global financial system, it is difficult to confine turbulence to specific market segments. A wave of exposure can spread swiftly to the whole system, even if it is overall more resilient than each national market individually. Regulators can help only up to a point in ensuring the sustainability of a global market. The players themselves must follow a prudent approach in pricing their instruments, and this depends on the availability of sufficient information on:

- Business partners,
- Market conditions,
- Implicit volatility,
- Implicit exposure, and
- The quality of risk management by counterparties.

A relevant legal framework valid across jurisdictions should give investors, banks and asset managers the incentives they need to carry out a thorough check of their borrowers' creditworthiness. It is also important to take account of the interdependence of different risks, as these do not occur in isolation and, when they occur, they tend to cause spikes in the distribution of unexpected risk that usually have a high impact.[10]

4.8   An introduction to stress testing

When the Basel Committee or a central bank decides that it is time for the institutions under its jurisdiction to implement a new risk management system, the time comes for a decision on whether to build internally or purchase commercially available risk management tools. Both options have advantages and disadvantages, and neither is without surprises for the bank.

The advantage of building internal tools and systems for risk control is that these will be built specifically for the institution's own needs, by means of constant and detailed involvement of all major users. In addition, risk management operation procedures and the risk control system's output can be developed to fit with the bank's:

- Investment,
- Lending, and
- Trading processes.

However, there is a number of disadvantages to a risk control system built in-house. At top of the list lies the fact tools and systems needed for risk management are complex. The larger the scope and complexity of asset classes in the bank universe, the more complex this project becomes. Other drawbacks are time and cost.

- In-house developments usually take a long time, and
- In some cases, the cost of a risk control system and its tools, built in-house, can be prohibitive.

Although the implementation of commodity solutions may not be as easy as hoped for, other things being equal, the time needed to build a risk management system in-house will tend to be considerably longer than the time to implement a commercially available product. One way around this problem is to purchase off-the-shelf tools for normal testing, but develop an in-house methodology and value-added approaches for *stress testing*.

There is a plethora of definitions regarding stress testing, but the one the reader may wish to retain is that it concerns testing for risks and their impact falling outside the three standard deviations left and right of the expected value of the normal distribution. In other words, stress testing targets risk at the long tail of the distribution. In the background of this procedure is the desire to account for:

- Outliers, and
- Extreme events.

For instance, because of volatility and liquidity constraints, tier-one commercial and investment banks regularly subject their portfolios to stress tests, simulating significant market changes and, at the limit, crashes. Not only do regulators welcome this practice, they are also quite often at its origin.

Since the crash of the savings and loans (S&Ls, thrifts, building societies) in the USA in the late 1980s, the Office of Thrift Supervision (OTS) requires all S&Ls in its jurisdiction (some 1100 entities) to submit daily the result of:

- Normal tests, and
- Stress tests.

These focus on the effect of changes in interest rates on the thrifts portfolio of mortgages and other loans. Current interest rates ±100 and ±200 basis points (bp) are normal tests. Current interest rates ±300 and ±400 bp are stress tests.

As this example demonstrates, stress testing not only concerns a worst case scenario, but may also include other, more likely market changes. The criterion in the preceding example was stress testing the effect of changes in interest rates on the survivability of the institution. Other stress tests may focus on:

- Changes in the slope of the yield curve,
- Currency exchange rates,
- Liquidity in one or more markets, and
- Volatility, both current and implied.

Another critical reason why stress tests have become so important along the aforementioned dimensions is the rapid inflation in financial assets. Figure 4.5 gives a snapshot of this exponential growth in derivatives, debt instruments and equity prices, in the 1990s in the USA. When financial aggregates reach for the stars, normal tests are absolutely incapable of unearthing underlying exposure.

All tests addressed to the long tail of the distribution must give special consideration to instruments or positions that may be difficult to liquidate in a crisis, or to offset. In principle, stress test criteria should be defined by the board of directors and senior management. This definition is part of their effort to ensure that appropriate contingency plans are in place.

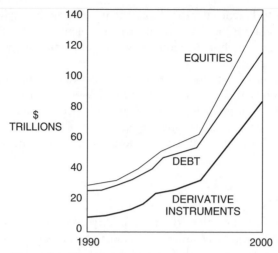

Figure 4.5 The exponential growth in US financial
aggregates: 1990–2000

In outlining the areas where stress tests should be done, and the criteria to be observed, account should be taken of the fact that the basic aim of stress tests is to go to the roots of risk. Basically, a stress test is a rigorous evaluation of the exposure that has been assumed, or is to be taken, as well as of crucial factors characterizing this exposure. A stress test can be done at various levels, through any of four methods:

- Scenario writing,
- Sensitivity analysis,
- Statistical inference under extreme conditions,
- Drills for a meltdown (extreme conditions).

It should be noted that scenario writing, sensitivity analysis and statistical inference are widely used tools for risk management. They become part of stress testing specifically when they are applied to extreme conditions. Hence, not all scenarios are connected with stress testing, and stress testing is more than classical scenario writing.[11] Stress tests can be done:

- A priori, before entering into an investment,
- In the course of managing a portfolio, and
- Post-mortem to evaluate 'what would have happened if . . .'.

As the best bankers and fund managers know, it is important to take a critical look at any investment's risk factors before being committed to it. Since investments are typically made up of common stocks and debt instruments, the risks inherent in any equity and bond should be flushed out. This procedure is more important with derivatives, because derivatives are leveraged instruments.

Stress tests that aim at investigating outliers can be effectively assisted by expert opinion about future unexpected but not impossible events. The Delphi method is recommended in this connection.[12] Banks that have acquired experience in stress testing are increasingly using complexity theory, involving:

- Frequency of events, such as credit losses, and
- Impact of each type of loss on the institution, or on a given portfolio.

Events happening over a given period may be high frequency but low impact (HF/LI), or they may be low frequency but high impact (LF/HI). In general,

- It is easier to identify HF/LI events than LF/HI events, and
- Unexpected risks are usually associated with LF/HI events.

It is also appropriate to keep in mind that, even for the same bank, the pattern of HF/LI, LF/HI is not the same at all times, or at the same time in all countries. An example is risks assumed in south-east Asia, before the 1997 crash. In the late 1980s and up to the mid-1990s, seven south-east Asian economies were characterized by Western analysts as 'tigers'.

Notes

1 D.N. Chorafas, *Managing Credit Risk*, Volume 1, *Analysing, Rating and Pricing the Probability of Default*, Euromoney, London, 2000; D.N. Chorafas, *Managing Credit Risk*, Volume 2, *The Lessons of VAR Failures and Imprudent Exposure*, Euromoney, London, 2000.
2 D.N. Chorafas, *The 1996 Market Risk Amendment. Understanding the Marking-to-Model and Value-at-Risk*, McGraw-Hill, Burr Ridge, IL, 1998.
3 D.N. Chorafas, *Operational Risk Control with Basel II. Basic Principles and Capital Requirements*, Butterworth-Heinemann, London, 2004.
4 D.N. Chorafas, *Implementing and Auditing the Internal Control System*, Macmillan, London, 2001.
5 Basle Committee, *Risk Management Practices and Regulatory Capital. A Cross-Sectoral Comparison*, Basle, November 2001.
6 D.N. Chorafas, *Management Risk. The Bottleneck is at the Top of the Bottle*, Macmillan/Palgrave, London, 2004.
7 *The Economist*, 18 December 2004.
8 D.N. Chorafas, *Liabilities, Liquidity and Cash Management. Balancing Financial Risk*, Wiley, New York, 2002.
9 D.N. Chorafas, *Managing Risk in the New Economy*, New York Institute of Finance, New York, 2001.
10 D.N. Chorafas, *Economic Capital Allocation with Basel II. Cost and Benefit Analysis*, Butterworth-Heinemann, London, 2004.
11 D.N. Chorafas, *Stress Testing. Risk Management Strategies for Extreme Events*, Euromoney, London, 2003.
12 D.N. Chorafas, *Modelling the Survival of Financial and Industrial Enterprises. Advantages, Challenges, and Problems with the Internal Rating-Based (IRB) Method*, Palgrave/Macmillan, London, 2002.

Part 2
Asset management

5 Asset management defined

5.1 Introduction

Since the 1990s, in the Group of Ten (G10) countries, there has been a trend towards the institutionalization of fund management, including asset selection for risk and return optimization, and administration of wealth. This is what private banking and asset management are all about, both terms identifying a process of *outsourcing* the administration of wealth, albeit with reference to different populations of investors. (The concept of outsourcing and some of its functions are discussed in Chapter 7.)

This evolution in the management of one's fortune is characterized by the notion that professionals in the investment business can offer, to a diverse range of investors, wealth management practical capabilities better than each investor can provide for himself. Many of the *insourcers* of wealth management focus on price/value, exploiting periodic discrepancies between an investment's:

- Market values, and
- Intrinsic value (see section 5.7).

Because the experts are supposed to know better, companies outsource asset management to specialized firms or do it in-house in a separate business unit. This is the policy practised by many insurance companies in the UK. Besides managing their parent institution's wealth, asset management divisions or subsidiaries aim at becoming leading wealth administrators and mutual fund providers. They do so by offering a broad range of services and products:

- To institutional clients across the world, and
- To high net worth individuals and retail clients, frequently through the personal banking division of a bank.

Wealth management is generally undertaken as an umbrella function, with some individual investment fund units concentrating on the administration of assets, and others addressing product development and distribution functions. This polyvalence of approach makes possible a wider range of investment styles and a more diversified asset management strategy.

As discussed in Part 1, flexibility and adaptability are at a premium because asset management strategies addressed to institutional investors must be tailored to each major client's risk and return objectives. This requires both human skills for personalization of portfolios and a sophisticated technological support, as well as an international presence to keep close track of all major investment markets.

Well-managed private banking outfits ensure that the personalization of investments also characterizes the provision of retail investment products. This is widening the reach of private banking, and generally of fund management, to individual clients. When this strategy is executed in a successful manner, it sets a financial institution apart in its ability to customize global investments:

- Matching local requirements of its clients,
- Paying attention to risk management, and
- Complying with different regulatory constraints.

As explained in Chapter 4, a rigorous exposure control programme will induce fund managers to introduce risk-adjusted pricing, pay greater attention in selecting investment with proven risk and return ratios, and increase their focus on investment choices with attractive risk/reward characteristics. Favourable macroeconomic events influence the portfolio's performance in a positive way.

Increasingly, asset management is targeting not only domestic but also foreign investments. Based on German statistics, Figure 5.1 shows that between 1990 and 2000 the share of funds' assets invested in equities rose from around 20 per cent in 1990 to over 50 per cent at the end of 2000. While much of this growth in equities investments reflected the herd syndrome of the late 1990s and rapid increase in the share prices, even after the bubble burst the trend towards domestic and foreign shareholding continued to characterize the German market.

Throughout the G10 countries, one of the forces behind the trends towards investments in securities is that private individuals are increasingly resorting to investment funds. In general, this practice is also followed by institutional investors such as pension funds and insurance companies; although each institution, and its assets manager(s), tend to have its own asset allocation strategy.

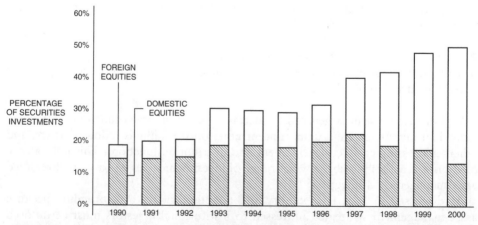

Figure 5.1 Domestic and foreign equity investment as a proportion of assets of German securities-based funds

5.2   Asset management and capital mobility

Let us start with the bigger picture. As discussed in Chapter 3, asset management, to a significant extent, is today done within an integrated financial market. This is the policy followed by the most proactive funds managers, to which a great deal of investors subscribe. A prerequisite to this is capital mobility. The hypothesis of perfect capital mobility implies the existence of a global capital market, which is not realizable because of differences prevailing among jurisdictions. From the point of view of a single country, particularly among the smaller countries, participation in a global capital market requires that:

- National savings are supplied to the global capital market, and
- Capital is obtained from that global capital market for local investment purposes.

If this were the case, the more or less perfect correlation between savings and investment in a closed national economy would tend to disappear. This 'perfect correlation' is a theoretical underpinning of findings by empirical analyses that point against a high degree of international capital mobility, at least at present.

There are also other reasons why capital mobility for investment purposes is imperfect, in a global sense. For example, there is dispersion of securities portfolios characterized by significant differences in the rules used to construct them. Comparative studies still support the hypothesis of clear preference for domestic stocks, bonds and notes, although this may be changing.

Unknowns embedded in credit risk, market risk, volatility and liquidity add to the reasons why asset managers do not fully subscribe to the concept of wholly integrated financial markets. This is understandable inasmuch as fund management deals with credit decisions, and in the global market many credit issues are obscure, although universal credit rating may help in risk and return trade-offs across an aggregation of individual markets. Other challenges include:

- Pricing to fair value
- Profit and loss evaluation
- The aftermath of hedging
- Portfolio segmentation
- Limit-setting for each segment
- Current and further out risk assessment
- Real or fancy diversification.

As shown in Chapter 3, and discussed in Chapter 6, a portfolio can be segmented on the basis of criteria, geography, industry and product type. It is important to estimate the volatility between segments and within segments, as well as credit exposure, and the other factors that have been outlined in Part 1.

The careful reader will recall that credit risk estimates are generally based on empirical analysis of rating migrations and actual loss experience. Market risk estimates will be based on asset volatilities, the analysis of equity share prices, econometric modelling and the all-important *leveraging* factor of the investment.

As with local markets, in the integrated financial landscape specific limits are necessary to contain total exposure within each portfolio segment. Limits, however, are not enough. There is also a need for a transfer pricing mechanism that calculates incremental risk by capital market, as considered in the opening paragraphs of this section.

Asset managers belonging to different investment philosophies tend to use a variety of theories, models, liability characteristics and benchmarks in making up their mind in terms of allocation of wealth. This has an evident impact on their recommended list and resulting commitments. Examples of different popular theories are:

- Mean-Variance Portfolio Theory, of 1952, and Efficient Market Theory (EMT) by Dr Harry Markowitz
- Capital Asset Pricing Model (CAPM), of 1964, where Dr William Sharpe made a contribution
- Universal Hedging Model, elaborated in 1989, by Dr Fischer Black.

Theories, however, are not set in stone. Over time, they tend to act as a guide, until they are challenged, disproved or demolished by other theories. However, neither the older nor newer theories should be *the* basis for investment decisions and commitments. Clear-eyed asset managers appreciate that investments are too serious a matter to be left to theories. Factual and documented investment decisions require:

- A great deal of homework,
- Plenty of analytics, and
- Steady vigilance,

which a theory does not provide. In addition, stress tests are needed before confirming the allocation of money (stress testing has been discussed in Chapter 4). Theories provide none of these prerequisites. By contrast, always keeping in mind the dictum that: 'All models are wrong, but some are useful', mathematical models can be helpful in:

- Monitoring portfolio risk,
- Keeping track of limits,
- Helping in benchmarks, and
- Assisting in performance of tests regarding investment criteria.

The use of models, rather than theories, can at times be instrumental in identifying the best next trade for rebalancing a portfolio or the likelihood that a given bet may turn out to be right. But it is human experience and skill, rather than models, that will handle the framework of asset allocation, which is studied in section 5.3.

Last but not least, astute asset managers appreciate that they need a fairly reliable pricing mechanism, and they understand that when using this mechanism, potential unexpected losses must be evaluated for each portfolio position, as well as for new transactions. Measures of incremental unexpected losses, as well as simulated market gains, should give input to a risk and return.

These are, in a nutshell, approaches that highlight the homework that needs to be done for globalized investing. Starting with these premises, investors, bankers and fund managers position themselves against market forces. This permits them to proceed, on a fairly firm basis, with asset allocation strategies.

5.3   Asset allocation strategies

The classical way of thinking of asset allocation is in reference to a big plan that involves major choices: stocks, bonds, derivative instruments, real estate, cash and other commodities. Below that level, however, there should be a finer grain of alternatives, and therefore of choices.

In the decisions to be made between fixed income and equities, subjects regarding fixed income involve term structure, projection of changes in interest rate(s), yield estimation, duration, convexity, credit quality and the selection of the debt instruments.[1] Each one of these references requires human expertise, although experimentation through models and assistance by expert systems can help.

Equity investments call for a decision on individual stocks and/or index tracking, multinationals versus national companies and country of origin, among the crucial factors. Figure 5.2 shows country allocation by a major investment fund. Beyond this comes the choice of industry to which the company or companies belong, product line(s), price/earnings (P/E) ratios, growth potential, dividends and other criteria leading to individual stock picking and stock rotation.[2] Figure 5.3 presents an example of industry sector allocation.

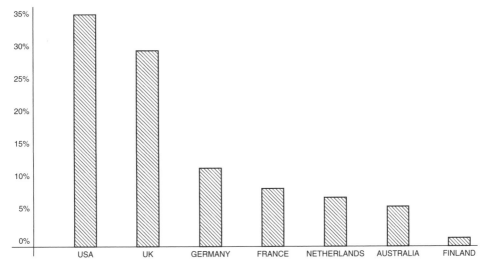

Figure 5.2 Example of country allocation of equity investments, by a major fund that is targeting the global market

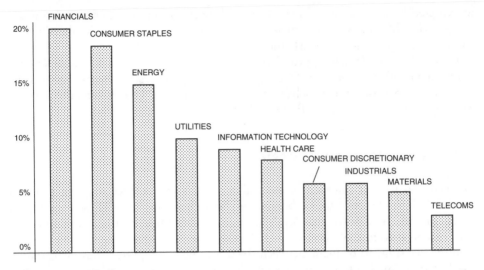

Figure 5.3 Diversified industry sector allocation by an equity portfolio. This is an example, not investment advice

Currency trading and associated investments are usually done in blocs: US dollars, sterling, euro, yen. They may also involve interbloc and intrabloc allocations. Typically, currency is managed as a separate asset class, requiring specific expertise and having its own rules. (Chapter 16 addresses currency exchange structured products.)

If the investor decides to include derivative financial instruments in his or her portfolio, a basic decision should be made as to whether this is done for hedging or for speculation. Companies and institutional investors trade in derivative instruments, whereas retail investors choose structured products such as fixed income derivatives (Chapters 12 and 13), equity-type structured products (Chapters 14 and 15) or currency exchange derivatives.

Within a general framework that should be consistent with an institutional investor's or private banking client's objectives, investment advisors usually provide target asset allocation guidelines, as well as ranges. Usually, but not always, the midpoint of ranges is the long-term neutral benchmark allocation for a particular investor profile. Much depends on the choices of active or passive investment strategies, discussed in section 5.6.

Following this general framework, and the investor's or asset manager's personalized decisions, investment advisors suggest what they call *actionable* ideas. These are usually based on investment themes prevailing at a given moment in the financial market. For instance, at end of 2004 the themes brought forward by an investment newsletter have been US dollar weaknesses, projected Asia boom and risk of inflation. Based on these premises, the fund management outfit that wrote this newsletter gave the following investment advice:

■ Stay invested in equities.
■ Overweight the Eurozone in fixed income portfolios.

- Remove US dollar hedges (by euro-based investors).
- Maintain exposure to Asia, in general, and Japan.

Investment advisors and asset managers may also follow a more holistic approach, as shown by the following quotation from another newsletter: 'One of the most important decisions in investment is if you are pessimistic or bullish about the market's prospects.' As advice, this is an oxymoron, because the typical investor would like to hear from the investment expert whether he or she should be bullish or pessimistic about the market's prospects.

A similar reference is valid regarding asset allocation to different investment classes. Tim Tacchi, TT's senior partner, said during a meeting on 22 October 2001 that according to this opinion net asset value (NAV) allocation in equities should be 20 per cent if the fund manager is pessimistic and 80 per cent if he is bullish. Among the factors that enter into this evaluation are:

- The fund manager's own appreciation of market sentiment,
- The usual macroeconomic decision criteria, and
- Trends in market behaviour, as well as in the securities themselves.

Depending on the economy, market psychology, the time when investments are made and, in many cases, the country, other criteria, too, are important because value selection needs milestones and triggers to release value. Besides such general principles, experts also have their own criteria. Tacchi underlined that a big question with equities is that of hidden liabilities.

The type of market that one targets in asset allocation brings specific criteria into decision making. Investing in the macromarkets provides an example. This is often leveraged trading, particularly when investing in interest rates and currencies. It is not a hedge. For several asset managers, the macromarket is treated as a self-standing, independent profit centre with that part of NAV allocated to it that is not in equities, fixed income, cash and liquid instruments. The latter include liquid government securities, futures, options and money market futures contracts.

Macrotrading is done in forex, government securities, emerging market exposure, other products and a permutation of different instruments. At the time of the meeting on 22 October 2001, Henry Bedford, the co-partner of TT, said that he was agnostic about strengths and weaknesses of the euro, but he saw a tactical opportunity to shorten it. At that time, Bedford used to be 80 per cent long in euro/dollar exchange rates, then his feeling became negative and he positioned himself 30 per cent short. The market rewarded that position, and the euro fell significantly during that week.

The best investment managers ensure that their opinion is kept dynamic, fully accounting for prevailing trends. 'From time to time I eat my words, and I find them a very tasty diet', Lord Allanbrook, the chief of the British General Staff during World War II, used to say. When Konrad Adenauer, the late German chancellor, was reminded that he changed his opinion, he answered: 'What can I do? God makes me wiser and wiser.'

Investment advisors and asset management would be well advised to change their opinion when necessary, rather than stay on the wrong side. Investment newsletters

often contain the phrase 'We are making two significant changes to our asset allocation recommendations for the period ahead . . .'. For instance, in connection to debt
instruments, the asset manager may be significantly reducing exposure to the five to
ten-year yield curve, while increasing the one to five-year cash exposure.

As expected, the attitude of investment advisors and asset managers is influenced
not only by market forces, but also by the prevailing culture in terms of investments.
This is often reflected in the type of funds offering their services to the market. This
statement is better explained through the histogram in Figure 5.4 based on statistics
by the European Central Bank (ECB), which shows the prevailing general European
and American patterns in terms of investment funds. ECB compiles euro area aggregates for:

- All investment funds,
- Investment funds broken down by investment policy, and
- Investment funds classified by restrictions on the purchase of the funds' shares.

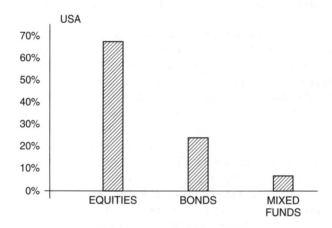

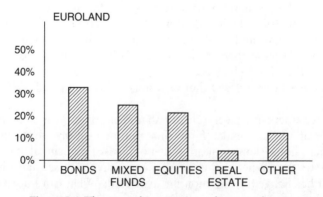

Figure 5.4 The general investment culture can be seen
through the prevailing pattern of investments. (Statistics by
European Central Bank, Monthly Bulletin, January 2003)

The statistics in Figure 5.4 regard the second bullet point. The categories that have been identified are: equity funds, bond funds, mixed funds, real estate funds and other investment funds. The classification indicates the type of asset in which the fund primarily invests. Mixed funds are those investing in both equity and bonds, where neither of the two prevails a priori.

5.4   Asset allocation and the shift in economic activity

Asset allocation strategies discussed in section 5.2 have focused on financial instruments, and hence on virtual assets, not on real assets such as real estate, gold, silver, base metals or other commodities. This is the prevailing trend, and it represents a significant cultural change in the investing population. Many investors who still think of real assets now prefer to buy an option on them.

- Purchasing the shares of a gold mining company is like buying an option on gold.
- Purchasing the equity of an oil company is like buying an option on oil.

The shift in economic activity from the real world of assets to the virtual world of finance is an event to which there exists no precedence. Therefore, there are no standard rules through which an evaluation can be made regarding opportunities, risks and effects. What can be said is that, by all evidence, the new economy is likely to give rise to business cycles characterized by swings in implied volatility (see Chapter 4), including both:

- Credit volatility, and
- Market volatility.

Investors should take note of this likelihood. With a certain periodicity that is difficult to establish a priori, credit and market volatility will probably reach new heights that are, at present, unfamiliar to the experts. This gives a new twist to the concept of *risk-weighted assets* (RWA). The problem is that, at present, risk differentiation between various credit exposures is too crude and market risk is underestimated by worn-out metrics such as value at risk (VAR).[3] With VAR, this and similar models:

- Concentration risk is typically ignored.
- Forex risk and interest rate risk in the banking book are not covered.
- The treatment of securitization and risk mitigation is half-baked.
- The handling of business risk (see Chapter 3), insurance and operational risk is left for tomorrow.

There are many issues that have not been adequately addressed by Basle II, although some independent rating agencies and certain financial institutions bring them into perspective. Because there is no precedence to the twists that may characterize the virtual economy, both bulls and bears can make a point that is difficult to refute. One thing that can be said with relative certainty is that because of globalization and financial instrument innovation, the new economy has a deflationary effect:

- Globalization not only provides worldwide markets, but also gives companies one more incentive to shift labour-intensive tasks to lower wages.
- The increasingly networked economy adds to the possibility of swamping costs, by igniting a race to execute formerly complex jobs such as purchasing on the internet.
- Financial innovation means that the time-honoured law of supply and demand does not always prevail, because the supply of new instruments is nearly infinite (see the case study in section 5.5).

At the same time, steady financial innovation is not possible without high technology and rocket science. Even in the more classical evaluation of equities, the sophistication of information technology (IT) used by the asset manager has become most important, although in this case technology is one of the factors, not the whole story.

During one of the research meetings that led to this book reference was made to a well-known insurance company that has low IT, but a huge domestic market and tremendous margins in it life and non-life product lines. 'Almost obscene margins', said one of the asset managers, adding that when one is picking equities he wants to have:

- Visibility of earning,
- Transparency of accounts, and
- Some evidence that profit margins have not been severely squeezed.

The answer to this argument is that in a highly competitive global economy 'obscene margins' do not last for long, even if in violation of the accords that it has signed, 'this' or 'that' government tries to erect artificial barriers to entry by competitors. An example is the recent efforts by the Bank of Italy to fence off other European Union banks from buying control of two major Italian banks.

Investment advisors and asset managers should appreciate that financial might and huge margins are, in general, temporary phenomena. Financial might can quickly turn to ashes. In 1989, at the apogee of the Japanese banks' brief rise in the world's financial capitalization, they had an impressive $400 billion in unrealized profits. Then, this turned into a $1.2 trillion torrent of red ink, which is very serious because:

- Japanese banks were never strongly capitalized, and
- Their special reserves were trivial or outright non-existent.

Globalization so far has had rather negative effects in connection to the preservation of acquired financial might. The way to exploit the positive effects of globalization is not through ever bigger size but by means of better and better management, and the prudence to have sufficient capital to absorb all risks through a period when the market does not support replenishment. A rigorous capital model advanced by Standard & Poor's assumes the following recession scenario, of which the reader should take notice:

- Three years without access to capital markets,
- Forced rollover of maturing loans,
- Unavailability of liquidity of loans, and
- Enough capital at the end, to be in business.

These scenarios have been written for credit institutions, but they can be extended to all commercial and industrial organizations, as value added to current methods for valuation of equities that are based on earnings; cash flow; earnings before interest, taxes, depreciation and amortization (EBITDA); return on assets; and return on equity. Within the context of asset allocation for investment reasons, the primary search must be for:

- Quality,
- Franchise value, and
- Financial staying power.

Among the catalysts in investment decisions, as much for equity as for debt, are soundness of corporate governance, the management change, realization of hidden value and dependable accounting practices. Fund managers should always be alert to taking advantage of quality of management, while avoiding buying the equity, or debt instruments, of companies known for their management risk.[4]

The quality of management plays a crucial role in the success or failure of any enterprise; hence the need faced by asset managers and financial analysts to meet periodically with company executives and estimate their intellect, character, decision-making process, marketing skills, products in the pipeline, research and development (R&D) breakthroughs, inventories and sales effectiveness.

Moreover, it is a sound investment policy to verify choices made by the assets managers, and by industry specialists and academic experts, acting as external consultants. What the asset manager would like to hear from them is an *independent* opinion that challenges what is contemplated or has been done. It is always rewarding to challenge the 'obvious'.

5.5 Real estate property derivatives: a case study

In mid-2004 the race began to create derivatives in the real estate property market, substituting real assets with virtual assets. Although there were several attempts during the 1990s to create such products, only in September 2004 was tax treatment under British law changed to make them attractive. Until then, capital gains tax was payable on profits from property derivatives, while losses did not qualify for relief.

Another push in the same direction has come from the Financial Services Authority (FSA), which allowed insurance companies to use property derivatives for portfolio management reasons. With approval from supervisors and tax advantages assured by law, Britain became the first country in the world with a property derivatives market.

In all likelihood, another contributor has been the fact that the UK is considered to have reliable property data, collated by the Investment Property Databank (IPD). This is an independent research company whose index tracks the return on £102 billion of property. Experts believe that, among themselves, these three factors:

- Reliabile property data,
- A friendly nod by supervisors, and
- Taxation that promotes virtual assets

are instrumental in defining the landscape in that can develop, and may prosper, different types of real estate derivatives. Some of the experts add that (if and) when property-type derivative instruments pick up momentum, their business is going to be exactly the opposite to a succession of 'ordinary days'.

Could real estate derivative instruments follow on the tracks of the equity derivatives market? It is too early to give an answer to this query, but one should keep in perspective certain analogies. The trend lines in Figure 5.5 show that over two periods doing the past 23 years: 1982–1987 and 2000–2004, values in the equity market and real estate market in the UK have moved remarkably close together.

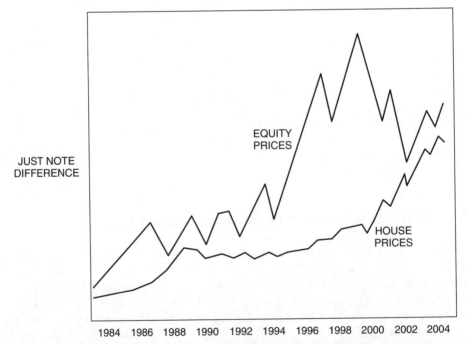

Figure 5.5 Trend curves in the values characterizing the UK real estate and equities markets

Different derivative instruments may qualify. The case study in this section involves real estate swaps, but these are not the first financial product based on the property market. Barclays has offered bonds and Abbey National saving products, where the payout depends on movements in real estate prices. Real estate swaps are, however, the first derivative in the sense that no money changes hands at the point at which the product is set up.

- Former products did not allow investors to bet against the property market.
- Swaps make it possible to take positions such as reducing exposure to retail warehouses and increasing exposure to offices.

Within the aforementioned setting, 13 January 2005 saw the completion of the first property swaps deal, consisting of a £40 million contract for difference that involves the exchange of exposure to the property market, without transfer of physical assets. Swaps of that type may enable traders and investors to increase or decrease instantly their exposure to real estate property, and game the taxation system too (for tax issues see the Appendix).

Promoters of the new instrument capitalize on the fact that real estate is a very *illiquid* market in which deals can take months, with charges reaching 6–8 per cent. This is one of the major challenges characterizing physical properties. The real estate derivatives swap is done without the costs and delays of a physical deal.

The 13 January 2005 contract for difference was arranged by Deutsche Bank and Eurohypo, the German bank specializing in real estate. This £40 million is almost pocket money, but experts estimate that the market's potential size, in the UK alone, could range from several billion pounds to £3 trillion. Other banks are said to be considering similar moves, not only in Britain but also in Sweden and the USA. Specifically in the mid-January 2005 three-year swap,

- An unnamed life insurer wanted to decrease its exposure to property by £40 million.
- A property company, acting as counterparty, wanted to assume increased exposure.

If returns from the UK property market outperform the Libor interest rate, the insurer will simply pay the difference. If the returns trail Libor, the property company will pay the difference. In both cases, the investor's estimate on how the market will move provides the difference between winning and losing.

Some people say that real estate swaps came at the right time, as an estimated £4 billion is expected to be unlocked from people's property over the next five years, as elderly homeowners look for ways to boost their retirement income. The more classical way of doing this is by remortgaging or selling part of their homes, but certain experts are of the opinion it will not take long before derivative financial instruments offered to home owners:

- Amplify, and
- Leverage this process.

At consumer level, the leveraging of real estate deals may find eager participants in the equity release market. This market involves risks, but it also has the potential for huge growth given that people are forced to take more responsibility for:

■ Funding pensions,
■ Taking long-term health care, and
■ Facing growing education costs.

A motor behind potential growth is the significant gap between current and planned pension provision and people's needs. What are the alternatives?

In their more classical incarnation, equity release mortgages are aimed at home-owners who may have paid off their mortgage, or have only a small amount out-standing. However, such deals attracted a bad name in the late 1980s because many were linked to variable interest rates, which hit a peak of 15 per cent in 1989. It will be interesting to see what happens when property derivative instruments come into the wider market.

At the high end of the real estate market, property derivative transactions are likely to take the form of risk swaps between two different sectors. One counter-party, for example, may wish to increase its exposure to business parks and decrease its exposure to shopping centres, while another may take the opposite view.

One opinion that is heard is that some traders, investors or companies will take synthetic exposure to the real estate market rather than buying properties. As more banks and other entities exchange derivatives, the market could create international swaps, for instance, between London offices and New York or Tokyo warehouses, as well as assume a more complex nature by including in one deal:

■ Real estate,
■ Interest rates,
■ Currencies, and
■ Other commodities such as energy.

That day is some time away as the new financial instruments must adapt to the idiosyncracies of the property market and create for themselves a niche from which they can grow further. Also to be seen is whether the real estate property derivatives market will have enough liquidity, and how frequently estates will be valued. Will marking to market be done on a regular quarterly or annual basis, or at a higher fre-quency?

5.6 Passive and active investment strategies

In classical investment jargon, a *passive strategy*, such as index-linked, is usually based on the investor's, investment advisor's or asset manager's view that signifi-cant pricing errors on equity markets are rather rare. This approach accepts that financial markets are efficient and that no mispriced securities exist, there-fore there is no incentive to trade actively in securities. The added value that passively managed funds are able to offer primarily consists of reducing price risks by means of:

- Broad equity risk diversification, such as linkage to an index, and
- Possibly hedging approaches related to certain portfolio items with greater exposure.

The concept underpinning passive portfolio management can be expressed as 'buy and hold' or 'buy and sell', the latter if the overall benchmark return is negative. In the background of this strategy is buying a combination of assets and holding them for a relatively long period, with only a few minor adjustments over their life cycle because of market changes.

Alternatively, passive management can be performed by *index-matching*, through different approaches known as complete, stratified sampling, factor matching and so on. The investor or asset manager makes no attempt to beat the market, but follows some consensus estimates of risk and return, which he or she adopts as his or her own. Based on risk tolerance, a mixture of treasuries and AAA equities may be selected. The portfolio changes only if:

- The market consensus changes drastically, or
- The investor's risk preferences are altered.

An *active strategy* in investment management, by contrast, aims at realizing above-average returns on equity investments. The way to do so is by beating the market and the different indices. With an active strategy, value is generally derived from deliberate exploitation of real or hypothetical information advantages, on which the investor or asset manager aims to capitalize.

For this reason, active portfolio management involves frequent and relatively substantial adjustments to the portfolio. An active strategy does not accept that markets behave according to EMT (see section 5.2). The guiding light is that the search for greater return justifies the resources, commissions and risks involved in:

- Forecasting of financial market developments,
- Analysing their likely effects, and
- Trading to reposition the portfolio's contents.

Active assets managers do not always accept the market consensus regarding risk and return based, for instance, on historical mean and standard deviation. Instead, they have their own criteria for equity selection, as well as for buying and selling different positions. Active portfolio managers develop and follow their own estimates by:

- General asset category: shares, bonds, derivatives, other commodities, and
- Individual securities within each investment class, such as specific stocks or debt instruments.

The first decision in an active strategy is the asset allocation decision, roughly along the lines examined in section 5.3. The second is the security selection decision.

Moreover, active portfolio managers indulge in market timing of their investment decisions. In so doing, they are based on their expectations about the future, supported by fundamental and technical analysis.[5]

There is, of course, a question of whether or not some investors and asset managers can obtain consistently superior information in the longer term. This argument of more competitive information is one that is often heard but rarely documented. One who has superior information capitalizes on the fact that in the general case, new information is not being immediately reflected in market prices. With the exception of panics, the impact of fresh data is gradual.

Contrarians say, and some evidence suggests, that the concept of short-term share price distortions might be introduced in the aftermath of initially inappropriate responses to new information on the part of investors. The pros answer that this is of secondary importance, although it could happen from time to time. Only the more theoretically inclined people:

■ Ascribe a comparatively high degree of efficiency to the equity market, and
■ Consider shares to be valued correctly, on the whole.

A middle way of looking at these statements for and against market efficiency is that *information asymmetries* do matter, but how they are conceived and used is by no means self-evident. To make up for the missing linkages, academics, and some investment managers, develop or adopt theories such as CAPM and its variants, which they consider to be of assistance in active portfolio management. In principle,

■ If the market is expected to move upwards, then the correct strategy would be to select high volatility (beta) shares.
■ If a bear market is expected, then the proper strategy would be to select low-beta shares, go liquid or short the market.

Other active investment approaches centre around the identification of undervalued or overvalued securities by targeting the *intrinsic value* (see section 5.8). A positive abnormal return, known as alpha value, would indicate an underpriced security. The active portfolio manager seeks to select portfolios of securities with positive alphas. Alternatively, he or she can short overpriced securities with negative alpha values.

Still other active portfolio management techniques rest on the belief that market anomalies will result in groups of stocks that will outperform the overall equity market. According to this approach, also known as style-based portfolio management, investors target different groups of equities, such as growth stocks, value stocks and cyclical stocks. In so doing, they are choosing between:

■ *Style-based*, therefore homogeneous, and
■ *Style-diversified* portfolios of assets.

Basically, the search is one for anomalies that can be exploited. Another strategy is that of choosing a portfolio of assets that have the highest expected geometric mean return. This approach makes no assumptions about investors' behaviour or distribution of returns. It is based on the hypothesis that the portfolio with the maximum geometric return tends to have the highest likelihood of reaching, or exceeding, any given wealth level in a relatively short time. This is often a diversified portfolio. (The geometric mean return penalizes extreme observations.)

Still another technique is to select an investment portfolio on the basis of the first three moments of return distributions: mean, standard deviation and skewness. Skewness, the third moment, measures the asymmetry of a distribution. A symmetrical distribution should have a skewness around zero. A positive (or negative) skewness coefficient indicates that:

■ The distribution is asymmetrical, and
■ It has a tail extending towards the right (or left).

Further on, the distribution's fourth moment can be exploited. This is known as kyrtosis. Some statistical distributions have *fat tails*. The underlying concept, the technical term for which is Hurst's exponent (or coefficient), is that certain events tend to repeat themselves rather than being normally distributed.[6] An example of a normal and a leptokyrtotic distribution is given in Figure 5.6. Being able to study in an analytical way the tail of a distribution is most valuable, because it provides:

■ A more wholesome view of risk, and
■ A broader picture of unlikely but possible events that may represent gains or losses.

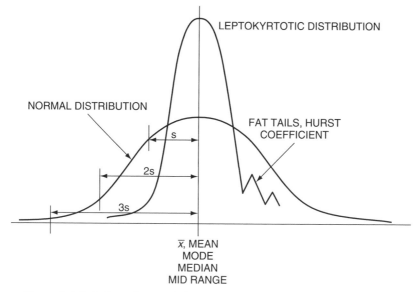

Figure 5.6 Bell-shaped normal distribution and leptokyrtotic distribution

There is risk associated with both passive and active funds management. Meetings in New York and London, in the aftermath of the year 2000 market collapse, brought into view that financial analysts were worried about certain types of investment strategies. In late October 2000, one of them was to say that as stockmarkets everywhere have slumped, active fund managers have performed on average even worse than the indices, and in some cases this has led to legal risk (more on this in section 5.7).

5.7 A critical view of alternative solutions

No investment strategy is foolproof. Leaving aside the case of trends followed by investors, private bankers and assets managers from time to time, practically everybody in this industry tries to do a decent job. However, there are no self-evident truths about how money can be made, and risk controlled in the longer term, even though diversification in exposure is often voted as 'the best possible solution'.

Diversification is an alternative which, however, has limits. Although the equities portfolio may include a lower to medium two-digit number of positions, it is four or five of these positions that will really contribute to the year's profit and loss (P&L). The problem is that, typically, asset managers do not know from the beginning which will be the winners; also, the definition of a 'winner' will be influenced by the strategy being followed, whether the goal is:

- Value investing, or
- Growth investing.

In principle, a value-orientated investment favours shares with a relatively low valuation. A growth-orientated strategy targets equities with a significant potential for earnings growth. These short sentences bring into perspective a practical distinction, and indicate the reason for investor preference for certain equity classes.

Contrary to what is generally said, value investing and growth investing have similitudes, one of them being the approach towards analysis of fundamentals characterizing any stock. This consists of taking five to ten-year cash flow, adding a residual value on it. It is also advisable to look into longer term prospects regarding the evolution of:

- A particular equity,
- The industry to which it belongs, and
- The market as a whole.

The assets manager's research department, for example, will be asked by the investment advisors to respond to the query: 'Is the big bear market in telecommunications, media, and technology (TMT) done?' The answer should be factual and documented, not hearsay. Generalities such as, 'Many market players think that as 2004 came to an end there have been some very undervalued TMT stocks around, but not all of them are appealing' are of no value whatsoever.

Say that the asset manager wishes to pay a premium for growth stocks. Which one should he or she choose? As a practical example, Vodaphone, the mobile telephony operator, has a high multiple to Novo, the pharmaceutical company, but its earnings are not better. In addition, Vodaphone has no free cash flow, and financial history suggests that the stock of phone companies does not rise until they have free cash flow.

What this example brings into perspective is the need for industry-specific investment criteria, that should always be used to compare one equity to another, within and between industry sectors. Cash flow is a good criterion, but it is even better to link it to historical evidence within the industry to which an equity belongs. Investment decisions cannot and should not be made independently of criteria underlying the health of a market, including:

- Breadth,
- Volume,
- New highs/new lows, and
- Annual rate of change.

A given equity's measures may or may not be in gear with the market's trend, or with that of its industry. Investors want to be in a market that has the potential to move ahead. The same is valid about choosing equities. Foremost in their mind are the queries: Which is the better place to make money? Will this be a growth market? Many investment advisors and asset managers tend to change their equity strategy depending on the response to these queries.

Major external events can influence significantly the course of the market. Before 11 September 2001, the US economy was nose-diving, because of a drop in consumer confidence. After September 11, market watchers saw that the direct effect of terrorist acts had been minor and not long lasting. In fact, from an economic view September 11 was a 'plus' for the US economy, although it was a very tragic event, and one that also showed that some industries need to consolidate more rapidly, airlines being an example.

Sometimes investment advice that is perceived, through its aftermath, to be wrong may lead to legal risk. In other cases, to gain business asset managers offer investors, and confirm in writing, a return that is difficult to sustain under prevailing market conditions. When this happens, and the results being obtained do not correspond to contractual clauses, investors ask the asset manager to compensate them. Alternatively, they sue in court.

In London, in a court case that began on 15 October 2001, pension-fund trustees for Unilever sued Merrill Lynch Investment Managers (MLIM) for negligence. The Unilever pension fund sought £130 million ($250 million) in damages for alleged mismanagement of their £1 billion ($1.8 billion) account, saying that the extent of underperformance at Mercury Asset Management amounted to negligence.

- The contractually agreed performance target was to beat the benchmark by one percentage point.
- Instead, between January 1997 and March 1998, Mercury underperformed the benchmark by one percentage point.

In its defence, MLIM said that neither performance target nor floor was guaranteed, and they could not mean that the fund would never perform outside the range in a given period. While this was a judicial test of underperformance (eventually settled out of court), analysts were concerned that it would be likely to be followed by other legal arguments on whether the assets manager:

- Took excessive risks when responsible for pension-fund property,
- Failed to diversify sufficiently, or
- Was stopped by his superiors when investment decisions diverged greatly from the fund manager's house policy.

Arguments about underperformance are more frequent when the equity markets are in a tailspin. Firms that are active managers of money are taking significant risks to come up with double-digit annual profits. When they do not show extraordinary results under their management assets shrink. For instance, in the 2000–2001 timeframe, Britain's twenty biggest fund-management firms have lost 14 per cent of institutional assets under their wings, while costs have climbed.

This in no way means that passive asset management (discussed in section 5.6) is the preferred solution. Passive management often underperforms, even if at times it is better to do nothing than to switch investments. For these reasons, some experts suggest that a sensible strategy is to use a mixture of active and passive strategies by dividing the available resources in:

- A well-diversified core portfolio that is traded very seldom, and
- A relatively smaller speculative portfolio that is traded actively.

This poses the problem of first class focus on asset allocation, and equity picks, as well as market timing. It also has prerequisites such as obtaining and sustaining a rich information flow, and being supported by high technology. Another prerequisite is the use of advanced modelling techniques, in full appreciation of the fact that there is model risk involved in this exercise.

5.8   The portfolio's intrinsic value

Reference was made in the Introduction to *intrinsic value*. This is the discounted value of cash that can be taken out of a business, or an investment, during its remaining life. The calculation of intrinsic value is a 'must' with any investment, but computing intrinsic value is not that simple, because:

- It is a metric based on estimates rather than on precise figures, and
- Such estimates must be changed if interest rates move, or forecasts of future cash flows are revised.

One of the key points of interest in analysing an equity for intrinsic value, or for that matter of analysing any other acquisition, is the relationship between this metric and the market price of the same asset. Theoretically, but only theoretically, the future income to be derived from holding the asset should be reflected in its market value. However, markets are not efficient and therefore this rarely happens in real life.

Intrinsic value is a dynamic concept and two analysts or investors looking at the same facts may come up with somewhat different intrinsic value figures. By contrast, another metric, the *per-share book value*, is easy to calculate, being based on accrual accounting, but it reflects obsolete figures that have little to do with market reality. Therefore, book value is of limited use and, sometimes, it may even be meaningless.

One way to do away with the limitations characterizing book value is to carry holdings of marketable securities at fair value, precisely at current market prices. It is not only today that experts appreciate that the values stated in books are often obsolete, and different from market value and from intrinsic value. This has been known since the time of Luca Paciolo and his seminal 1495 work. However:

■ When the market moved very slowly, and the assets were largely physical and well known, the accruals method made sense.

After all, book value has the advantage that it is based on facts, documented by invoices, as well as on a methodology (such as linear or dynamic depreciation) approved by the government and by regulators.

■ The problem arises in a dynamic market where commodity prices move very quickly, and assets are now largely virtual for which there exist no vouchers for authenticity test.

A paradigm that Warren Buffett uses to explain the differences between book value and intrinsic value is that of looking at college education as a form of investment. One can think of education's cost as its book value. If this cost is to be accurate, it should include:

■ The earnings that were forgone by the student because he or she chose college education rather than a job, and
■ The earnings that the graduate would receive over a lifetime, subtracting those that he or she would have gained without college education.

In this example, the investment horizon is one's lifetime. The resulting excess earnings figure, which can be credited to having undertaken higher education, must be discounted at an appropriate interest rate back to graduation day. This computation will give the intrinsic value of education.

Intrinsic value is used by savvy investors, who are, nevertheless, a minority. The majority goes after other criteria such as P/E ratios, largely based on future growth rates, although they may also involve a dividend discount model that assumes that the market is fairly priced. Hence, the investor is looking at relative valuations, as well as at whether a company can sustain a growth rate different to that of the market for five years. In this case, too, measurements and opinions differ, because everyone has a different view of:

- Long-term growth rates, and
- The sustainability of excess growth.

The aforementioned process becomes more complex with globalization because no two markets have the same relative levels of P/E ratios, as shown in Figure 5.7. The examples come from the USA and Europe in the 2003 and 2004 time-frame. From this figure, the Standard & Poor's 500 has had consistently a higher P/E than Euro Stoxx. By contrast, with the exception of a couple of quarters, the German DAX index and Euro Stoxx tend to correlate.

Apart from the more generally used standards, such as P/E and earnings per share (EPS), many investment experts have their own metrics and strategies, which they often keep close to their chest. Secrecy gives a false sense of security, while the most outspoken investors are also more successful. If you choose to construct a portfolio of individual shares, suggests Warren Buffett, forget betas, efficient markets, modern portfolio theory, option pricing and emerging markets;

- What you need is the ability to select businesses correctly (hence the intrinsic value concept), and
- You have to be able to evaluate companies within your circle of competence and experience.

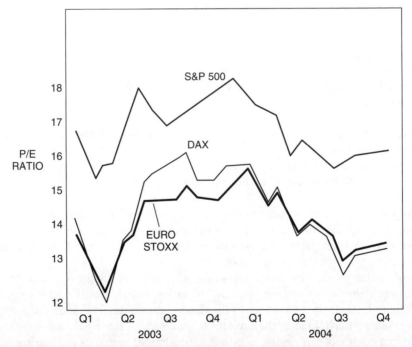

Figure 5.7 Comparison of price/earnings ratios of three major stock indices

The size of this circle or sample of companies where one has analytical expertise is bound to be small, and the way to bet is that in many cases it will be limited. It is vital to know its boundaries. In line with this strategy, the investor's goal must be to purchase at a rational price part interest in an easily understandable business whose earnings should be:

- Virtually certain, and
- Materially higher five to ten years from now.

In addition, what matters is not that all chosen companies of proven intrinsic value should remain leaders of the pack, in the longer term. History shows that they will not. Therefore, periodically and steadily these companies must be re-evaluated. The fact that they are in the lead today is no guarantee that they will remain there because:

- There are challengers for every leader, and
- Companies now riding high are vulnerable to competitive pressures, some of which one day will outstrip the leaders.

The course suggested by the foregoing paragraphs is a different, more well founded than the classical active portfolio management approach. Taken together, financial analysis focusing on intrinsic value and steady re-evaluation suggest that the crucial criterion that every investor should observe is *focus*. Loss of focus is worrisome even when one contemplates investing in businesses that, in general, look outstanding. All too often, we see value stagnate in the presence of hubris, lowered governance standards or other reasons causing the downturn of companies.

Notes

1 D.N. Chorafas, *The Management of Bond Investments and Trading of Debt*, Butterworth-Heinemann, London, 2005.
2 D.N. Chorafas, *The Management of Equity Investments*, Butterworth-Heinemann, London, 2005.
3 D.N. Chorafas, *Modelling the Survival of Financial and Industrial Enterprises. Advantages, Challenges, and Problems with the Internal Rating-Based (IRB) Method*, Palgrave/Macmillan, London, 2002.
4 D.N. Chorafas, *Management Risk. The Bottleneck is at the Top of the Bottle*, Macmillan/Palgrave, London, 2004.
5 D.N. Chorafas, *The Management of Equity Investments*, Butterworth-Heinemann, London, 2005.
6 D.N. Chorafas, *Chaos Theory in the Financial Markets*, Probus, Chicago, 1994.

6 Business models for asset management

6.1 Introduction

To be effective in asset management, private investors, institutional investors and other companies must be confident in their business model, as well as in the investment strategies of their business partners to whom they outsource the management of their wealth. Plenty of research is necessary to acquire confidence in investments, and with it vision. (More on outsourcing in Chapter 7.)

Chapter 5 introduced plenty of concepts underpinning investment strategies, including the strengths and weaknesses each one has. To be successful with the investment strategy they choose, asset managers and private bankers must have a business model, with deliverables that are satisfactory to their clients. Successful business models have more than one dimension. The recent round of consolidation in the financial services industry suggests that neither of two product lines,

■ Product-based content, and
■ Client-based distribution,

can thrive separately: the two have to work in synergy. Product-based choices are central to enhancing client offerings. A bank targeting private banking and/or asset management for institutional investors must remain committed to increasing product choice by supporting both in-house developments and quality selection of third party financial instruments. One of the better known asset managers described in the following terms his fund's strategy:

■ We look for outperforming sectors, by means of a top down macroeconomic analysis,
■ We combine a highly structured and disciplined bottom-up approach to stock selection, and
■ We direct our research on critical factors that can affect earnings growth and cash flow.

Based on this input, the investment policy committee of this asset management outfit sets the investment strategy, including sector concentrations, general orientation in regard to capitalization and other targets. The research department analyses cash flow, earnings growth and other fundamentals of portfolio candidates, seeking dominant companies with sustainable growth rates.

For its part, the asset management entity's risk control unit quantitatively monitors the risk and reward profile of the portfolio, analysing stock, industry and sector exposures, and doing sensitivity analysis. Trading systems are used to provide timely information on market activities and trends, and this helps in developing timing strategies.

Such a holistic approach to a business model is not everybody's policy. Other asset managers, with investment banking background, emphasize to their client the know-how they possess in designing a suitable issue: bonds, shares, derivatives products and structured instruments, and the fact that they go through the appropriate regulatory approval chores. However, some business models along this line of reference leave something wanting.

Practically all asset managers pride themselves on exercising due diligence and ensuring that investors receive all relative information on the status of their wealth. Some assets managers, particularly those belonging to big financial institutions, act as underwriters, whereas others outsource the underwriting activity or put together a group of underwriting institutions. Practically all distribute the newly created financial instruments to:

- Institutional investors, and
- High net worth individuals.

Notice that the activities outlined in the preceding paragraphs involve a great deal of *productizing*, which is a fairly recent term, coined to differentiate between a product that is still at the research and development (R&D) stage and one that is ready to be launched on the market. Securitization of mortgages, credit card receivables, car loans and corporates is an example of productization. Sometimes productization is only sugar-coating aimed at increasing the attractiveness of an already existing product or group of products.

Sugar-coating is often practised in an effort to make an existing product look new and different. In its effort to recover lost market share in credit cards, in 1994 American Express introduced Optima True Grace and revolving credit, which was half-way between an innovation at card level and the revamping of an ageing product. The further aim was to offer consumers the flexibility to *create their own card*, which would let them add some of their favoured features such as:

- A buyer protection plan, and
- A frequent-flier programme.

They could do so by paying for each facility separately. This has been a business model whose concept was not easy to sell, and in the end its success was questionable. At the time, some experts said that if American Express wanted to recapture a large market share it needed to develop a new generation of plastic money to lead the way, not face-lifting solutions.

Of course, the credit card boom that started in the USA in the late 1960s and in Europe two decades later is an example of spending policies, not of investments. But investing and spending should be seen as two sides of the same coin, as we have seen in Chapter 1. First, because someone's liabilities find a way of becoming someone else's assets, and second, because both assets and liabilities have to be managed in the most effective manner.

6.2 Choosing the investment manager

Many people are looking for ways and means to increase their net worth and supplement what social security, the classical safety net, can or could offer. For this reason, as has been discussed since Chapter 1, personal banking has acquired a greater status than ever before, within the societal structure. The same is true of asset management by, or for, institutional investors.

The keyphrase in this process, which is attracting a growing amount of attention, is *effective wealth management* to be done by experts, including investment advice, administration of assets and trust functions (see Chapter 8). At the same time, however, this growing emphasis on outsourcing wealth administration brings to the foreground some interesting questions:

- How is wealth management in the new economy different from wealth management in the old economy?
- What short of investment planning can take advantage of globalization; and of deregulation?
- How important is brand name to a financial institution targeting the role of an insourcer in wealth management?
- Is it true that in today's internationalized but fragmented financial services market, a recognized and trusted brand is a priceless asset?

The answer to such queries should by no means be academic. The choice made by the private or institutional investor among a myriad of name plates depends, to a significant extent, on the answer that is given.

Other questions that are critical to the choice of investment experts are raised when one considers what is told to an investor at *product* offering time, and the queries that the investor poses to the vendor: Which are the product characteristics that make your financial services company more serious and more effective than its competitors? What will really value differentiate the product you are offering from that of the next assets manager?

In the background of similar queries lies the fact that in their role as administrators of individual wealth, mutual funds have had a most asymmetric appeal to investors in the different countries. This has spread to other asset managers, who do not work like mutual funds.

The reason has to do with population dynamics. In the USA, an estimated 16–20 per cent of adult population is in a mutual fund. By contrast, in flourishing cities such as Singapore and Hong Kong, whose mutual funds have the highest penetration in Asia, only 2–3 per cent of the population subscribe to them, even though Asia, in general, has a very high ratio of savings.

In other countries, too, there is a large untapped population of potential savers and investors, because there exists a growing middle class, and fairly good, or at least improving, economic prospects. Experts say that in these cases the brand name plays a role. Other things being equal, banks that market mutual funds among their products have a better chance of capturing the customer's retention, compared with a mutual fund start-up.

In connection to the query regarding the administration of wealth in the new economy, globalization, innovation and technology aside, the functions of assets management have many common characteristics, no matter what the specific investment environment may be. These common characteristics include:

■ Financial discipline,
■ The bottom line,
■ Handholding with customers,
■ Answering customer needs, and
■ Building an *investment advisory* service that gains the client's confidence.

These five bullets create a frame of reference that can help the individual or institutional investor in selecting a private banker or an asset manager. In more sophisticated societies other criteria need to be added to assist the investor in tracking the assets manager's performance (see section 6.6). Examples are:

■ Portfolio content,
■ Consistency in selection,
■ Cash flow,
■ Growth prospects, and
■ Performance benchmark(s).

Some investors are particularly sensitive to the assets manager's and private bank's sales policies and methods. Targeting investments clients requires procedures that are friendly to the individual or institutional investor, who seeks to trust his or her money to an insourcer with asset management expertise.

The marketing practices of an insourcer must be much deeper than just defining the level of commission, performance targets, and absolute or relative return. The investor must become convinced that the investment processes and procedures that the asset manager follows really make sense.

For their part, investors should appreciate that no two insourcers have the same frame of mind. Every assets manager has his or her own personality, priorities, strengths and weaknesses. All of these characteristics show up in running a fund. Not only the quantitative criteria of a portfolio's contents, but also qualitative issues such as the investment advisor's and asset manager's personality, are part of the efficient frontier that, in the investor's eyes, links risk and return. Figure 6.1 presents a template.

Because of the importance of qualitative factors, since the beginning of this book a great deal has been said about the quality, honesty and ethics that should characterize the investment advisor and manager of accounts. A short story from the early years of the twentieth century helps to convey this message. Andrew Carnegie, the great Scottish–American industrialist and philanthropist, was invited to meet Emperor Wilhelm II of Germany. When Carnegie and his wife arrived in the seaport of Kiel, US Ambassador Tower accompanied them to the emperor's yacht.

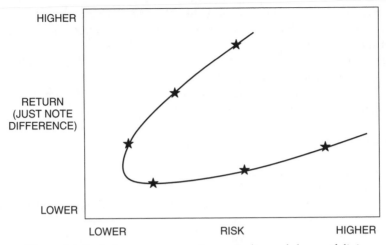

Figure 6.1 Both the asset manager's personality and the portfolio's
contents make up the efficient frontier

The Carnegies were first introduced to various admirals and dignitaries, and were
deep in conversation when the emperor unexpectedly approached from behind.
'Mr Carnegie, the Emperor', Tower said. Carnegie raised both hands in delight
and exclaimed: 'Your Majesty, I have traveled two nights to accept your generous
invitation, and never did so before to meet a crowned head.' 'Oh yes, yes. I have
read your books. You do like kings', said Wilhelm II. Andrew Carnegie answered:
'No. Your Majesty, I do not like kings, but I do like a man behind a king when I find
him.'[1] That is precisely what the educated investor likes.

6.3   Don't kill the goose that lays the golden egg

Investors, whether individual or institutional, must like the man behind the function.
On behalf of the company for which he or she works, the investment manager acts
as trustee. Some of the roles that have to be performed in answering the responsibilities involved in this duty are:

- Observance of the investor's objectives, guidelines and restrictions
- Safety of wealth being entrusted through careful selection, diversification and risk
  management
- Able handling of the investment's prospects by being alert to business opportunities
- Other critical functions, such as custody, trust and secrecy.

Something that investment advisors and assets managers should not do to gear up
the investor, supposedly to maximize returns, but really assuming inordinate risks. If
and when the investment advisor promotes alternative investments,[2] he or she should
ensure that the customer fully understands the product and its risks. The assets
manager should ensure that as appropriate reference framework is in place, like the
one shown in Figure 6.2.

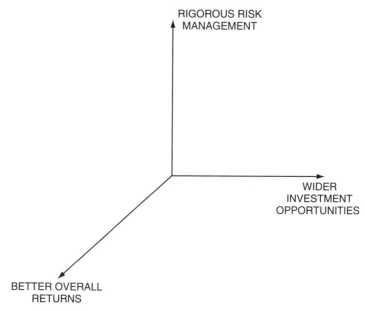

Figure 6.2 Not only should the customer fully understand the
product in which he invests, but the asset manager must also have in
place the appropriate framework

Scandals are poisoning the investments practice. There is nothing more effective
than malfeasance in killing the goose that lays the golden egg. The year 2001 had
Enron; 2002, WorldCom; 2003, Parmalat. In 2004 big banks put aside huge reserves
for legal risk, and then came 2005.

Mid-March 2005, an investigation into whether American International Group
(AIG) distorted its financial results resulted in the resignation of its long-time CEO,
Maurice 'Hank' R. Greenberg. Analysts say that regardless of whether AIG broke the
law, or must report lower earnings for past periods, the case is likely to prompt executives at other financial companies to be more conservative in stating their numbers.

Investigations into whether American International Group manipulated its financial
results to mislead investors have been increasingly focused on the insurance industry's
Bermuda triangle, where businesses can escape disclosure radar screens. As one of the
world's biggest sellers of property-casualty insurance, AIG:

■ Buys billions of dollars of reinsurance policies to protect itself from bigger than
expected claims on policies, and
■ Obtains some of these policies from obscure companies in lightly regulated offshores, such as Bermuda, Barbados and Cayman Islands.

As far as AIG investors are concerned, the problem is that companies in these
places are not always required to disclose who really owns and controls them, or to
report on other details of their operation, as insurers in the USA must do in filings
with state insurance departments and the Securities and Exchange Commission

(SEC). As a result of this lack of transparency, both investors and investigators are trying to figure out whether New York-based AIG secretly controlled some of the reinsurers that it listed on financial filings as unaffiliated. If so, it might have:

- Bought reinsurance from itself, and
- Benefited by stuffing bad claims onto these companies' books and otherwise burnished its results.

Financial companies are generally opaque and, as some experts say, their quarterly and annual statements are like black boxes. But the fact regulators and the New York attorney general were following up with their investigation of AIG made many analysts wonder how and why, on 6 March 2005, two Wall Street firms upgraded the insurance company's investment outlook.

As this and many similar cases demonstrate, a great deal of attention should always be paid to compliance with rules and regulations. This must be done not only in the home country but also, individually, in each host country where the firm operates. Globalization leaves much to be desired in regard to standard rules and unity of supervision. For example, there is no single regulator for all of the European Union; neither is there a single regulator for North America (particularly the NAFTA region), south-east Asia, or any other major group of nations with tightly linked economies. Every country has its own:

- Laws,
- Regulations, and
- Ways of supervision.

Compliance with a mosaic or rules and regulations is difficult at best. Yet, today, this is more crucial than at any other time, because investments are subject to a diversity of jurisdictions that defy globalization; and to a multiplicity of versions because of growing customization of financial instruments.

A lesson that asset managers should learn from the manufacturing industry is that satisfied customers come back for more. In IBM's heyday, in the 1960s and 1970s, 70 per cent of its steadily growing annual turnover came from its existing customer base. This is a good rule for banking, too.

Management makes the difference. An old adage has it, 'More security does not make you more secure. Better management does.' In the 1960s and early 1970s IBM had first class management. From time to time, many companies have good management but, as profitability and cash flow accelerate, their executives forget where the brakes are.

In AIG's case, among authorities exploring its dealings with offshore entities are state insurance regulators in New York, who have been working with SEC and New York state's attorney general, Eliot Spitzer. This investigation is intensifying even as other investigators from the SEC and the attorney general's office continue their probe of a transaction between AIG and a Stamford, Connecticut, unit of Berkshire Hathaway.

American authorities are looking at whether AIG used the transaction with Berkshire's reinsurance subsidiary to pump premium revenue and claims reserves.

Indeed, this seems to be the mother of inquiries, which led to the abrupt retirement of Maurice Greenberg as AIG's chief executive in mid-March 2005, although he remains chairman.

One theory is that Mr Greenberg was laid low by transactions he personally arranged in 2000 with General Re, owned by Warren Buffett's Berkshire, which had the appearance of boosting AIG's reserves without actually doing so. Although Maurice Greenberg was a careful executive who largely avoided e-mails, General Re apparently did keep detailed records.

All this is indeed a pity, and a deception of AIG's investors. Over the years, from 1968 to 2005, Greenberg had build AIG into a financial giant. Apart from being the largest insurance company in the world, the entity is known for its flat management structure, with 90 000 employees allegedly reporting to Maurice Greenberg.

- Anyone could get a call from the CEO at any time, even on holiday,
- That this call was likely to demand information on the tiniest detail.

It would therefore be rather surprising if Greenberg did not know what was going on in the Bermuda triangle or the Berkshire affair. Neither are these AIG's only problems. Four former employees have pleaded guilty in a bid-rigging case centred on Marsh & McLennan, the world's largest insurance broker, whose chief executive, Jeffrey Greenberg, is the son of the former AIG CEO.

Regulators are also scrutinizing alleged attempts by Maurice Greenberg to put pressure on specialists on the floor of the New York Stock Exchange (NYSE) to support AIG's share price in 2001. This happened while the company was consummating the acquisition, paid for with stock, of American General. Greenberg's efforts included lobbying the NYSE's then chief executive, Richard Grasso, while the AIG CEO himself sat on the compensation committee of the NYSE.[3]

Delaware insurance regulators, meanwhile, are looking into AIG's relationship with two companies with which it has disclosed ties: deferred compensation and investment firm Starr International, and insurance agency C.V. Starr & Co. Several years ago, Delaware regulators investigated AIG's use of a Barbados-based Coral Reinsurance to determine whether the firm was controlled by AIG.

At the time, AIG said that it voluntarily would phase out its use of the company, and the state of Delaware levied no penalties. The times, however, have changed. The Sarbanes–Oxley Act, passed in 2002 in the wake of major bankruptcies and fraud cases such as Enron, Global Crossing, Adelphia Communications and WorldCom, made regulators much more inquisitive and rigorous in their work than they used to be. It also made investors more alert to what is happening with their money.

6.4 The contribution to asset management by contrarians

Basically, the contrarian spirit says: 'Never follow conventional wisdom in the market'. To go counter, however, investors, their advisors and assets managers, have to learn how to think for themselves in alternative ways than those promoted by 'traditional wisdom'. The problem is that most people do not want to make the effort to do it. They prefer being the followers of a trend rather than taking the risk of having an independent opinion. This state of mind does not appreciate that even riding the wave requires thinking. In market terms:

- Contrarians bring liquidity to the market through their action, which goes against the trend, and
- By challenging the obvious, they help in renewing the market's thinking and, eventually, its behaviour.

Some contrarians are among the most respected names in asset management. They have made a lot of money for many of their clients, which is not forgotten. This, however, does not mean that contrarians are always right. If a contrarian opinion can prove to be quite valuable, it is just as true that in other cases the contrarian's judgement on the timing of a stockmarket crash is indeed premature. The question then becomes, which is more honourable:

- To keep out of equities when one thinks they are overvalued?
- Or, to keep on buying and remain fully invested since this is only the clients' money anyway?

In regard to the framework characterizing their investments initiatives, decisions and actions, contrary to the classical wisdom based on investment criteria such as price/earnings ratio, dividend yield, normal growth rate and balance-sheet strength, contrarians in the investments arena use as indicators:

- Earnings expectations,
- Estimate revisions,
- Price momentum, and
- Killer product stories that may be hearsay.

When they are criticized for this policy, contrarians point out the shortcoming of classical analysis. For instance, stocks of companies likely to beat expectations rise rapidly. Rising earnings estimates from analysts lure more buyers, and the equity zooms even more. Rising stock prices attract fund managers who do not want to be left behind, and dazzling products that may 'change the world' make stocks seem priceless, leading to even more price leverage, eventually to be paid by those who come in late; the market laggards.

Contrarians do not go for such fads. They judge the situation on their terms, making up their mind and moving quickly. While acting in this way, they prove to be more conceptual than analytical. This is a dichotomy that identifies a basic difference between trading and portfolio management. Classically,

- Portfolio management is 80 per cent analytical and 20 per cent conceptual.
- By contrast, trading is 80 per cent conceptual and 20 per cent analytical.

This most significant difference in way of thinking reflects itself in the contents of the investment portfolio and of the trading book. A conceptual strategy is cost-effective for temporary shifts in risk exposure, using short-term risk management products. For instance, a contrarian may exchange traded futures to increase his or her exposure to a given stockmarket, without incurring massive dealing costs.

Like traders, contrarians are intuitive. They rely mainly on their imagination, although sometimes they help themselves through real-time simulation. Notice, as well, that there is an important difference between a theoretical contrarian and one dealing in pragmatic terms. In practice, to win as a contrarian one has to have both:

- The proper strategy, and
- The right timing for moves.

The true contrarian is not going against *any* trend, because he or she appreciates that there is no general pattern of successful activity. Sometimes one does exceptionally well on the strength of a few chosen stock, temporarily leaving other investors by the wayside. In other years one makes a fortune because he or she is the first to be on the right side of the market, which swallows as others come on board.

Neither are contrarians limiting their options to market trends and timing in coming in and out of investment positions. One of the characteristics of several contrarians is their disdain for diversification. They believe that diversification is a *hedge for ignorance*, and that one can be much better off:

- Owing only a few stocks, and
- Knowing a great deal about them.

Notice that conceptual investors follow more or less the same line of thinking, and most often they end up with a concentrated portfolio. A few securities come to represent a very large portion of their assets, and many of them warn vehemently against diversification for diversification's sake.

Summing up, contrarian opinions are important and they should always be considered because of the strength that comes from dissent and the associated breadth of vision. Their implementation, however, requires strength of character to break with the past, or with the ongoing trend, which could no longer serve as a reliable guide to the future. A great deal can be learned, in that respect, from the leaders of industry, particularly those who had a vision as well as the skill to see this vision through.

A practical example from the post-World War II years helps in better appreciating this reference. The late Dr W. Edwards Deming was the first to support publicly the thesis that the system of mass production, which propelled American manufacturing firms to worldwide domination in the 1950s, was hugely wasteful of:

- Talent,
- Materials, and
- Labour.

Deming's solution is most valid today in the financial industry. It consists of personalizing work by involving workers more closely in production, dividing them into teams, granting them responsibility for the quality of what they make and instructing them to check continuously for flaws in the goods. In his time, Dr Deming was largely ignored in America, but postwar Japan followed closely his ideas, which rapidly became central to lean production, just-in-time inventories, high-quality deliverables and team-based work.

6.5 Asset management as an enterprise

In the course of the research that led to this book, a senior banker phrased his mission in the following way: 'Our business in investment management is delivering value performance and excellence in service to a diverse international client base.' This client base, the banker said, ranges from major institutions to individual mutual fund clients. He then added that what distinguishes his bank from its peers is its:

■ Global scope,
■ Investment capabilities,
■ Financial research, and
■ Risk management.

In the opinion of another top executive of a well-known financial institution, the key elements of investment solutions that his bank offers to its clients are: a global perspective on markets and economies; a high-quality investment management platform; research dedicated to valuing markets, currencies and securities around the world; and a range of investment styles, with particular expertise in identifying price/value discrepancies and capitalizing on them.

A third executive cognizant in asset management and investment banking suggested that his bank has historically been closely associated with a price/intrinsic value investment style (see Chapter 5). He then added that, to enlarge the range of its market appeal, more recently his institution had:

■ Broadened its capabilities, and
■ Developed a multiparadigm investment strategy.

The same executive pointed out that over the years, with the evolution that characterized investing, from private banking to asset management for institutional investors, the bank's investment strategy had an impact on its structure. Figure 6.3 presents the chosen fund management structure, which links in an effective manner private banking, institutional asset management and the administration of the bank's own assets.

These three references document that from private banking to institutional asset management, a credit institution's client mandates reflect a broad range of services characterized by certain overlaps. In terms of content, these go from fully discretionary global asset allocation portfolios to equity or fixed income, and structured product portfolios where asset selection and reallocation are in the client's hands. Investment policies vary, including emphasis on specific investment limits. Regarding market appeal, all three institutions address both:

■ Private banking clients, and
■ Asset management for institutional investors.

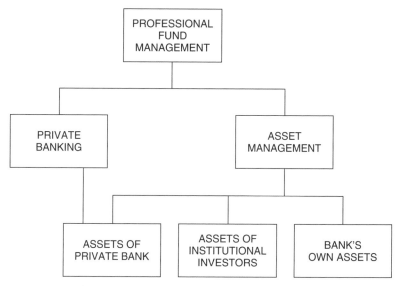

Figure 6.3 A holistic approach to the management of wealth, appealing to diverse client populations

Deutsche Bank offers a good case study on the complexities and challenges of the asset management product line provided by major credit institutions. As reported in 2004, its asset management product line was losing more business than it could attract, and its equities division had slumped.[4]

To appreciate the difference that exists between a plan for asset management, as a major product line, and its execution, it should be recalled that the asset management division has been Deutsche's strategic line following the 2001 acquisition of Scudder, in the USA, for €2.5 billion. It got dragged in the aftermath of that deal and by restrictions about how soon acquisition costs can be written down. Moreover, in the opinion of some experts,

- The asset management division has suffered outflows of funds at a rate of €8 billion a quarter, over several quarters, and
- This took place at the time when the bank's old industrial shareholdings were downgraded, and ended by generating only a 1 per cent return.

Along with these challenges came that of a too high overhead. Deutsche Bank's cost/income ratio has been 69 per cent, which is worse than its big rivals, and analysts look at overhead as a measure of the company's efficiency. Analysts therefore say that the credit institution needs a combination of cost savings and revenue growth, which could boost the bottom line by €1 billion or more, over the next year or two.

There is a pervasive trend in business today, described by many as 'the tyranny of success', in which successful organizations face considerable difficulty in maintaining their strength and their innovative edge in the face of changing markets, new technologies and more sophisticated consumer demands. This is not one bank's problem; it is a worldwide dilemma.

■ The very factors that lead to a firm's success can also play a significant role in its demise.

The leadership, vision, strategic focus, valued competencies, structures, policies, rewards and corporate culture, critical in building the company's growth and competitive advantage during one period, can become its Achilles' heel in another, as market conditions change over time.

■ To overcome adversity, senior management must learn to innovate effectively for the future, while paying attention to both risks and costs.

Cost savings, particularly in regard to personnel, are difficult to make when personal banking and asset management at large call for the recruitment and maintenance of the highest quality investment talent. It is not easy being in charge of the cost structure, but it is possible.

Practical cases that come to public attention provide good evidence about what needs to be done. A recent article in *Business Week* stated that, at Citigroup, 'expenses exceeded revenues in seven of Citi's nine units'. Sallie L. Krawcheck, Citi's chief financial officer, says that this is due in part to the cost of:

■ Upgrading technology in the investment bank,
■ Training Smith Barney brokers, and
■ Legal expenses from run-ins with regulators and investors, which the bank is 'managing aggressively'.[5]

Krawcheck's remarks are instrumental in pinpointing many of the challenges faced by an institution in controlling its cost base.[6] If fund management is run as an enterprise able to customize the client's deliverables, then both skill and technology must be on hand to enhance short-, medium- and long-term results. This is no mean task, because it has inherent in itself a contradiction.

Investors often tend to expect that short-term results, when positive, will hold true in the long term. For instance, in the go-go late 1990s many investors believed that the great returns they achieved on their capital signalled that big gains would continue indefinitely. Then pessimism set in, and by 2002, some investors were just as sure that stocks would not rise again.

As stated in the Introduction through reference to productization, basically investments are like any other product that may have market highs and lows. The key is capturing value. It is not enough to have a great idea. If one is going to spend R&D money to develop products and services that customers want, one needs to think about:

■ How to continue moving forward through steady market-orientated development, and
■ How to prevent the competition taking the market away.

Since banking has become an industry, credit institutions and asset managers need people who fuel and run the customer sales effort, effectively manage the fuzzy front end of innovation, have the ability to see clearly in uncertain environments and never forget about risk control. All this makes a culture that enables and supports corporate survival.

6.6   Hedging strategies followed by portfolio managers

One of the crucial issues that many investors, private as well as institutional, often fail to decipher is the strategy followed by the fund manager in making the money work. A business model described in a short sentence is not self-explanatory. Usually, the investment managers present to the client a nice-looking chart like the one in Figure 6.4, which emphasizes performance against an index; but little is supplied in terms of detail as to *why* and *how* the strategy being followed performed so much better than the index.

During the years of investment performance mapped into Figure 6.4, the index tanked, because it is equity based and the early years of the twenty-first century were a disaster for equities. This result runs contrary to a saying at Wall Street that in the longer run return on equity investments outperforms return on bonds. However, if the asset manager keeps his business model close to his chest, there is no way to tell why his fund outperformed.

Notice that the hypothesis of better performance by equities is not necessarily valid in the short term. Statistics show that during any five-year holding period, there is a 26.7 per cent chance that stocks will not outperform US Treasury Bills. This is what research by Professor Jeremy Siegel, of Wharton School of the University of Pennsylvania, in 1997, has shown.

To be at least 90 per cent sure of beating Treasury Bills returns, investors historically have had to hold stocks for twenty years or more.[7] Siegel, however, speaks of market risk connected to equities, and of credit risk-free Treasury Bills, not of any bond instrument. There is plenty of credit risk with corporate bonds, even debt instruments of big corporations, as the General Motors events of March 2005 demonstrate.

Figure 6.4 Comparison to an index. Has this been a sound investment strategy?

Sometimes asset managers explain their strategy for greater investment performance in terms that the average investor hardly understands. This is the case of an asset manager who, in an investors' meeting, spoke of *stochastic dominance* as an approach that makes minimal assumptions about:

■ Investors' preferences, and
■ Statistical nature of returns.

For starters, stochastic dominance involves the comparison of cumulative distribution of returns between alternative portfolios, using skewness and other risk metrics in 'case' investment strategies (such as writing call or put options), studying whether they affect the distribution of returns in an asymmetrical way. In the background to this approach lies the fact that relying on the mean and variance of risk and return can be misleading, because with the normal distribution one assumes that both tails are affected equally by changes in the variance; hence the wisdom of studying the distribution's long tail.[8]

Other portfolio managers use a business model known as *spectral analysis*, targeting returns that have a cyclical component that can be represented in sine waves. Fourier analysis makes it possible to represent investment returns that have multiple cyclic characteristics and/or regularities that depend on specific periods. These calendar effects are explained on the basis that:

■ News is of an institutional nature, and
■ They are reported at regular time intervals.

Under these conditions, investors do not perceive risk as a random event. Instead, uncertainty can be seen as periodic, with risk regarded as a harmonic process, under the hypothesis that isolated cyclical components are not correlated. This approach contradicts many of the prevailing theories, by pushing the point that, when assessing risk, investors form expectations regarding the periodic arrival of critical information.

These and most of the other theories, business models and procedures developed and used by investment specialists focus not on opportunity analysis but on *hedging*. No asset manager would ever say that he or she is not using a hedging strategy, with the objective of transferring risk 'somewhere else'. In principle,

■ The person off-loading the risk is the hedger, and
■ The person accepting the risk is a trader or speculator.

Like freedom and democracy, however, hedging is very often a misused word. Those who love the practice of hedging tend to forget that perfect hedging implies no losses or gains. A perfectly hedged portfolio is characterized by the fact that its price fluctuations are fully negatively correlated with price fluctuations of the underlying security, which is a practical impossibility, and is not really wanted because no risk means no gain.

Within the limits of what is feasible, a hedging strategy helps against unexpected or undefinable losses, and it can be performed in a number of ways using derivative financial instruments such as options, futures, forwards and swaps (see Chapter 9). One of the methods of risk hedging attempts to replicate the outcome of a put option on a portfolio of securities to:

■ Maintain an upside potential, and
■ Limit the associated downside risk.

Another hedging approach uses portfolio insurance, by buying a protective put or an insurance policy, or by means of dynamic asset allocation. Asset managers are usually thrifty regarding information on their preferred hedging strategy. Sometimes they keep it as their trade secret, and in other cases they do not want the investors to know how often they change their approach to hedging.

Not all investment types, and not all clients, require the same hedging strategy. The best approach is to custom-design the hedging solution, accounting for investment decision factors characterizing the portfolio under management. Moreover, market conditions impact on opportunistic investment strategies and hedging choices.

In the 2002–2004 time-frame, for example, in practically all G10 government bonds, and other highly rated government securities, investors have been facing historically low yields on the instruments to which they have traditionally devoted the bulk of their portfolios. With this, both institutional asset managers and private bankers proposed alternative investments to their clients, and in particular structured financial instruments (see Part 3).

Rather than coming up with miracle solutions, it would be so much better to explain to all investors that outperformance and underperformance are both natural parts of complete market cycles. Between 1945 and 2000 the S&P 500 slid into ten bear markets, defined as declines of 20 per cent or more. Reaching the bottom took from three months, in 1990, to thirty-seven months in 1946–48 and 2000–03, well within historical precedent. After bottoming, the stockmarket has typically recovered in less than twenty months,[9] but this is in no way sure that it will repeat itself in the future.

These facts are a reminder that all investments, and particularly so equities, are volatile in the short term. During the fifty-five years before the year 2000 downturn, the Dow Jones Industrial Average (DJIA) highest average annual gain was 43.96 per cent in 1954. The largest one-year decline was –27.57 per cent, in 1974. This negative market performance by the DJIA was not historically unusual. This is the investment horizon concept. Turnarounds tend to suggest that:

■ The longer the investor holds his or her portfolio positions,
■ The better the chances of being rewarded for his or her patience.

A long investment horizon may be the best investment strategy. Further, in conclusion, sound advice that can be given to investors, private bankers, institutional asset managers and risk controllers comes from the way in which Andrew Carnegie instructed the directors of his factories: 'You have only to rise to the occasion, but no half-way measures. If you are not going to cross the stream, do not enter at all and be content to dwindle into second place'.[10]

6.7   Deliverables and performance in administration of assets

In a narrow sense, the performance of an assets manager is the return on investments that he or she attains for the client, the investors. In a much broader sense, however, performance is a complex issue involving asset selection, risk control processes, culture, skills, the detailed attention paid to portfolio returns and attitudes that altogether impact upon the asset manager's deliverables to the investor.

All asset managers, more or less, say that they are well positioned for the economic upturn or downturn projected to occur in the world or, more specifically in 'this' or 'that' economy. Behind this statement is the implication that their performance will be helped by relative overweighs regarding certain assets, such as high yield and emerging market debt, equities or other commodities.

The usual argument is that within each asset class, individual security or commodity selection will contribute significantly to strong relative performance of the fund. Other asset managers emphasize that their superior performance is a direct result of the integration of their investment advisory services, sharing knowledge and research across the globe. To be satisfied, however, investors may require some greater detail rather than vague statements about competitive advantages, deliverables and performance. For instance:

- What kinds of people and critical skills will be available for continuing performance?
- What kind of risk will these people be willing to take, and how will they see things others do not?
- How will the asset manager reward and motivate its investment experts, on a day-to-day basis and in the longer run?
- What technological processes are required to support these people, and how will they be enhanced over time?

Investors who know what to expect from outsourcing the management of their wealth appreciate that answers to these queries are not self-evident. Several asset managers fail in their attempts to motivate because they rely too much on throwing money at the problem, and their culture is inappropriate. This raises the question: How must cultures that support greater investment performance differ from those required by more traditional business activities?

In the background of the cultural question lies the fact that wealth management is no linear business. Neither are its deliverables going along a straight line. This poses several challenges regarding how these deliverables should be judged. A basic approach when measuring portfolio performance is to assess some type of risk and return in:

- Absolute terms
- Relative terms, and
- Some combination of both.

The *relative* assessment compares performance of the portfolio to some benchmark, such as a general index or credit risk-free rate of return. This approach has been often criticized as allowing mediocrity, since the direction of the market is irrelevant because the asset manager should be able, on average, to make a profit by taking the appropriate long or short positions.

The use of *absolute* returns does not make for unanimity of opinions either. Critics of performance measurements based on absolute return say that although it may be superior to relative return, it should be corrected for assumed risk. In addition, that it should be combined with relative performance measures to provide a more reliable picture of risk and return in the investment world.

The divergence of opinions about methods and metrics for measurement of performance is by no means a theoretical issue. It is a present and real subject because in asset management investment performance is a core factor in determining client satisfaction, and therefore a growth in assets under management, as well as good commissions.

In a stockmarket environment characterized by soaring share values for fast growing, high-technology companies, like that of the late 1990s, it is not difficult to achieve above-average investment performance. The challenge is to do so in a falling market, as below-average, let alone negative, performance leads to client defections and attrition in assets.

Therefore, it is not surprising that asset managers pride themselves in showing superior performance against a recognized standard. An example is shown in Figure 6.5, based on statistics published by Goldman Sachs. These compare the annual return of the investment bank's priority list against a market index in three

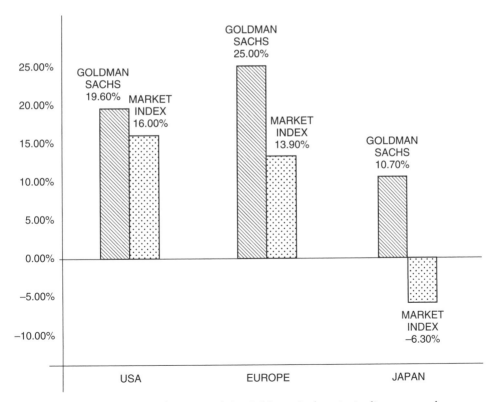

Figure 6.5 Annual performance of the Goldman Sachs priority list compared to market index (1987–1993) with values from the USA, Europe and Japan. (Statistics from Goldman Sachs)

distinct geographical areas: the USA, Europe and Japan. On average, performance is measured over half a dozen years.

In principle, although not always, investment research and asset management performance correlate. To attract clients, investment bankers must use both new research and their track record, an integral part of the latter being the quality of their services. Not surprisingly, however, investment research, not just investment decisions, involves risk.

On 12 January 2004, Bernard Arnault, the chairman of LVHM, the French luxury-goods conglomerate, scored a personal victory in his long-running feud with Gucci. A Paris court ordered Morgan Stanley to pay LVMH €30 million ($40 million) in compensation for alleged bias in its investment research on the company.[11] The way that LVMH's camp had it, the motive for luxury-goods analyst Claire Kent's 'systematic denigration' of LVMH was the investment bank's lucrative advisory work for Gucci. (With Morgan Stanley's help, Gucci foiled a takeover attempt by LVHM a couple of years earlier.)

Kent had a negative investment opinion about LVMH. That is what independence of opinion is all about. She argued that the Louis Vuitton handbag brand may have reached 'maturity', and raised the possibility of a downgrade of the group by Standard & Poor's, the credit-rating agency, which had placed LVMH on negative outlook. Kent also reminded investors that LVMH had 'destroyed value' when it lost money investing in Sephora, a cosmetics chain. Experts said that it is difficult to see how this amounts to tort, as the court found.

Post-mortem, lawyers were to suggest that such evidence would not have been enough to make a case against Morgan Stanley in the USA or the UK. There was no damning e-mail by analysts of the kind that got Merrill Lynch and its star analyst, Henry Blodget, into trouble for hyping internet shares to the public while saying something different internally. Nor was there a case advising investors to buy AT&T shares just before they tanked, as Jack Grubman, of Citigroup had done.[12]

The LVMH/Morgan Stanley case, and some others, make the point that deliverables connected to investment analysis are not free of risk. Take as another example Sodexho, which asked French regulators to investigate Smith Barney, Citigroup's investment banking arm. The bank issued an analyst's report revealing what it claims was debt unacknowledged in the catering firm's accounts. Sodexho said that the arrangement had been disclosed in the accounts of a subsidiary.

In conclusion, independence of the analyst's opinion is a measure of performance. Independence of opinion is so crucial because, without it, the contents of analytical reports would be damaged goods. Another enemy of objectivity in analytics, and a major one for that matter, is conflict of interest between investment banking business connected to mergers and acquisitions, and equity research. This has been in the background of a huge April 2003 settlement between the SEC and a group of ten Wall Street firms, to the tune of $1 billion.

6.8   Past performance is no prognosticator of future results

Past performance in return on investment, and other criteria connected to deliverables, is not necessarily a prognosticator of future performance. Stockmarket volatility, currency exchange rate and interest rate movements may cause the capital, and income from it, to go down rather than up as expected. Therefore, the investor may not get back the amount originally invested, no matter what sort of trend was shown to him or her a priori. For instance, see the trend line shown in Figure 6.4.

For these reasons, prudence advises that rather than accepting at face value a graph on past performance as being indicative of future performance, the investor should investigate whether the asset manager has the necessary skill and know-how to provide good performance in the future. As with implied volatility (see Chapter 4), what is important is *implied performance*.

Stated in the clearest terms possible, with investments and so many other enterprises, the past may be a reference, but it is not a goal. The goal is implied performance without inordinate risk. That is why in the USA some asset managers who were considered to be fairly high performers have been fired.

- Either they used money for the wrong reasons,
- Or they were falling out of line with developments in the market.

Trend curves and fact sheets usually shown to investors at the time of the sales pitch really say nothing. In fact, almost all asset managers carefully write as a footnote to the fact sheet: 'This is neither an offer to sell nor a solicitation of an offer to buy any securities described herein. Any offer can only be made by the memorandum which contains important information concerning risk factors, performance information, and other material aspects of the fund, and must be read carefully before any decision to invest is made.'

To be on the right side of the balance sheet in case of legal risk, other footnotes add: 'An investment in the fund is speculative and involves a high degree of risk. There can be no assurance that the fund will achieve its objectives, or avoid substantial losses.' This is tantamount to admitting that past results are no assurance of how an investment will perform in the future, and therefore investors are asked to ascertain on their own that:

- The investment in the fund is suitable to them,
- They are able to bear the risk of an investment in the fund, including that of the limited liquidity of the shares, or even of losing the entire capital, and
- Either alone or together with the person(s) advising them in connection with that investment, they have enough knowledge and experience to evaluate merits and exposures.

This puts squarely on the investor's shoulders the responsibility to understand the risks being involved, and make all appropriate considerations related to the investment. As discussed in Chapter 4, such understanding is in no way a foregone conclusion. Few institutional investors, let alone private individuals, really understand all of the risk factors entering a proposed investment, let alone their future behaviour.

A sound policy for asset managers and private bankers is that of advising investors, in advance of a commitment, that above-average price movements should always be expected. It is also necessary to point out to the investor that information being provided should never be taken as advice or personal recommendation. Information ranging from past performance to current market trends:

- Is a non-committal expression of facts and opinions, and
- Should not be misinterpreted as forecasting favourable future events.

Another fact of which investors must be aware is that no matter what the business model is, their financial interest in any entity or programme is always subject to dilution. Impairment of assets is an example. In their financial reporting, companies are obliged to recognize an impairment charge when declines in fair value of their publicly traded securities, below their cost basis, are judged to be other than passing factors. There are rules in recognizing an impairment charge, including:

- Length of time and extent to which the fair value has been less than cost basis, and
- Management intent and ability to hold the investment for a period sufficient to allow for any anticipated recovery in market value.

Goodwill impairments, mainly related to mergers and acquisitions, have become a class of particular prominence in the last few years, following new rules by the Financial Accounting Standards Board (FASB). *Goodwill* is measured as the excess cost of acquisition over the sum of the amounts assigned to tangible and identifiable assets acquired less liabilities assumed. Goodwill impairment tests must be performed on an annual basis and between annual tests in certain circumstances. A likely consequence is goodwill write-offs.

There may also be other reasons turning projections on future performance on their head. In mid-2002, in the UK, Aberdeen Asset Management was the group at the forefront of the split capital investment trust debacle. In the aftermath, it put some of its trusts into receivership and made eight of its leading fund managers redundant.

By late September 2002, Aberdeen's share price hit a four-year low, and Aberdeen Preferred Income Trust, with about 12 000 private investors, was put into administrative receivership. This was the fourth Aberdeen split capital investment trust to go into receivership. With these failures, thousands of investors have lost their savings which they put in split capital trusts. Such outfits have different classes of shares aiming to:

- Pay out income to one set of holders, and
- Provide capital growth to others over a set period.

Notice that while the going was good, Aberdeen was a leading firm, with nineteen trusts under its management. Private investors saw split trusts as a low-risk option able to assure a steady retirement income. What these investors did not know is that many trusts took on a high level of debt, and their leveraged portfolios were subsequently hit by asset falls that went spiralling through. As a result, in the UK alone eighteen trusts have asked for their shares to be suspended.

Neither are prognostications about volatility smiles and the likelihood of rising markets a sure thing. Not without reason, in late November 2002, at the *Institutional Investor* magazine's All-American Research Team Awards dinner, Eliot Spitzer,

New York State Attorney General, said that his office had commissioned independent research firms to analyse recommendations made by more than 400 analysts, covering fifty-one industries, who had been ranked at or near the top in their profession.

Based on their actual stock picks over the 1999–2002 time-frame, analysts who were ranked number one in their fields actually had pretty mediocre performances. Spitzer went on to say that average investors would not know the truth because Wall Street promoted the rankings of their analysts, but withheld data on their effectiveness in stock-picking.[13]

Spitzer has not been alone in his comments about stock picks. Since June 2002, the SEC has said that it requires Wall Street analysts to certify that their stock picks are not influenced by pay packages or investment banking relationships. The SEC now asks that analysts ratings, included in the information they give in interviews, public appearances and reports, must incorporate statements pledging that such ratings were not influenced by:

- Compensation, or
- Any relationships with companies.

This can be stated in conclusion. Investors should be fully aware that past investment performance is not a guide to implied performance. Asset managers use past performance as a reference because they cannot sell without a good track record. Appreciating the fact that uncertainty dominates future events is part of the investor's responsibility in the management of his or her assets. That is the sense of caveat emptor.

Notes

1 P. Grass, *Carnegie*, Wiley, New York, 2002.
2 D.N. Chorafas, *Alternative Investments and the Mismanagement of Risk*, Macmillan/Palgrave, London, 2003.
3 *Economist*, 19 March 2005.
4 *Financial Times*, 16 September 2004.
5 *BusinessWeek*, 14 February 2005.
6 D.N. Chorafas, *Operational Risk Control with Basel II. Basic Principles and Capital Requirements*, Butterworth-Heinemann, London, 2004.
7 *New York Times*, 4 August 2002.
8 D.N. Chorafas, *Economic Capital Allocation with Basel II. Cost and Benefit Analysis*, Butterworth-Heinemann, London, 2004.
9 *Wall Street Journal*, 6 March 2001.
10 P. Krass, *Carnegie*, Wiley, New York, 2002.
11 *Economist*, 17 January 2004.
12 D.N. Chorafas, *Management Risk. The Bottleneck is at the Top of the Bottle*, Macmillan/Palgrave, London, 2004.
13 *BusinessWeek*, 2 December 2002.

7 Outsourcing and insourcing wealth management

7.1 Introduction

That which connects the individual investor to the private bank and the institutional investor to the asset manager is essentially one of outsourcing one's duties and responsibilities to a third party. This relationship has become one of the ownership society's basic characteristics, because the management of wealth calls for skills that are not widespread, and also involves plenty of administrative duties.

Outsourcing is the delegation to the *insourcer* of the authority for the provision of investment management services. This is done under a contract that typically incorporates a *service-level agreement* (SLA). While no two SLAs are exactly the same in scope and content, the way to bet is that their core will include issues such as:

- Functionality,
- Cost,
- Quality of service, and
- Timeliness of deliverables.

The entity hiring the third party to perform investment specific services is the *outsourcer*. The party accepting such authority, and responsibility that goes with it, is the *insourcer*. In the business partnership which is being established, *outsourcing* and *insourcing* agreements and contracts define the different aspects of two-way investment management contracts. Ideally such agreements should also include:

- The reward for getting it right, and
- The cost or penalty for getting it wrong.[1]

Insourcing and outsourcing have become core issues because the complexity of technology used in banking, as well as in other domains, puts the supplier of goods and services at the centre of the system as an insourcer, while the outsourcer must focus much more on the development of its produce. The statement is valid in the supply of physical wares as well as with investment issues.

Seen in a much broader perspective, insourcing and outsourcing affect the way in which a national economy is run. As would be expected, there are winners and losers in insourcing and outsourcing.

Politicians hint at cross-border outsourcing as being a principal reason for unemployment, but a recent article stated that American companies earn more money from foreign firms outsourcing service jobs in the USA than the economy loses from domestic firms sending service jobs overseas. In numbers, in 2003 American businesses:

- Took in $61.4 billion by insourcing,
- Outsourced $43.6 billion worth of jobs.[2]

The fact behind these numbers is that when it comes to supplying expertise in areas such as accounting and legal services to other countries, corporate America runs a healthy surplus. This should be good news for US employment. The downside is that if every country in the world decided to cut down on service outsourcing, then countries with insourcing surplus would be likely to lose the most.

Among the ten countries whose balance of outsourcing and insourcing activities is shown in Table 7.1,

- The USA, UK, India, Singapore and China have a positive balance;
- Germany, Japan, Austria and the Netherlands have a negative balance, while France just breaks even.

In private banking, as well as in assets management for institutional investors, typically high net worth individual and institutions act as outsourcers, because they feel that they can get a better deal than if they were managing their wealth by themselves. Private banks and assets managers act as insourcers, exploiting their worth as service providers and making a profit by selling investment management services.

The concept underpinning outsourcing and insourcing of investment services, or of any other type of services, is that of using complementary resources existing in co-operating firms. It is this complementarity that should be subject to functional

Table 7.1 Insourcing and outsourcing activities characterizing ten countries in 2003 (in $ billion)[a]

	Insourcing	Outsourcing	Difference
Net insourcers			
USA	61.4	43.5	+17.9
UK	41.2	19.7	+21.5
India	18.6	11.8	+6.8
Singapore	13.0	9.2	+3.8
Net outsourcers			
Germany	26.5	41.4	−14.9
Japan	17.4	24.7	−7.3
Austria	13.8	16.6	−2.8
Netherlands	19.2	20.1	−0.9
Balancing-out			
France	23.2	23.1	−0.1

[a] Statistics on insourcing and outsourcing by *Wired*, April 2005.

definition, as well as to the definition of cost and quality of deliverables. To appreciate better the evolution in insourcing and outsourcing practice, it is proper to record that originally outsourcing was a rather temporary relationship, but the time-frame has changed:

- Today, instead of being a stop-gap, outsourcing sometimes transforms itself into a long-term policy.
- Consequently, insourcing and outsourcing are no longer the exception; they become mainstream issues subject to strategic review.

At the same time, however, nobody should believe that outsourcing and insourcing are without risk, including legal risk (see Chapter 8). Therefore, a significant number of preparatory steps and prudential policy decisions are necessary to field potentially negative effects of outsourcing, and to support in an able manner an insourcing policy.

The serious person or organization will be neither 'for' nor 'against' outsourcing. Rather, one should examine costs, risks and benefits, and therefore 'pluses' and 'minuses', connected to outsourcing. This must be done in an analytical, objective, factual and documented manner. Functionality, cost, quality and timeliness of deliverables should not only be studied in a rigorous way but also be explicitly written in the SLA.

7.2   Risk and return with outsourcing

Without a clear and unambiguous functional definition, as well as specification on quality of deliverables, timeliness and cost, it is not possible to speak of risk and return with outsourcing. In wealth management, this is a demanding task, but it is possible. Wealth creation by the entrepreneurs of the 1980s and 1990s has fuelled the demand for asset management services, and these entrepreneurs are sophisticated investors who appreciate that a thorough conceptual definition of outsourcing and insourcing obligations and requirements makes it possible to improve significantly the deliverable.

- Private banks, many of them family owned or controlled, traditionally provided high levels of personal service to their customers.
- But several private banks lost ground to international asset managers because by majority, these banks remained untouched by modern management techniques and technological advances.

To be properly executed, an outsourcing/insourcing relationship requires that both counterparties make explicit their goals and the way they should be fulfilled (see section 7.5 on building up the investor's portfolio). The fact that other people outsource the management of *their* wealth does not automatically mean that this answers everybody's requirements. Leaving aside the fact that outsourcing is *en vogue*, one has to accept that, although it may be beneficial, it does not solve as a matter of course all of one's investment management problems.

For instance, as far as institutional investors are concerned, outsourcing asset management requires a great deal of research effort, focused senior management attention, expertise and organizational wizardry, practically on a par with in-house solutions. Outsourcing is a delegation of authority, and delegation should never mean relegation. Appropriate delegation requires well-documented answers to:

- Functional queries,
- Performance targets, and
- Issues related to the cost of deliverables.

In the background of the third bullet point lies the fact that as far as the outsourcer is concerned, one of the main reasons for entering into such a relationship is cost reduction. The insourcer is supposed to benefit from economies of scale. Another reason that is rather prominent in assets management is a lack of skill on the outsourcer's side in terms of managing one's wealth in a cost-effective manner; or, at least, the outsourcer believes that for asset management purposes, the insourcer has better know-how and technology than his own.

Still another reason given for outsourcing is operations orientated, even though, in the majority of cases, the associated operational risk (Chapter 1) is not appropriately brought into perspective. Further reasons (particularly in the manufacturing and merchandising business) are:

- The breaking down of traditional product and provider barriers,
- The changing nature of distribution channels, and
- The fact that clients are becoming increasingly more demanding in their requirements.

That is the general coverage. In specific cases, however, not all of these reasons make sense, and poor decisions are aggravated by the fact that, often, outsourcing decisions are made in a rush. Such is the case of the alleged drive to avoid increases in operational and infrastructural costs, and the often stated (but vague) goal of raising profitability. These issues are rather general in nature, but also apply to a significant degree to investments.

Good governance requirements impose that, like any other skill, outsourcing must be learned. Moreover, what we learn about the manner in which we apply it should answer the prerequisites of efficient account management. An integral part of efficient account management is the quality of deliverable to the client of which the insourcer can be proud.

A good point to start an investment management outsourcing study is the guidelines established by regulators. In banking, new directives by the Basel Committee on Banking Supervision bring attention to six basic requirements connected to outsourcing/insourcing contracts. The first is that a credit institution should be very careful when entering into an outsourcing arrangement, because it *increases* its operational risk.

The second requirement outlined by the Basel Committee is that the outsourcing vendor, that is the insourcer, must be competent, financially sound, and endowed with appropriate knowledge and expertise. Third, senior management of the outsourcing entity must ensure that it concludes a contract that can remain valid over a long period. Insourcing/outsourcing is essentially a business partnership and, as such, it is a strategic issue.

The fourth requirement by the Basel Committee is that the outsourcing contract (that is, the SLA) should *clearly* define the insourcer's assignments and responsibilities. In terms of responsibilities, risk analysis is included on both the insourcer's and the outsourcer's side. Take, as an example, product pricing where an insourcer's opinion is requested in terms of implied volatility. In option pricing,

- The practice of using brokers as consultants presents problems of conflict of interest.
- Such practice is questionable because brokers have business incentives to lean towards volatility estimates that assist in deals, the so-called *volatility smile*.

The price paid by Natwest Markets, the investment banking arm of National Westminster Bank, for mispricing its options is that it ceased to exist. Yet, in its heyday NatWest was the second largest credit institution in the UK. After the announcement of huge losses, the bank's top management admitted that:

- Risk management did not have good enough computer models, and
- The bank had accepted outsourced brokers' estimates of volatility, which turned out to be overgenerous to the pricing of options.

This example helps in documenting the wisdom of the fifth directive on outsourcing by the Basel Committee, that a credit institution must analyse the impact that outsourcing will have on its risk profile, and on the way its internal control system works. The sixth outsourcing requirement outlined by Basle is that overall accountability for outsourced services remains with the board and senior management of the bank that has called in an insourcer. Responsibility is never delegated.

7.3   Internal control and security are not negotiable

Internal control, at the outsourcer's side, and *security* problems, at the insourcer entity, always exist when companies outsource and outskill some of their *basic functions*. Outsourcing is no excuse to lower internal control standards, and no SLA should be soft on security issues. Although the directives by the Basel Committee discussed in section 7.2 address credit institutions, their applicability is far more general covering all companies outsourcing part of their authority on products and processes.

Internal control and security are not negotiable. American regulators have issued similar guidelines. An example is the rules set down by the Federal Deposit Insurance Corporation (FDIC) in connection to the year 2000 (Y2K) problem (the risk that the millennium change will bring computer systems to a halt because of past patchwork with software). The FDIC rules:

- Focused on the dependability of the insourcers in terms of solving Y2K problems, and
- Outlined basic guidelines for choosing a software house or service bureau operation for outsourcing Y2K solutions.

Lessons learned during the Y2K exercise document that, in many cases, the customization of the insourcer's system solution to meet the outsourcer's requirements is a source of breeding trouble. Answering the question: 'How much do you go for customization?' in a conference on outsourcing in London, in December 2001 (which I was co-chairing),[3] the representative of an insourcer said: 'Early customers have much better chance of getting customization. As business piles up, people and time become limited resources.' Limited resources can have detrimental effects on security and the quality of deliverables.

Customization may be necessary in asset management because no two investors' requirements are the same. In customizing, a great deal depends on both the technology and the skills of the insourcer. Notice that risks exist at both the insourcer's and the outsourcer's side, including issues such as:

- Top-notch information technology and its fitness to the job on hand,
- Effective risk management regarding every position in the portfolio,
- Privacy and confidentiality, and hence security, regarding the client's account (see Chapter 8).

If the board of directors, CEO and other senior executives of the outsourcer are personally responsible for whatever happens with the insourcer's contribution, as the Basle Committee says, then it follows that the outsourcer's internal control system should be extended all the way into the insourcer's operations. This is also what the FDIC, Federal Reserve and Office of the Controller of the Currency (OCC) have said in connection to the Y2K problem.

Does this sound too much? If yes, then take note of the following event, which took place in April 2005. In late 2004, five workers of an Indian insourcer, illegally obtained passwords from four US Citibank customers. They then quit the Indian company and set up their own shop. In December 2004, these five and nine others started setting up bank accounts using false identification. They logged on to Citibank on-line and transferred at least $426 000 to Indian accounts.

Sometime thereafter, Citibank customers discovered the transfers and alerted the bank, which informed the Indian police, and Citibank traced the funds to five banks in Pune, the embezzlers' hometown, and asked branch managers to watch for the account holders. When two ringleaders visited a branch on 4 April 2005 to check on the funds, they were arrested by the police.[4]

Another of the challenges associated with outsourcing is due to false expectations. Often the outsourcer expects things that the insourcer is not in a position to deliver. A widespread example in the financial industry is improvements connected to the outsourcer's internal control and compliance requirements.

- If a company has limitations in the domains of internal control and of compliance,
- Then the thing to do is to correct them by itself, not through relegation of its responsibilities to a third party.

The process of identifying and correcting functions and services that are wanting should never be outsourced. The same is true about the execution of *core functions* by the outsourcing entity. (By definition, core functions are those essential to engaging in the provision of products or services to which an organization primarily addresses itself.)

Beyond this, any functions delegated to the insourcer should be under steady supervision and quality control by the outsourcing organization. In regard to asset management, outsourcing is not an off-the-shelf delivery of services such as back-office functions. In fact, this 'ready-made' idea, borrowed from merchandising packaged foods or home appliances, is one of several misconceptions regarding what outsourcing is and is not.

Finally, institutional investors and other companies contemplating outsourcing of asset management functions should be aware that one of the obstacles in this business has traditionally ranged between miscommunication of goals and wishful thinking. Insourcers simply do not have the fantastic solution the outsourcer desires, which can handle everybody's problem and this outsourcer's problem in particular.

Many years of experience have taught me that, as far as outsourcing results are concerned, much depends on what each party brings to the table. In this respect, some of the critical questions that should receive well-documented answers are:

- Is the service to be outsourced core or non-core?
- Is the service to be outsourced self-contained?
- Is outsourcing consuming substantial management time?
- Is there evidence that outsourcing will provide a competitive advantage?

The answers must be precise. The same is true of another query: Is our company ready to exploit the advantage outsourcing is said to present? If not, what else must be done to gain from an outsourcing relationship? What are the costs associated with the contemplated solution? Are the advantages covering them with a margin? Are the risks we will be taking well understood? Are these risks acceptable? All these are queries to which the following sections address themselves.

7.4 Custody only, mid-way solutions and discretionary powers

The relationship that prevails between investors on the one side, and private bankers and asset managers on the other, may take different forms. At one extreme of an outsourcing/insourcing agreement, the client assigns to the private banker only the custody of his or her securities (see Chapter 8), and takes care himself of all investment decisions. Investment trades may be done using different brokers.

This is the policy followed by sophisticated investors, who take charge of managing their wealth. They look at maximizing the security and yield of their investments as being their own responsibility. Indeed, these two factors, security and yield, remain the sophisticated investor's primary concerns irrespective of whether he or she:

- Uses new or already existing financial instruments, or
- Chooses local financial products or products that have evolved in the international financial market.

Also known as *lone-wolf* investors, those taking this road must understand that reaping the benefit from any financial instrument requires constant observation of the market(s), and a level of information that normally exceeds the average investor's capability. If this is not feasible then one must examine other options regarding asset management.

A slightly different version is that, along with custody, the assets manager acts as a broker. Therefore, not only is he gaining brokerage fees, but he also influences the client's choices. As portfolios of securities must be kept dynamic, and therefore there is unavoidable buying and selling, the client needs to ask the broker for investment advice. Alternatively, he may take input from different banks where he has accounts, and make up his own mind.

As far as the asset manager is concerned, the solution that offers an advantage in brokerage is *mid-way*, with the investor remaining the final decision maker. This is also the solution that I follow with my accounts because brokerage fees are negotiated and I find such an approach quite rewarding. With it, the investor:

- Outsources the transaction execution and back-office part of the job, and
- Retains for himself all of the investment responsibility, having only himself to blame when things go wrong.

The investment opinions heard from a group of selected international institutions are often contradictory; but this is normal. Divergence of outlook and of advice is what makes the market. The challenge consists of bringing these opinions together, and coming up with a conclusion in terms of investment choices. The portfolio of non-speculative investors in this category is likely to resemble the pattern presented in Figure 7.1.

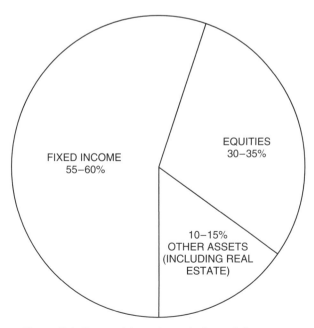

Figure 7.1 Composition of a typical portfolio among
non-speculating investors

At the other end of the spectrum in outsourcing asset management responsibilities is *discretionary* portfolio management (full powers). Many banks say that discretionary asset management is the most important service that the financial industry can offer to high net worth individuals and institutional investors. In these cases, the client issues the bank *a mandate* to manage his or her portfolio, having formulated investment objectives on the basis of personal preferences. For example, a client may prefer to:

- Earn regular income from fixed-interest securities,
- Maximize near-future profits,
- Target long-term growth of his assets, and so on.

There are several reasons why the client may not choose to manage his assets by himself. He may live in a different country to the one in which the custody takes place, may not have asset management skills, or simply may not care to manage a securities account. Cognizant investors do, however, appreciate that they face some penalties if they follow the road of assigning to the bank a mandate for discretionary account management. These include the risks of:

- Changes in the portfolio that do not correspond to the investor's profile,
- Too much switching around of portfolio's contents, to generate fees, and
- Inadequate investment performance, which is a key reason why clients leave a private bank or asset management outfit.

While performance is one of the basic issues facing asset management in private banking (see Chapter 6), few institutions have in-house the required skill and high technology to face the market's whims without much damage to the assets of which they are in charge. Ten years ago, rolling out the red carpet was cornerstone in attracting private banking customers, but as the latter gained investment experience, today the crucial subject is:

- Providing substance, and
- Delivering profits.

To round up this discussion, Figure 7.2 presents four quarters formed by non-discretionary and discretionary solutions at two different levels of invention. Some of the bankers who participated in the research project leading to this book commented that several of their high net worth clients in private banking have started to behave like institutional investors who prefer:

- Brokerage-level relationships, and
- Services such as safekeeping and investment advice.

Alert asset management outsourcers have taken note of this developing trend. One institution, a Dutch asset management company, said that its business is now characterized by the statistics shown in Figure 7.3. Notice that while 15 per cent of clients ask for mainly brokerage-level services, brokerage fees give this institution 50 per cent of its profits.

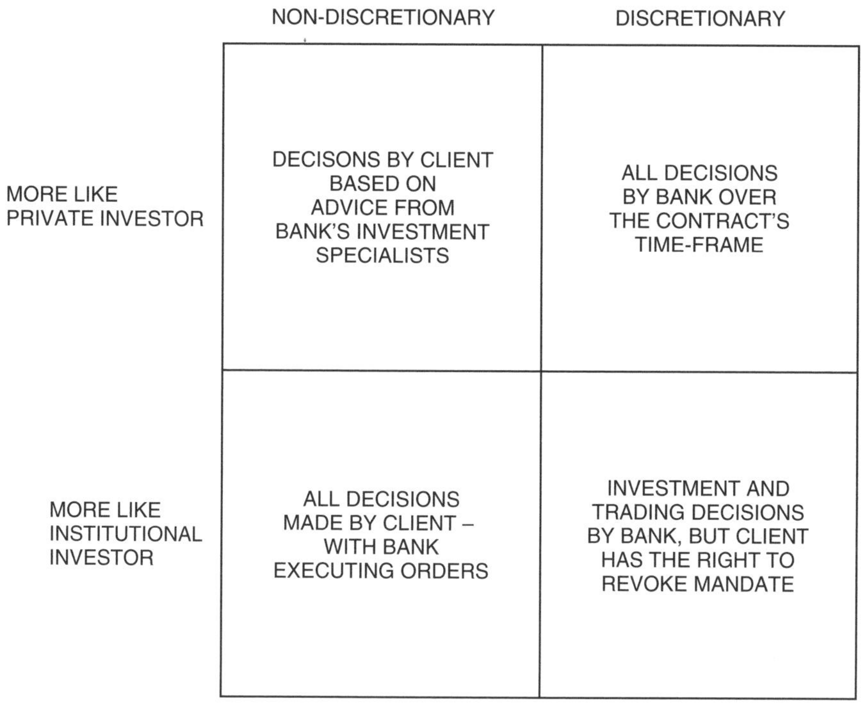

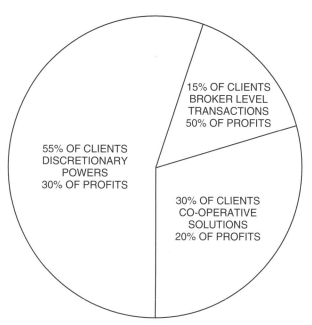

	NON-DISCRETIONARY	DISCRETIONARY
MORE LIKE PRIVATE INVESTOR	DECISONS BY CLIENT BASED ON ADVICE FROM BANK'S INVESTMENT SPECIALISTS	ALL DECISIONS BY BANK OVER THE CONTRACT'S TIME-FRAME
MORE LIKE INSTITUTIONAL INVESTOR	ALL DECISIONS MADE BY CLIENT – WITH BANK EXECUTING ORDERS	INVESTMENT AND TRADING DECISIONS BY BANK, BUT CLIENT HAS THE RIGHT TO REVOKE MANDATE

Figure 7.2 Quarters in outsourcing/insourcing agreements regarding private banking and assets management

15% OF CLIENTS
BROKER LEVEL
TRANSACTIONS
50% OF PROFITS

55% OF CLIENTS
DISCRETIONARY
POWERS
30% OF PROFITS

30% OF CLIENTS
CO-OPERATIVE
SOLUTIONS
20% OF PROFITS

Figure 7.3 A Dutch example of investment management: percentage of clients and corresponding share of profits

For sophisticated clients who still follow the discretionary portfolio management approach, good performance does not necessarily mean the greatest possible capital gain, because greater gain necessarily involves greater risk. What they want is for the asset manager to work out a risk profile appropriate to their needs and requirements, observe established benchmarks and deliver much better results than they can achieve themselves.

Moreover, sophisticated wealth clients appreciate when the boss takes personal care of their account, particularly at the time of a major market switch. Here is an example from the early 1930s.

In 1933, in the midst of the disorder that followed the Great Depression, Jackson E. Reynolds, chief executive of New York's First National Bank, was asked by one of the bank's clients, a woman who was a writer and a friend of his wife, to switch her account from bonds to stocks. The woman's estate consisted of $100 000 entirely invested in US Treasury 4.25 per cent bonds.

The investor profile was conservative, with her income derived from her writing and the interest on the bonds. The woman asked the bank to prepare for her a list of good common stocks. 'We'll go over them, and then you can sell the governments and use the proceeds for the common stocks', she said to the banker.

Reynolds took charge, ordering one of his assistants to prepare the equities list. 'Mr Reynolds', the assistant exclaimed, 'You are not serious! Selling the primest of investments at a time when stocks have dropped through the floor, and no one knows what's going to happen or when the end has been reached.' But the CEO replied, 'I certainly mean to do this. Run along and get the list ready.'[5]

Jackson Reynolds could not have known that US economic conditions would not deteriorate further, although that was precisely what the large majority of investors feared. But he knew that these fears were already reflected in stock prices. Therefore, he did not try to convince the client to stay on the safe side and hang on to the debt instruments in her portfolio. What happened next demonstrated that both he and his client were right (more on market turnarounds in section 7.5).

7.5 Building up the investor's portfolio

Two alternative approaches are favoured by asset management insourcers in developing an investor's portfolio. One is known as *bottom–up* and the other as *top–down*. Both have advantages as well as limitations. Typically, the bottom–up approach starts with different stocks and bonds and is constructed on a microeconomic basis. A first concept about what should be in the portfolio is tested against the market.

- Results are analysed, and
- They are summed up, with both return on investment and assumed risk appropriately evaluated.

Along the lines of this solution, primary attention is paid to the component parts of a simulated portfolio: which includes bonds, stocks and maybe structured financial instruments (see Part 3). This is done in relation to risk and return accounting for:

- Interest rate developments,
- Projected changes in currency rates,
- Implied equity volatility, and
- Ways and means for hedging risk.

By contrast, the top–down approach starts with a macroeconomic basis. It looks at developments taking place in the global economy, and most particularly in economies where investments are or will be made, as well as how these may impact the market, rather than at the instruments. After a decision has been made about economies and markets in which to invest, the focus is placed on the instruments.

In general, some investment advisors, and several investors themselves, favour the top–down approach, while others believe that bottom–up is better. In the majority of cases, the choice between the two methods is a matter of people's training, experience and culture. Neither method has indisputable advantages to help to determine which one to choose.

Beyond background, cultural issues and their aftermath, the choice between the two methods depends on other factors such as currency exposure, country risk and some particular characteristics of the market(s) in which one wants to invest. A number of analysts suggests that when it comes to return on investment,

- About 80 per cent is a function of choice of markets, and
- Only the remaining 20 per cent is a question of cherry-picking.

Up to a point, the 'choice of markets' argument presupposes that the market is efficient, which is far from being a self-evident truth. If the market were efficient it would be hard to beat the index. The concept of market efficiency has something to do with the fact that many investment managers today choose to play the index rather than investing in discrete stocks, or make their picks by focusing on stocks that replicate the index, but this is not the most rewarding strategy.

Betting on the index rather than on individual stocks practically eliminates the bottom–up component of an investment policy. By contrast, the fact that many private bankers and asset management insourcers prefer the bottom–up method suggests that traders and investment advisors believe previous little in market efficiency. They believe even less in the 'perfect relation between markets'. Had this been the case, there would be no reason for global diversification.

However, during the last quarter century globalization has meant that there is a correlation between markets, and this needs to be established and accounted for in evaluating exposure or risk. There is also a need for estimating liquidity and volatility, interest rates and currency exchange rates. None of these factors behaves linearly, and therefore risk and return with investment is not a simple proposition.

With regard to the preceding paragraphs, it is proper to stress that while investors may choose to outsource the management of their wealth to the experts, there are some principles that should be observed. The first and foremost rule in an ownership society is that *all investors must be and continue to be in charge of their wealth*. The more important next principles are described under nine headings.

Decide what your risk appetite is, and never lose track of it

Like everything else in life, investments involve risks. This is true of all sorts of investment, although with some of them, particularly those that are leveraged, the investor assumes a much greater exposure than with others. Moreover, as shown in Figure 7.4, risk and return are not linearly related. Beyond a certain point risk grows much more rapidly than return.

Own your stocks, and never borrow money for investments

The golden rule is to own all the components of your portfolio of financial instruments. If you borrow money or take a mortgage on your house to play in the stockmarket you will be the loser. This is what Amadeo Giannini, who built up the Bank of America, advised his friends, clients and employees. 'Own your stock' is excellent advice. Worry is the extra interest that investors pay when they buy stock on margin or with borrowed money.

Examine the pluses and minuses of diversification

As already shown, one of the basic investment choices is concentration versus diversification. Theoretically, diversification is good for an investor. Practically, however, holding too many different positions makes it difficult to follow their fortunes. As far as the typical investor is concerned, four to six stocks are enough for a portfolio, albeit in different industries for diversification reasons. If an investor knows what he is doing, he needs no more. If he does not, he should not be in the stockmarket.

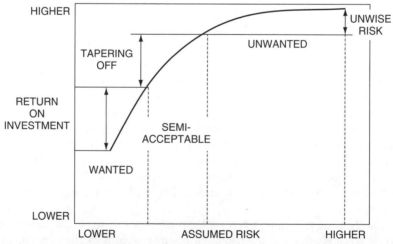

Figure 7.4 Risk and return are non-linearly correlated. Investors must appreciate the shape of the risk and return curve

Unless you are a long-term investor, put a target on the profits you expect

Like any other commodity, equities have ups and downs. In the current market, the advice 'Cut your losses and let your profits ride', meaning hold onto winning stocks for a long time, is full of risks. A sound rule is to set an objective of X return on the investment. The difficulty associated with this advice is finding another situation that meets the initial requirements for equity investing.

Follow the challenger

Some investment experts advise buying only the common stock of companies that are second or third in their respective fields. The investment reason in the background of such advice is that their further growth will provide specialists with built-in support for a 'bull raid' that they will conduct in the shares of these companies.[6] Most of these bull raids will occur before the company's potential is publicized in terms of significant earnings or market share announcements.

Invest in stocks quoted in big boards

The New York Stock Exchange, London Stock Exchange and NASDAQ, for example, fall under this heading, whereas small local exchanges do not. The investment experts' argument is that an absence of significant institutional participation on small exchanges makes it possible for speculators to conduct bear or bull raids that can peak in an hour's time. Moreover, because of a stock's bigger capitalization and larger quantity of institutional sales, equities in big boards tend to give investors advance warning as institutions begin selling near to or at a stock's high.

Play down the use of stop and limit orders

The best investment experts advise against entering stop or limit orders with the broker. These land on the specialist's book, giving him insight information on the stocks that he is handling. Besides that, it is better to follow the market prices dynamically, and make up one's mind, rather than setting limits based on guesses. Markets can turn around and/or have a step-down well below the buy limit one has placed.

Do not buy at peak quotations

A sure way to get burned is to buy at peak values, or jump on an upswing to be on the bandwagon. The best investment managers advise restricting purchases to stocks that have declined by at least 35–50 per cent from their highs. It is a bad investment policy to wait to buy until stocks are making new highs, following something that is attracting public attention. In general, such highs tend to make their appearance after the halfway mark in a bull market, and in this case it is better to begin thinking of sales rather than acquisitions.

Do not sell short and do not allow your equities to be borrowed

Another sound rule is not to sell short, because your potential losses are unlimited, and not to allow one's stock to be borrowed. These two issues correlate. Speculators borrow equities from brokers to sell them short, and brokers rent out equities of their clients who are on margin. A corollary to this is not to leave one's stock with the broker in street name. It is within the broker's ability to vote this stock as the owner of record, which gives the stock exchange brokers their power over the economy.

7.6 The option model of investing

Portfolio managers are often selected on their ability to perform in up and down markets. Like all investment outfits, private banks and asset managers search for people who have proven track records, and are able to reposition dynamically the portfolios under their authority while adhering to company goals and strategies, as well as their customers' guidelines. These are the quantitative criteria.

Qualitative criteria for selection of portfolio managers are whether they have an edge, are experienced and have a stable organization of assistants ready to support them. Many experts believe that qualitative measures in selection of the appropriate insourcing firm are more important than quantitative factors. The latter can be learned, while qualitative factors are closely linked to a person's decision profile.[7]

One of the foremost qualitative elements is that of a *conceptual* mind, able to size up the market's moves and direction. Conceptual capabilities are right brain characteristics, and they contrast to analytics, digging deep into issues, which is left brain. A conceptual mind examines alternatives and the expected aftermath. It is 'challenging the obvious', while at the same time being characterized by an orderly decision-making process.

The ability to structure and price *options* is conceptual. Options challenge the obvious because they are contrarian to prevailing culture, and to the way in which we usually think. For starters, an organization's *culture* is made up of its shared values and beliefs. As such, they are both a promoter of legacy actions and an impedance to research. This statement can be best appreciated through a recent example from natural science.

A basic problem in our search for life in the universe is that this is too Earth-centric, says Steven Benner, Professor of Chemistry at the University of Florida. Yet, if some aspects of life on Earth are historical accidents, as we think is the case, then there could be other chemical solutions to the problem of building life out of non-living materials. As the Huygens mission to Saturn's moon Titan seems to have shown, the fact that life on Earth:

- Builds living organisms out of carbon,
- Encodes genetic information in DNA, and
- Uses water as a solvent to bring chemicals close enough to each other, to undergo biological reactions,

in no way means that is the only way to do it. Organic chemicals may be just as prone to undergo biochemical reactions in methane and ethane as they are in water. Benner suggests that in natural science some bonds may be formed even more readily in methane and ethane than in water and, moreover, such solutions may be less likely to fall apart.

Thinking by analogy, solutions and instruments used today in economics and finance in no way need to be the only approach possible. In terms of concepts, structures, products, risks and other effects we are, so to speak, too Earth-centric.

- A priori, the after-effect of challenging the obvious way of doing things is as clear as a desert sandstorm.
- A posteriori, this is the only way to reveal major breakthroughs, as Dr Roentgen found out by discovering X-rays.

Challenges can be made effectively only by minds that combine conceptual and analytical capabilities. Conceptual approaches to business decisions have amplitude rather than great depth. They also exhibit significant stability, because of being based on a more rounded view. An analytical approach, in contrast, is fundamental in breaking down old structures by revealing new but 'nasty' facts that destroy old theories.

One of the important characteristics of a conceptual mind, which is a bonus in asset management, is the ability to live with uncertainty. A proxy to that is the concept of options, which increases obligations to the writer, one of the contractual parties, while the buyer has the right, but not the obligation, to purchase or sell a stated quantity of the underlying commodity or asset. Furthermore, the buyer can do so:

- Sometime in the future, and
- At a price agreed upon when the contract is first entered into.

The extent of applicability of this conceptual characteristic has meant that option pricing models have been applied with increasing success to all kinds of securities, as well as in connection to credit risk evaluation and measurement.[8] Indeed, option premiums are computed as the sum of intrinsic value and time value, this sum being the amount of money that buyers are willing to pay for an option in anticipation that, over time, a change in the underlying asset price will cause the option to increase in value.

An example of the wider application of this concept is the *option model of investing*, a relatively recent development in risk management. Traditional approaches to risk control, and their models, account for uncertainty by converting expected returns into a *certainty equivalent*. They do so by including a risk premium in the discount factor.

In a way similar to the Earth-centric example, because this certainty equivalent is the most commonly used algorithm, very few people appreciate its shortcomings; namely, that it involves asymmetrical adjustment costs. In principle, it is relatively easy to enter into an investment position, but it is often only possible to get rid of it by either:

- Selling it well below its original price, or
- Going through a fire sale, and eventually even scrapping it.

The new way of looking at projects that involve uncertainty and therefore risk is that investors have the option of postponing their commitment. Conceptually speaking, the less they know about future developments the more reserved they should become about tying up capital irreversibly. Any kind of commitment becomes more expensive if the degree of uncertainty associated with it is high.

For this reason, an analysis based on options concepts can provide vital information on assumed exposure. As an MIT study has shown, when it comes to investments, savings and other financial activities, our behaviour can often be irrational and occasionally self-destructive.[9] Irrational behaviour by market players has significant impact on financial markets and the economic system as a whole. An option model will ensure the investor has two hats:

■ As an option writer he or she would put a premium commensurate to the risk taken if the option is exercised.
■ As an option buyer, he or she will not enter into such a contract unless the option has a high probability of being exercised, and the transaction leaves a profit.

The conceptual thinking required to proceed along this line of reasoning relieves the dampening impact of uncertainty on investment activity, particularly when market players are able to evaluate implicit risk and return. Concomitant to the concept underpinning the option model is the realization that microeconomic data are fundamentally better suited to explain the role of uncertainty than macroeconomic data, which are classically used. Microeconomic information is most helpful in investment analytics, particularly when the option models open up the conceptual perspective.

7.7   Efficiency in private banking and asset management

Associated with the issues discussed in the preceding sections is the efficiency with which private banking and assets management operations are executed. Industrial engineering may be used as a proxy. In the early part of twentieth century, Frederick Winslow Taylor toiled to uncover the scientific principles underpinning workmen's efficiency. Taylor developed the methodology of *time studies* by carefully observing, watch in hand, how workers work. His goal was to redesign work habits to make them:

■ More rational, and
■ More productive.

He addressed himself primarily to manufacturing *skills*. He wrote about the 'law of heavy labouring' and the science of shovelling, in the belief that every act a worker does could be optimized and made more efficient. From 1910 to the mid-1920s, H.L. Gantt (inventor of the Gantt chart), F.B. and L.M. Gilbreth (who developed the *motion study*) and other industrial engineers brought into existence what became known as principles of scientific management.

In industrial history, this concept of efficiency acquired meaning at the end of the nineteenth century and this probably led to the events mentioned in preceding paragraphs. Efficiency came into perspective when the newly discovered laws of thermodynamics were used to analyse energy input/output of the steam engine. Thanks to the mathematical and technical calculations of mechanical engineers,

- Efficiency attained quantitative precision, and
- It began to be applied to the industrial workplace.

Like advanced business knowledge, efficiency has prerequisites that are not completely fulfilled in the domain of finance. Yet investors are really after greater efficiency than their own when they outsource creation, supervision and administration of their portfolio. This poses the critical question of whether self-managed investment accounts can perform better than those entrusted to:

- Private bankers,
- Assets managers, and
- Highly leveraged funds.

What the reader should retain from the efforts of Taylor, Gantt and the Gilbreths is that their methods were rooted in observation and experiment. They were motivated by the search for general laws concerning work that paralleled the laws of nature. Their conviction was that science could foster harmony and co-operation in the workplace, along with greater efficiency, and they succeeded in proving their point.

In contrast to the pioneering industrial engineering work of the early twentieth century, during the past fifty years efforts have been focusing not on skills but on executive knowledge, performance and professionalism; on decision support, management information systems, knowledge artefacts and the real-time enterprise.[10] This has led to a 'try anything' philosophy that produced some tangible results, exemplified by the fact that tier-one managers:

- Prefer talk and debate to reports and memorandums, and
- Know how to use a circle of experts that may be wide and informal.

Both bullet points identify principles of good governance widely applicable to outsourcing and insourcing, and by consequence to modern industry at large. If we were to carry into investment management a lesson from industrial engineering, this should be that our actions must always examine available alternatives, which presupposes that we do our homework through analysis and experimentation.

Greater efficiency in management requires that the decision maker is a 'ganglion for reception, expression, transmission, combination, and realization', as the author H.G. Wells said of Franklin Delano Roosevelt. Like Roosevelt, investors should be delighted in playing off their advisers, private bankers and asset managers:

- Using their disputes as a means of screening and developing investment ideas,
- But retaining control of what truly matters: the power to decide.

As far as efficiency is concerned, the principle behind the oral debate is that talk keeps ideas from being prematurely fixed. While a sense of the meeting filters through, the executive's attention may move to the next intellectual puzzle. Efficiency requires fact-finding, but it does not call for deliberation that inhibits action until all evidence is in hand. The lacking evidence should be made up by testing methods, particularly stress testing (see Chapter 4).[11]

Efficiency also calls for intuition which, in many cases, helps in penetrating a situation that is otherwise impossible to value. Together with imagination, intuition helps to recast a complex problem, reducing it to some crucial elements. Moreover, intuition gives a 'feel' of a situation:

- Placing more reliance on hunch than on conscious reasoning, and
- Providing an ability to anticipate the future, a characteristic often given to successful leaders.

Take as an example the case of First National bank's Jackson E. Reynolds and the sophisticated investor who decided to switch from Treasuries to equities in the middle of the Great Depression (mentioned in section 7.4). In the exact reverse of the 1929 pattern, virtually all surprise by the market was likely to be positive.

The younger people working for Reynolds did not have that perception, but as events unfolded, there were indeed some positive surprises. By virtue of a change in the US Administration, the natural dynamics of the business cycle, deficit spending and inflationary monetary policies, the US economy recovered significantly during Franklin Roosevelt's first term.

- For investors who bought stocks in 1933, returns were spectacular.
- The Dow rose 288 per cent from 1933 to its 1937 high, rewarding the intuitive people's foresight.

Intuition aside, advanced business knowledge is acquired through a combination of research and practical experience. Its antithesis is a hotchpotch of defensive positions, and often biased opinions, checked only here and there by sporadic statistics. Advanced knowledge in a business environment also contrasts with that of scholarly investigators because, while their work may be underpinned by analytics, results never really pass laboratory status.

The idea of efficiency to which this section addresses itself is, as shown in the earlier paragraphs, a notion drawn from physics. Physics helps in supplying a rationale for the use of experts, and analytics redefines their participation in the decision-making process. This concept of the consultative role of expertise is a most delicate one in the domains of:

- Investments, and
- Outsourcing investment skills.

In the natural sciences, leverage helps only up to a point. Beyond this, it becomes a liability. Natural selection is based on genetic choices, adaptation and mutation, not on leverage. Something similar applies with investments.

Take the following example. Figure 7.5 shows the performance over 1998 of an account based on Microsoft, Cisco, Dell and AOL versus the results obtained by a highly leveraged fund. 1998 was a bumper crop year for technology stocks, but in terms of deliverables the difference is striking: the results represent a growth of 68 per cent for the self-managed account versus 31 per cent for the leveraged fund whose asset allocation is shown in Figure 7.6. Worse still,

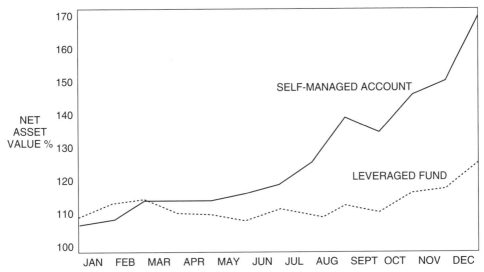

Figure 7.5 Performance of a self-managed account with technology stocks versus the lower performance of a leveraged fund in 1998 (100 per cent corresponds to mid-1997)

- The leveraged fund's annualized return since inception was a mere 8.5 per cent, and
- The annual volatility characterizing its assets was 28.3 per cent.

Any distribution whose standard deviation is four times its mean shows extremely bad quality. The leveraged fund also suffered a draw-down of nearly half its value at the end of the period. As far as the investor is concerned, what he received as a return

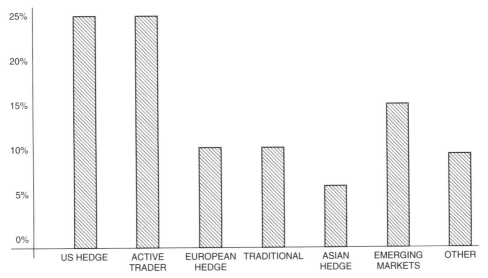

Figure 7.6 Asset allocation of investment holdings by a hedge fund

Table 7.2 Monthly market value over one year of investments holdings in a hedge fund, starting on 1 January of a given year

1 February	+11.39%
1 March	+8.72%
1 April	+1.54%
1 May	−3.01%
1 June	−7.95%
1 July	−9.66%
1 August	−9.57%
1 September	−10.63%
1 October	−10.21%
1 November	−8.60%
1 December	−8.26%
1 January	−2.03%

is shown through the monthly statistics on market value shown in Table 7.2, taking the status at the beginning of the year as 100 per cent.

Among other leveraged funds administered by the same assets manager, the currency fund lost money; real-time trading lost money; while commodities made a profit of 7 per cent during the same one-year period. Moreover, come rain or shine the investor still had to pay the assets manager fees for advisory services and administrative expenses, plus a 20 per cent appreciation fee, *if* there was an appreciation.

Of course, these two examples of Reynolds and the hedge fund are extreme cases. Many shades of grey lie between them. It may always be that the exercise in self-management of an investment portfolio turns on its head. Avoiding the deflationary effects of a down market that they find difficult to time, is one of the reasons why the ownership society tends to outsource the administration of its wealth to professional asset managers.

7.8   The private banking profit centre

Private banking is by no means an activity free of cost. Commercial activities associated with asset management; know-how of the people employed as investment advisors and portfolio administrators; custody services provided by the bank itself or outsourced; different functions bought from insourcers, such as information providers; and high technology that needs to be used, involve both set-up costs and running costs.

■ The income from fees by private bankers and asset managers must cover all these expenses and leave a good profit.
■ Therefore, private banking should be treated as a *profit centre*, subject to a well-established strategy and clearly defined profitability targets.

Costs matter, particularly so because the pricing of private banking services is not as elastic as many people think. This has become a highly competitive field and competition means that there are limits to fees and commissions. The most important private banking clients know how to shop around for the best deal.

Steadily increasing effectiveness and swamping costs should be a profit centre's credo. In the author's experience, a private banking/assets management business unit can really operate as a profit centre on a sustained basis if the management of wealth is profitable to the bank's customers, not only to the bank itself, and also if:

■ Its efficiency is high, and
■ There is a lid on expenses. Management should look at every dollar or pound being spent as a hawk.

A private bank with substandard cost structure has little if any idea of where its expenses go, nor can it project whether revenues will cover costs and leave a profit. In these cases, it is likely that:

■ A small percentage of profitable clients will end up subsidizing the rest, and
■ The bank will find it increasingly difficult to establish a proactive approach to enlarging its client base and improving its profitability.

As explained in section 7.7, greater efficiency in wealth management operations calls for significant productivity improvements, while maintaining a high quality of customer services. In turn, this requires a streamlined organizational structure, all the way down to the nucleus responsible for relationship banking (more on this nucleus later).

Experienced hands in assets management operations suggest that the profit centre will be much more successful if the wealth manager delivers within the three-dimensional frame of reference presented in Figure 7.7, and also, if he or she observes

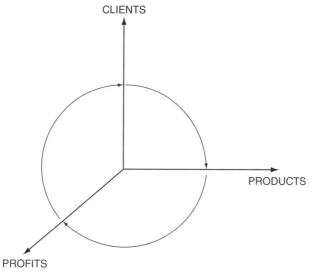

Figure 7.7 As the name implies, the goal of a profit centre
is growing income and profits

the obligation to inform the client, and handhold with him, at a level commensurate to the client's:

■ Investment experience, and
■ Importance of account with the bank.

An effective wealth management policy will make sure that clients are informed regarding the types of transaction that entail a higher level of risk, or have an exposure profile quite different to that of better known instruments. Case studies can be quite helpful in explaining the kind of exposure faced by investors. Plenty of examples and case studies on risks involved with structured products are presented in Chapters 12–16.

An investment advisor respecting himself and the bank for which he or she is working should be familiar with these and other case studies on assumed exposure. Telling a customer that 'there is no risk with structured products' destroys the profit centre's reason for being. It is also part of the responsibility of the wealth manager, and of the bank for which he works, to explain the likelihood of upside and downside associated with non-traditional investments, including investments in the emerging markets.

The more investors become knowledgeable and savvy, the more this issue of risk analysis becomes important. At the same time, private banks and asset managers who share with their clients their best estimates in terms of exposure, find themselves ahead of the curve in marketing their investment services. Once regarded as rather undignified, effective marketing of private banking, asset management and other financial services is today cornerstone to the effort of:

■ Winning new customers, and
■ Obtaining a greater share of existing customers' wealth.

Organization is another variable affecting the efficiency of a private banking profit centre. There is no universally valid answer on how wealth management profit centres should be organized. A great deal depends on:

■ Their client base, and
■ The type of services they offer.

An example from Swiss private banking helps in explaining what should be the target, and composition, of the most elementary business unit responsible for client support. This nucleus is typically composed of three or four people:

■ A very qualified, mature private banker, who is in charge,
■ One or two assistants, who at the same time are developing their skills, and
■ A secretary, also trained in client handling.

Although the boss of this small business unit has the final account management responsibility, both the assistant(s) and the secretary are able to execute many routine jobs. This evidently magnifies the time of the senior professional and, most importantly, provides the basis for continuity in handholding with private banking customers.

At no time during working hours will this nucleus private banking office be unattended. There is always a person available to talk to the customer when he or she calls. Compare this with the pitiful policy of many private banks, for instance British banks, where investment advisors can be reached only through their mobiles. Even then they are often not available and all the client can do is to leave voicemail. With this sort of wealth management the telephone tag starts, a practice most disgusting to high net worth individuals.

In early 2005 one of the best known high street banks in London, where I have a current account, asked me to open an account with them. The person to be responsible for my account was not available; but I was told not to worry; 'he will call me soon'. When he called, it was I who was unavailable. To test him, I sent him an e-mail:

Dear Mr . . .

I have tried twice to reach you while in London, at . . . – but without success.

Can you kindly let me know, at your earliest convenience, what your bank offers in the following products:

Fixed Income Derivatives
Equity Derivatives
Currency Derivatives

along with literature explaining the characteristics of each instrument you offer, including risk and return. The same reference is true of:

European Medium Term Notes (EMTN)
Absorber Certificates (Airbugs).

Finally I will appreciate to know what your bank offers in:

Constant Proportion Portfolio Insurance (CPPI).

After having studied your reply and associated conditions, I will get in contact with you.

With best regards

A whole month passed by with no reply. Then I sent him a new e-mail asking whether he was still labouring to collect this information. This time the reply came rather quickly.

Dear Professor,

I can only apologise for the delay: I have been sick for the better part of the last two weeks.

I had started to collect all the information you asked us prior to that and I will complete the work in the next couple of days. You will receive an answer by e-mail no later than next Tuesday.

Apologies again.

Kind regards

A couple of Tuesdays elapsed before the information in reference showed up. This is an anti-private banking paradigm. It would have never happened in a Swiss bank. This does not mean that the Swiss approach to private banking is the one and only, but from my experience with asset management operations with banks from ten different countries, it is the best. Other asset managers should therefore be keen to take notice and learn from it.

In general, other things being equal, the contact with the client is much closer when the private banking unit is small, because big private banking operations have inefficiencies of scale. Large-scale units breed a lack of personal accountability as well as complexity; both can lead to mini-catastrophes in terms of customer contact and satisfaction. Beyond a certain point, as size increases, efficiencies of scale turn into inefficiencies, the planning and control mechanisms necessary to the effective functioning of any organization move out of gear.

Moreover, with the growing size of the private banking unit and a flood of innovate financial instruments (read derivatives based alternative investments), financial institutions lose contact even with the products they sell, if not with investment realities altogether (see the case study in the Appendix).

Notes

1 D.N. Chorafas, *Outsourcing, Insourcing and IT for Enterprise Management*, Macmillan/Palgrave, London, 2003.
2 *Wired*, April 2005.
3 *Outsourcing for Financial Services*, Conference organized by IIR, London, 11 and 12 December 2001.
4 *BusinessWeek*, 25 April 2005.
5 J. Grant, *Money of the Mind*, Farrar Straus Giroux, New York, 1992.
6 D.N. Chorafas, *The Management of Equity Investments*, Butterworth-Heinemann, London, 2005.
7 D.N. Chorafas, *Membership to the Board of Directors*, Macmillan, London, 1988.
8 D.N. Chorafas, *Economic Capital Allocation with Basel II. Cost and Benefit Analysis*, Butterworth-Heinemann, London, 2004.
9 *MIT Report*, October 2001.
10 D.N. Chorafas, *The Real-time Enterprise*, Auerbach, New York, 2005.
11 D.N. Chorafas, *Stress Testing. Risk Management Strategies for Extreme Events*, Euromoney, London, 2003.

8 Trust duties and legal risk

8.1 Introduction

Etymologically, *trust* means faith, confidence, reliance, conviction, certitude. In credit terms, trust is used to describe the reliability of a business partnership; most specifically its credibility and trustworthiness. Trust is confidence, and as Demosthenes, the Ancient Greek orator and politician said: 'Business depends on confidence'.

In connection to securities, the meaning of trust underpins operations such as custody, care, charge, guardianship, protection and safekeeping. The term trust is also used to describe a monopoly or cartel, as in the phrase 'an international trust controls the market in diamonds'.

In banking and finance, the trust function is important for many purposes. Basically, it involves the holding of property by a trustee who has power to administer it. The trustee receives the benefits from the assets in trust, both property and income, to be used as directed by the trust agreement. This scheme has often been used by persons and entities wishing to have funds held safely and/or administered by a trustworthy institution.

Every trust function involves legal responsibilities and is, therefore, confronted with the likelihood of legal risk. One of the many aspects of legal risk is that of loss arising from misbehaviour, inability or unwillingness to comply with assigned trust function(s). Legal risk can also come from unexpected application of a law or regulation, or for other reasons such as impossibility to enforce a contract.

Most often, the amount of assumed legal risk depends on the law of the land and on law enforcement practices that vary by jurisdiction. Therefore, legal risk can best be judged within the jurisdiction in which the transaction takes place and/or the counterparty is established. Knowledge of the law of the land constitutes the basis for controlling many of the factors entering legal risk.

Stress tests could be used to examine 'what if' the legal system does not function well because of nepotism, corruption, occult influences, and political interference with the way the police and judiciary systems work. Another important test regards how counterparties react to reputational risk. There are three main reasons why legal risk has been increasing over the past two decades:

1. *Globalization*: business is conducted cross-border and differences across jurisdictions add to legal risk. Also, for many legal cases there is no cross-border precedence, and the laws of one country may contradict those of another.
2. *Complexity of financial instruments*: innovation brings into the legal risk equation many unknowns. With the exception of custody, which is a specialized business,

bankers, asset managers and investors have not been forthcoming in their examination of *implicit legal risk*.

3. *Our society is more prone to litigation than previous social structures*: this is true of both individual actions and class actions, which are multiplying, putting the legal system under stress. In connection to Vioxx, which it withdrew from the market, the pharmaceutical company Merck faces 850 lawsuits, plus ninety putative class actions, as well as lawsuits by its own shareholders and by its own employees (see section 8.8).[1] As another example, during the research that led to this book, reference was made to a bank with ninety-four cases in court.

One way of controlling the expansion of legal risk is to apply a priori the *six evidentiary questions*, by Marcus Tullius Cicero, the famous Roman senator and orator (106–43 BC). The first two concern personal accountability: *Who*, apart the person who signed, contributed to or was witness to this decision or act? *How* did the persons involved, alone or by committee, come to this decision (or perform that act)?

The next two of Cicero's evidentiary questions provide background evidence: *Where* has the decision (or act) been made that led to the commitment being made? *When* was this decision originally made, and under *which* conditions? The last two of Cicero's questions are the all-important 'what' and 'why': *What* exactly did the decision involve? Was it subsequently changed or manipulated? *Why* was the decision made? What precise goal did it target or intend to avoid? Was there a conflict of interest?

Even after nearly twenty-one centuries, Cicero's queries are as valid today as at any time. Not only are they renowned for their lucidity, but they also constitute the pillars on which rests every legal discovery process, and practically every case of breach of trust.

8.2   Trusts and trustee responsibilities

Trust has been defined in the Introduction. *Trust* and *agency* services are rendered, largely by the financial sector, to individuals, institutional investors and corporations, as well as other entities such as hospitals, colleges and communities. The concept of *trusteeship* can be traced back to antiquity. Fundamentally, trust functions include service both as *trustee* and as *agent*. A trust exists where a *trustor*, settler or creator commits property to a trustee to administer:

- In accordance with terms of a trust agreement, and
- For the benefit of a well-defined beneficiary.

The main difference between an agent and a trustee is that the agent does not take title to the property involved. He usually transacts business under the name of the principal. In an agency relationship, a specified agent is authorized to represent and act for a principal in his or her business, or contractual dealings with third parties.

In contrast to the agent, the trustee takes legal title to the property and does business in his own name, even if title to and interest in the property remain with the beneficiary. Trust functions are an integral part of private banking and in many cases of asset management. They are also being performed to an increasing extent by credit institutions which provide accessible, continuous and impartial administration:

- Under financial responsibility, and
- Subject to strict governmental regulation.

As legal structures, trusts are rather complex. They are recognized as self-standing by those countries that follow an Anglo-Saxon-type legal system. In the USA, for example, the trust institution dates back to 1818 in Massachusetts, and 1822 in New York.

In terms of the contributions that they provide, trusts can be useful vehicles to safeguard assets from rapid spoilage by beneficiaries, overeager tax authorities or plain mismanagement of investments. They also carry risks. As has been the case (rather recently) with personal banking, the trust business grew with:

- The development of large private fortunes, and
- The emergence of big corporations, accompanied by a shift in emphasis from tangible wealth to intangible property, such as securities.

On setting up a trust, the investor who places the assets into this trust become the *trustor* empowering another party to act on his or her behalf, whether the wealth is real estate property, cash, stocks, bonds or any other commodity. For this purpose, the trustor appoints at least one manager, the trustee, and often more than one, to:

- Manage the trust's wealth, and
- Make disbursements to beneficiaries.

On completion of all necessary documentation, the most important being the trust deed, the trustee has total control over what is done with the assets. At the same time, the trustee is accountable for acting in accordance with the trustor's wishes, the by-laws of the trust and prevailing legislation.

In the USA, national banks were first empowered to add trust activities by the Federal Reserve Act of 1913. A 1918 amendment required them to obtain approval from the Federal Reserve Board to exercise all trust functions, and also permitted state banks and other entities to become trust companies in the state in which the national bank was located. Their participation was made complete in 1927, when they were granted indeterminate existence.

In 1940, the US Congress enacted the Investment Company Act to cover phases of investment company operation not regulated under either the Securities Act of 1933 or the Securities Exchange Act of 1934. Although registration under the act is optional, trust activities of unregistered companies are so severely limited that registration becomes practically compulsory.

Legislation and regulation ensure that the activities of trust companies, or departments, must be conducted in accordance with the terms of the trust instrument and state law. In banking, trust activities must be carried on by a separate department of the institution, with separate records and funds. Records and funds of individual trusts may not, in general, be mingled. Serving both users and suppliers of capital, the trust function makes three broad economic contributions.

- It conserves wealth or private property, safekeeping accumulated capital and avoiding its wasteful use.
- It assists in stabilizing investments, placing funds in productive use through the large volume of funds it controls as well as by means of its advice to clients.
- It encourages the collective ownership of industry, both in its handling of estates and in its services to corporations in connection with security issues.

Trust legislation varies by jurisdiction. In the USA, only public trusts may be created in perpetuity; all others are limited in duration. *Voluntary*, or *living trusts*, are created through deed or agreement with a living person, and may be revocable or irrevocable. The assets of the latter are essentially gifts. Important trusts that can be created by living persons only are:

- *Retirement trusts*, made to build up an estate during the productive years of an individual, while providing relief from the problems of managing property during declining years,
- *Life insurance trusts*, which consist of the proceeds of policies on the creator's life. Such policies are made payable to the trustee with whom they have been deposited, and
- *Pension trusts*, under which trust funds are set up by corporations for payment of retirement and other benefits to employees.

Retirement trust, life insurance trusts and pension trusts have in common the fact that their primary aim is assuring that an adequate standard of living is maintained throughout life and after retirement. This is fairly comparable to the aims of private banking, examined in Part 1. It also means that there is no room for risky investment policies.

In some countries, financial guarantees are mandated by law, or are often demanded by policyholders themselves who want to be certain of their future standards of living. These guarantees can pose serious risks to the trustee. If the financial management cannot achieve expected returns, the company has to resort to shareholders' money. Therefore, financial guarantees must be consistent with:

- The opportunities offered by financial markets, and
- Honest, ethical and good governance of the trustor's money by the trustee.

Other types of personal trust include *sheltering trusts*. These are set up, for example, by parents to ensure the support of their children. Still other types are spendthrift trusts, to protect improvident beneficiaries from their lack of responsibility in money matters; and charitable trusts, such as for religious, educational, literary or scientific purposes.

In conjunction with personal banking, personal trusts may perform both trust and agency functions for individuals. An example is the settling of estates of deceased persons. This is not necessarily a handover, as exemplified by the will of Henry Kaiser, the great American industrialist, signed two years before his death. In this will, Kaiser's grandchildren are listed along with his son Edgar, followed by this provision:

> In the knowledge that they are otherwise provided for, I have intentionally and in full knowledge omitted any provision herein for . . . [them].[2]

An *executor* acts under the last will and testament of a deceased person, whereas an *administrator* is appointed by the court of jurisdiction, if the individual dies without leaving a will or naming an executor in his will. The duties of both are, however, similar: collect the assets of the estate, pay debts, taxes and other charges, and distribute the balance according to the terms of the will, where one exists.

Trust departments established by banks also render the outlined trust and agency services to corporations. Their principal trust function is to act as trustee under the *indenture* or *mortgage* securing a bond issue. The bank's trust department:

- Co-operates in drafting the indenture, and
- Authenticates each bond.

During the life of the bonds, on behalf of the many widely scattered bondholders, the trust department watches for any breach of the agreement by the issuer(s), serves notice of a breach on the issuer(s) and, if not remedied, may start an action to protect the bondholders. In the USA, the performance of these duties is governed by the Trust Indenture Act of 1939.

Agency functions for corporations may take several forms. For instance, a *transfer agent* keeps a record of transfers of the ownership of stock, issuing new certificates and cancelling the old ones. A *registrar* prevents overissue of shares by keeping a record of the issued and outstanding shares. The registrar's duty is primarily to the public, whereas the transfer agent serves the company.

8.3 Legal risk and the case of tort

Legal risk and business risk (see Chapter 3) can have a very significant impact on the fortune of investors. Legal risk, which is a major component of operational risk under the new Capital Adequacy Framework of the Basle Committee (Basle II),[3] can have devastating consequences on an equity. Moreover, legal risk, business risk and *reputational risk* correlate.

Tort is any legal case other than breach of contract that includes economic and non-economic damages. The American tort system has been designed to compensate accident victims and deter negligence. Over the years, however, it has been widely abused and is becoming a very expensive and economically distorting proposition (see section 8.4 on cost of litigation).

The USA spends over $230 billion a year, or around 2 per cent of gross domestic product (GDP), on tort-type legal actions, while victims of negligence get a very bad deal. In America, tort is twice as expensive as the liability systems of other industrialized nations. Over half of the compensation goes towards legal fees and administrative costs. With the exception of trial lawyers, who benefit from the current system, few deny that the US tort laws need reform. No wonder that George W. Bush wants to:

- Cap non-economic damages at $250 000,
- Reform the rules for asbestos compensation, and
- Shift national class-action lawsuits from state to federal courts to stop plaintiffs shopping among the states for the highest payouts.

Shaking up the tort system, however, is no easy matter because of a high level of embedded interests. As long as this system lasts, it is a duty of senior management to provide economic capital commensurate to assumed legal risk. For this purpose, *intrinsic legal risk* estimates are necessarily based on:

- Assumptions, and
- Hypotheses.

Assumptions must be based on current evidence of what might come a legal penalty, versus the cost of an off-court settlement. Hypotheses must be documented through historical precedence concerning similar cases confronted by a company, as well as the markets and jurisdictions in which it operates.

Assumptions and hypotheses are more sound when they overcome the usual resistance: 'A major legal risk would not happen to us'. There is no reason to believe that Bank of America was deliberately taking legal risk, yet in February 2005 five of its units settled charges of improper mutual-fund trading with the Securities and Exchange Commission by agreeing to pay a total of $515 million.[4]

In one case, Bank of America Capital Management, BACAP Distributors and Bank of America Securities agreed to pay $375 million to settle charges that they let large investors make rapid and illegal late mutual-fund trades. In a second case, Bank of America's mutual-fund unit Columbia Management Group, and its distributor, agreed to pay $140 million to settle charges related to undisclosed market timing. The best policy for being in charge of legal risk is:

- Actively involving board members and senior management,
- Developing a well-documented system on legal exposure, with regular reporting,
- Verifying that internal control functions properly without cover-ups, and
- Reviewing results by internal and external auditing.

Because it has generated escalating losses, the US tort system has become a major worry to insurers, financial institutions and industrial companies. A case of tort that has rocked an already wounded company and hampered its recovery is that of Lucent Technologies. This has been a securities litigation concerning misinformation by Lucent which allegedly damaged shareholder interests. The case lasted for several years, with:

- The lawyers asking for multibillion dollar compensation, and
- The judge limiting this compensation to $500 million, on the grounds that this was all Lucent could afford to pay without going bankrupt.

In all, over 680 000 proofs of claim were submitted, representing total recognized claims of $15.4 billion. Given the money available to satisfy these claims, and the heavy lawyers' fees, each authorized claimant received approximately 3 cents per dollar of his or her recognized claim, and even this has been paid in instalments, with the first distribution of 2 per cent made in December 2004.

For the investors, such compensation represented peanuts, and what they finally received from this tort litigation was a very small fraction of what they lost, because in the last analysis the $500 million that Lucent paid came out of the pocket of its shareholders. Foreign corporations, too, are exposed to risks of the US tort through exports, offices or factories in the USA. The most vulnerable lines of business are:

- Product liability,
- Medical malpractice,
- Directors and officers,
- Errors and omissions, and
- Employment practices liability.

It is not without reason that many experts consider those payments economically wasteful. Research suggests weak performance of juries in allocating non-economic awards, as well as overgenerous amounts that have no relation to an objective tort. Compensation for non-economic damages comprises about one-quarter of total tort costs.

Asbestos cases have been among the most famous in tort. Many companies sank because of them, while others tried legal means to escape. Honeywell's attempts to avoid problems with asbestos foundered after it failed to sell Bendix, a car-parts subsidiary with significant asbestos-related liabilities. For their part, creditors of Federal-Mogul, another car-parts firm in bankruptcy protection since 2001, were not prepared to take over around $2 billion in damages and wrote off their loans. Federal-Mogul had collapsed beneath its asbestos liabilities.

Another famous tort case is that of Dow Corning. The company was formed in 1943 and it was fairly prosperous. But in the 1960s, Dow Corning hit on the idea of making breast implants with silicone. Originally designed for women who had mastectomies, the implant became a very popular cosmetic device among many women, particularly in the USA.

Adversity hit when some women developed autoimmune diseases such as lupus, which they attributed to the implants. Although the allegations were never scientifically proven, Dow Corning pulled the product in 1992, but this did not immunize the company from a wave of injury lawsuits, which brought it to bankruptcy.

There is a myriad of reasons for suing for damages, with litigation hitting investors like a hammer. The restaurant chain McDonald's had to settle a lawsuit after a customer spilled a cup of its scalding-hot coffee on her lap. The court said that the company was responsible for not telling its customers about the damage the product might cause. McDonald's had to issue a printed warning on its coffee cups, bringing its customers' attention to the fact the coffee they 'are about to enjoy' is 'extremely hot'.[5]

In 2004, the large retailer WalMart was sued by the US government for illegally using foreign workers to clean its floors. They were working for a subcontractor, allegedly without WalMart's knowledge, but the retailer got the blame. This is a good example of how the legal misdeeds of one firm can tarnish others.

Another legal concern, which arises particularly for intermediaries, is *settlement risk* because of differing or incomplete confirmations of financial transactions. This is an operational risk. In trading markets, many concerns appear to centre on payments and settlements, as well as the system's ability to keep pace with market developments. A case in point is the time it takes to obtain confirmations of transactions.

A critical aspect of legal risk involves *documentation risk*. An example is the case of financial contracts that may not prove legally robust. For instance, the protection of a buyer's understanding of contractual arrangement may be wanting, with the result that such arrangements could be overturned by a court challenge.

A case in point involving both documentation risk and settlement risk is the documentation of derivatives transactions. The documentation of derivatives deals, including International Securities Dealers Association (ISDA)-type contracts and guarantee instruments, leave some aspects wanting. Documentation risk persists even if ISDA-type contracts have been subject to market tests, because they have not yet been subject to tests in the courts.

Other related legal concerns revolve around the definition of a *credit event*, as well as restructuring of debt. These are among the major teething problems in new instruments and in new markets, with plenty of potential to develop into structural problems, and from there into legal risk that falls on the borderline between:

- Plain tort, and
- Contractual breach, because of different interpretations.

In terms of economic policy, liability relating to *emerging risks* poses major challenges, particularly to the insurance industry. Tort cannot be assessed using traditional actuarial methods. Therefore, insurers must collect a risk premium that factors-in the possibility of a tort case developing unexpectedly, while defences built for damage control limit accumulation risk.

8.4 Reasons behind legal risk and cost of litigation

The Introduction stated that legal risk is one of the major *operational risks*. Most operational risks happen because of wanting definition of the job to be done, lack of training or plain incompetence. Examples are booking errors and execution errors. Fraud is people's risk translated into legal risk. Most forms of legal risk affect the way in which an ownership society operates.

Some operational risks that can have legal consequences are technology orientated; for instance, modelling error, programming error, database failure, telecommunications network failure and overall system failure. Product complexity, too, can lead to legal risk. The same is true of vulnerabilities associated with security, which are another type of operational risk.

There is also the omnipresent case of *deception*, or Andersen risk. Risk connected to auditing, balance sheet analysis certification of financial statement and other activities is often associated with conflicts of interest. Conflicts of interest can bring down in flames a major company, as the Arthur Andersen case demonstrates. Risk of deception also has other origins:

- Incompetence,
- Repeated errors,
- Lack of information, and
- Lack of transparency.

Some operational risks are morphing into perpetual legal risk, the cost of which is measured not just in billions of dollars, but also in the growing perimeter of a cemetery of formerly prosperous companies. Even former 'miracle products' can bring a company down. The case of asbestos, treated in section 8.3 in connection to tort, provides an example.

According to some estimates, more than 100 000 American workers died after being exposed to asbestos. Yet, until the 1970s asbestos was a widely used material, used to insulate buildings, to protect from fire and for many other purposes.

Only later was it discovered that breathing asbestos material can cause mesothelioma, a cancer, or other lung problems, which led to a flood of legal cases. Claimants' first targets were asbestos manufacturers, accused of failing to disclose the dangers. As most of these went bust, trial lawyers went after companies that used asbestos, distributed products containing it or assumed part of the liability, as in the case of insurers.

The legal risk of asbestos is also a first class example of how compensation can fall into the wrong hands. Lester Brickman, a law professor at Yeshiva University, in New York, told President George Bush recently that 'out of approximately 850 000 claimants since asbestos litigation began, perhaps 600 000 of these are largely baseless claims'. Worse, more than half of the cost of litigation is paid to lawyers or spent on administration.[6]

Here is another example of the cost of litigation. In mid-May 2004 Microsoft achieved a new record: the lawyers who handled the case against the software manufacturer Sun Microsystems, and seem to have convinced Bill Gates to sign the $1.1 billion settlement, sent in a bill for $258 million for their services.[7] This is another case of the cost of legal risk.

New instruments and new processes, too, may be incubators of legal risk. The internet, and on-line banking at large, brought many challenges to financial institutions in connection to existing legal frameworks and regulatory rules originally designed to address issues affecting the physical world. Moreover, when laws and regulations are interpreted by the courts under a new perspective, such as on-line networking, cross-border interpretations may vary in a significant way. Issues affecting the e-banking delivery channels include the facts that:

- On-line offerings may be considered solicitations not permitted by the law,
- Relationships created with customers in different jurisdictions may become legally unstable, and
- Different regulations applying to internet banking, and traditional delivery mechanisms, may impact products with multichannel delivery.

Core to all these references is the fact that on-line media exist and operate in a multijurisdictional world. Legal problems surfacing on the internet do so not because there is no law, but because it is not clear which country's laws apply in each specific case, or what should be done when there are legal contradictions from one jurisdiction to the next.

Many British laws are not valid in countries of continental Europe which are, more or less, under Napoleonic law; for example, Bills of Exchange Act 1882, Copyright Act 1911, Companies Act 1985, Consumer Credit Act 1974, Patents Act 1977, Unfair Contract Terms Act 1977, Forgery and Counterfeiting Act 1981, Consumer Protection Act 1987, Control and Misleading Advertisements Regulations 1988, Copyright Designs and Patents Act 1988, Trade Marks Act 1994, Data Protection Act 1984 and 1998, Contracts Protection Act 1990, Electronic Communications Act 2000, Regulation of Investigatory Powers Act 2000, Unfair Terms in Consumer Contracts Regulations 2001.

Apart from legal incompatibilities from state to state that create havoc in terms of legal risk, new laws and regulations are necessary to cover issues specific to on-line banking. For instance, the credit risk of a bank can be affected by internet banking activities because:

- Remote communication can make it much more difficult to assess the creditworthiness of both existing and potential customers;
- The internet allows banks to expand very rapidly, leading to weakened internal control;
- There is a tendency to pay higher rates on e-banking deposits, squeezing the profit margin, and
- A new practice is to grant sub-prime credits without appropriate investigation, leading to heightened credit risk.

Another example of background factors of legal risk is liquidity risk precipitated by adverse information about a credit institution that can be easily disseminated over the internet. Bulletin boards and news groups transmit effectively both information and misinformation. When this happens, the aftermath is likely to cause depositors to withdraw their funds in large number at any time of the day.

8.5 Legal risk and management risk correlate

On 21 September 2004, six former Enron and Merrill Lynch executives were accused by a US prosecutor of disguising a $7 million loan as a sale of energy-producing barges to 'help Enron out of a jam'. This is what John Hemann, assistant US attorney, in Federal court in Houston, said as he accused two former Enron executives and four former Merrill executives of inflating Enron's finances by $12 million with the sham sale of energy-producing Nigerian barges to Merrill.

This court case marked the start of the first criminal trial stemming from the 2001 collapse of Enron. The Nigerian barges transaction is an example of a new generation of financial manipulations that were used to hide debt and artificially inflate profit at Enron. Their effect was negative because they ultimately led to its collapse.

Experts said that behind this trial was the US government's wish to test evidence that it will eventually use against more senior Enron officials, including former chief executives Kenneth Lay and Jeffrey Skilling, who are charged with directing the fraud that forced Enron into the second largest bankruptcy in US history. What the top brass of the defunct company is accused of by the prosecutors is an example of *management risk* which, like legal exposure, is a fully fledged operational risk.[8]

Indeed, coming thirty-one months after the bankruptcy of Enron, the July 2004 indictment of ex-Enron CEO Kenneth Lay has been long overdue. On 8 July 2004, Lay was indicted in Houston on eleven counts, including conspiracy and multiple counts of fraud; all part of management risk. This indictment came on top of that of Enron's former president and Lay protégé Jeffrey Skilling, and former chief accounting officer Richard Causey.

In the go-go 1990s, Enron had become one of the darlings of the ownership society. To bring this court case into perspective, it should be recalled that before the Ken Lay years Enron was a company that owned a gas pipeline. Lay turned it into a huge hedge fund with a gas pipeline on the side. He did so:

- By exploiting loopholes in deregulated markets, and
- Through energy derivative speculation.

Moreover, Enron was a product of the junk bond-financed sprawling mergers and acquisitions activities, which made it possible for a small company to acquire a great number of other bigger and financially healthier entities than itself. Enron's management risk, and subsequent legal risk, started with the speculative big financial games of the 1980s.

It was Michael Milken, of now bankrupt Drexel Burnham Lambert investment bank, who in 1985 provided the financing for Kenneth Lay to engineer the takeover of Houston Natural Gas by Omaha-based InterNorth. Through debt financing, Enron was transformed by Lay:

- From a firm owning a gas pipeline company
- Into a major energy investment bank and speculator.

With leverage reaching for the stars, the company's shareholders, bondholders, employees and pensioners were taken to the cleaners. Among other banks that helped Enron in its metamorphosis were Chase Manhattan, Citibank, Lazard Frères, First Boston and Salomon Brothers. The transformation that took place was described as the 'financialization of energy' by Jeffrey Skilling.

According to expert opinion, Enron played a major role in every change in regulatory policy that took place in the USA in the late 1980s and the 1990s, from lobbying the Commodity Future Trading Commission (CFTC) to decree regulatory exemptions for over-the-counter derivatives, to lobbying the US President's Working Group on Financial Markets to prevent moves towards regulation of derivatives. This working group came alive in the Bill Clinton years, following the collapse of Long Term Capital Management (LTCM) in September 1998 and the imminent danger of a systemic meltdown.

By means of higher and higher leveraging, and by exploiting the system, Enron grew to be the seventh largest company in America. A mountain of indebtedness, however, can keep a company going in short term, but eventually the day of reckoning will come. When Enron collapsed in early December 2001, many people were hurt.

- Stockholders and bondholders lost practically all of their savings.
- Investment bankers who recommended Enron as a sound investment until a short time before its collapse were left with egg on their face.
- Worst of all fared Enron's employees, who lost their jobs, their pension rights and their investment in the company they were working for.

Post-mortem, the skeletons the defunct company was carefully hiding started to come out of the cupboard. One of them has been the energy scandal in California. Energy prices in California first jumped in the summer of 2000. Enron and its allies in the California energy bubble started by blaming the state, even as their traders were pushing up prices through various kinds of practices with code names such as 'Death Star', 'Fat Boy' and 'Get Shorty'. The goal was to:

- Game the market, and
- Make a fast megabuck.

There is a parallel between this California energy bubble of 2000 and the global energy bubble of 2004 and 2005 which, according to expert opinion, has been engineered by hedge funds. Therefore, lessons learned from California's experience when, at the dawn of the twenty-first century, the electricity price became disconnected from supply and demand, can help us to appreciate what has happened with oil prices four years later.

During the California power crisis of 2000 and 2001, the state was hit with rolling blackouts, soaring rates and the bankruptcy of a major utility company, Pacific Gas and Electric (PG&E). Timothy Belden, a now-jailed Enron operative and chief of the company's West Coast trading division, boasted on one of the recorded tapes that one trader 'steals money from California to the tune of about a million dollars a day'. As energy prices skyrocketed, traders pumped each other up with stories of how they were 'f***ing California'.[9] Figure 8.1 shows how quickly energy prices moved.

The damage done to California by this unwarranted looting of energy resources has plunged the state into near bankruptcy. More than $70 billion was taken away from the state by speculators, leading to a budget deficit of $38 billion to be paid by the citizen. The president of the state's senate, John Burton, said, 'Sooner or later, we've got to let these buccaneers know that we're not going to tolerate what they're doing to us. The only thing these exploiters would understand is a little counterterrorism'.

The indictment of Ken Lay opens the opportunity to correct the balance. His case, however, is just one out of many. Omega Advisors provides another example of the existing correlation between management risk and legal risk. In early October 2003, a financier was indicted on charges of stealing $182 million from fifteen investment funds run by Omega Advisors, a New York-based hedge fund consultancy.

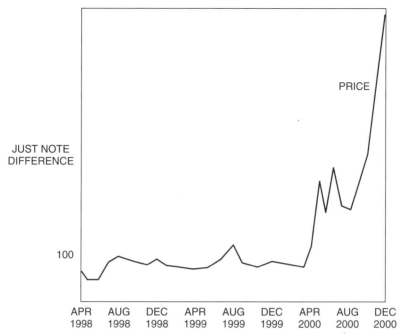

Figure 8.1 California's electricity price reaches for the stars (constant dollars, indexed to August 1998 = 100). (*Sources*: California Power Exchange, US Department of Energy, EIR, 23 July 2004)

Manhattan's district attorney Robert Morgenthau charged thirty-nine-year-old Viktor Kozeny, who lived in Lyford Cay, the Bahamas, with:

■ fifteen counts of first degree grand larceny, and
■ two counts of first degree criminal possession of stolen property.

According to the district attorney's office, the thefts took place between March and June 1998. Morgenthau said that investors hurt by Kozeny's activities included Columbia University, which lost $15 million, and The Common Fund, a fund for universities and other not-for-profit organizations, which lost $4.5 million.[10]

While outright fraud is a major management risk, and most evidently a legal risk, other lesser cases, too, may qualify for that heading. Anything that violates the mission and code of ethics of a corporate executive, investment advisor, asset manager or banker can bring its author to the courtroom.

During the first week of September 2004, former star technology banker Frank Quattrone was sentenced to eighteen months in prison after his conviction for obstruction of justice. He also was fined $90 000 and sentenced to two years' probation by US District Judge Richard Owen. The judge concluded that Quattrone had lied on the witness stand, and therefore granted a government request to give Quattrone a prison term above the sentencing guidelines range.

Quattrone was tried on the same three charges on which he was first accused in an earlier trial: obstructing a grand jury, obstructing federal regulators and witness tampering, in autumn 2003; but that trial ended in a hung jury. For its part, however, Quattrone's employer Credit Suisse First Boston (CSFB) paid $100 million to settle related civil charges. Quattrone left the bank in early 2004.

In their plea for acquittal, or at least a light sentence, the investment banker's lawyers said that his wife was chronically ill, and his fifteen-year-old daughter has had psychological problems. Correctly, neither the prosecutor nor the court bought these arguments. In fact, some people pointed out that the impact on the Quattrone family would be softened by its financial assets. The wife had $50 million and the daughter had $26 million in a trust fund. Nobody seems to have asked how a fifteen-year-old had made such a fortune.

8.6   Mishandling the client: small cases that can lead to legal risk

The message in Chapter 7 is that outsourcing wealth management should be no relegation of responsibilities on behalf of investors. Outsourcing has its risks, ranging from the more classical operational risk type[11] to conflict of interest and strong-arm tactics that sometimes border on malfeasance. This section includes four short case studies, two from each class. The first is an operational risk-type failure that had a reputational aftermath for the bank.

For more than twenty years I have held a current account with a high street bank in London. There were no problems over the years until, suddenly, one day in late 2004 two cheques were returned unpaid to their beneficiaries with a note: 'There is no such account'. This was surprising because both cheques were well covered by the balance in the account. The bank gave the following reply after an internal investigation brought to light the reason for these failures:

> I understand that you issued two cheques from a cheque book that had been discontinued due to merge of sortcodes. These cheques were returned unpaid and charges were incurred by yourself as a result.

> I am aware that we should have advised you of the change of situation with the merge of sortcodes, and that responsibility for the error lies with the bank. Please accept my sincere apologies for any inconvenience that this matter may have caused.

This settled the matter. But a few months later another international bank made a mess of its payment and settlements responsibility, in an operating risk case. By 15 March 2005, the 25 February order for money transfer had not yet been executed. It took ten days of telephone calls and pressure on the credit institution to find out where the money was, and to obtain an answer that it had finally been found and credited to the account.

This information was false. The lost and supposedly found money had not been credited to the client's account as promised. As a result, when the client gave a new order to transfer this money his account was in debit, with the bank applying debit charges to the client's account for something that was entierly its own fault. It took another ten days of client pressure to have the balances corrected; an inexcusable and protracted operational risk on the bank's part.

The third case is much more serious, because it concerns something amounting to outright theft. This concerns a current account with another European bank, standing for nearly twenty-five years. Over that period, the charges were nominal. But suddenly, in March 2005, a major debit was made to the account without the client being informed of tariff changes, let alone having given his consent.

Immediately after learning about these charges through the monthly statement, the client wrote to the bank. The bank answered, with some delay, that there has been a tariff change. The client responded that the tariff sent to him post-mortem, after his complaint, is not applicable to his account, and this was so for two reasons, each being enough on its own.

First, the charges identified in the new tariff concern 'Gestion de Portefeuille' (portfolio management). The client has entrusted no portfolio management functions whatsoever to this bank. All it has had for a quarter of a century has been a banal classical current account. Therefore, such charges were absolutely out of context and, as such, they were irrelevant and illegal.

Second, before applying a changed tariff, the bank should always communicate the new charges to its clients, because they may wish to opt out and transfer their account(s) to another bank. This had not been done. Arbitrarily charging a client's account, without informing this account's owner in advance, is like stealing money. A self-respecting bank does not do so. The client expected to see the illegally charged amount recredited and have this confirmed in writing. The bank did not even bother to answer this correspondence, obliging the client to return time and again on this issue.

What has happened with the fourth case is complex and bad business on the part of the bank, because there has been intentional verbal aggression by a major broker's and asset manager's agent, who paraded himself as 'director of marketing'. The person in question tried through most dubious means to press the customer into an investment he did not want. This led to several customer complaints to the bank's senior management. The complaints became a torrent because senior management was very slow to respond and gave evidence of intent to cover the marketing manager's acts. Here is the opening salvo written by the investor:

> Let me start with a point I hope we are in accord: 'Business is based on Confidence.' What your director of marketing has tried to do is a breach of confidence which reflects badly on your bank.

> Let me add one more reference, this one a dictum guiding the hand of American companies: 'The Client Is Always Right.' Yours is an American company.

The letter to a top executive, indeed, the chief operating officer of the bank, mentioned by name the misbehaving 'director of marketing', but it fell on deaf ears. This letter was therefore followed by another call to duty:

> If I understand right, your company approves the behavior of . . .. The only comment I have on this coverage on your behalf is a quotation from Shakespeare's 'Timon of Athens': 'Nothing emboldens sin so much as mercy.'

> There has been too much sin around the investment banking industry as the 2002 court cases in New York demonstrate. It is the duty of senior management to penalize improper behavior of the company's agents – not to condone it.

A couple of more salvoes down the line, senior management decided to respond, by whitewashing its 'director of marketing'. A letter by the president of the International Private Client Operations said:

> We have reviewed with [the director of marketing who misbehaved] and his superior the discussion which occurred [with you]. What [the director of marketing] attempted to make was a presentation to you concerning the . . . [a highly leveraged and risky derivative instrument].
>
> At no time, we were advised, were any inappropriate selling tactics employed . . . [They were advised wrongly]. Having reviewed the record, it would appear that [our bank] has been offering free custodian services to you and very little else over the last two years.

This statement was wrong all around. The account did not belong to me, but to a company I manage. The nearly 'free custodian policy' was this broker's practice anyway, because it made its money out of commissions. Moreover, customers are not around just to be charged the fees. They open an account with private bankers and assets managers to be served; not to be insulted or misled.

The worst part in this case study is the elusive reply by senior management, which left no option other than to ask the president of the division if pushing any sort of 'investment plan down the client's throat is his company's new policy', in which case I stood ready to transfer the account to a competitor. The answer has been 'no, no', and since then (at least in this particular account) no strong-arm tactics have been repeated.

The lesson the reader should learn from this case is that even outsourced investment accounts have to be managed by the person who puts his, or his company's, money on the line. 'A man can stand anything except succession of ordinary days', Goethe once opined; or a succession of extrordinary tricks that trap the customer and bring to the company doing them nothing but reputational risk and discredit (see the case study in the appendix).

8.7   Big cases of legal risk: high-tech crime and identity theft

In mid-March 2005 it was reported that half a year earlier a high-tech crime ring tried to steal £220 million from the London offices of Sumitomo, the Japanese banking group. This was one of the most audacious thefts attempted in the City of London for many years. Police have been investigating the theft since October 2004, when the gang:

- Gained access to Sumitomo's computer systems, and
- Tried to transfer the cash electronically to ten bank accounts around the world.

Financial theft has been globalized. The gang's plan was uncovered before any cash was transferred, but this case highlights the growing threat posed by organized gangs of criminal computer hackers to credit institutions, other companies and consumers.

While it is not quite clear exactly how the gang gained access to Sumitomo's computer systems, some evidence is provided by the fact that police subsequently warned financial institutions in the City to be on the alert for criminals using technology that can record every keystroke made on a computer.

Allegedly, the gang used *keyloggers*. These are devices typically used to steal passwords controlling access to important computer systems. At the time this information came to the public eye, it was not clear whether the computer hackers and their criminal friends:

- Gained physical access to the Sumitomo Mitsui bank and installed keylogging hardware, or
- Hacked into the institution's computers from afar and installed malicious software.

The police investigation has extended as far as Israel, one of the countries to which the gang attempted to transfer the money. Israeli police arrested a man whose business account had been the intended recipient of some of the cash. Israeli police said that there had been an attempt to transfer €20 million into the account 'by deception in a sophisticated manner'.[12]

For their part, security experts have been warning for some time about the risks from keyloggers and other devices that can secretly gather information. In 2003 alone, high-tech crime affected more than 450 people in the UK, proof that the rise of keyloggers and other high-tech criminals poses a real threat not only to companies but also to individuals. The investigation into the Sumitomo Mitsui bank robbery, conducted by the national High-Tech Crime Unit of the British police, is ongoing.

One thing that has become clear after successive security breaches is how much supervision is necessary on behalf of governments to ensure that banks and other information brokers adequately protect the financial data of citizens. For instance, in March 2005, in the USA, Reed Elsevier Group's LexisNexis unit disclosed that hackers had gained access to roughly 32 000 of its consumer accounts.[13] A month later, at the end of April 2005, the tally grew to 310 000 customer accounts and this is still only an estimated number of people whose personal information was stolen from LexisNexis databases; an order of magnitude as many as the company originally thought.[14]

Since, one piece of bad news never comes alone, also in April 2005 it was revealed that 180 000 people were notified by HSBC bank that their credit-card data may have been stolen after shopping with a MasterCard. Moreover, according to the Federal Trade Commission (FTC), there were 246 570 US complaints of identity theft in 2004, up from a mere 1380 in 1999. The FTC estimated that 2003 annual losses from such fraud stood at about $47.6 billion.

Solutions to the problem of identity theft are far from being clear or easy to implement, because finding the right balance between securing private data without irrevocably harming information providers can be tricky. Data collected by what is known as 'information brokers' play a role in the economy because they allow:

- Credit institutions to offer loans,
- Employers to check out potential employees, and
- Landlords to assess the credit histories of prospective tenants.

Some states have been more active than others in the search for solutions, which invariably favour either security or data communication. For instance, California and Texas permit individuals across the country to place a security freeze on their credit history. Because such a freeze makes it hard for merchants and other providers of credit to review an applicant's credit history without permission, it is much more difficult for thieves to advance unauthorized applications for credit or perform similar criminal acts.

Experts say that the information brokers should bear greater liability than is presently the case when a breach occurs. Until now, courts have refused to allow defrauded consumers to bring suits against information brokers for the reason that individual consumers:

- Are not their customers, and
- Have no business relationship with the brokers.

However, without the threat of fines or other penalties connected to law security and privacy protection, information brokers have little economic incentive to increase the amount of attention they pay to data theft. Yet, this is precisely what is needed the most: a great deal of responsibility and measures to see it through.

8.8   Merck and Co.: legal risk with Vioxx

In its Annual Report 2004, Merck states that it is involved in various claims and legal proceedings of a nature considered normal to its business. The term 'normal' is, however, questionable because of the huge number of pending legal actions. These actions include:

- Product liability,
- Intellectual property,
- Commercial litigation, and
- Additional matters such as antitrust cases.

Merck states that it records accruals for contingencies when it is probable that a liability has been incurred, and the amount can be reasonably estimated. As should always be the case, such accruals are periodically adjusted, because assessments change or additional information becomes available.

For product liability claims, a portion of the overall amount is actuarially determined. This approach considers factors such as past experience, number of claims reported and estimates of claims, when such claims are probable and reasonably estimable. Legal defence costs expected to be incurred in connection with a loss contingency are also accrued, when probable and reasonably estimable.

As already seen in connection to other cases, both damages and legal costs can be high. With regard to Merck, a case in point is the *Vioxx litigation* in late 2003, 2004 and following years. Federal and state product liability lawsuits involving individual claims, as well as several putative class actions, have been filed against the company with respect to Vioxx. These have been product liability lawsuits. As of

31 January 2005, Merck had been served, or was aware that it has been named as a defendant, in:

- Approximately 850 lawsuits,
- Including some 2425 plaintiff groups alleging personal injuries resulting from the use of Vioxx.

An interesting lesson to be learned from Merck's case is that certain of these lawsuits include allegations regarding gastrointestinal bleeding, cardiovascular events, thrombotic events or kidney damage. The company has also been named as a defendant in approximately 90 putative class actions alleging personal injuries or seeking:

- Medical monitoring as a result of putative class members' use of Vioxx,
- Disgorgement of certain profits under common law unjust enrichment theories, and/or
- Various remedies under state consumer fraud and fair business practice statutes.

The latter include recovering the cost of Vioxx purchased by individuals and third party payers, such as union health plans. In addition to the Vioxx product liability lawsuits, in late 2003 and early 2004 a number of purported class action lawsuits was filed by several shareholders naming as defendants the company and several of its current or former officers.

This is, indeed, one of the crazy aspects of legal risk. Shareholders are supposed to go to court against the company in which they are investing; for practical purposes they are moving against themselves and they are cheated by the usually astronomical legal fees.

This is not all. After it announced the withdrawal of Vioxx, Merck was named as a defendant in additional purported securities class action lawsuits. Such actions alleged that the defendants made false and misleading statements regarding Vioxx in violation of sections 10(b) and 20(a) of the Securities Exchange Act of 1934, and they have been seeking:

- Unspecified compensatory damages, and
- The costs of suit, including attorney's fees.

If there was any question about whether we live in a litigative society, this has been answered by the fact that in addition to the aforementioned patient and shareholder actions, since the announcement of the withdrawal of Vioxx, putative class actions have been filed against Merck on behalf of certain of the company's current and former employees.

Employees and shareholders are stakeholders in a firm. In this particular case, employees are participants in certain of Merck's retirement plans asserting claims under the Employee Retirement Income Security Act (ERISA). The lawsuits make similar allegations to those contained in the Vioxx securities lawsuits. As of 31 January 2005, eleven Vioxx ERISA lawsuits were pending.

Moreover, in addition to the lawsuits discussed above, Merck & Co. has been named as a defendant in actions in various countries in Europe, as well as Australia,

Canada, Brazil and Israel; all related to Vioxx. As the Annual Report 2004 points out, based on media reports and other sources, the company anticipates that additional Vioxx product liability lawsuits and Vioxx shareholder lawsuits will be filed against it and/or certain of its current and former officers and directors in the future.

One of the most interesting issues with the Vioxx litigation is that while it may have had detrimental effects on some clients, it benefited others. The reader should keep that in mind when the pluses and minuses of structured financial products are discussed in Parts 3 and 4. Eventually there will be legal actions with them that will make Vioxx look like small game.

Of course, Merck has product liability insurance for claims brought in the Vioxx product liability lawsuits. Reportedly, it is up to $630 million after deductibles and co-insurance. This insurance provides coverage for legal defence costs and potential damage amounts that have been or will be incurred in connection with the Vioxx product liability lawsuits. However, $630 million may prove peanuts when confronted by all of these claims.

Neither is it sure that the insurers will come up with the money. While the company believes that this insurance coverage extends to additional Vioxx product liability lawsuits that may be filed in the future, certain of its insurers have reserved their rights to take a contrary position with respect to certain coverage. There could very well be disputes with insurance companies about coverage matters.

This section has highlighted issues of interest to the ownership society's stakeholders. Legal risk can hit them whether they are shareholders, bondholders, employees or pensioners, to name only a few. The curious thing with so many legal cases, including Merck's, is that the ownership society's stakeholders themselves have instituted the legal action.

Notes

1 Merck, Annual Report 2004.
2 A.P. Heiner and H.J. Kaiser, *Western Colossus*, Halo Books, San Francisco, 1991.
3 D.N. Chorafas, *Operational Risk Control with Basel II. Basic Principles and Capital Requirements*, Butterworth-Heinemann, London, 2004.
4 *BusinessWeek*, 21 February 2005.
5 *Economist*, 24 January 2004.
6 *Economist*, 29 January 2005.
7 *Sole-24 Ore*, 13 May 2004.
8 D.N. Chorafas, *Management Risk. The Bottleneck is at the Top of the Bottle*, Macmillan/Palgrave, London, 2004.
9 *EIR*, 23 July 2004.
10 *USA Today*, 3 October 2003.
11 D.N. Chorafas, *Operational Risk Control with Basel II. Basic Principles and Capital Requirements*, Butterworth-Heinemann, London, 2004.
12 *Financial Times*, 17 March 2005.
13 *BusinessWeek*, 28 March 2005.
14 *Time*, 25 April 2005.

Part 3

Derivative financial instruments, structured products and risk control

9 Derivative financial instruments defined

9.1 Introduction

If a company is in the business of making a product that has become indistinguishable from those of its rivals, this means that its goods have turned into a commodity. Therefore, they will sell chiefly on price. This has happened with all sort of wares, including those of technology, enabling low-cost clone makers to knock down famous names such as IBM.

There used to be a time when low cost frequently meant low quality. Today, this is not necessarily the case. *Low cost* has become a relative term in the sense that, with globalization, costs continue to drop. In America, the makers of many goods now live in daily terror of what is known as *China price*, which means that even their best price 'made in the USA' can be undercut by the much lower cost of 'made in China' products.

The answer to this challenge is steady innovation and this applies all the way to financial products. 'Clothes and automobiles change every year. But because the currency remains the same in appearance, although its value steadily declines, most people believe that finance does not change. Actually, debt financing changes like everything else', advises M. Mazur of Lehman Brothers, adding that:

- We must remain inventive architects of the money business, and
- We have to find new models in financing, just as in clothes and automobiles, if we want to stay on top.[1]

This evidently poses a challenge. In terms of classical banking, it has become very hard to make a product that is genuinely different to, or better than, a competitor's. Personalized *private banking* is an example of innovation in services offered by a credit institution, but as shown in Parts 1 and 2, being a player in private banking has prerequisites that are not that easy to meet. Moreover,

- Population-wise private banking has its limits, and
- Innovation associated with private banking is conditioned by the development of new financial instruments.

As far as the development of new financial instruments is concerned, the banking industry today is in a race to stay ahead. This is a basic reason why, since the 1980s, many banks, particularly the bigger ones, have sought technical expertise in new derivative financial instruments (the definition of a derivative is given in section 9.2).

Another reason that pushed banks in the direction of trading and investing in derivatives has been the dual effect of:

- Deregulation, and
- Loss of intermediation.

With non-banks, such as insurance companies, credit associations and acceptance corporations, entering into lending, credit institutions lost a great deal of their role in financial intermediation between depositors and borrowers. This loss has been aggravated by the fact that big names in manufacturing and merchandising now raise money in the capital markets at better rates than banks can offer.

Deregulation, which for practical purposes started in America in the late 1970s, the Jimmy Carter years, allowed banks to enter domains that used to be out of bounds. This accelerated in the early 1980s when the Federal Reserve permitted credit institutions to write *off-balance sheet* (OBS) their gains and losses with derivative products. With Financial Accounting Statement No. 133 (FAS 133), in the late 1990s, by the Financial Accounting Standards Board (FASB) this has changed. Yet, the fact remains that many banks enter into derivatives:

- Without having the needed expertise in this trade, and
- Without really being able to control the huge amount of assumed risk.

Options, futures, forwards, swaps (see section 9.5) and other derivative financial instruments are today widely traded by an expanding universe of credit institutions and other companies. Morphing into what is known as *structured products* derivatives (Chapter 10) are disseminating at fast speed in the personal banking market. So are the risks that accompany them; and these risks, which are explained in Chapter 11, are not well understood.

9.2 Derivatives and hedging

The classical definition of a derivative instrument is that this is a future, forward, swap or option contract. (Derivatives that became institutionalized are discussed in section 9.5.) In 1998, however, the FASB refrained from defining derivative instruments only by example because the existing distinctions between many types of contracts have become blurred, and they are likely to become even more so during the coming years.

Instead of defining derivatives by example, FASB opted for a different, more generic approach. In FAS 133, derivatives are defined as financial instruments with the following characteristics:

- They have one or more *underlying* (see section 9.3) and one or more *notional amount* (see section 9.4), as well as payment provisions.
- Usually, they require no initial net investment, and when this is needed it is smaller than that characterizing other instruments.
- They neither call for nor permit net settlements, or provide for delivery of an asset that practically puts the buyer at a net settlement position.

Between the lines, the provisions outlined by these three bullet points by FAS 133 make up the ideal domain for leveraging. *Leveraging*, or gearing, means living beyond one's present means through easy money that typically is not invested, or spent, in a prudent manner. This means that liabilities will balloon relative to one's assets.

Dr Marrinner Eccles, the chairman of the Federal Reserve in the Franklin D. Roosevelt years, stated that, 'There is no limit to the amount of money that can be created by the banking system. But there are limits to our productive facilities and our labor supply, which can be only slowly increased.'[2] The fact that physical limits continue to exist ensures that financial staying power is *weakened* by leveraging.

- In the short term, provided the markets move in the way investors and bankers bet, leveraging helps to improve profit figures.
- In the longer term, however, leveraging makes it very difficult, if not outright impossible to face adversity. Long-Term Capital Management (LTCM), when it practically crashed, was geared up 292 times (see section 9.5).

This does not mean that derivatives are not useful financial instruments. They are, but they must be traded and inventoried for *true hedging* reasons, not for speculation, as is usually done (more on this later). Most importantly, derivatives should be used in conjunction with a *rigorous risk management* system. These are important pre-conditions, and they are not always fulfilled. Derivatives traded in exchanges are part of the ever-growing number of gross issues of securities.

In the banking industry at large, trading and investing in derivatives accelerated in the boom years of the late 1990s. This led to a structural change in the financial industry, which became fast paced, taking on significant dimensions and also leading to concentration of *risks* assumed with derivatives. Part of the reason for such concentration is the merger activity that piled one trading book upon another, and also:

- Reduced the number of big players among credit institutions,
- But increased the number of hedge funds, which are most active in derivatives.

So far, the most famed hedge fund failure took place because of an inordinate amount of derivatives exposure. The failure of LTCM in September 1998 nearly tore apart the world's financial fabric.[3] To rein in the amount of gambling taking place with derivative financial instruments, the FASB has established a rule requiring companies to show whether:

- They are using derivatives to hedge risks connected to their business, or
- They are just taking a risky bet in the hope of making extra profits.

True hedging, such as buying forward against a rise in the exchange rate of the dollar, euro, pound, yen or any other currency, is directly connected to current business commitments. *Speculative hedging* is another matter. New regulations ensure that such hedges made for trading purposes have to be carried on a bank's books at their market value. This can cause wild fluctuations in the entity's:

- Income, and
- Exposure.

By contrast, current regulations are very light regarding derivative instruments sold to private investors. The expectation is that this will change in the coming years, to protect the banking public at large, and savers in particular, in spite of opposition by embedded interests. We shall see.

An example of true hedging is provided by the management of foreign currency risk, the way it is practised today by practically all global manufacturing and merchandising firms. While the US dollar is the functional currency of many American global companies and their foreign subsidiaries, a significant portion of their revenues is denominated from foreign currencies. For instance, Merck & Co. made a statement on this issue in its Annual Report 2004.

To appreciate the reasons for currency hedging, the reader must remember that global firms rely on sustained cash flows generated from foreign sources to support the long-term commitment to their home currency-based research, development, and exploitation of research results. In Merck's case, to the extent that the dollar value of cash flows is diminished as a result of a strengthening dollar, its ability to fund research and other dollar-based strategic initiatives at a consistent level can be impaired. This underpins the need for revenue hedging and balance sheet risk management programmes to protect against:

- Volatility of future foreign currency cash flows, and
- Changes in fair value caused by volatility in foreign exchange rates.

The objective of a revenue hedging programme, says Merck, is to reduce the potential for longer term unfavourable changes in foreign exchange to decrease the dollar value of future cash flows derived from foreign currency denominated sales, primarily the euro, Japanese yen and British pound.

To achieve this objective, companies partially hedge anticipated third party sales expected to occur over a given planning cycle, typically no more than three years into the future. Over time, this strategy leads to layers in hedges, increasing the portion of sales hedged as one gets closer to the probable date on which the hedged transaction will occur. This portion of sales hedged should be based on assessments of cost/benefit profiles that consider:

- Types of offsetting exposures,
- Revenue and exchange rate volatilities and correlations, and
- The cost of hedging instruments, which itself may be significant because *all hedges involve risk*.

The hedged anticipated sales must be a specified component of a portfolio of similarly denominated foreign currency-based sales transactions, each of which responds, in its way, to the hedged risk. Well-managed companies ensure that their anticipated transaction exposure is principally hedged with purchased local currency put options, which provide the right, but not an obligation, to sell foreign currencies in the future at a predetermined price.

For instance, if the US dollar strengthens relative to the currency of the hedged anticipated sales, total changes in the options' cash flows should fully, or nearly fully, offset the decline in the expected future US dollar cash flows of the hedged foreign currency sales. By contrast, if the dollar weakens, the options' value reduces to zero, but the company benefits, in a way, from the increase in the value of the anticipated foreign currency cash flows.

Seen from the above perspective, the primary objective of a balance sheet risk management programme is to protect the dollar value of foreign currency denominated net monetary assets from the effects of volatility in foreign exchange that may occur before their conversion to US dollars. Apart from the options, companies use forward exchange contracts, which enable them to buy and sell foreign currencies in the future at fixed exchange rates, and offset the consequences of changes in foreign exchange on the amount of cash flows derived from net assets.

This is true for euro, pound and yen exposures. Conversely, for exposures in developing country currencies, companies tend to enter into forward contracts on a more limited basis and only when it is deemed economical to do so, based on cost/benefit analysis that considers the:

- Magnitude of exposure,
- Volatility of the exchange rate, and
- Cost and risk associated with the hedging instrument.

Merck states in its Annual Report 2004 that it also uses forward contracts to hedge the changes in fair value of certain foreign currency denominated available-for-sale securities, attributable to fluctuations in foreign currency exchange rates. Such decisions are usually based on a sensitivity analysis to changes in the value of the US dollar on foreign currency denominated:

- Derivatives,
- Investments, and
- Monetary assets and liabilities.

However, even if such a careful elaborated strategy prevails, derivatives contracts can go wrong. Mitsubishi Motors found this, to its cost, when it bet against further strengthening of the yen against the dollar and, instead, the yen weakened significantly, going from 80 to the dollar to 115 instead of going 'as expected' to 70 or lower. This is a good example of how currency exchange hedges can backfire.

9.3   Underlying and notional principal amount

As stated in section 9.2, derivative financial instruments include forward and futures contracts, interest rate swaps, forward rate agreements, options, and transactions relating to underwriting and 'when issued' commitments. Usually, although not necessarily always, derivatives instruments represent future obligations to:

- Purchase or sell the underlying at specific terms on specified future dates,
- Exchange currencies, or other commodities,
- Swap interest payment streams, and
- Perform other activities characterizing custom-made products that have an underlying and (usually) a notional principal amount.

The *underlying* in a derivatives transaction may be the *price* or *rate* of an asset or liability, but it is not itself a liability or an asset.[4] Examples of underlyings are interest rates, currency exchange rates, share prices, other commodity prices, an index of prices or some other variable that is used in conjunction with the notional principal amount (see section 9.4).

For instance, the price of a security involved in an options contract is the underlying (or underlying security). The volatility characterizing this price is used to determine cash flows or other exchanges required by the contract. The price at which the security may be bought is the *exercise price* or strike price. The last date on which the option (see section 9.5) may be exercised is the *expiration date* or maturity date.

As a writer of options, a bank receives a premium in exchange for bearing the risk of unfavourable changes in the price of the underlying index, security, currency or other commodity. In principle, this premium is computed on the likelihood of adverse financial conditions to the writer of the option, which would lead the buyer to exercise it. But:

- If the market turns against the writer,
- Then red ink can run like a torrent, with the premium falling short of covering the losses.

This is an example of risk contained in derivatives, as changes in market values may result in losses in excess of a worst case scenario that has been developed a priori. Moreover, securities sold but not yet purchased represent obligations on the seller (writer) of the option to deliver specific assets at contracted prices, thereby creating a liability to purchase the securities at prevailing market prices. These transactions result in exposure to market risk as the bank's ultimate obligation may exceed the amount recognized.

Besides having one or more underlyings, a derivative financial instrument is characterized by a *notional principal amount*. This is a term borrowed from the swaps market (see section 9.5), where it signifies the contractual quantity of money, never actually to be paid or received.

A notional principal amount, also called face amount, is a metric of currency, number of shares or number of other units specified in the contract. In a derivatives contract, neither the writer not the buyer is required to invest, pay or receive the notional amount, but they are responsible for the effects of market risk computed through an agreed-upon algorithm characterizing a derivatives contract. Such a contract may be:

- An interest rate swap (IRS),
- A forward rate agreement (FRA),
- An inverse floater,
- A knock-in/knock-out derivative, or
- Any other type of contractually specified instrument.

The notional principal amount will be used to determine the actual cash flows paid or received, for instance, by applying the corresponding interest rates for the appropriate calendar periods. As an example, it may be used as the basis for calculating the periodic payments of fixed or floating interest. The same notional principal concept applies to a variety of derivative instruments:

- From caps and floors,
- To futures or forward contracts regarding practically any commodity.

These contracts are made either for hedging or for speculative reasons. The difference between the two has been explained in section 9.2, and it can be summarized in one short sentence: 'The dose was toxic waste' (see section 9.4).

Trading positions in financial derivatives include interest rate and currency swaps; options on equities and equity indices; foreign exchange futures and forwards, forward rate agreements and a growing range of instruments that start as 'exotic' but over time enter the mainstream (see section 9.5). To some of these instruments are assimilated others with similar characteristics. For instance, interest rate caps or floors and fixed-rate loan commitments have notions similar to options because:

- They provide the holder with the benefits of favourable movements in the price of an underlying asset or index, and
- They ask, in return, a premium to be paid at inception by the buyer to the writer (issuer).

Variable rate loan commitments, and other variable rate financial instruments, may also have characteristics similar to option contracts, and the same is true of different kinds of commitments to purchase stocks or bonds. Currency products, interest rate products, equity derivatives and derivatives of other commodities can be exchange traded or dealt with over the counter (OTC). Overall, in terms of notional amount, OTC trades tend to exceed exchange-based transactions by a ratio of 3.34 to 1, as shown in Tables 9.1 and 9.2 (based on statistics by big banks).

Not all instruments that derive their values, or required cash flows, from the price of some other security or index are by definition derivatives. Because a very extended scope of derivatives definition can be inconsistent with the objective of improving

Table 9.1 Notional principal in derivatives: over-the-counter (OTC) versus exchange-traded derivatives

OTC	**77.1%**
Currency products	41.0%
Interest rate products	30.0%
Equity derivatives	5.0%
Precious metals/commodities	1.1%
Exchange-traded	**22.9%**
Currency products	1.0%
Interest rate products	21.0%
Equity derivatives	0.5%
Precious metals/commodities	0.4%

Table 9.2 Notional principal amounts by taxonomy
of derivative instruments[a]

Currency products	**42.0%**
OTC	41.0%
Exchange-traded	1.0%
Interest rate products	**51.0%**
OTC	30.0%
Exchange-traded	21.0%
Equity derivatives	**5.5%**
OTC	5.0%
Exchange-traded	0.5%
Precious metals and other commodities	**1.5%**
OTC	1.1%
Exchange-traded	0.4%

[a] The gross volume of buy and sell contracts is combined.
The percentages include unsettled spot transactions.

OTC, over-the-counter.

financial reporting, it is wiser to follow a narrower usage of the term, within the limits set by regulators and supervisors.

For instance, before the recent change in regulation, banks tended to exclude on-balance sheet receivables and payables, as well as optional features embedded in them. This dichotomy, however, is far from being unambiguous. Because the rapid development of new derivative instruments makes past definitions obsolete, in major jurisdictions such as the USA and UK, banking regulators have been striving for modernization of accounting and disclosure standards in a way that makes it possible to address effectively:

■ New financial products, and
■ New risk management techniques.

Indeed, some regulators have cited serious deficiencies in prevailing financial disclosures particularly connected to market-risk exposure. Legislators, too, have been preoccupied with the aftermath of *creative accounting* and of unreliable financial reporting. An example is the 1992 Sarbanes–Oxley Act in the USA, enacted after the Enron, Global Crossing, Adelphia, WorldCom and other scams, which made a company's chief executive officer (CEO) and chief financial officer (CFO) personally accountable for the contents of the financial statement.

Regarding financial reporting connected to derivatives, it is no secret that bankers, treasurers, investors, financial analysts and regulators are confronted by interrelations and complexity embedded in modern financial instruments. There is also the fact that in many countries disclosures are:

■ Scattered throughout the financial statement notes, and
■ Often understood only by a relatively small sophisticated group of people.

The majority of bankers, treasurers, managers and accountants are mystified and frustrated about the effects of derivatives on their balance sheet and, by extension, on their companies, because derivatives instruments do more than allow them to take risks or hedge risk. They permit the holder to simulate virtually any financial activity by:

- Redrawing assets and liabilities,
- Separating and recombining risks, and
- Bypassing what regulators can prohibit.

A little appreciated fact about derivatives is that they blur distinctions between instruments regulated by different authorities responsible for market discipline. In this way, they virtually eliminate functional and other distinctions among commercial banks, investment banks, insurance companies and non-bank companies acting along the line characterizing past dichotomies among financial institutions. Further, they can turn the notional principal amount of a contract into financial toxic waste.

9.4 From notional principal to financial toxic waste

Section 9.3 stated that, in the large majority of cases, the whole notional principal amount is not at play. Indeed, with the exception of *binary* options, where all of the notional principal may be at risk, usually the contractually specified notional amount must be *demodulated* (downsized) to a core exposure, to establish the amount of risk assumed with a given contract (more on this later). The most common binary options, which are becoming more popular than in the past, are all-or-nothing and one-touch.

- The rapport of an *all-or-nothing* depends on the option's value at expiration.

  An option with intrinsic value is said to be *in the money*. If the strike price is equal to current market price, the option is *at the money*. An option with no intrinsic value is *out of the money*. If the option is in the money at maturity, the buyer will receive an amount equal to the notional principal of the contract. If at maturity the option is out of the money, the buyer will receive nothing and the writer will have no further obligation in regard to this option.

- *One-touch* options are similar to all-or-nothing, but they are exercisable as soon as the strike price is reached.

  In either case, with binary options the whole notional principal amount is at play. This, however, is not true of other options where only part of the notional principal is exposed. The question then is: How much?
  A rather linear answer to this query is to find out the *fair value* of each derivative instrument in the portfolio. Defined by Financial Accounting Statement No. 107 (FAS 107) as a reporting criterion, fair value stands for market value, if there is a market for that instrument. For instance, the large majority of OTC derivatives contracts are not traded and, hence, have no current market value.

If there is no market for the instrument whose value is sought, the fair value must be computed through *option pricing models* such as Black–Scholes, the binomial or Poisson distribution, or the Monte Carlo method. Current models have a common weakness in that they do not examine worst case scenarios. Yet, it is very important to account for fair value in case of nervous markets, and even more so in market panics or collapse. Banks must do so for:

- Their own portfolio,
- That of their clients, and
- What is known about their counterparties.

A frequent policy among banks is to compute the *credit equivalent* value of portfolio positions as the replacement value, and add-on value factors. *Replacement value* typically is the *present value* (PV) of a financial transaction. It represents cost at the present time for the replacement of a given inventoried contract in the event of the counterparty's default; hence the credit equivalent label.

Add-ons are additional charges for already recognized expenses connected to the replacement; for instance, owing to volatility in currency exchange rates, interest rates, and other *current* and *future* factors taken into account in the replacement value algorithm. *Net present value* (NPV) is calculated as the sum of PV and future cash flows.

Much of what comes into replacement value, PV and NPV is subjective. A much more objective way of proceeding, which makes feasible experimentation and stress testing, is the *demodulation* of notional principal amount to core exposure, or *financial toxic waste*. The concept is that of downsizing the notional principal through a divisor that:

- Accounts for the prevailing pattern of risk, regarding a particular instrument and its underlying, and
- Makes it possible to use effectively applicable historical and/or hypothetical simulated economic and financial conditions.

The conceptual frame of reference is shown in Figure 9.1. The demodulator can be calculated as follows.[5] Say that for an IRS the notional principal of a contract is $100 million. By mining the IRS database, it is found that in the distribution of *absolute values* of gains and losses in connection to fixed/floating rates:

- The mean is 2.4,
- The standard deviation is 1.

At a 99 per cent confidence level (two-tailed distribution) the risk being taken is: $x + 2.6s = 2.4 + 2.6 \times 1 = 5$, and the resulting demodulator is: $100/5 = 20$. This demodulator of 20, which effectively amounts to 5 per cent of notional principal subject to loss, may be good under normal market conditions, but not in a crisis.

The critical issue is to account for events that are at the tail of the distribution, all the way to the end of it, as shown by the spikes in Figure 9.2. Several factors affect the value of the demodulator. These can be divided into first and second order factors.

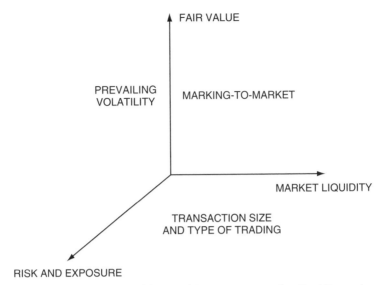

Figure 9.1 The value of financial instruments, market liquidity and exposure tend to correlate, forming a coordinate frame of reference

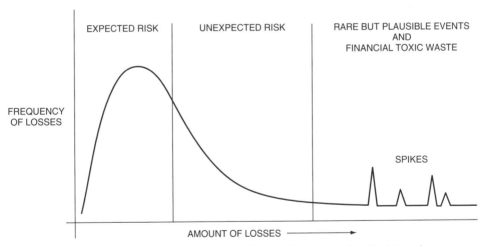

Figure 9.2 The statistical distribution of derivatives losses classified into three major categories

First order factors are the type of instrument (or mix of instruments in a portfolio), prevailing market volatility, prevailing market liquidity and goal of the test. This goal can be expressed by means of two bullets; the first has three options and the second has two:

■ Normal, reduced, tightened inspection, and
■ Classical type, or stress test.

Concepts underpinning normal, reduced and tightened inspection have been established through the seminal work done in World War II in connection with the Manhattan Project. They can be found in Military Standard 105A (MIL-STD-105A), Sampling Procedures and Tables for Inspection of Attributes, published by the US Printing Office, Washington DC. Corporate leveraging is usually accompanied by a severe drop in the company's credit quality.

Classical type tests address the high-frequency and relatively low-impact events. By contrast, stress tests target low-frequency but high-impact events. Second order factors that impact the demodulation of notional principal amount are:

- The entity's high or low gearing (see the LTCM example in following paragraphs),
- Transparency characterizing exposed positions,
- Implicit volatility, and
- Prevailing as well as projected market psychology.

A good example of the visibility offered by demodulation is LTCM's ratio of toxic waste in derivatives. The company had an estimated total derivatives portfolio of $1.4 trillion, pure risk embedded in its portfolio was $300 billion, its debt stood at over $100 billion and its capital base was $4.8 billion. Some interesting ratios can be derived from these statistics.

LTCM's gearing of capital to assumed debt was $100 billion/$4.8 billion = 20.8. This ratio, however, was further superleveraged through derivatives. The gearing of its capital to assumed risk stood at $300 billion/£4.8 billion = 62.5, and even this was dwarfed by its derivatives exposure.

LTCM's leveraging of capital to derivatives contracts was indeed huge, standing at $1400 billion/$4.8 billion = 292. In the last analysis, this is the company's effective leveraging factor eventually leading it to the abyss, as the LTCM case documents. When it approaches the precipice, the demodulator of derivatives exposure to credit-equivalent risk (the toxic waste) is no more 20, as in the preceding example, but:

$$\frac{\$1400 \text{ billion}}{\$300 \text{ billion}} = 4.66$$

Dr Henry Kaufman aptly suggests in his seminal book that LTCM's 'problems centered on leverage so excessive that it could not be unwound in a manageable fashion without endangering key institutions involved in open market financing'.[6] Kaufman further brings attention to the limited power of quantitative risk modelling, upon which many institutional lenders and investors rely as they funnel their funds. He also makes the point that LTCM's plight revealed weaknesses in the dubious value of marking to market.

The capital of $4.8 billion that LTCM mastered in its heyday may seem a lot of money, but with derivatives bets of $1.4 trillion it is really peanuts, dropping to a 'mere' $600 million at the time of bailout in September 1998, at the eleventh hour before the hedge fund's crash. It might be said that LTCM has been an extreme case, but several other corporate failures involving leveraged entities demonstrate that in a crisis the demodulator of notional principal shrinks to about 5.

For instance, when the Bank of New England went into bankruptcy in the early 1990s, it had $36 billion in its derivatives portfolio. The Fed of Boston tried for a whole year to clear this derivatives mess, and finally found that the financial toxic waste in it was $6 billion. This gives a demodulator of 6. In the 1997 East Asian crisis, banks that failed (particularly in South Korea) had a derivatives demodulator of 5. This is the number that should be used in stress tests.

9.5 Derivatives that became institutionalized

The preceding sections have explained that derivatives are financial instruments with a payoff that depends on the future price of an underlying asset or liability. The majority of such contracts, particularly forward and swaps, are handled OTC, and generally do not have a secondary market. The two main types of derivatives that are actively traded on exchanges around the world are:

- Futures, and
- Options.

However, there is also a variety of other derivative instruments that have been institutionalized because they have entered into daily business practice and therefore become more or less commonplace. Examples are:

- Forward rate agreements (FRA),
- Interest rate swaps (IRS),
- Foreign currency swaps,
- Interest rate foreign currency swaps,
- Stripped treasuries (where STRIP is an acronym for separate trading or registered interest and principal securities),
- Mortgage-backed securities (MBS), and
- Asset-backed securities (ABS).

To these should be added other instruments, originally used by FASB in its 'by-example' definition of derivative products, such as commitments to extend credit, standby letters of credit, financial guarantees written (sold), interest rate caps and floors, exchange-traded futures contracts, resource obligations under foreign currency exchange contracts, obligations to repurchase securities sold (repos), outstanding commitments to purchase or sell at predetermined prices, and obligations arising from financial instruments sold short.

Four terms that are often repeated in these lists are futures, forwards, options and swaps. *Futures contracts* are standardized in terms of maturity, notional principal amount and other variables, and they are traded on exchanges. In the case of futures contracts, payment into a margin account is required, against which gains and losses are settled on a daily basis.

By contrast, a *forward contract* is executed OTC. It is an agreement to buy or sell a specific underlying asset at predetermined delivery price, on a certain maturity date. The buyer of the forward agrees to purchase the underlying asset, while the seller of the forward agrees to sell the underlying asset on the maturity date for the delivery price, which is usually referred to as the *forward price*.

An *option* is an instrument giving the owner the right, but not the obligation, to buy and sell the underlying asset at a predetermined price, on the exercise or maturity date. A *call option* gives the buyer the right to acquire the underlying asset; a *put option* gives the holder the right to sell it. It is the buyer of the option who decides about exercising it. There are several types of options, American, European and Asian, but they are not the theme of this book.

A *swap* is a financial transaction in which two counterparties agree to exchange streams of payments over time, according to a predetermined rule applying to both of them. For instance, an *interest rate swap* is a transaction in which the two counterparties exchange interest payment streams of differing character, based on an underlying notional principal amount.

A *currency swap* involves an initial exchange of principal of two different currencies. Interest payments are exchanged over the life of the contract, and the principal amounts are repaid either at maturity or according to a predetermined amortization schedule defined at contractual time.

Because futures and options are traded in exchanges, there is available fair value information by marking to market each instrument's and the portfolio's value. As such, futures and options are the best for hedging activities. Component parts of a fairly simple system that can be supportive to a heading strategy are shown in Figure 9.3.

Although there are difficult scientific-looking methods for derivatives pricing, how to do it remains more of an art (and guesswork) than a science. With forwards, for instance, the most interesting issue is the determination of the forward price. Assuming that the underlying asset is a traded security that does not make payoffs during the period to maturity, the forward price is given by:

- The current value of the underlying, and
- The interest rate earned on this value during the period to maturity of the contract.

The reason behind this approach is that the cash flow of a forward contract, settled at maturity, can be replicated by a two-step strategy that involves buying the underlying asset today and financing such purchase by borrowing at the available interest rate, and selling the underlying on the delivery date at the prevailing market price and repaying the loan.

In connection to options, the most commonly used formula for pricing European-type options was developed by Black and Scholes in 1973. A European option contract can be exercised only on its expiration date. The value of such an option is determined by five factors:

- Current price of underlying,
- Strike price,
- Time to expiration of option,
- Risk-free interest rate during the life of the option,
- Volatility of return on the underlying asset.

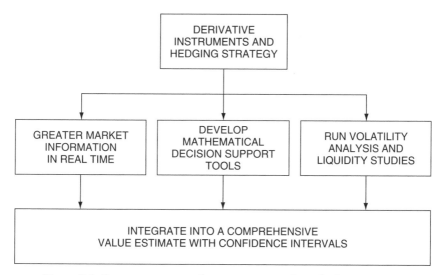

Figure 9.3 Component parts of a system supporting a hedging strategy

Several assumptions underpin this approach, the main one being that the price of underlying asset follows a process that implies that returns are normally distributed with constant mean and volatility. This is, of course, an approximation. Notice that such a calculation can be reversed, in the sense that given an observed option price, a value for volatility can be found that, by means of an option pricing model, produces an option price corresponding to the observed market price. This is essentially the process leading to *implied volatility* (see Chapter 4).

While option pricing is no exact science, and as Warren Buffett suggests sometimes marking to models is like marking to myth, the real challenge in the financial industry is not with products that have become *commodities*; it is with the so-called *exotics*, which are complex derivatives with plenty of financial toxic waste. Complex derivatives are not the subject of this book, except with the reference to the fact that they are revolutionizing the global banking industry and, at the same time, they are putting global financial systems under stress.

9.6 Private banking derivatives and the paper money trauma

Structured financial products offered to retail investors are the theme of Chapter 10. This chapter, however, is a good place to bring the reader's attention to the broader issue of risks associated with navigating in uncharted waters. George Bernard Shaw once said: 'No one has satisfactorily placed a boundary between myth and history.' Paraphrasing Shaw's concept, as far as retail investors are concerned no one has satisfactorily proven the relation between risk and return with derivative instruments.

Since the 1990s the private banking operations of major financial institutions have been promoting among their wealthy clients, in the USA and beyond, the more settled type of derivative financial instruments. This push accelerated after the stockmarket crash of 2000. The products being sold are mainly structured:

- They are thought as a way of preserving capital, and
- They are offering the potential for returns, if the market moves the way the investor hopes.

From the start, derivatives are offered to private banking clients as the way to eliminate capital risk, and reduce the volatility of yields, which is half true at best. Some banks have added another twist to this argument by suggesting that the structured products they sell enable their clients to 'benefit' from the movements of an underlying asset: equity, currency or index, without being directly exposed to that equity, currency or index.

This second argument is, of course, bordering hype. As an example, one of the customized products of the mid-1990s based on two 'exotic' currencies, Thai baht and the Indonesian rupiah, was supposed to allow the investor to name his or her view of the currency market and look accordingly to the rewards. Nobody bothered to inform the private banking clients that such currency deals also carry a very high amount of risk. Suddenly:

- In the wake of the East Asian crisis of 1997, both the Thai baht and Indonesian rupiah collapsed, and
- Their collapse left the private banking investors in trouble.

Although the collapse of the 'East Asia Tigers' and its aftermath on exotic currency derivatives is now history, it would be good to learn a lesson from it. Major economic and financial events are fairly unpredictable and, like a tropical storm, a financial catastrophe may come from nowhere. This is what is taught by chaos theory.

Thinking by analogy, perhaps the best example to date on what should be expected in terms of risk is the case study of European paper money at its very origins in the early eighteenth century. The underlying of this paper money was gold coins and, in that sense, the paper was a derivative.

Paper money was invented in China, in about 300 BC. Its first appearance in Europe was in France in the 1710s, by John Law and the Royal Bank. The latter's bankruptcy left so deep a trauma that, in France, paper money did not see the light of day again until after the 1790s. The French Revolution introduced the *assignats*, but in the turbulence of the terror and social upheaval that followed the revolution, the assignats also failed.

It was left to the *Directoir*, which in 1794 followed the reign of Maximilien Robespierre, to face the bankruptcy of the revolutionary assignats. New paper money was issued, the *mandats territoriaux*, and it met with the same lack of success. On 23 December 1795, the first day these mandats were issued, paper money of 100 livres fell to the parity of 18 livres in metallic money (the underlying). This greatly benefited speculators and profiteers at the expense of the whole French population.[7]

Investors should take note. Post-mortem, the trauma of a major failure leaves a great scar in the public mind, particularly among those who paid for it. The story that led to French paper money in the early eighteenth century is a great lesson to everybody and its origins lie both with John Law, the banker, and with Louis XIV, France's 'roi soleil' (sun king).

John Law was born in Edinburgh in 1671, and at an early age, for three years, Law worked for a firm, learning the principles of banking and being distinguished for mathematical brilliance. Then he left to seek his fortune in London, where he gambled, studied finance and practised gallantry. As early as 1705, Law argued in a pamphlet for the establishment of banks that would issue paper money backed by land or other collateral. He characterized money as:

- A functional medium, with no intrinsic value,
- Backed by something of stable value, to be accepted by the public.

It would be difficult to find a better definition for derivatives at large, and for structured financial products in particular (see Chapter 10). Of particular interest to Law was the fact that Louis XIV, who died just before 1715 when Law moved to Paris, had been living on loans, borrowing from his subjects and issuing worthless certificates that went by different names. In the last dozen years of his reign, Louis XIV had spent 2 billion livres, more than he had collected in taxes. As a result:

- The coinage had been so debased that it was almost worthless,
- A mass of workers was unemployed,
- Trade was at a standstill, and agriculture in distress.

Law believed that he could fix the finances of France by proposing a bank that would issue notes and hold and transfer deposits, much as the Bank of Amsterdam did; a process he had studied while living in Amsterdam. In 1716, Law managed to persuade the Regent, the Duc d'Orléans, to establish the Banque Générale with the aim of issuing paper money backed by deposits, and to install him at its head. His scheme was a success and the notes issued by the bank soon commanded a premium.

- The French economy was revived and Law became the nation's premier banker.
- In 1717, the notes were made receivable for taxes and other royal revenue.

With success came appreciation and Law's bank became the French state's Royal Bank. Thereafter, one of its first actions was to change the terms of the notes to be redeemable for current coins, subjecting the bank's notes to fluctuating values. In a way, this resembles current paper money, the value of which has been decoupled from gold.

In 1717, Law also proposed establishing a company that would have the exclusive rights to trade with and exploit the resources of the Mississippi River, the Louisiana Territory and Canada's fur trade, all under French control at the time. Part of this scheme was that it would also pay down, from the company's profits, some of the government's enormous debt.

The Law-founded Mississippi Company in North America was given the right to all trade between France and its Louisiana colony for twenty-five years. It also obtained permission to maintain its own army and navy, beyond farming and mining. Eventually, with plenty of leveraging, this would become the Mississippi bubble.

Since John Law needed more and more money, to underwrite his grandiose ventures he began issuing public shares at 500 livres a piece. During the summer of 1719, France saw a bull market. By the time the second instalment was due on the new issues, the share price had doubled to 1000 livres while, in effect, Law had become France's central banker.

- The printing presses were busy producing more paper currency, and
- With the inflated paper money speculators could buy more Mississippi Company shares.

At the same time, Law encouraged holders of government annuities, whose debt financing was crippling the Crown, to exchange their instruments for shares in the Mississippi Company. He issued 200 000 new shares and accepted discounted paper at face value. Some months later, he issued another 50 000 shares; and then still another 50 000 shares. Sounds familiar?

In September 1719, Law announced that he would buy the entire debt of France by issuing more shares of his company, basically swapping dividends. By the end of that year, he had sold 600 000 shares of Mississippi Company to a public ever more hungry for financial paper. There were three glory-years, from 1717 to 1720, with each Mississippi share hitting 10 000 livres. When share prices showed signs of softening, Law, who in the meantime had been promoted to controller general of France, issued edicts designed to keep investors:

- From stampeding out of Mississippi shares, and
- From dumping their paper currency.

These edicts outlawed the export of underlying coinage and ownership or purchase of gold, silver or other precious gems. Then it was announced that all gold and silver coins would be removed from circulation. The final blow came on 21 May 1720, when Law had to admit publicly that:

- The value of Mississippi shares would be cut in half, to 5000 livres, and
- The face value of banknotes would also be cut by 50 per cent.

Paris mobs rioted for three days. Mississippi shares crashed and John Law was soon under house arrest. It would be eighty years before France would introduce banknotes again. A satirical epitaph published in France after his death in 1729 read, 'Here lies that celebrated Scotsman, that peerless mathematician who, by the rules of algebra, sent France to the poorhouse.' Amen.

9.7 Dr Alan Greenspan on derivatives and the case of hedge funds

On 7 May 1998, Dr Alan Greenspan, the chairman of Federal Reserve, said that with financial leveraging there will always exist a possibility, however remote, of a chain reaction, a cascading sequence of defaults that will culminate in financial implosion if it proceeds unchecked. Greenspan added that only a central bank, with its unlimited power to create money, has a high probability of thwarting such a process before it becomes destructive.

Yes, the central bank can do it, but by putting its printing presses on high gear, like John Law did; but then the time comes when the bubble bursts. The story of the eighteenth century French Royal Bank is graphic enough to requiring no explanation about the perils of the 'day after'. If we do not learn from history, we are condemned to repeat the same serious mistakes.

One of the major risks to our economy lies in the fact that not only banks, who are at least regulated, but also (if not mainly) hedge funds, many of which are offshore, and practically non-regulated, are very big players in the derivatives market. There are today an estimated 10 000 hedge funds mastering among themselves more than $1 trillion at exponential progression, as shown in Figure 9.4. Leveraged by a factor of up to 50 (see the case of LTCM in section 9.4), hedge funds are in control of something like four times the gross domestic product (GDP) of the USA.

A hedge fund can be defined as a fund whose managers receive performance-related fees and freely use a number of financial leverage strategies, long and short positions in securities, directional hedging, market neutral approaches, and complex derivatives or other geared assets. Typically, hedge funds perform in a wide range of market sectors.

Despite what their name implies, the strategies followed by hedge funds rarely if ever involve hedging. Neither do hedge funds have any restrictions on the type of instruments they can use, owing to their unregulated or lightly regulated nature. Indeed, financial reporting by hedge funds is characterized by voluntary or very limited disclosure requirements. This contrasts with other registered investment funds

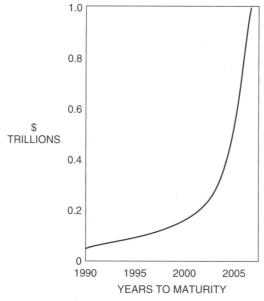

Figure 9.4 Fifteen years of rapid growth in hedge fund money

although, following a 2004 ruling by the Securities and Exchange Commission (SEC), in the USA they must now register with the SEC.

If hedge funds are coming under increasing regulatory scrutiny, this is because of concerns that some entities have overreached themselves. According to Stephen Cutler, head of enforcement at SEC, the SEC is keeping a 'very watchful eye' on hedge funds. In the background are two reasons:

■ The proliferation of hedge funds, and
■ The fact that pressure on them to maintain high returns has intensified.

Regulators are concerned that some hedge funds may collapse because of high-risk trading. In early March 2005, the SEC enforcement division sought to freeze the assets of KL Group, a Florida-based group of hedge funds, and its principals, saying that investors had lost most of the $81 million they put into the KL hedge funds because of a 'massive fraud'.

The SEC alleged that KL Group's principals raised money from wealthy individuals by boasting of above-market returns, at a time when the hedge funds in that group were suffering huge trading losses. Moreover, one of the regulators' main concerns is that hedge funds are:

■ Reaching out to retail investors, and
■ Approaching unsophisticated investors who do not understand the risks involved with structured products (see Chapter 11).

Another major concern is large-scale leveraging as more and more hedge funds are chasing the same investment ideas and market possibilities. To stand out from their competitors, hedge fund managers are taking increasing risk in pursuit of greater returns. In addition, hedge funds have become a good excuse for doing no matter what in the market. Indeed, recent data underline the growing significance of hedge funds and other non-bank professional traders to:

■ Fast growing trading volumes, and
■ Potentially disruptive trading patterns.

According to the Bank for International Settlements, as reported in its triennial report on the forex market, trading between banks and other financial institutions, including hedge funds, jumped by 78 per cent between 2001 and 2004. Specifically in currency trading, overall volumes rose 36 per cent during that period to a record level of nearly $1.9 trillion a day.

The Bank for International Settlements attributes this boom in foreign exchange trading to three main reasons: growing acceptance of forex as a distinct tradeable asset class; sizeable increase in activity by hedge funds; and speculatory activity after a trend in the market such as dollar weakness. This trend-following has encouraged:

■ Momentum traders who aim to ride a trade for as long as it runs, and
■ Traders pursuing *carry trades*, borrowing a low-cost currency and investing in higher yielding assets elsewhere.

Confronted with these facts, the SEC is taking no chances. Through proactive risk assessment it hopes to avoid another spate of scandals. Managers of hedge funds with assets of more than $25 million have to register with the SEC by February 2006 and will undergo periodic inspections by the regulator's compliance office. It is also worth noting that following risk assessment work, the SEC enforcement division has been increasing its investigations of another domain, that of small or microcap companies, suspending trading in shares of some microcaps over the past year, because of concern about their vulnerability to fraud.

The effort to see through what hedge funds are doing did not start in 2005. Ten years earlier, in January 1995, House Banking Committee chairman James A. Leach introduced a bill requiring more disclosure by derivatives dealers and buyers. His thesis was that Washington can no longer credibly continue to rationalize a laissez-faire approach to derivatives oversight. At the same time, then Senate Banking Committee Chairman Alfonse M. D'Amato started hearings in Orange County, California, after the rich Orange County collapse because of overexposure to derivatives instruments (more on Orange County in Chapter 13).

Not everyone, however, agrees with the need for regulating derivatives exposure. In the same month, January 1995, Dr Alan Greenspan stated at a Senate hearing that special legislation to control the use of derivatives was not really necessary. In his opinion, existing mandates by the supervising authorities could do the job. Ten years later, at the March 2005 hearings by the Senate Banking Committee, he told chairman Sabanes that he did not recall a letter he wrote the Senate arguing against hedge funds registration with the SEC, prompting Sabanes into saying: 'You don't recall?'

This is a ten-year long argument. In 1995 Greenspan essentially said that derivatives are a bit like electricity: dangerous if mishandled but bearing the potential to do tremendous good. Notice that John Law did not use the word 'tremendous' with his paper money. Indeed, derivatives could be used for good reasons if used principally for hedging, and if inordinate risk is kept under lock and key. The question, however, is:

- How to keep inordinate risk under lock and key, and
- How to keep the accumulating, potentially limitless, derivatives exposure under control.

Many knowledgeable people have volunteered advice on the risks embedded in derivatives: 'The growth and complexity of off-balance sheet activities and the nature of credit, price and settlement risk they entail, should give us all cause for concern', said Gerald Corrigan, former president of the New York Federal Reserve. 'Sophisticated trading strategies and complex instruments, by their nature, require robust risk management and controls', added C. Feldberg, also of the New York Federal Reserve; and W. Heyman of the SEC said, 'I cannot believe that all these derivatives people are competent.'

Neither, may I add, can I believe that all of the 'alternative investments' (read structured derivatives products) people are competent. Some bankers have been more direct in describing the risks with such instruments. '26-year-olds with computers are creating financial hydrogen bombs', said Felix Rohatyn, former senior executive of Lazard Brothers and US Ambassador to Paris.

'We do not know the web of interconnections between banks established through derivatives', said Alexander Lamfaslusssy, a former general manager of the Bank for International Settlements and of the European Monetary Institute, predecessor to the European Central Bank. 'Behind the big guns is a growing number of smaller outfits anxious not to miss the boat, who cobble together OTC derivatives capabilities in an attempt to keep up with the play and get their share of the market – with limited regard to the dangers', commented V. Fitt, of the UK Securities and Futures Authority.

Many knowledgeable people eager to avoid systemic risk have asked for new derivatives legislation, in full appreciation of the fact that this is an issue neither easy to settle, nor rapidly brought to conclusion. Banking industry lobbying against such a bill and the sheer complexity of the subject are two problems. An executive of a hedge fund was to suggest: 'You can't pass a law that prevents people from taking the wrong risks'; true enough, but you can pass a law keeping such risks below a prudent limit.

9.8 George Soros on derivatives

George Soros, the well-known and successful hedge fund manager, once said that there are so many derivatives with esoteric characteristics that they present a problem to investors. Moreover, in many cases the risks involved are not properly understood, while in other cases derivative instruments masquerade as 'low risk', which is not at all the case. This:

■ Means that supposedly conservative investors take major risks, and
■ Permits institutional investors to make gambles that are not allowed by their statutes.

In the background of these two points lies the fact that seemingly simple and straightforward business decisions can become unsound financial practices, with adverse effects on investors and systemic aftermath on financial markets. Major exposures hidden behind all sorts of derivatives could bring about commercial failures and losses with devastating financial consequences for individuals and organizations, in particular for:

■ Pension funds,
■ Mutual funds, and
■ Insurance companies,

which represent the finances and security of ordinary working people. Soros is not the only knowledgeable person to ring the alarm bell. Warren Buffett, another known and successful investor is another. Neither did Soros speak about derivatives risk just in the past few years. On 13 April 1994, in his testimony to the US House of Representatives Committee on Banking, Finance and Urban Affairs, Soros stated: 'We use derivative instruments to a much lesser extent than generally believed, very largely because *we don't really understand how they work*' (emphasis added).

If one of the smartest financial operators of the past two decades admits that this is the case, think about the myriad of bankers, treasurers, institutional investors and private people who do not even understand the fundamentals of derivatives, yet engage in very dangerous trades. The risks resulting from trading and investing in an uncharted domain have led to greater uncertainty regarding the financial market's future.

Lots of people and of companies have joined in risky derivatives trades, in the vain hope of making a quick buck. According to a March 2005 article in *BusinessWeek*, returns from gambling with financial instruments today supply 30 per cent of all US company profits, up from 21 per cent in the mid-1990s. Some of these profits come from manufacturers and retailers that rely on financial dealing for:

- Their earnings, and
- The market appreciation of their stock.

For instance, at the farm-equipment company Deere, financial deals produce nearly 25 per cent of earnings;[8] and while General Motors is having trouble selling cars, its ditech.com mortgage business is very profitable. GM's financing operations earned $2.9 billion in 2004, while the car-making operations lost money.

Apart the overriding risk that this leads to a casino society, a major problem with finance dominating the corporate landscape is that any threat to financial earnings has a magnified impact, and by 2005 several threats were gathering. Since the Federal Reserve started raising interest rates in June 2004 in quick succession, finance businesses have paid higher short-term rates on the funds they use.

- This is true even for banks that buy money to make loans,
- Whereas the rates they charge customers for longer term loans have not been rising nearly as quickly.

In essence, to the credit risk they traditionally take with loans, banks have added a wave of derivatives exposure, involving credit, market and operational risk. Because the issuers or co-sponsors of many derivative instruments are commercial and investment banks, in the case of systemic risk the regulatory authorities will find themselves obliged to step in to preserve the integrity of the system. Hence,

- The likelihood that they will use taxpayers' money to save overexposed credit institutions, as happened in Japan, and
- The amplified obligations to supervise and regulate *all* players in derivative instruments, including hedge funds, before a meltdown occurs.

What about being able to forecast future events in the financial markets, thereby turning the tide of risk before the financial tsunami hits? 'The financial markets cannot possibly count the future directly because they don't merely discount the future. They help to shape it', Soros suggests. Market players can:

- Affect the fundamentals, and
- Push towards a state of dynamic disequlibrium.

Soros advises that a boom/bust sequence can develop if the market is dominated by a trend following behaviour; that is, investors and traders buying in response to a rise in prices and selling because prices fall. This is a self-reinforcing cycle that can become vicious and produce a market crash. The likelihood of such as event obliges all investors, from institutional to private banking clients, to understand what is meant by exposure and learn to cope with risk.

While, as shown since Chapter 1, both institutions and people benefit from innovation, it is appropriate to appreciate that to a very large extent financial innovations are very *short lived* by their nature, while they have a great *long-term impact*. Financial innovations have changed and continue to change people's thinking with regard to investment, a theme that is elaborated in Chapter 10, but it is also wise not to forget the words of Dante Alighieri (1265–1321):

That which is called modern is perhaps that which will not endure.

Notes

1 J. Wechsberg, *The Merchant Bankers*, Pocket Books/Simon and Schuster, New York, 1966.
2 W. Greider, *Secrets of the Temple*, Touchstone/Simon & Schuster, New York, 1987.
3 D.N. Chorafas, *Managing Risk in the New Economy*, New York Institute of Finance, New York, 2001.
4 'Underlying' is used as a noun in this context.
5 For greater detail see D.N. Chorafas, *Stress Testing. Risk Management Strategies for Extreme Events*, Euromoney, London, 2003.
6 H. Kaufman, *On Money and Markets*, McGraw-Hill, New York, 2000.
7 R. Caratini, *Napoleon, Une Imposture*, Michel Lafon, Paris, 1998.
8 *Business Week*, 28 March 2005.

10 Structured financial products

10.1 Introduction

Chapter 9 indicated there is growing interest in investments in the retail derivatives market. Although this is still a relatively small percentage of overall derivatives business, a number of banks comment that, some years down the line, they can see it exploding to a third of their overall derivatives transactions. Cornerstone to this unprecedented growth would be structured financial products.

Structured products, also referred to as 'protected products' or 'guaranteed bonds' (which is a misnomer) are a novel asset class. The popularity of these instruments has increased in response to stockmarket volatility as misinformed investors sought to reduce risk. Another reason for the rather sudden popularity of structured products, which are essentially *alternative investments*, has been the very low interest rates which, in the first few years of the twenty-first century, dominated in the USA and in Euroland. Statistics from the European Central Bank show the trivial euro area bond yield in 2004 and first semester of 2005.

Basically, structured instruments are securities that provide investors with a redemption amount, which may be with either full or partial capital protection, and a certain type of return. The latter is paid in function of a specific investment strategy on selected underlying asset(s). This means that much depends on the performance of the financial product's underlying, often promoted through the purchase and sale of embedded options.

Structured products, and the use of options in their regard, are relatively new developments. The world of finance has been full of novel instruments that have had their day and eventually worn out, or their risks have became known, and therefore controllable, and the instruments have ended up being traditional. The most basic reasons making a new financial product attractive are that:

- People and companies want to believe that there is something great in it for them, and
- This new product they were dreaming of will make them rich in a short time (see the reference to John Law and the Mississippi bubble in Chapter 9).

In which markets do structured financial products have their believers? The answer is: Asia and Europe, in that order. Fixed income structured products (FISP, see Chapter 12) largely sell in Asia. Although since 2002 they have enlarged their customer base in the European market, they have done less well in America. 'Investors rather go for equities because the US is a mature equity market', said one of the investment bankers who participated in this research. Other structured products use as underlyings:

■ Equities (see Chapters 14 and 15),
■ Currency exchange (see Chapter 16),
■ Commodities, such as base metals and oil (which are not part of this book).

Because they are largely based on derivatives, and derivatives provide an array of options in the design of financial instruments, structured products sold by commercial and investment banks, hedge funds and other entities, come in a growing number of structures. Their variety enables cognizant investors to serve their financial objectives and risk tolerance. Not all investors are, however, knowledgeable of:

■ What a structured product is about, and
■ The amount of exposure that it brings to a person's or an entity's portfolio.

Early versions of structured financial instruments were known as 'precipice bonds'. Their name was, by all likelihood, one of the reasons why they failed to live up to their marketing expectations. It is like the 'Alaskan spider crab', which totally lacked market appeal, but sold like hot cakes after somebody changed its name to 'Alaskan king crab'. Another more fundamental reason for lack of market appeal has been that, in many cases, the capital invested was far from being protected. This led to design changes.

Today's standard structured product has a fixed term, usually six to seven years (although some products have more or less than that), and offers protection of the investor's initial capital, along with exposure to a variable such as an equity index. Underlying indices, for example, cover the world's main markets: the FTSE 100, S&P 500, Nikkei 225 and Dow Jones Eurostoxx 50. Other exposures are linked to single stocks, basket of stocks, interest rates and different commodities. There are also structured products, particularly those with currency exchange underlying (see Chapter 16) where maturities can range from one month to over six months.

Note that some structured products only offer what is referred to as *soft protection*, where losses may kick in when a safety level has been passed. Others offer *hard protection* with 100 per cent, or better than 90 per cent, capital guarantee. None, however, includes a clause compensating investors for lost interest on the capital over the life of the instrument, and that is the caveat.

Finally, one of the major and most important differences between guaranteed investments is how the returns are calculated. The investor should look into this issue most carefully before commitment, and seek advice about the twists associated with a structured instrument, as well as their aftermath. It is always vital to understand how and to what extent the product one buys can affect potential profits and losses.

10.2 Structured products and capital protection

According to an article in *Sigma* magazine, ours is the age of *equitization*.[1] While the root of this term is 'equity', behind equitization lies both equity and debt. Financial innovation, declining costs of securitization and the increasing sophistication of market participants have enabled securities issuance to:

- Replace bank lending as the major source of capital for large corporations, and
- Produce a torrent of new financial instruments, which find their way into the portfolio of investors.

As far as the second bullet point is concerned, *Sigma* noted that increasing demand for securities by pension funds and mutual funds has stimulated securities issuance. Between 1998 and 2000, worldwide debt and equity issuance exceeded $4 trillion each year. Although the pace of issuance slowed in late 2001, in subsequent years of the twenty-first century it picked up again. The difference is that over this time-frame:

- Issuance of equities has taken the back seat.
- By contrast, more and more emphasis has been placed on securitized liabilities.

Statistics from the financial markets of the USA and UK in the post-bubble years demonstrate that in both markets the issuance of equities has fizzled, and so have the prices. By contrast, the bond price index held its own, albeit with ups and downs. Other things being equal, a higher price for debt instruments means a lower interest rate and, as stated in the Introduction, this has been a motor behind the advent of structured financial products. Moreover,

- Rapid progress in the field of information and communications technology,
- More sophisticated financial modelling techniques, and
- Globalization of markets along with computerization of trading procedures

have contributed to the design and aggressive marketing of structured instruments, with private bankers and asset managers labouring to convince their clients that these products 'create added value by reducing risk'. This is most evidently hype, because the doors of risk and return are adjacent and indistinguishable.

One of the hypotheses that try to explain the growing popularity of structured products is that investors increasingly tend to leave key investment decisions to the experts. In its background is the assumption that, by outsourcing asset management, investors can bypass problems, caused by lack of time, information and market know-how (see Chapter 7). I do not buy this assumption. On the contrary, there is much to be said for the role played by technology in enabling experimentation on investment strategies, as well as:

- The term structure of new financial instruments,
- Dynamic changes in risk and return, at least from the issuer's viewpoint.

As the name implies, the *term structure* of an instrument or transaction defines a specific period over which condition(s) hold; for instance, a specific rate of interest. The term can be fixed at any date, but for some instruments, such as repurchase agreements, it is often set to mature on important dates, such as action settlements or tax payments.

The fact that many issuers today have real-time systems and powerful mathematical models for experimentation purposes is good for them, but not necessarily for the investors, who have neither the systems nor the experimental know-how. A significant amount of study and analysis by the issuer is necessary in order to come up with a structured instrument that would not be too onerous. Capital protection is an important part of this reference.

Fundamental *capital protection* should be seen as a market-and-product mechanism, originally invented by insurance companies, but widely used today by banks and hedge funds. The best way to appreciate the shortening of capital protection is through comparison to what is offered by AAA-rated government bonds.

Had the investor put his or her money in a credit risk-free government bond, he or she would have obtained, under current market conditions, 3.5 per cent interest (more than that in a market with high interest rates). Over a seven-year time-frame the investor's money is tied up in the structured product:

- This would amount to a compound 26 per cent.
- All of that money would be lost if the instrument has no return, even if the bank returned the capital at 100 per cent.

True enough, most structured instruments benefit from a secondary market. They are priced on a weekly or monthly basis depending on the underlying asset, and feature typically bid/offer spread of 1 or 1.5 per cent. The problem is that this secondary market is too esoteric and under the issuers' control. Therefore, investors in structured products are usually advised to hold them to maturity.

Moreover, although guaranteed capital investments look similar on the surface, they can actually be quite different when one looks at them closely. For this reason, it is important that the investor reads all the small print before choosing a structured product. Understanding what is written *between the lines* can ensure that what the investor chooses has a chance to live up to expectations.

For instance, many guaranteed capital equity investments limit the growth potential of the returns, either by applying a cap such as 70 per cent growth over six years, or by means of a limited level of participation in the rise of an index. Some combine both methods. There are other structured investments that offer unlimited growth potential, with no maximum limit on the return, but these may involve other restrictive conditions.

In other terms, there is no free lunch. The goal of the issuer is to increase his revenue and profitability, doing so by exercising pricing power. Capital protection is a flexible concept, and structured instruments with this feature exist in three markets:

- Equities,
- Fixed income, and
- Currencies.

Major clients of these products are private banks, which buy them for their clients, as well as institutional investors, which define the character of instruments they buy in function of their mandate. Pension funds, the second largest financial group in the USA today, are an example.

Among the most favoured structured financial techniques is pooling of underlying liabilities and assets and dividing the resulting security into senior/subordinated tranches. The sugar-coating is guarantees, such as 100 per cent capital repayment at maturity, which can transform the risk and return profile of a product, making it look like an acceptable solution for the retail investor, pension fund, insurance company or other entity.

The notion underpinning all securitizations is that taken one at a time, all mortgages, car loans or credit card receivables may not be of investment grade. Structured finance, however, labours to transform a pool of them into a security that qualifies as having a relatively low credit risk, depending on the tranche that the investor buys.

This type of sugar-coating is typically done at design level by the investment bank or hedge fund. The private bank may also do something about the risk embedded in the instrument. Some private banks also press the point that the investment bank that designs this derivative financial product makes a secondary market for it. Others tell the investor that they provide a secondary market in conjunction with the investment bank that designed the structured product.

In terms of marketing structured products, and selling them to willing investors, some private banks are only intermediaries, marketing to their clients what they buy from investment banks and hedge funds. In one of the meetings during the research that led to this book, reference was made to a £50 million package bought by a private bank, which it subsequently sold in £1 million lots to 50 clients.

In many cases ideas about the nature of a structured financial instrument come from the clients or specialists who are in close contact with the market. This is discussed in section 10.4, which addresses the role of strategists, traders and modelling controllers in the design of a new financial product.

10.3   Structured versus synthetic products

There is a certain confusion in the terminology of derivative financial instruments packaged and sold to institutional investors and retail investors. An example is the distinction, if any, between *structured* (defined in the Introduction) and *synthetic* products. It is important to clarify this issue before discussing the role of different players in the domain of popularized derivatives.

According to the International Financial Reporting Standard (IFRS) by the International Accounting Standards Board (IASB), a *synthetic instrument* is a financial product designed, acquired and held to emulate the characteristics of another instrument. Such is the case of floating rate long-term debt combined with an interest rate swap that involves:

■ Receiving floating payments, and
■ Making fixed payments.

This instrument synthesizes a fixed rate long-term debt. IFRS specifies that each of the individual financial instruments that together constitute such a synthetic product represents a contractual right or obligation with its own terms and conditions. Moreover:

■ Each may be transferred or settled separately, and
■ Each is exposed to risks that may differ from the risks to which other financial instruments are exposed.

It follows from these considerations that when one financial instrument in a synthetic instrument is an asset and another is a liability, these are not offsetting one another. Therefore, they should be presented on an entity's balance sheet on a net basis, unless they meet specific criteria outlined by the aforementioned international accounting standard. IFRS does not emphasize synthetic financial products.

Other entities do not have the same clarity of definition in differentiating between structured and synthetic financial instruments. Next to IASB's, in terms of scope and detail, comes Bloomberg's definition, which says that a *synthetic* security is a swap combined with a bond. By contrast, Bloomberg defines a *structured* note as hybrid security combining a fixed income instrument with one or more derivative components. As a result of this combination, the coupon's life, and/or redemption value, can become exposed to market forces such as forward movement in:

- Equity price indexes,
- Currency exchange rates, and
- Prepayment speeds of mortgage-backed securities.

Bloomberg also adds that when combined with the nature of options typically embedded within these structures, including complex call features and/or caps and floors, one can expect exotic payoff scenarios and random cash flows. Excluded from this class are fixed income securities issued by sovereign governments whose structure is considered to be standard domestic convention.

Barclays Bank gave a different definition of synthetics, based on the opinion of its structured instruments specialists. Having stated that his bank does not use synthetics, one of the Barclays executives said that the *synthetic* instruments are structured products with composition changing across the life of the note. By contrast, with the now typical structured instrument the composition is known in advance.

Another bank expressed a different opinion, saying, for example, that a *synthetic bond* is an asset swap, that is, a combination of a long-term fixed rate bond with an interest rate swap that converts it into a floating rate asset. The resulting synthetic product enables the investor to take on the credit risk of the issuer, without the market risk associated with the fixed interest rate over the longer term.

Still another opinion expressed by specialists who do not exactly espouse the aforementioned definitions is that *synthetic products* are, essentially, covered options and certificates. These are characterized by their identical or similar profit and loss structures, compared with specific traditional financial instruments such as equities or bonds. Basket certificates, for example, are based on a specific number of selected stocks.

Moreover, in the opinion of the latter entity, like structured financial instruments synthetic products can be traded in an exchange or over-the-counter (OTC). A point that was raised is that risks associated with synthetic products need to be the same as risks characterizing the financial instruments these contain.

A risk manager added that, in a way similar to what was said about structured instruments, it is important that investors are fully aware of the exposure they are about to assume, before acquiring synthetic products. Most particularly, investors should appreciate what is involved in risk and return, regarding a *covered option* which involves the purchase of an underlying asset:

- Equity,
- Bond, or
- Currency,

and the writing of a call option on that same asset. In return, the investor is paid a premium, which limits his or her loss in the event of a fall in the market value of the underlying. At the same time, however, the potential return from any increase in the asset's market value is limited to gains up to the option's strike price. If the underlying asset is lodged as collateral, then the product sold to investors is known as a *traditional covered option*.

Synthetic covered options are based on a process of duplicating traditional covered options, by means of a transaction. The purchase of the underlying asset and writing of the call option are effected using derivatives. Moreover, the purchase price of the synthetic covered option is equal to that of the underlying, less the premium received for the same call option.

The reader should notice from this discussion that unlike structured products with capital protection, synthetic covered options do not contain a hedge against losses in the market value of the underlying. This lack of capital protection could indeed be a basic element in the distinction between *structured* and *synthetic* products, but then again it would be enough to characterize synthetics as structured products without capital protection, rather than inventing a new and confusing term.

Basically, by writing a traditional covered option (which is a call option) or by calculating the return from the sale of a call option into the synthetic covered option price, any loss in market value of the underlying is lower than it would if this were a direct investment. The option premium limits the loss in market value of the underlying because of market risk.

- If the market value of the underlying on maturity is higher than the strike price, the investor is paid a specified cash amount as settlement.
- If it is lower than the strike price, he or she receives physical delivery of the underlying asset.

In the latter case, the investor carries the full risk associated with the underlying. Either cash settlement or physical delivery of the underlying takes place on the expiration date. Investors should also carefully examine what sort of risk and return can be provided by these certificates. Is the structured product according a right based on one or several underlyings? Is its value derived from different indicators? Accurate answers to these queries help in achieving diversification over a range of investment opportunities or risk factors. For instance:

- *Index certificates* reflect a whole market and are based on an official index.
- *Region certificates* are derived from a series of indices or companies, from a certain region.

In conclusion, a major part of risk assumed by investors in connection to synthetic products and certificates is lack of information. Many jurisdictions and stock exchange acts do not lay down an obligation to provide general information concerning the risks of investing in non-traditional funds.

There is also a wide variety of taxation rules and generally legal consequences pertaining to securities transactions that fall outside ordinary boundaries. Investors should therefore be very careful in regard to the tax treatment of gains and losses, as well as duties of disclosure (see the Appendix).

10.4 The role of strategists, traders and modelling controllers

At the origin of all new products, whether physical or financial, are ideas, concepts and research results. Let us start with the premise that the idea for a new structured financial instrument comes from the *clients* or, alternatively, from the bank's *specialists* who are in constant contact with the market. The latter are sometimes known as *developers* or *structurers*.

Clients and structurers are essentially 'idea persons'. Other inputs about novel financial instruments may come from the bank's *traders*. As Figure 10.1 shows, all of these inputs have to be elaborated, massaged, tested and eventually structured by the *quantitative analysts* (quants, rocket scientists). In investment banking jargon, the latter are also known as *strategists*.

'Strategists' may seem a strange title for these specialists, but the work they are doing is not just quantitative analysis. Product structuring requires a considerable amount of strategic perspective, accounting for the population of potential clients, its likes and what makes it tick. Otherwise, the structured product will not sell. (More on this later.)

Because, however, there is modelling risk,[2] and moreover both the bank structuring the product and its clients may be faced with a significant amount of exposure, the

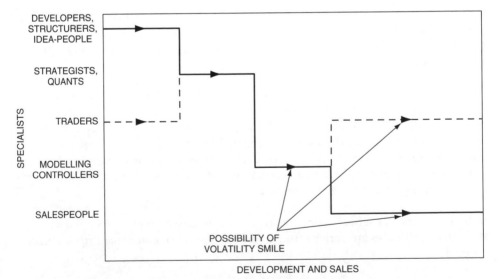

Figure 10.1 Birdseye view of stages involved in the development and marketing of a new financial instrument

work done by strategists, although necessary, is not enough. Somebody has to control the product being designed, and give a stamp of approval. This is the job of the *modelling controllers*.

Ideas people (developers, structurers), rocket scientists and modelling controllers are specialists whose role in banking may be likened to that of a research and development (R&D) laboratory in the manufacturing industry. In manufacturing, R&D laboratories developed in the late nineteenth and early twentieth century. In banking, R&D laboratories were born in the 1980s. Morgan Stanley was one of the first institutions with an R&D outfit.

Take as an example of product design for the ownership society a *podium note*, which is a hybrid bonds and equities structured instrument (see also Part 4). For example, a 5-year bond investment linked to the stocks currently contained in the Dow Jones Global Titans index,

- Provides 100 per cent capital protection,
- Has fixed coupon in year 1 and year 2, and
- Features full currency hedging in three currencies: US dollars, euros and Swiss francs.

However, the fixed coupon this podium note offers to investors differs by currency. It is 4.5 per cent for dollars, 5 per cent for euros and only 1.5 per cent for Swiss francs. The note features a 12.5 per cent target coupon for years 3 to 5, but also has some binary derivative features (see Chapter 9):

- A reduction of 2.5 per cent for each share that touched the barrier during the corresponding year (step-down coupon), and
- A barrier for each share, set at 67 per cent for US dollars, 65 per cent for euros and 75 per cent for Swiss francs.

The work done by modelling controllers led to an evaluation of best case and worst case returns as far as the end investor is concerned (private individual or institution). The scenarios for all three currencies are presented in Table 10.1.

The product development outline and sample results shown in preceding paragraphs are important elements in understanding the study, evolution and financial

Table 10.1 Best and worst case Podium note scenarios

Best case	Worst case
100% redemption plus fixed coupon in first 2 years	100% redemption plus fixed coupon in first 2 years
Annual coupon of 12.5% in years 3–5	No coupon in years 3–5
Likely return per year	
US$: 8.89%	US$: 1.85%
Euro: 9.10%	Euro: 2.06%
CHF: 7.61%	CHF: 0.61%

aftermath of structured products. As the careful reader will have noticed between the lines, three classes of people are involved in this financial R&D effort:

- Clients, developers, structurers and traders who have to deal with the client(s) and eventually sell the product,
- Strategists, essentially quants who think about the technical aspects of new product(s) and are mainly rocket scientists, and
- Modelling controllers, who must audit the model on which the new instrument is based and must approve that model, including its risk profile.

While the concept is contributed by developers, market research will be done by the strategists. Instrument development, and the inseparable modelling of it, is a joint effort of strategists and traders, followed by model audit and control. For instance, the control of volatility smile which may be involved in the pricing of the new instrument (see Figure 10.1) is the job of modelling controllers.

Once the new financial product has been designed and approved, the traders, or a separate group of salespeople, will take care of marketing it. This is the line shown at the bottom of Figure 10.1, which presented a birdseye view of perception, conception and interaction connected to the new structured instrument all the way to selling it to the market, either directly or through an intermediary such as another bank.

To cover sales expenditures, the entity developing the instrument and that selling it to retail clients or institutional investors will demand an upfront distribution fee. Often this is 2 per cent, but it can go to 4 per cent of the denomination of the note; or it may be zero, as a special condition or for promotional reasons. One of the features found in connection with some structured products is a borrowing charge for clients foolish enough to borrow money to buy the structured product.

Not only should investors never leverage themselves to buy structured instruments, or even equity traded in exchanges, but they should also be very careful about the cost of opting out of the instrument before maturity. Apart from the fact that pricing in the secondary market is not transparent, there is, in some cases, an *early close-out fee* determined in accordance with a published schedule. An example is:

- During the first year after strike date: 3.75 per cent
- During the second year after strike date: 2.50 per cent
- During the third year after strike date: 1.25 per cent
- Thereafter, the early close-out fee may be zero.

All elements presented in the foregoing examples count a great deal in terms of risk assumed by investors. As cannot be repeated too often, both private and institutional investors must always read the small print, and they should also be aware that past performance is no guarantee of future results.

Vendors of structured instruments often exaggerate their return and minimize their risk. This amplification of benefits takes place not just in words, but even when the structured product's salesperson presents the client with a simulation of historical performance as the nearest proxy to the 'real thing'. Figure 10.2 gives an example of an often seen comparison between the returns of a known index and those of a structured instrument. It is advisable not to believe in Santa Claus.

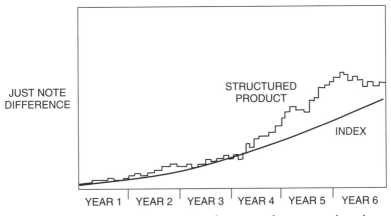

Figure 10.2 Simulation of historical performance of a structured product against an index

10.5   Aftermath of design factors on risk profile

The Introduction stated that, in the most general sense, the term *structured products* refers to combinations of two or more financial instruments, at least one of which must be a derivative. Together, these instruments form a new investment product, which is usually traded OTC, or placed through direct sale to a private banking client or an institutional investor.

Subsequent sections of this chapter explained why every structured product has its own characteristics and risk profile. Reference was made to *capital protection* in section 10.2. In this connection, it has been stated that while many structured instruments advertise a 100 per cent or 95 per cent capital protection, even 'all your money back' is insufficient because over a, say, six-year time-frame to maturity the investor would have received better than 26 per cent interest for his or her money by buying credit risk-free government bonds, and this interest is not protected.

With a 100 per cent capital protection this 26 per cent is lost because it is used to compensate the risk that the issuer of the structured product, bank or any other entity, takes because of market uncertainties. Indeed, the exposure that the issuer takes goes beyond the, so to speak, classical market risk. The risk profile of structured instruments is amplified, because these instruments are highly leveraged.

In principle, exposure associated with the individual components of a new structured instrument may be reduced or increased in a way that is difficult to foretell even with risk management expertise. The work of modelling controllers is centred around the risk protection of the issuer, not necessarily of the investor.

Because of reasons outlined in the preceding paragraphs, it is important that private banking and institutional investors are fully aware of the risks involved before acquiring any new product. As stated in section 10.2, the widely advertised *capital protection* offered by structured products essentially consists of two elements:

- An option, and
- An income investment.

Modelling controllers work to determine how much of the purchase price of the structured product is paid out when it expires. This provides them with an estimate of the capital protection's cost. They also work to establish the minimum return to be paid out independent of price movements in the option component.

Some interesting notions are connected to this work. Because the capital protection is linked to the nominal value rather than the issue price or the secondary market price, if the issue/purchase price paid by the investor exceeds the nominal value, then capital protection will concern only the nominal value. By contrast, if the issue/ purchase price is less than the nominal value, then the capital protection will rise accordingly.

Another twist along this frame of reference is that, depending on the product, the capital protection component can be well under 100 per cent of the capital invested. Investors should appreciate that capital protection does not mean 100 per cent repayment of purchase price for all products. The nominal price is usually different to the purchase price, and it is always wise to read the small print.

The income investment of the structured product may be of fixed-income type, like a bond or a money market instrument, but it may also be an equity-type investment. Investors will be well advised to inform themselves about both the income investment and embedded option before commitment. Other design factors connected to the structured product that should attract the investor's attention are:

- Mean monthly or annual return,
- Variance around this mean,
- Percentage of negative monthly or annual returns,
- Historical profit/loss ratio (from similar products),
- Maximum drawdown, and
- Maximum drawdown period.

Moreover, structured instruments are often characterized by adjustments and redemptions. The issuer of a structured product, or its agent, may adjust the terms of that product to cover unforeseen circumstances, such as changes to the index, interest rates, currency rates or other underlying factors. Adjustments may also be made in response to a corporate event, such as merger or insolvency, affecting any share on which the product is based.

In several cases, issuers may also entitle themselves to substitute different underlying indices, rates or shares. They may even be entitled to redeem the products before maturity, if they profit from doing so. Moreover, they usually have the right to amend the dates on which market levels are observed or payments are made, to reflect the business days applicable in the underlying markets. All this speaks volumes about 'guaranteed capital' and its exceptions.

- Nothing is really guaranteed when the terms of the contract can be changed unilaterally, and
- Apart from the interest on capital forgone by the investor, there may be other design factors affecting the risk and return equation.

Investors should therefore inform themselves in the most rigorous way before entering into a commitment involving structured products. Figure 10.3 gives an

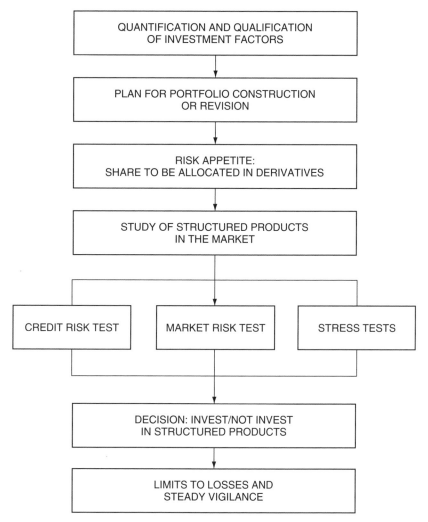

Figure 10.3 Wealth management is a learning process where structured products must be thoroughly tested

integrated view of steps necessary to arrive at a factual and documented decision. Note that the amount of investment in structured products is closely linked to the investor's risk appetite.

- Low-risk investors should buy no derivative instruments.
- Medium-risk investors could allocate no more than 1 per cent of their funds to structured products.
- High-risk investors could allocate up to 5 per cent, but under the conditions of stress testing and steady vigilance.

The fourth decision box in Figure 10.3 advises a careful study of past and current behaviour of structured products in the market. The choice should fall on instruments with characteristics sought out by the investor, because there are thousands of different products and new ones come out every day. Chapters 12–16 address the nature of these instruments. Examples of structured products are:

■ *Interest rate notes*, such as step-ups (stairway notes), crescendos and inflation-linked notes, as well as fixed and variable interest rate notes,
■ *Structured credit products*, such as single credit linked notes, first to default baskets, bearish on credit notes (yogi) and CPPI credit funds,
■ *Collateralized debt obligations* (CDO): asset-backed securities, leveraged loans, bank/insurance trust preferred and synthetic credit (CDOs are not treated in this book),
■ *Equity-type derivatives*, such as certificates of securitized equities, certificates of underlying's performance, absorber certificates, early repayment certificates and enhanced yield certificates,
■ *Currency exchange products*, where the investor usually makes poorly documented bets about future foreign exchange rates.

There are also the so-called *A&L management products*, such as asset inflation swaps, interest rate swaps and quantos. The first choice, therefore, is which class of structured products the investor wants to enter. After a strategic decision has been made comes the choice of which instrument can best contribute in attaining predefined goals and realizing a satisfactory performance.

Some products offer an option of *participation component* which enables the holder to take part in price movements of one or more variable (e.g. indices), while limiting potential losses because of the capital protection component. Notice, however, that usually in these cases capital protection may only cover a portion of capital invested. Moreover, depending on product design, the participation and protection elements can be separated, and there may be also limitations and ceilings attached to this facility.

10.6 Structured investments are not liquid

Apart from the problems associated with capital protection that have been discussed in sections 10.2 and 10.5, investors should always remember that this clause works only at maturity. From day of purchase to expiration, structured instruments are *not liquid* and their quotation in the secondary market is not necessarily free of bias. To obtain a better deal, investors have to wait until they mature. If an investor must access his or her funds during the term of the note, then the choice lies between two possibilities:

■ Put it up as collateral to a loan,
■ Or try to sell the structured product in the secondary market, if there is one (see section 10.7).

Banks are usually prepared to consider structured products as collateral, often with a 30 per cent haircut, which speaks volumes about the risk assumed by investors. The exact loan-to-value ratio to be applied when calculating the collateral value of the note depends on the structured product's design, as well as on the way this note fits into the investors portfolio of other securities. Furthermore, the provision of a loan is subject to:

- Credit approval, which may involve other considerations, and
- Completion of relevant documentation, which evidently adds to the costs of the credit facility.

Borrowing money to buy structured instruments is one of the most foolish actions one could make. Apart from the fact that it is likely to end up as a lose–lose proposition, using a credit facility to fund the purchase of derivative-based notes can significantly:

- Alter the investor's risk profile, and
- Increase the amount of leverage in the portfolio.

In principle, the general effect of borrowing for investment reasons is to magnify gains and losses of the underlying portfolio, depending on the market's behaviour. Where the cost of borrowing to buy structured products is greater than the return generated by the note, the investor would suffer a net loss in value on an aggregate basis. This is true even if the return of the structured instrument is positive but less than the cost of the loan.

Indeed, not only in connection to derivatives but also in the general case, borrowing for investment purposes is one of the major misconceptions by the investing public, often fed by brokerage houses and other investment advisors. Amadeo Giannini, the man who made Bank of America, advised his friends, employees and clients never to borrow to bet on the stockmarket. Borrowing becomes even more illogical when one wants to invest in complex and barely comprehensible hedging strategies involving the use of derivatives.

Borrowing is leveraging, and leveraging with structured instruments is not unheard of. One of the earliest deals that came to my attention concerned a highly leveraged structured instrument, launched in 1998 when a Cayman Islands special purpose vehicle (SPV) issued AAA-rated euro medium-term notes and commercial paper.

- The objective was that of leveraging equity capital raised from institutional investments, and
- The proceeds were invested in a portfolio of assets managed on a daily basis through hedging.

The structured instrument underpinning this offer has been primarily medium- to long-term asset-backed debt. Issuers of the debt were financial institutions, corporates and sovereigns. The cost of the instrument's debt was low, because of good credit rating. The underwriter received a continuing fee for its role as investment manager. The equity investors expected to receive a Libor-plus return from the credit spread between the companies' assets and the cost of their debt.

In the years that elapsed since this issue came to the market, structured instruments have become much more complex and risky. In many cases, high credit rating has taken a leave, and therefore investors must learn how to factor in credit risk. Another 'must' for investors in structured products is to become familiar with options and their pricing.

Section 10.5 mentioned that investors in structured financial instruments should understand the role of the 'option component' that determines how and to what extent the buyer of a structured product with capital protection benefits from price movements in the underlying. This is important inasmuch as:

- The option component establishes the potential return above the capital protection component, and
- It may comprise not just one option but a combination of options, depending on product design.

The risk the option component entails corresponds to the risks of the option(s) comprising it. As with every option, depending on the underlying's market value, this component can expire without value to the investor. All these factors lie behind the statement that every structured product has its own characteristics and risk profile. Because there is almost limitless potential to combine product elements, no two structured products entail the same:

- Credit risk,
- Market risk, and
- Liquidity risk (regarding volatility in liquidity, see Chapter 11).

All structured products involve credit risk because investors can only assert their rights against the issuer if this entity is still in business. Therefore, particular attention needs to be paid to *issuer risk*, over and above market risk, which is omnipresent.

With regard to market risk, investors are exposed to a potential loss owing to a fall in the market value of the underlying, but they also face a total loss of their investment if the issuer defaults. Moreover, liquidity risks cannot be excluded. At times, happily not very frequently, investors are advised to 'take advantage' of a facility to exchange certificates currently in their possession with others characterized as being 'more liquid'. Any advice promoting the liquidity of structured products borders on conflict of interest. There are, however, people and entities who buy it.

While market markers, who in many cases are the issuers of structured instruments, guarantee that these are tradeable, there is always the risk that a counterparty (or a participant in a settlement system) will not settle an obligation for full value when due. In a way, liquidity risk may be only temporary; its existence does not necessarily imply that a counterparty or participant is insolvent.

- There are cases where the counterparty may be able to settle the required debit obligations at some unspecified time thereafter,
- But there are also other cases when it is difficult to distinguish between liquidity risk and plain insolvency.

Solvency risk aside, the maximum possible loss for the buyer of a structured product with capital protection is the difference between the purchase price and both the amount of capital protection and the forgone interest on credit risk-free bonds (see section 10.2). There is always potential loss on the structured product's wings.

10.7   A secondary market for structured instruments

An investor could liquidate a structured instrument in his or her portfolio before maturity, *if* and *when* there is a secondary market for it. Typically, this secondary market is arranged by the market maker. In principle, a secondary market will only be available under normal market conditions. Therefore, this is:

- A restricted market for transactions in derivative products, and
- One in which it may be difficult to obtain reliable independent information as to the structured product's fair value.

In theory, in secondary market transactions, the current value of the product is calculated by the market maker based on its features, its underlying and prevailing market conditions. In practice, while movements on the underlying market factors affect the value of the instrument during its term, this may also be affected by other factors such as changes in:

- Level of interest rates,
- Characteristics of currency of issuance, and
- Time to maturity.

In practice, the value of a structured product will be influenced by complex and interrelated political, economic, financial and other factors that affect capital markets. The market maker has the know-how and information necessary to follow those changes and decide on instrument pricing. The typical investor does not.

In terms of valuation, the instrument's ownership exposes the investor to many different risks, including interest rate, foreign exchange, corporate, time value and/or political risks. Investors are also exposed to forex risk, to the extent that they invest in products denominated in a currency other than their home currency.

The valuation of structured instruments in the secondary market is so complex because, for any practical purpose, it is impossible to predict whether the fair price of the product will rise or fall. It follows that, at any time, its value may be less than the sum of money invested. Investors should also take note of the fact that secondary market transactions may be subject to:

- Dealing or commission charges, and
- A bid/offer spread, which characterizes every commodity.

Reverse engineering the value of an instrument does not ensure a dependable discovery process, no matter what the underlying instrument: home mortgages, commercial mortgages, car loans, credit card debt, corporate debt, trade receivable or any other. One of the issues faced by reverse engineering in a process of discovering underlying value is the sugar-coating that has been added. Another problem lies in the fact the new securities have been structured to achieve a desired credit rating level, which is now an integral part of the instrument's strengths and weaknesses.

Still another obstacle in an analytical price discovery process is the way the system works. Structured finance transactions pool assets and transfer the whole or part of the originator's risk to the investors purchasing such securities. Between the originator and the investors may come obligors, or guarantors, and the argument remains as to which way this *risk transfer* should be priced.

A lesson could be learned from computing the fair value of debt instruments. The fair value of a company's debt is determined using pricing models reflecting one percentage point shifts in appropriate yield curves. The fair value of an investment can be calculated through a combination of pricing and duration models.[3] Duration is a linear approximation that works well for modest changes in yields and generates a symmetrical result. By contrast, pricing models reflect the convexity of the price/yield relationship. They:

■ Provide greater precision, and
■ Reflect the asymmetry of price movements for interest rate changes in opposite directions.

The impact of convexity is more pronounced in longer term maturities and low interest-rate environments. Another way of dealing with the pricing query is by borrowing a leaf from leveraging in the housing market. The concept is known as *cash-on-cash*, and as any good hedge fund manager knows:

■ Cash-on-cash returns are a more accurate measure of investment performance than ordinary returns.
■ As leverage is rising in the housing market, traditional statistics of home price appreciation become misleading.

American financial analysts working towards a solution to this pricing puzzle have come up with an approach which calculates cash-on-cash returns by combining data on home equity ownership from the Federal Reserve's Flow of Funds reports with the traditional home price appreciation index. The algorithm is:

$$\text{Cash-on-cash return} = \frac{\text{Actual price appreciation in year 2}}{\text{Owner's equity at year 1 end}}$$

Figure 10.4 shows the magnitude of the difference between the compound appreciation in home prices as they are traditionally measured, and the compound returns when prices are computed using a cash-on-cash approach. A Merrill Lynch study shows that, during the past twenty years, home prices have:

■ Roughly tripled using the traditional methodology,
■ But more than quintupled using the cash-on-cash approach.[4]

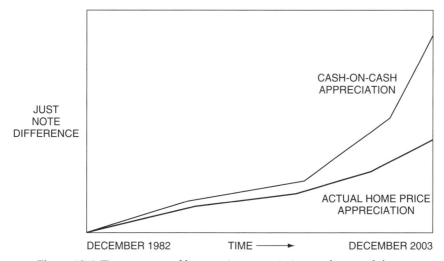

JUST
NOTE
DIFFERENCE

CASH-ON-CASH
APPRECIATION

ACTUAL HOME PRICE
APPRECIATION

DECEMBER 1982   TIME ———►   DECEMBER 2003

Figure 10.4 Twenty years of home price appreciation: cash-on-cash home
price appreciation versus actual home price appreciation. (By Merrill Lynch,
with permission)

There is another interesting finding from the same Merrill Lynch study. Many
observers have suggested that home prices have not risen enough to create a
housing bubble. According to the US data, house prices have appreciated by about
7 per cent a year in the 1999–2003 time-frame. That is the traditional approach.
By contrast, cash-on-cash returns have risen by about 12.5 per cent a year. Such
returns are lower than equity-market returns during the late 1990s, but they
significantly exceed the often quoted historical average of 5 per cent a year for the
housing market.

10.8   Dynamic threshold mechanism

One of the high street banks in London offers structured instruments based on
what it calls a dynamic threshold mechanism (DTM). These notes have been
created to maximize exposure to the underlying portfolio while providing capital
protection at the maturity of the note. DTM has a duality of price dependence in
its background, because rather than being linked exclusively to the underlying
portfolio, the notes' performance is computed with reference to the level of an
index.

The process underpinning dynamic management of exposure uses a test T and a
multiplier, defining asset allocation within the index in three steps. In step 1, at each
weekly monitoring date the computation agent determines the distance between the
value of the index and the value of a zero coupon bond (ZCB) of the same maturity:

$$T_t = \frac{1 - \text{ZCB}_t}{\text{Index}_t}$$

Step 2 takes a risk measure of the underlying portfolio, defined at inception. The multiplier typically ranges from 2 for an emerging market fund to 12 for a government bond. Step 3 defines the maximum allocation (MA) to the portfolio on the basis of the algorithm:

$$\text{MA}_t = T_t \cdot \text{multiplier}$$

As another example of the DTM approach, one of the major banks has designed a US dollar denominated hedge fund index note, aiming to provide, over a six-year term, exposure to positive performance of the Hedge Fund Research Global Index (HFRX). This structured performance-linked product is coupled with reference to an index that targets managed exposure to HFRX. The index comprises notional exposures to:

- HFRX,
- Deposits with the same maturity as the note, and
- Loan units that enable the introduction of leverage.

The weightings of these three components in the index are determined monthly using a dynamic threshold mechanism. During the term of the note, the DTM is used to compare the actual level of the index to the minimum level consistent with returning investors' capital at maturity. At maturity of the note, investors receive 100 per cent of any positive performance of the index over the term. Capital protection applies only at maturity.

Minimum HFRX weighting within the index is zero and maximum weighting is 150 per cent. When the relative performance of the index is sufficiently strong, HFRX weighting is increased. If the relative performance of the index falls, the deposit weighting is increased. Among the disadvantages of this issue is a barrier function (see Chapter 9): if the index weighting for HFRX ever falls below zero, investors will not participate in its subsequent performance. Moreover, this particular structured instrument has a very restricted secondary market.

Notes

1 Sigma No. 7/2001, Swiss Re, Zurich.
2 D.N. Chorafas, *Stress Testing. Risk Management Strategies for Extreme Events*, Euromoney, London, 2003.
3 D.N. Chorafas, *The Management of Bond Investments and Trading of Debt*, Butterworth-Heinemann, London, 2005.
4 Merrill Lynch, *Global Research Highlights*, 18 June 2004.

11 Controlling the risk taken with structured products

11.1 Introduction

The concepts underpinning risk management have been discussed in Chapter 4. Subsequently, Chapter 8 brought to the reader's attention the omnipresent legal risk. All investments involve exposure, therefore private banks and asset managers would be well advised to ask themselves: What is the client's motivation for buying 'this structured product'? Does the transaction require particular attention to credit risk, liquidity risk, market risk or any other risk?

Indivisible from this question is another query: Are term sheets and descriptive notes designed to convey the particulars of this derivatives investment in a clear fashion? Has the client signed, or will he sign, standard documentation, including a master agreement? Can this transaction carry any special legal or operational considerations? Does it require any special attention?

There are plenty of questions that the issuer of a structured instrument should ask him or herself to avoid losing a client, and to avoid becoming tangled in legal risk. A most crucial question is whether this transaction warrants the allocation of supplemental reserves and/or credit capital, including the reason why this might be needed. As all investors, private bankers and asset managers should know, the value of all investments, and income derived from it, may go down, not only up.

- Changes in equity prices, interest rates and currency exchange rates may have adverse effects on an investor's portfolio.
- Certain events may result in the investor's worth rising or falling dramatically, and
- The more leveraged, or derivatives based, the instruments in the portfolio, the greater the risk of financial loss.

Under adverse market conditions, it is most unlikely that the investor will get back the full amount paid for certain securities. Further, past performance is not indicative of future results. Investors should fully appreciate that no projection or presentation made by the structured instrument's vendor is a guarantee of performance in the future.

Moreover, illiquid investments, such as real estate, many derivative financial instruments, structured products and private equity deals, may not be suitable for an investor's risk profile and/or cash needs. Illiquid investments cannot be turned into cash under other than fire sale conditions. Structured products, and other derivatives deals, may not be listed or traded on any exchange. Hence, as has already been emphasized,

- It may be difficult to realize the investment before its maturity,
- Or even to obtain reliable information about its market value.

Worse yet, included in most leveraged investment is the risk of total loss of capital. Wherever and whenever it is part of a deal, leverage can carry a high degree of exposure. A comparatively small movement in the value of the underlying can lead to a large change in the value of a position in the investor's portfolio. Volatility works against both the investor and for the investor. As Figure 11.1 suggests, whether we talk of private investors, institutional investors or asset managers in general, at the core of risk and return is *volatility*.

Certain derivative instruments, for instance, futures contracts where the investor is on margin, may involve the risk of losing not only the amount invested, but also additional amounts in the aftermath of margin calls by the broker. Transactions in derivatives that are not traded on a recognized stock exchange may only be suitable for people and companies who have experience in them and/or do not care about blood-letting. Illiquid investments such as many over-the-counter (OTC) derivatives

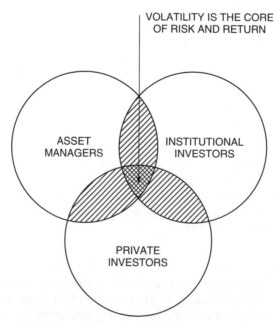

Figure 11.1 Functions of institutional investors, private investors and asset managers partly complement one another and partly overlap

may not be transferable. Therefore, investors are well advised to risk-weight their assets for:

- Credit volatility (section 11.4)
- Volatility in liquidity (section 11.6)
- Market volatility (section 11.7).

Either of them may reach new heights in the months and years ahead, hitting levels that are, at present, unfamiliar to investors. Investors must be familiar with the concept of *risk-weighted assets*. The problem is that, at present, the risk differentiation between various credit exposures is too crude, liquidity risk is a moving target and market risk is underestimated by metrics such as value at risk (VAR).[1] Moreover,

- Concentration risk is typically ignored,
- Forex risk and interest rate risk are not always well covered,
- The treatment of securitized tranches and risk mitigation is often half-baked, and
- The handling of business risk (see Chapter 3), insurance coverage and operational risk is frequently substandard.

Audits that I have done in connection to risk profile have shown that most of the structured instruments in a portfolio were not suitable for the investor who bought them, and that many investors had underestimated the risks being involved, including, but not limited to, interest rate risk, price risk, liquidity risk, redemption risk and credit risk.

To put it bluntly, investors should not purchase structured instruments, or any other type of investments, unless they understand the risks and have sufficient financial resources to bear the credit, market, liquidity, structure, redemption and other risks associated with the products they buy. Moreover, investors should intend to purchase and hold structured products to maturity. Mid-term unloading can create financial wounds.

11.2 Credit risk and exposure at default

Charles Munger, of Berkshire Hathaway, once said to the treasurer of an American company after having examined the company's holdings, 'This is a perfectly respectable BAA list. But for (your company) I don't want anything other than A1.' This is what every investor should think and say about the counterparty's dependability, when it comes to evaluating credit risk.

Chapter 4 explained that what underpins credit risk is the likelihood that the counterparty in a transaction may default. This does not mean that we must deal only with AAA-rated entities, if for no other reason than because as investors we can make more money by taking credit risk than by taking market risk. However, we should know the exposure we are assuming, and monetize it by:

- Calculating credit risk-adjusted return on capital, and
- Requiring an extra premium to cover assumed credit risk, even if the rating of the structured product's issuer is investment grade.

Risk-adjusted return on capital is a process rarely applied by investors, or for that matter by the credit institutions themselves. When there is too much money chasing too few debt instruments, credit risk standards bend. This has happened, for instance, after mid-2001 as issuance of bonds by Euroland corporations tapered off; a pattern fairly common across the credit quality spectrum.

Even after late 2002, when corporate bond spreads (see section 11.4) began to respond to the efforts made by management to repair their balance sheets, issuance of debt instruments only picked up mildly. Furthermore, differences in the issuing patterns of firms with high and low credit ratings really became apparent only after mid-2003, while the issuance of bonds by firms with subinvestment-grade ratings, that is *junk bonds*, increased significantly.

The fact that issuers with low and subinvestment-grade ratings have been accumulating additional debt is not necessarily raising financial stability concerns in the immediate future, but the story is different in the longer run. Based on European Central Bank (ECB) statistics, Figure 11.2 presents a most interesting pattern. The long leg of the distribution indicates that investors and lenders are assuming a fairly significant exposure at default (EAD).

Not everything is negative about non-investment credit debt. Junk bonds facilitate the financing of higher risk, but potentially highly profitable companies and projects, which might not otherwise have been undertaken. Non-investment-grade credit may also reflect that firms that found it more difficult to restructure their balance sheets on account of:

■ Inadequate profits, and
■ Limited cash flow

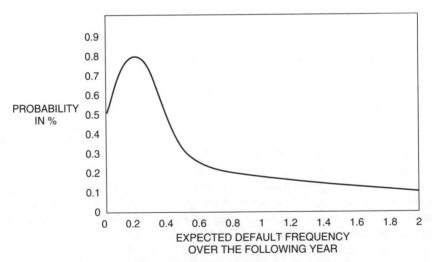

Figure 11.2 Expected default frequency distribution for European non-financial companies in March 2004. (Statistics by European Central Bank)

continue to have great capital needs. However, the fact that this doubtful debt is financed by banks and investors raises significant concerns in terms of EAD. Therefore, a proper methodology should fully account for:

- The magnitude of assumed credit risk, and
- Expected default frequency by the counterparty or counterparties.

The *annual default rate* is expressed as a percentage of formerly creditworthy enterprises that have become insolvent during the course of a given year. This percentage is the ratio of defaulted firms to the total number of companies certified as eligible for loans at the start of the year. Default rates should be computed by threshold established by independent credit rating agencies. An example of a one-year transition matrix in credit ratings is given in Table 11.1.

With all structured products, and even more so with those featuring guaranty of capital, the investor assumes the full credit risk of the issuer. He or she is also reliant on the issuer and the market maker, to fulfil their obligations in respect of the product. Hence, investors should carefully consider the credit quality of the issuer before deciding to invest in a given structured instrument.

While structured instruments are defined as *market risk* products, and have to be risk adjusted to reflect assumed exposure in interest rate, currency exchange rate or other underlying, there is also *credit risk* attached to them. It is therefore proper that the investor makes allowances for credit exposure in regard to all instruments in his or her portfolio, particularly those with:

- Longer maturity, and/or
- Other than AAA and AA issuers.

For instance, the credit risk of an *up and in* barrier option (see Chapter 9) is two-fold: premium, plus the risk that the counterparty will not perform if the option is exercised. While the investor purchasing the option will be faced with market risk, he or she will be looking to the option seller to perform once it comes into being. Here is where the credit risk generally lies. Therefore, the investor is well advised to do a worst case credit risk scenario.

Table 11.1 Transition matrix based on average one-year transition rates (in per cent)[a]

Initial rating	AAA	AA	A	BBB	BB	B	CCC	D
AAA	88.72	8.14	0.66	0.06	0.12	0.00	0.00	0.00
AA	0.68	88.31	7.59	0.62	0.06	0.14	0.02	0.00
A	0.09	2.19	87.74	5.32	0.71	0.25	0.01	0.06
BBB	0.02	0.31	5.61	81.95	5.00	1.10	0.11	0.18
BB	0.01	0.13	0.61	7.03	73.27	8.01	0.91	1.06
B	0.00	0.10	0.21	0.38	5.66	72.91	3.56	5.20
CCC	0.00	0.00	0.18	1.07	1.96	9.27	53.48	19.79

[a] Courtesy of Standard & Poor's.

All investors, and most particularly those assuming credit risk associated with derivative financial instruments, will be well advised to learn from the new capital adequacy framework (Basle II) by the Basle Committee on Banking Supervision. Basle II specifies a very important requirement in respect to the bank's internal estimates of EAD,[2] which can also be used by investors.

Although EAD concentrates on on-balance sheet transactions, off-balance sheet (OBS) can also be included. Trades in derivatives are an ever-present problem in determining drawn credit line amounts at the time of default. Several studies indicate that there are significant correlations between:

- EAD and residual maturity of the loan,
- EAD and the borrower's credit card rating,
- EAD and exposure to derivative instruments.

All three correlations are important to investors who include structured products in their portfolio. In banking, utilization of credit line by a counterparty for OBS transactions tends to increase the EAD significantly. Moreover, the longer the residual maturity of a loan, the greater the probability that:

- The borrower's credit rating will deteriorate,
- Its potential access to alternative financing sources will diminish, and
- Its continuing exposure to derivatives may damage the balance sheet, sometimes beyond repair.

A damaged creditworthiness also has a snowball effect. Faced with a borrower with a poor credit rating, a bank may insert clauses into the credit agreement that put the brakes on the borrower's use of an approved credit line in the event of derivatives losses. Sooner rather than later, the latter become known to the market and leads to deterioration of the borrower's rating.

Exposure at default estimates can be significantly simplified if dependencies on some of factors affecting creditworthiness, derivatives exposure and residual maturity are not taken into account. However, neglecting these dependencies greatly increases the unreliability of credit risk estimates being made. Hence, this is not an advisable policy. Investors, bankers and assets managers must be very pragmatic about assumed credit risk.

11.3   Credit risk transfer and hazard rate models

The discussion on credit risk in section 11.2 showed how important it is to draw attention to EAD embedded in a derivatives portfolio, whether this belongs to a bank, an institutional investor or a private individual. This statement is particularly true of derivative contracts because they are leveraged. A counterparty may not pay because of being:

- Unable, or
- Unwilling to do so.

This happened in both Russian and Asian crises of 1998 and 1997, respectively. To appreciate the magnitude of the risk it is important to keep in perspective that the amounts being involved are large, many times the capital of banks engaged in derivatives, even after the notional principal amount has been demodulated.[3] While so far pure credit losses in the derivatives have been small, it should not be forgotten that in the early years of derivatives trading counterparties have generally been of high quality. Competition in this business means that:

- Margins are being steadily reduced, and
- The creditworthiness of counterparties is falling, leading to a greater potential for losses.

All this is most relevant to institutional and private investors, because the structured instruments that they buy are based on derivative contracts. Whether or not it is explicitly stated, counterparty risk is an integral part not only in connection to the issuer and market maker, as stated so far, but also in relation to farther out counterparty risks that the issuer has assumed.

A lesson learned by proxy can provide insight. Take as an example classical loans at a time when lending to riskier credits increased sharply. In retail banking, lending to subprime retail borrowers has rocketed, and in business lending money has been given to property companies and other entities with non-investment-level rating.

Experts suggest that technically speaking this has been unavoidable, since better quality borrowers have turned their back on banks, preferring to tap the capital market. At the same time, however, EAD has increased. Moreover, in an effort to keep up their profits, banks started by having plenty of *retail assets*, such as mortgages (at razor-thin spreads) and credit cards, on their balance sheets, and they expanded their private banking activities, through structured products sold to retail investors.

Contrarians to this policy of feeding retail investors with structured products, and the risk embedded into them, point out that the most significant innovation with OTC derivatives has been the growth of *credit risk transfer*. The objective of instruments such as credit derivatives is to facilitate the trading and transfer of credit risk:[4]

- From loan originators,
- To investors willing to assume credit exposure.

Among business entities, for instance, insurance companies are seen as important risk-takers. Theoretically, but only theoretically, through credit derivatives credit risk is spread more evenly over the financial system, making it easier to absorb large corporate defaults. Practically, however, the credit derivatives market has raised a number of major concerns about the management of exposure. These are related to the:

- Ability of late-day credit risk players to absorb the shock of major bankruptcies,
- Effect of such bankruptcies on the solvency of insurers and other credit derivatives writers,
- Transparency of risks incurred by naive market players, as credit institutions increasingly transfer their risks to other market participants.

The third bullet points to retail investors and, to a lesser extent, to institutional investors. One of the experts participating in the research that led to this book pointed out that by adding structured products to their portfolio, retail investors became like the 'names' in old Lloyd's insurance, who were very badly burned when, in the early 1990s, poorly scrutinized insurance underwriting wiped out all the assets of many of Lloyd's names.[5] The only difference, this expert said, is that, as far as individual investors are concerned, most of the derivative instruments can zero out the money you invest in them, rather than your whole fortune.

In this connection, however, credit institutions accumulating toxic waste are faced with a concentration effect. Global OTC interest-rate derivative markets are known to be highly concentrated among certain banks, which face considerable strains from dynamic hedging activities. The concentration in these markets, where several large financial institutions have counterparty exposures, can:

■ Reduce the ability of a bank to position itself against market forces, and
■ Raise the vulnerability of the global financial system.

Credit risks can spill over through channels of contagion to other institutions in the global financial system who were more prudent in their exposure. Such risks could arise, for example, through correlation between US and euro-area long-term bond yields, which tends to be high at times of market stress, and also through unhedged interest rate exposures of some financial institutions, as well as because of exposures to hedge funds.

In the early part of the twenty-first century, in the aftermath of the market bubble of the late 1990s, low official interest rates in major currencies, as well as a recovery of risk appetite, encouraged substantial growth in the global hedge fund industry. As section 11.2 pointed out, faced with long-term government bond yields at historical lows and relatively cheap and abundant sources of liquidity, investors sought alternative instruments with:

■ Higher yields, and
■ Much greater risk.

For all these reasons, not only prudence in investments is highly recommended, but also the use of real-time information systems and modelling methodologies allowing investors, bankers and asset managers to be ahead of the curve. An example is *hazard rate* models, used to determine probability of default over a given time-frame. Such models are distinguished by the fact that data collected both over time and in a cross-sector analysis are processed simultaneously, a method known as the *panel data* approach.

Supervisory authorities use hazard rate methodology for macroprudential reasons, when assessing risks in the banking industry. Several hazard rate models are calibrated to a one-year forecast horizon, in estimating the probability of default over the coming twelve months. This is necessary but not sufficient. Eventually the hazard rate methodology needs to be extended well beyond the rolling year.

Basically, the concept underpinning the hazard rate is based on hypotheses regarding the likelihood of survivability of a given entity when confronted by

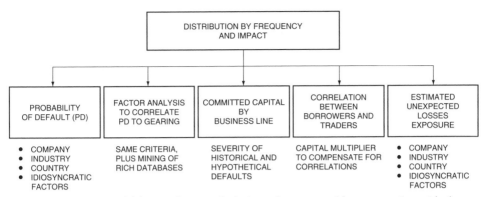

Figure 11.3 A model for stochastic calculation of unexpected losses, starting with the probability of default and following with business commitments

financial shocks. The probability of a credit institution defaulting is determined by means of bank-specific, regional and macroeconomic ratios, relating to the institution's:

■ Capital base,
■ Profitability,
■ Credit risk,
■ Market risk, and
■ Macroeconomic factors.

Taken together, these help in determining the development of the average probability of default over time. An interesting finding by supervisory authorities is that the capital base is by far the most important feature for expected default frequency discrimination; hence the emphasis that Basel II places on capital requirement. Figure 11.3 suggests a model for stochastic calculation of unexpected losses, starting with probability of default and ending by estimating unexpected losses exposure.

11.4   Credit risk volatility and bond spreads

The year 2004 has been the first since 1998 when upgrades exceeded downgrades in credit ratings. Standard & Poor's (S&P) had 101 upgrades and seventy-seven downgrades in that year, among 1443 non-sovereign bond issuers. Moreover, among these companies only two failed, compared with eight in 2003 and twenty in 2002. There were five 'fallen angels' (junk bond issuers) in 2004 versus eleven in 2003. But S&P has been much more prudent about 2005. Other independent rating agencies, too, think that in 2005 credit risk will probably deteriorate.

■ Like any other characteristic factor of an important commodity, credit risk is volatile.
■ The creditworthiness of any company or commodity changes over time, which is why credit rating is a steady process.

The rating of a company and its bonds does not have a one-to-one correspondence. As of November 2004 the credit risk involved in investing in European companies has been increasing, although bond market prices did not reflect this increase in credit exposure. 'Credit markets have run ahead of themselves and appear oblivious to the underlying fragility of creditworthiness', said Barbara Ridpath, S&P's chief credit officer for Europe.[6]

Credit risk volatility can be *general* or *specific* to a company, industry or country. Specific credit risk volatility is reflected in and expressed by *credit spreads* (more on this later). The reasons behind general credit volatility are that:

- The economic outlook changes from cloudy to bright, and vice versa, and
- There is a cyclical effect in terms of corporate profitability, which increases and decreases based on demand.

General market volatility and credit rating of debt issues correlate. In her doctorate research, Paraskevi Dimou, of Cass School of Business, City University, London (now with Joint Research Center, Ispra), has come up with an impressive family of curves with AAA to B-rated bonds, under observed equity volatility ranging between 25 and 50 per cent. The pattern is shown in Figure 11.4. As this family of default probability curves demonstrates:

- Equity volatility affects a great deal the default probability of rated bonds, and
- This is particularly pronounced in the longer term, over a ten-year horizon.

For greater precision, the statistics mapped into this family of curves are shown in Table 11.2.

If the market was efficient, then growing credit risk should have been immediately expressed in widening *bond spreads* between different credit ratings by bonds issuers. This is logical and normal since the prices of bonds reflect the probability that bondholders will not be repaid in case of default. Slow response to credit facts is an anomaly in market pricing.

Bond spreads exist, but they do not work themselves out immediately. There is always market latency in factoring-in assumed risk. When the probability of the issuer's default is higher, its bonds trade at a price that is lower than the price of highly rated companies. Even the debt instrument of the latter firms traded lower than those of a Western government's bond of comparable:

- Maturity, and
- Coupon.

The difference in price, which translates into a difference in yield, is the corporate bond yield spread, which measures the additional premium required by investors to accept incurring a credit risk, in addition to the market risk associated with the interest rate. The *bond spread* provides the link between corporate bond yield and market volatility. A *real bond spread* is derived from:

- Market prices of credit risk-free bonds,
- Computed on the basis of the real interest rate.

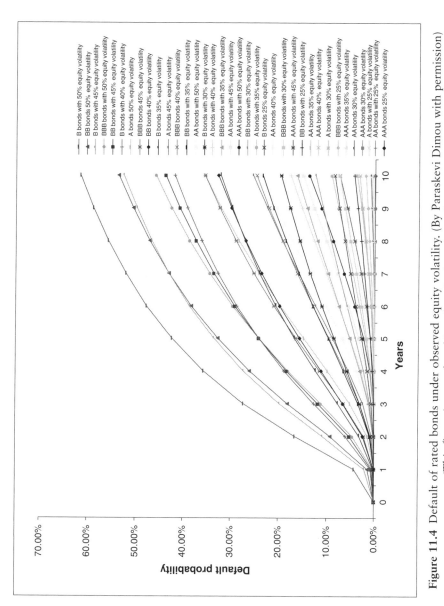

Figure 11.4 Default of rated bonds under observed equity volatility. (By Paraskevi Dimou with permission) (This figure is reproduced in colour in the colour plate section.)

Table 11.2 Equity volatility impacts upon the probability of default of a Company's debt, beyond bond rating

Years	AAA bonds 30% equity volatility	AAA bonds 35% equity volatility	AAA bonds 40% equity volatility	AAA bonds 45% equity volatility	AAA bonds 50% equity volatility	AA bonds 30% equity volatility	AA bonds 35% equity volatility	AA bonds 40% equity volatility	AA bonds 45% equity volatility	AA bonds 50% equity volatility	A bonds 30% equity volatility	A bonds 35% equity volatility	A bonds 40% equity volatility	A bonds 45% equity volatility	A bonds 50% equity volatility
0	0.00%	0.00%	0.00%	0.00%	0.00%	0.00%	0.00%	0.00%	0.00%	0.00%	0.00%	0.00%	0.00%	0.00%	0.00%
1	0.00%	0.00%	0.00%	0.00%	0.00%	0.00%	0.00%	0.00%	0.00%	0.00%	0.00%	0.00%	0.00%	0.01%	0.04%
2	0.00%	0.00%	0.00%	0.00%	0.02%	0.00%	0.00%	0.01%	0.05%	0.22%	0.00%	0.02%	0.16%	0.50%	1.43%
3	0.00%	0.00%	0.01%	0.05%	0.24%	0.00%	0.02%	0.10%	0.48%	1.43%	0.02%	0.24%	1.05%	2.38%	5.09%
4	0.00%	0.01%	0.07%	0.28%	0.97%	0.01%	0.11%	0.46%	1.57%	3.75%	0.14%	0.85%	2.75%	5.34%	9.85%
5	0.00%	0.04%	0.26%	0.82%	2.30%	0.04%	0.35%	1.15%	3.25%	6.80%	0.38%	1.82%	4.99%	8.79%	14.82%
6	0.01%	0.11%	0.63%	1.67%	4.12%	0.11%	0.76%	2.14%	5.35%	10.21%	0.77%	3.07%	7.49%	12.38%	19.63%
7	0.02%	0.24%	1.17%	2.82%	6.29%	0.23%	1.32%	3.37%	7.68%	13.72%	1.27%	4.50%	10.09%	15.90%	24.12%
8	0.05%	0.45%	1.88%	4.18%	8.69%	0.40%	2.02%	4.77%	10.13%	17.21%	1.87%	6.01%	12.68%	19.27%	28.25%
9	0.09%	0.73%	2.73%	5.72%	11.20%	0.63%	2.82%	6.27%	12.61%	20.58%	2.54%	7.57%	15.20%	22.45%	32.03%
10	0.16%	1.08%	3.70%	7.36%	13.76%	0.90%	3.70%	7.82%	15.06%	23.81%	3.25%	9.13%	17.61%	25.42%	35.49%

Years	BBB bonds 30% equity volatility	BBB bonds 35% equity volatility	BBB bonds 40% equity volatility	BBB bonds 45% equity volatility	BBB bonds 50% equity volatility	BB bonds 30% equity volatility	BB bonds 35% equity volatility	BB bonds 40% equity volatility	BB bonds 45% equity volatility	BB bonds 50% equity volatility	B bonds 30% equity volatility	B bonds 35% equity volatility	B bonds 40% equity volatility	B bonds 45% equity volatility	B bonds 50% equity volatility
0	0.00%	0.00%	0.00%	0.00%	0.00%	0.00%	0.00%	0.00%	0.00%	0.00%	0.00%	0.00%	0.00%	0.00%	0.00%
1	0.00%	0.00%	0.01%	0.09%	0.36%	0.00%	0.02%	0.12%	0.50%	1.37%	0.03%	0.24%	0.74%	2.04%	4.20%
2	0.02%	0.23%	0.74%	2.14%	4.55%	0.17%	0.93%	2.31%	5.17%	9.17%	0.89%	3.08%	5.99%	10.84%	16.58%
3	0.24%	1.23%	2.97%	6.45%	11.20%	0.94%	3.31%	6.50%	11.83%	18.13%	3.01%	7.66%	12.67%	19.84%	27.35%
4	0.78%	2.97%	6.08%	11.46%	17.98%	2.28%	6.42%	11.18%	18.31%	26.02%	5.68%	12.38%	18.84%	27.37%	35.74%
5	1.62%	5.12%	9.50%	16.40%	24.16%	3.93%	9.68%	15.69%	24.08%	32.66%	8.42%	16.72%	24.17%	33.54%	42.34%
6	2.65%	7.43%	12.90%	20.99%	29.63%	5.70%	12.84%	19.83%	29.12%	38.23%	11.04%	20.59%	28.75%	38.65%	47.66%
7	3.80%	9.76%	16.15%	25.18%	34.43%	7.48%	15.80%	23.56%	33.50%	42.96%	13.47%	24.01%	32.69%	42.94%	52.04%
8	5.00%	12.03%	19.20%	28.97%	38.67%	9.21%	18.54%	26.91%	37.35%	47.01%	15.70%	27.04%	36.12%	46.60%	55.72%
9	6.21%	14.20%	22.04%	32.39%	42.41%	10.87%	21.07%	29.94%	40.73%	50.53%	17.74%	29.74%	39.13%	49.76%	58.87%
10	7.41%	16.26%	24.66%	35.49%	45.74%	12.44%	23.38%	32.67%	43.74%	53.61%	19.60%	32.16%	41.79%	52.52%	61.58%

The real interest rate is established after deducting the inflation rate from the market interest rate. Corporates usually offer a premium over the real bond spread, with corporate bond spreads computed as the difference between seven to ten-year corporate bond yields and seven to ten-year government bond yields.

In the background of bond spreads lies the fact that a company with volatile assets is more likely to reach the conditions of default, since there is a higher likelihood that the value of its assets will be lower than the value of its debt. When asset volatility is high, bond investors require additional compensation in the form of higher yield spread over the market rate. This helps in establishing a positive relationship between corporate:

- Bond spreads, and
- Asset volatility.

Practically all of these basic notions are forgotten with credit risk calculations in connection with structured products, where debt is king. Yet, as a study by the ECB points out, the probability of default is related to the firm's indebtedness. The latter can be measured by the debt-to-equity ratio. When the size of a company's debt is high compared with the value of its equity, it becomes difficult for the firm to meet its debt obligations.[7]

11.5   A case study on General Motors

Because structured products are most complex in their design, they are capable of hiding the credit volatility underpinning them. A similar statement is valid about market risk. Their long time-frame, amounting to six or more years to maturity, makes them most exposed to market volatility. This is something that neither their issuers nor their investors can do anything about, short of selling them at cut price.

Even if the debt underlying a structured product belongs to a big corporate name, the impact of credit volatility can be devastating. Take the General Motors (GM) bonds as an example. In March 2005, the likelihood of downgrading GM's and General Motors Acceptance Corporation's (GMAC's) debt by rating agencies created a big soft spot in the globalized higher interest and high-risk debt bubble.

Part of the problem faced by investors lay in the fact that in 2005 GM reached the state of having more pensioners than employees, with an evident impact on its financial condition. The company's US car workforce had shrunk by 70 per cent since 1980, while GM lost a big chunk of its market share. On 26 February 2005, in an article under the headline 'Thunderstorm over Detroit', Zürich's Neue Züricher Zeitung forecast dramatic turbulence as:

- GM prepared to refinance or pay $44.7 billion in debt in 2006, and
- Ford has also been faced with refinancing or paying $37.1 billion on its $174 billion total debt.

One of the outstanding challenges of an economy based on debt lies in the ability of its companies and its citizens to issue new debt in order to pay a large share of old debt which becomes due. Depending on the time when this happens, debt refinancing may need to be done amidst rising interest rates and falling credit ratings. This is a situation at the edge of chaos, because

- If a company cannot generate enough cash to face its obligations,
- Then its troubles become a vicious cycle that can spread over the economy like an oil slick.

Because they are faced with greater credit risk, in an efficient and *transparent* market bondholders require a higher premium as compensation for the risk of default with which they are faced. This makes corporate bond spreads linked to the debt-to-equity ratio. The underlying concept runs parallel to the Basle II approach to credit risk measurement, which represents a significant step forward in banking regulation because it is suitable for implementation by banks of different:

- Sizes,
- Business goals, and
- Risk profiles.

Based on practical results obtained through credit risk studies, the internal ratings-based (IRB) approach integrates credit exposure through a model that establishes the likelihood of a borrowing company being unable to repay its debt. The outcome of whether or not the company is able to meet its obligations is determined by the ratio of:

- Market value of its assets taken equal to its capitalization, and
- Nominal value of its debt, which is computed through an accruals method.

In brief, the value of the firm's assets is modelled as a variable that changes over time, partly because of the impact of random shocks. Default is assumed to occur when a firm's assets are insufficient to cover its debt obligations. With the time-frame at one year, the corresponding measure of credit risk is the probability of the firm's default.

While, however, the regulators have developed a rational approach able to account for credit exposure, the markets are not necessarily rational. According to the experts, the sharp tightening of corporate bond spreads in 2004 has been due more to a steep decline in new issues than to any improvement in the quality of the bonds on offer. Weak issuance has pushed investments lower down the ratings scale in search of yield.

- This has been good for debt issuers,
- But investors have not been adequately compensated for default risk.

After the equities bubble market burst, the spreads of long-term corporate bond yields over government bond yields became a barometer of investors' response to assumed risk. The spread narrowed considerably between early October 2002 and April 2003. Compared with the peak reached on October 2002, the differential between the yields on long-term bonds issued by BBB-rated corporations and government bond yields in the euro area narrowed by 110 basis points by early April 2003.

- Between early October and late November 2002, this narrowing of spreads mirrored a rebound in the stockmarket.
- Subsequently, however, stock prices and corporate bond spreads started to decouple.

The aforementioned developments took place in an environment in which macroeconomic data releases gave mixed signals, with some corporate earnings forecasts being revised downwards. At the same time, geopolitical tensions were intensified, contributing to the continued downward pressure on stock prices. The impact of major credit risk events, however, is a different pattern. When GM's credit rating came to the edge of being downgraded, in early March 2005, both its equity and the price of its bonds fell sharply.

11.6   Liquidity risk in an ownership society

Liquidity risk in connection to structured instruments was discussed in Chapter 10. The objective of the present section is to take a more general perspective identifying exposure associated with *liquidity risk* in an ownership society. Because it is so dependent on issuance and placement of debt instruments, an ownership society is most vulnerable to the drying up of *market liquidity*, with resulting potential inability to execute financial transactions, over a short period, in the desired:

- Date,
- Type of instrument, and
- Size of transaction.

For instance, in the specific case of credit risk transfer the desire for liquidity could include a significant reduction of exposure by protection sellers following some company news, intermediaries adjusting hedges following a large price movement, and issuers of securitizations seeking a funding source in a hurry.

Classical economics books advise that, in the more general case, market liquidity is synonymous with the ease with which financial instruments can be traded. As far as the better known (and transparent) debt instruments are concerned, market liquidity depends on the:

- Tightness,
- Depth, and
- Resilience of a market.

All three contribute to the immediate executability of orders. A market is *tight* if limited buying and selling orders are on hand, or new orders cannot be executed without triggering major price movements. Lack of transparency increases this risk, as buyers do not come forward, fearing unexpected losses.

A market is *deep* if orders placed in it reach a volume that suffices to execute even large volumes without exerting marked price effects. It is *resilient* if price movements triggered by excess demand, or excess supply, attract new orders that tend to offset prevailing imbalances.

Typically, the liquidity of a market is measured through indicators of trading activity. However, with OTC transactions and massive sales of structured products to private banking clients and institutional investors, a better methodology for measuring market liquidity is necessary, beyond trading activity in the exchanges. For instance, in a market with a central order book for electric trading, tightness may be judged by:

■ The bid/ask spread in bank quotations, and
■ The total volume of buying or selling OTC.

The downside of this approach is that there are no precise records on these two variables in OTC trading, which accounts for the bulk of derivatives transactions. It has to be admitted that the tools available for measuring market liquidity have not kept up with other developments that have taken place in finance over the last two decades.

Liquidity metrics are a little better on a case-by-case basis. One way to judge a bank's liquidity is to take a close look at the liquidity of its portfolio positions. During the past half a dozen years, this seems to be deteriorating, as documented in statistics by the ECB.

■ The growth in equity holdings, which are exchange traded and liquid, has fallen sharply, and
■ These have been overtaken by securities other than shares, including debt instruments and illiquid derivatives, to the ratio of 2 to 1.

This trend can have wide ramifications in the banking industry's assets and liabilities, including risks associated with interbank positions. To appreciate this argument it is important to keep in mind that risks faced by credit institutions in their interbank positions are different on the side of assets and on that of liabilities.

Liquidity shocks can be quickly transmitted within the banking system through the interbank market, making mandatory regular monitoring of interbank linkages. However, the simple mapping of interbank relationships is not sufficient to measure *contagion risk* in interbank markets. The proper measurement of contagion:

■ Calls for detailed consolidated data on each bank's interbank exposures, and
■ Requires taking into account the different risk mitigation measures, such as collateralization, netting and hedging.

Liquidity is the fluid through which interbank asset positions create a channel for contagion by means of credit risk and other exposures. Interbank liability positions expose institutions to *funding risk*. Ready access to a large pool of interbank lenders reduces the risk of a loss of liquidity for financially sound institutions in the case of withdrawal of funds by a creditor bank. Moreover, cross-border interbank credit risk implies an increase in cross-border creditor exposure.

All this points to correlations in market liquidity. Several studies indicate that, to permit a more comprehensive assessment of the impact of crises on the functionality of markets, price and volatility movements due to crises and panics must be considered in both a national and global portfolio context. Decisions by investors on the size of equity, debt or derivatives holding will depend on both:

- The expected level and volatility of returns on domestic holdings, and
- Their relationship to the risk and return characteristics of investments made in the global market.

Up to a point, global price and yield correlations can be described in the form of a number of factors that could apply not merely to crises but also at more normal times. Research and analysis show that short-term price fluctuations are mostly synchronous, and a rise in volatility is normally accompanied by closer correlations.

Other studies document that crises in global equity markets hit most particularly the less liquid markets of smaller countries, especially the emerging economies. For example, as reported in the Monthly Bulletin of the Deutsche Bundesbank, during the 1997 Asian crisis, the daily volatility of returns on shares in the entire German equity market rose from 1.25 per cent to over 3 per cent. By contrast, in the Asian emerging economies it almost quadrupled.

During periods of ebbing market confidence or outright turbulence, observed international correlations tend to increase significantly. This pattern implies that the diversification advantages of a globally based equity portfolio may be severely curtailed under market stress. Such findings are most relevant to risk management, because they indicate that exposure can snowball if market players, in response to the outbreak of a crisis, try to exit simultaneously through the same door.

The lesson to be retained from the preceding paragraphs is the growing need for awareness of financial risks, and for assessing liquidity exposure more realistically. This is written in the understanding that many market players often fail to gauge correctly risks posed by financial assets and correlations between the different risk categories. The draining of liquidity causes enormous disruption, and attempts to mitigate risks by selling affected securities dramatically depress their price.

11.7 General and specific market risk

Every company is exposed to market risks, including changes in interest rates, foreign currency exchange rates and marketable equity security prices. One way to mitigate these risks is to use derivative financial instruments, but prudence requires that derivatives are used for hedging open positions and not for speculative purposes (see Chapter 9).

Banks, as well as manufacturing firms, hedge the currency risks of lending (or investments) denominated in foreign currencies, with foreign currency borrowings, currency forward contracts and currency interest rate swaps. However, gains and losses on foreign currency investments are not necessarily offset by corresponding losses and gains on the related hedging instruments.

Even a well-studied hedging programme helps to reduce, but does not entirely eliminate the impact of foreign currency exchange rate movements. A similar statement is valid with regard to interest rates. Hedging is often asymmetric, as the German

Metallgesellschaft found to its dismay when it almost went bankrupt because of an inordinate exposure in oil delivery contracts, in the USA, hedged imperfectly.

Market risk can be classified into *general* and *specific*. General market risk is connected to the whole market activity. For instance, it can be expressed as risk associated with the volatility of an equity index. Specific market risk reflects the price behaviour of one company. This may work in synergy with general market risk or it may exhibit a countertrend.

The *general market risk* is relatively easy to understand. In the case of interest rates, for example, the general risk results from the change in the yield curve because of higher interest rates than those contracted, or from changes characterizing the stock-market index, exposure connected to currency exchange, and so on. In principle, changes in prices of key commodities with wide consumption have direct, indirect and second level effects, as shown in the block diagram in Figure 11.5.

One issue that is not clearly defined by the 1996 Market Risk Amendment[8] is specific market risk. In a way that follows financial reporting practice in America, the Amendment says that there is a link between specific risk and the standardized method of reporting exposure to regulators, but specific market risk is not defined in unambiguous terms; rather, it is lumped together into a VAR measure.

Specific risk is connected to an instrument, and/or the issuer of the instrument. In the case of assumed counterparty risk, different issuers and different debt instruments have different spreads. Such spreads are defined by the market on the basis of the information that it possesses on that particular instrument, or on the rating of the issuer and associated rumours.

The discussion in section 11.4 indicated that other factors, too, can influence the spread. To these should be added the possibility of cornering the market, whereby a

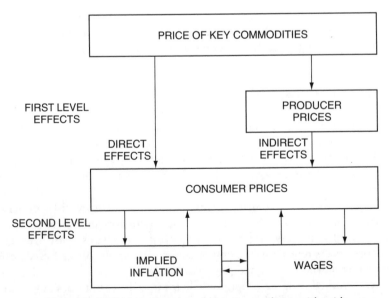

Figure 11.5 Changes in price of key commodities with wide consumption have direct, indirect and second level effects

small number of players impact on market price(s). Liquidity reasons relating to the type of instrument, which may be independent of the issuer, also add their weight.

Apart from specific market risk concerning a company or instrument, there is also specific market risk by industry and by country. The transport industry or the utilities industry, for example, may behave erratically while, in general, the stockmarket shows a positive trend. In the opinion of some experts, the best way to describe specific market risk is as a reference to:

- What is not explained by general market movements,
- But is specific to a single issue or entity.

Different financial institutions, and different analysts within the same bank, use their own criteria in analysing general and specific market risk. No two methods are exactly the same, and none of those available is definitely better than its alternatives.

Moreover, in terms of volatility, specific market risk can be significantly greater than general market risk, because it is influenced by so many factors involving unknowns. A good example is *event risk*, which can happen at any moment. Therefore, tier-one banks have developed expertise on how to simulate event risk.

Behind general market risk are all sorts of uncertainties in regard to price movements of equities, debt, interest rates, currencies, base metals, precious metals, energy and other commodities. Expected price changes in different commodities may be quite positive to some investors, but in the general case they can cause:

- Capital losses, or
- Lower income in the future.

The market is no zero sum game, and to be ahead of the curve investors, bankers, treasurers and market makers, among others, must closely study macroeconomic impact, short-term volatilities, non-linearity between profit and loss and risk factors, instability in correlations, impact of defaults and credit cycles, and other factors such as yield curve changes and spreads.

This is a most challenging task in connection to complex financial instruments, because our current know-how, tools and methods have not been made for them. Complexity means that, in a growing number of cases, market risk is morphing into credit risk, and vice versa. This is true of both general and specific market risk. Moreover, the global financial system evolves:

- From one dominated by banks
- To one with deep and liquid capital markets.

With this major structural change credit risk becomes market-tied. Unknowns embedded in structural changes turn some of our time-honoured notions of the economy and of finance on their head. Structural changes increase both price volatility and transborder financial flows. Structural changes can be costly in capital adequacy terms. For instance, experts think that loan loss provisioning may become unstable because of market risk morphing into credit risk, as well as because of growing derivatives exposure.

11.8 Stockmarket bubbles and damage control

'I don't think there is anyone in Congress who is supportive of doing anything meaningful about the bubble', said Dr Henry Kaufman. 'The Fed and the chairman really don't believe in selection intervention in the marketplace . . . I know of no time in the post-World War II period, when so much of the economic well-being of the United States and the world, hinges on the level of American stock prices'.[9]

In the late go-go 1990s, when this statement was made, the problem was not just hedge funds, although there has been a lot of focus on what hedge funds were doing and on what might be the aftermath. Most large financial institutions – commercial and investment banks, securities houses and insurance companies – conducted so much proprietary trading and positioning, that:

- The extent of their exposure was most difficult to quantify, and
- The accounting profession had not caught up with the challenge of measuring a mounting wave of general market risk.

Even if hedge funds had been to slow down their leveraging, which they did not, the gap between real and virtual economy created by stock price inflation would not have been filled by traditional financial institutions. At the same time, in the late 1990s, risk-taking was rapidly moving into the open credit market through credit derivatives and other (then) novel instruments.

Yet, precedence to these late 1990s conditions and their possible aftereffect could be found in the recent past. In terms of stockmarket bubbles the precedence was the September 1987 burst of the US stockmarket followed by that of other countries. Debt instruments, too, faced several headwinds, reminiscent of:

- The junk bonds bubble which, in the late 1980s, devastated American savings and loans, and
- The 1994 precipice which engulfed many highly leveraged investors, state agencies and well-known hedge funds, after the Federal Reserve raised interest rates in six consecutive steps.

The currency market was not sheltered and this had an impact on equities. Here, a precedence could be found in September 1992, when the European Exchange Rate Mechanism (ERM) fell apart, the British pound dropped out of the ERM, and George Soros made a profit between £800 million and £1 billion.

Damage control is complicated by collateral effects. Disruption in equities alone normally produces inertia among traders and other professionals. With the September 1992 events, however, bond and currency instability compounded the problem and made risk management so much more complex, particularly in the equity derivatives market.

Market makers in equity derivatives[10] tend to be option writers, and therefore the market as a whole tends to loop back. This is alright if the market's volatility is below what is assumed in the implied volatility of the option, since *delta hedging* with futures could make the option writer money. (For delta hedging and the 'Greeks' see section 11.9.) By contrast, if volatility flares up option writers who are short of volatility are faced with a difficult choice:

- They can try to weather the storm on the assumption that volatility will come down again, or
- They can cover themselves and buy back volatility by purchasing options from other issuers.

Either way, they lose money as higher implied volatility increases option deltas and sometimes the move is dramatic. This is one of the most challenging problems in risk control because, to a significant extent, changes in volatility are characterized by uncertainty, as far as their prognostication is concerned.

Algorithms from applied mathematics can help in keeping exposure under control, provided banks, treasurers, traders and investors are alert to the signals that these models give; but, while necessary, models are not enough. A rigorous policy of damage control requires:

- A thorough structure of checks and balances,
- Properly defined procedures as well as system engineering solutions.

A sound approach to risk control is to allocate limits to investment positions and trading lines. For instance, well-managed banks ensure that equity trading limits are established by operating unit and trading line, down to the detail of the trader. The risk associated with each limit is measured on the basis of:

- Position, and
- Market price.

With exchange-traded equities marking-to-market is preferable to marking-to-model, because stocks are traded and have an active market, which is not necessarily the case with equity derivatives. The best way to compute the sensitivity of present value per individual equity is to consider thresholds of change in market price. Such thresholds are usually established in percentage change and address both:

- Equity risk, and
- Currency risk (for international investments).

The value of portfolio and trading positions changes owing to equity price and currency exchange volatility. The two must be taken in unison when comparing results to reference currency. This is valid for each investment position and for the entire portfolio.

In any risk management system, special attention should be placed to the *worst case*, with scenarios associated with it. With most commodities, the worst case for investing and/or for trading is the largest change in market prices, based on historical references or hypothetical values. Both should be taken into account in stress tests. Retroactive walkthroughs provide useful lessons, with worst case results compared to limits established for price risk.

11.9   Risk management and the 'Greeks'

In the background of all hedging, and of the metrics used to measure its effectiveness, is the price change relationship between the option and the underlying futures. A critical question is:

■ How will the changing price of an option relate to changes in the price of the underlying futures contract?

Experience teaches that this relationship is usually not one-to-one. In most cases we do not know its exact pattern. This leads to another query:

■ What kind of metrics can we use to gauge change in the price of the derivatives vehicle for a given change in the futures price?

To appreciate the answer to this question one must understand that the option's price consists of *intrinsic value* (if any) and *time value*. Intrinsic value is the value of the option if it were exercised immediately. Time value is the time to the option's maturity or expiration. The greater the intrinsic value, the more responsive the option is to change in futures price. The *delta* metric addresses itself to this price dependency.

An option whose price changes, for instance, by $10 for every $20 change in the price of the underlying, has a delta of 0.5. Delta rises towards 1 for options deep in-the-money and approaches 0 (zero) for deep out-of-the-money, but it is never negative. Delta is the first derivative of the payoff function F(x):

$$\frac{dF(x)}{dx}$$

Delta is also known as *hedge ratio* because it expresses the ratio of underlying to option contracts, for a neutral hedge. *Delta neutral* positions are established through hedging.

Another important metric is *gamma*. It gives the change in the delta of the option induced by a small change in the price of the underlying asset. Gamma is the first derivative of delta, and the second derivative of F(x):

$$\frac{d^2F(x)}{dx^2}$$

As second derivative of F(x), gamma expresses *the rate of change*. If an option has a delta of 75 and a gamma of 10, then the option's expected delta will be:

■ 85 if the underlying goes up 100 basis points, and
■ 65 if the underlying goes down 100 base points.

Still another important metric is *theta*. It quantifies the loss of computed value for each day with no movement in the price of the underlying. It makes sense to follow both *change* and *no change* in an option's price. Theta exposure is closely related to

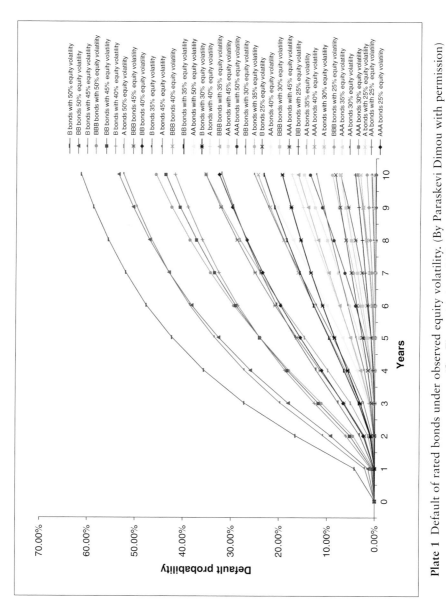

Plate 1 Default of rated bonds under observed equity volatility. (By Paraskevi Dimou with permission) (See Figure 11.4, p. 239)

gamma exposure. Theoretically, when hedging delta and gamma risk, theta exposure is also hedged.

■ The theta factor is sometimes referred to as the option's time decay.
■ Basically, it reflects price stability, rather than turbulence.

Also theoretically, a delta-gamma neutral position tends to be theta neutral as well, but many financial analysts consider this a weak proposition. The best approach is to have the underlying hypothesis evaluated in real-time and the position hedged according to the obtained results.

Another one of the Greeks is *kappa* or vega. As a measurement, it addresses the impact of fairly small changes in volatility affecting a given position. For instance, it is quite helpful to be able to measure the change in the option value for 1 per cent change in volatility.

Longer dated options have a higher kappa because they are more sensitive to changes in *implied volatility* (see Chapter 4). An option with a kappa 0.20 can be expected to gain (lose) in theoretical value 20 per cent of each percentage point increase (decrease) in volatility. Kappa-neutral positions, if ever they exist, are supposed to make investors indifferent to shift in volatility parameters; but they also raise the question 'What for?'

Rho reflects options carrying cost. It gives the change in the option price per 1 per cent change in *interest rate*. The sensitivity of an option's computed value to change in interest rate is estimated through rho.

Moreover, since all options have a degree of exposure to carrying costs, *weights* need to be set in a portfolio for neutrality in delta, gamma, theta, kappa and rho. Weights are, however, subjective and they change with time. Therefore, they must not only be chosen carefully but also be carefully adjusted.

Although it is not part of the Greeks, it is important to add to this list the beta metric. *Beta* stands for volatility and it is expressed as standard deviation of price distribution. An individual stock has its beta.

In conclusion, the Greeks are useful metrics contributing to prudential risk management. They carry a message such as 'Positions that are long gamma are those that benefit if options prices go up.' Notice that the only way to be long gamma is to buy options, but:

■ Most market makers are option sellers, and
■ Therefore, they short both volatility and gamma.

In their wish to cover short gamma positions by buying options, professionals tend to drive market volatility even higher. The same happens when people are panicking and try to obtain cover at any cost. In fact, some of the more conservative houses would push their derivative books into taking short-term cover, regardless of how expensive this may be.

Several market makers, traders and speculators short volatility by choice, because hedging it out is expensive. Given that short-term volatility is usually higher than longer volatility, rolling over short-term options to cover the gamma of a long-term option usually eats into profits. The same is true about using out-of-the-money options, the volatility of which is invariably higher than in-the-money options.

Notes

1 D.N. Chorafas, *Modelling the Survival of Financial and Industrial Enterprises. Advantages, Challenges, and Problems with the Internal Rating-Based (IRB) Method*, Palgrave/Macmillan, London, 2002.
2 D.N. Chorafas, *Economic Capital Allocation with Basel II. Cost and Benefit Analysis*, Butterworth-Heinemann, London, 2004.
3 D.N. Chorafas, *Stress Testing. Risk Management Strategies for Extreme Events*, Euromoney, London, 2003.
4 D.N. Chorafas, *Credit Derivatives and the Management of Risk*, New York Institute of Finance, New York, 2000.
5 D.N. Chorafas, *Managing Credit Risk, Volume 2. The Lessons of VAR Failures and Imprudent Exposure*, Euromoney, London, 2000.
6 *Financial Times*, 15 December 2004.
7 D.N. Chorafas, *Economic Capital Allocation with Basel II. Cost and Benefit Analysis*, Butterworth-Heinemann, London, 2004.
8 D.N. Chorafas, *The 1996 Market Risk Amendment. Understanding the Marking-to-Model and Value-at-Risk*, McGraw-Hill, Burr Ridge, IL, 1998.
9 *EIR*, 13 August 1999.
10 D.N. Chorafas, *Credit Derivatives and the Management of Risk*, New York Institute of Finance, New York, 2000.

Part 4

Case studies with the three main classes of structured products

12 Fixed income structured products

12.1 Introduction

From an investment viewpoint, *fixed income structured products* (FISPs) are comparable to unsecured unsubordinated debt by the issuer (for the definition of FISP see section 12.2). Usually, although not always, FISPs have debt instruments as underlying. With the exception of products involving equities, FISPs could be compared to classical bonds offered by the issuer. Up to a point, the underlying is the same; however, the result is different because the capital protection offered by FISPs has a cost. In terms of popularity, there is no free lunch. Today:

- The different types of classical bonds master a huge market share.
- By contrast, the market for FISPs is fairly small, but their proponents say that it is growing at rapid pace.

This is a statement that should be considered with caution. Caution is also necessary in deciding about investing in FISPs, for reasons to be examined in this chapter. Notice, too, that the reference to 'fixed income' is a misnomer, because FISPs are derivatives and derivatives are versatile. The resulting products may:

- Feature fixed or variable interest rate,
- Combine bond-type and equity-type characteristics, or
- Target credit risk associated with debt issuance.

Still, as far as this whole class of financial instruments is concerned (essentially the text in this chapter and in Chapter 13), it is advisable to stick with the market term of *fixed income derivatives*, even though this is not a precise title. Furthermore, there is a certain overlap between FISPs and equity-based structured products (discussed in Chapters 14 and 15), as shown in Figure 12.1.

To appreciate better the place of FISPs in the current market, it is advisable to start with the fundamentals underpinning debt instruments. Bonds used to be a fairly straightforward investment vehicle, appealing to relatively conservative longer term investors. They provided their holder with a regular income in the form of an interest rate or yield. In addition, assuming that no credit risk event took place, they assured the repayment of initially invested capital if held to maturity.[1]

In the general case, however, bondholders took a certain amount of credit risk, depending on the issuer's credit rating, or events taking place after the debt instrument's

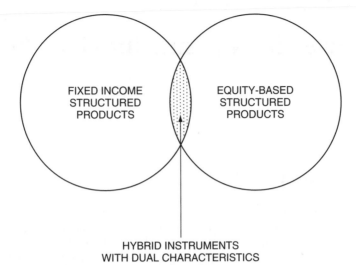

FIXED INCOME
STRUCTURED
PRODUCTS

EQUITY-BASED
STRUCTURED
PRODUCTS

HYBRID INSTRUMENTS
WITH DUAL CHARACTERISTICS

Figure 12.1 Fixed income structured products and
equity-based structured instruments have a certain amount
of overlap

issuance; events that had a negative impact on original credit rating. Securitized and/or structured debt alters this equation. Credit risk embedded in a pool of loans serving as underlying always remains an exposure, and to this is added the credit risk of the structured instrument's issuer, if the latter provides a guarantee for capital repayment at maturity (more on this later).

In which markets are FISPs being traded? There is no unique answer to this query. Some FISPs are pure *money market* products. Others are much more complex, also covering forex (see Chapter 16), oil, base metals and other commodities markets. FISPs are traded over-the-counter (OTC). With this in mind:

■ Their market has no resemblance to the classical money market and capital market.
■ The rapid evolution of hybrid structured instruments sees to it that traditional boundaries between markets are no longer as clear as they used to be.

One of the arguments frequently made in regard to classical debt instruments is that they offer their holder no opportunity to profit from the success of a company, as equities do. Investment banks that have designed FISPs as alternatives to traditional bond investments say that their offerings correct this shortcoming. Theoretically, but only theoretically, their buyer:

■ Enjoys a higher return, and
■ Depending on the instrument he or she buys, may even participate in corporate profitability.

Practically, this argument is highly situational, and even at best conditions it is only half true. As shown in Chapter 11, the low interest rates of the first years of twenty-first century, together with low-lying equity markets, led investors to look for attractive potential returns in what became known as alternative investments;[2] but this in no way means that alternative investments have no caveats and no downsides.

Before closing these introductory notes on FISPs, it is appropriate to bring to the reader's attention the fact that, as far as the European financial market is concerned, they are part of the *European medium term notes* (EMTN) universe. So are the *constant proportion portfolio insurance* (CPPI) structured products (see section 12.3). FISPs and CPPIs are not the same type of instruments:

■ FISPs are derivatives based.
■ By contrast, CPPIs involve (in principle) no derivatives.

These two bullet points trace a dichotomy between FISPs and CPPIs, but the dividing line is thin and twisted. As Figure 12.2 shows, there are possible overlaps between FISPs and CPPIs. Finally, the whole European medium-term market is not exchange traded. Deals are done OTC between financial institutions, as well as bilaterally between banks and their clients.

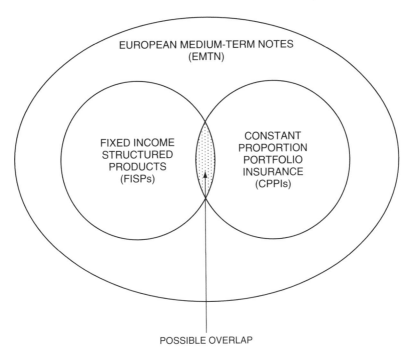

Figure 12.2 FISPs and CPPIs are part of the European medium-term note (EMTN) universe of financial instruments

12.2   Fixed interest structured products defined

Every financial instrument has a characteristic pattern, and to gain insight into this pattern it is necessary to know something about its development, as well as the market's response to it. During the early 1990s, fixed income derivatives started to proliferate rapidly, thriving on the uncertainty created by:

- Massive restructuring of corporate debt,
- A 300 basis points drop in US interest rates in just one year, and
- Volatility in European currency differentials following the demise of the Exchange Rate Mechanism (ERM).

During the course of 1992, corporate treasurers switched in a big way from fixed rate obligations, which looked very attractive only a few months earlier, to lower cost floating-rate debt. Indeed, even the US government shifted its debt sales to shorter maturities.

In these early years, the use of interest rate derivatives was for the big banks, not for retail investors and smaller companies. This use, however, trickled down from banks to corporate treasurers, then to asset managers, and eventually reached individual investors seeking higher yields by derivative-driven mutual funds. Note that there was an underlying bifurcation in market behaviour:

- Futures traders have been speculating in derivatives for years,
- By contrast, portfolio managers were latecomers to tailored OTC deals.

This popularization and generalization of derivative products has been seen, by many, as a way of creating a healthy 'buy side' audience for structured debt, able to provide an alter-ego to the wholesale derivatives industry. In the early 1990s some critics dared to say that by piling into derivative instruments in a frantic search for yield, asset managers could get burned if there is an unexpected interest rate shock. The events of February and March 1994 proved these critics right.

- With successive interest rate hikes by the Federal Reserve, the bottom fell out of the fixed interest derivatives market.
- With speculators being overrun by events, bankers, treasurers and investors have been running for cover.

The bonds debacle of 1994 took the steam out of fixed income derivative products, but the low did not last for long. Past the big scare of 1994, the market for fixed income derivatives again started to grow, because bankers, treasurers and institutional investors looked at these instruments as a way to enhanced interest rate management. The challenge has been that most players were not in a position to understand complex risk and return profiles.

- The growing breed of fixed income securities in the mid- to late 1990s included caps and floors, floaters and inverse floaters.

Theoretically, the methods for valuing these securities and measuring their interest rate risk are highly complicated and beyond the reach of many practitioners. Practically, however, as experience was accumulating, tier-one banks developed an integrated approach to understanding the valuation and interest rate sensitivity of fixed income derivatives.

■ The strategy has been to construct arbitrage-free interest rate models, and value all fixed income securities from a specified term structure.

To do so, it is necessary to appreciate how to measure *fair value*, and to be in a position to gauge interest rate sensitivity of a variety of important fixed income securities. This requires familiarity with the concepts of valuation and interest rate sensitivity of fixed cash-flow instruments. Knowledge of duration and convexity is also necessary.[3]

While the better known investment banks and some commercial banks possess the aforementioned know-how, this is true of neither individual investors nor several institutional investors, two populations that found it difficult to understand the exposure they were assuming. Risk control becomes most complex because most structured instruments:

■ Are novel,
■ Come in different versions, and
■ Keep on evolving all the time.

Moreover, terms used to describe them may be misleading, as is the case with structured 'bonds'. In addition, their characteristics are not commonplace when compared with past terminology. Inflation-linked notes, for example, target rising inflation, usually American or European, and their underlying is an inflation index.

Yet, the fact that many structured products are esoteric does not mean that they do not find buyers. The market expectation by investors willing to buy callable reverse floaters rose sharply in 1993 because interest rates were believed to remain below a given barrier. Then, in 1994, adversity hit and many entities went under, the most glaring example being the bankruptcy of California's Orange County. (More on this in Chapter 13.)

Several FISPs are in a class of their own. What they have in common is that their performance is linked to positive price development of the underlying that can be diversified:

■ Equity index
■ Currency, or
■ Other commodity.

In terms of the capital protection that they offer (see section 12.4), the amount depends on the instrument and its stated conditions. This is particularly true of capital protection units where the bar may be either above or below 100 per cent. No definite statement can be made about interest to be gained by a capital protection unit because this comes in a number of different structures. Moreover, given the cost of capital protection, this instrument usually underperforms when returns are compared with those of a direct investment.

It comes as no surprise that market expectations play a crucial role in terms of obtainable results. The market expectations for *podium notes* is that as a holding they are fairly equivalent to shares in the portfolio. Still, the pros say that the risk profile of a podium note is comparable to that of a bond investment, despite the underlying being an equity.

- The alchemy is achieved by setting the barriers at different levels for individual shares.
- With bull notes, by contrast, the bonus calculation is based on index returns periodically taken into account over the whole term (see Chapter 13).

Another feature of structured products is the existence or absence of a secondary market for investors. The first three instruments in Table 12.1, inflation linked notes,

Table 12.1 A pallet of fixed income structured products commonly available in the financial market

Instrument	Characteristics	Underlying	Secondary market
Inflation-linked note	Protection from rising inflation	Inflation index	Only for sellers. Product cannot be bought in secondary market
Stairway or step-up note	Variable coupon payments depending on performance of a short-term interest rate, with upper ceiling	Short-term interest rates, like 6-month US $ Libor or Euribor	Only for sellers. Product cannot be bought in secondary market
Callable reverse floater	Fixed interest rate (set at start minus short-term reference interest rate)	Short-term interest rates, like 6-month US $ Libor or 3-month Euribor	Only for sellers. Product cannot be bought in secondary market
Capital protection note	Participation in upside potential of an underlying, to a defined percentage set at the start	A hybrid with equity indices, commodities and currencies	Secondary market, with usual bid/offer spread of 1%
Fixed and variable rate note	Fixed coupon during the initial years; thereafter, variable interest depending on price performance of an equity portfolio	A hybrid with equity portfolio, often of 20–50 shares	Secondary market, with usual bid/offer spread of 1%
Bull note	This usually offers on maturity a minimum return plus a bonus, as a function of performance	A hybrid with different equity indices	Secondary market, with usual bid/offer spread of 1%

stairway notes and callable reverse floaters, have no secondary market for investors. This market is only for sellers. The other three instruments, capital protection units, fixed and variable rate notes and bull notes, do have a secondary market for investors, with bid/offer spread typically at 1 per cent. Notice that over and above that spread is a commission, usually expressed in a number of basis points. This commission is negotiable depending on the customer's weight with the seller and his or her negotiating skills.

- Nothing is cast in stone with sales conditions concerning structured financial instruments.
- The overriding need for the bank designing or marketing these instruments is to *sell them*, and move their financial toxic waste out of its portfolio.

There are also some special points to keep in mind. As their name implies, a real return with inflation-linked notes can be gained in a climate of sharply rising inflation, while in an environment of deflation the investor receives much less than he or she hoped for. A major risk to the investor associated with the callable reverse floater is that the issue has the right to redeem the note early, usually at 100 per cent, but under conditions leaving the holder exposed to adverse market forces. Investment in stairway notes sees rising coupon payments only when interest rates rise.

These are the most interesting historical developments and characteristics of FISP. The examples given in the preceding paragraphs define their pattern. Chapter 13 will look in more detail into the financial instruments outlined in Table 12.1, as well as several others. Before this, however, the more general economic variables defining the environment in which structured products exist must be considered.

12.3   Constant proportion portfolio insurance

As noted in the Introduction, CPPI products are quite distinct from FISPs. Moreover, they do not use derivative financial instruments. For these reasons, theoretically at least, CPPIs should not have been included in this chapter. Practically, as the reader is already aware:

- FISP and CPPIs overlap under certain aspects,
- They more or less appeal to the same population of investors, and
- They are both part of the EMTNs, as shown in Figure 12.2.

A standard CPPI instrument is not a bond. It is a product that consists of two asset categories: one is the *underlying fund*, which is essentially risky assets; the other is so-called risk-free assets, referred to as the *reverse account*. This second component is usually cash and therefore of lower risk, but it may be consumed over the product's life cycle. CPPIs have a maturity of five or six years.

In terms of asset management, the principle underpinning CPPIs is that total asset value must never fall below the present value, known as the *floor*, of the protected amount to be paid back at maturity. In terms of assets management, over the life of a CPPI the proportion of risky assets in the portfolio is:

■ Increased when the portfolio value moves away from the floor, and
■ Reduced when the portfolio value moves towards the floor.

A sound approach to risk management requires that exposure is steadily monitored. Daily allocation changes as interest rates, or generally the performance of the underlying, change. For capital guarantee purposes, as interest rates increase the assets manager increases his or her exposure to the asset.

As financial instruments, CPPIs are usually used in connection with non-liquid underlyings. Structured products along this line of reference are offered by many single-manager hedge funds, and they are often based on the outlined approach. Management-wise, the portfolio insurance strategy that is followed can be static or dynamic. The static strategy is characterized by:

■ Stop loss,
■ A protective put, and
■ A participatory call.

The dynamic strategy is more complex, involving CPPI, with synthetic puts and calls. Like a static strategy, a dynamic approach targets the protection of initial investment at maturity, either in part or in full.

The return of a CPPI depends on the underlying and on different performance lock-in features, chosen as part of the adopted strategy. As an example, Figure 12.3 presents the pattern of CPPI returns with level of downside protection set at 80 per cent, one-year maturity and an expected return of 2.5 per cent. Associated with this is an unprotected investment component, expressed as quantile of a normal distribution.

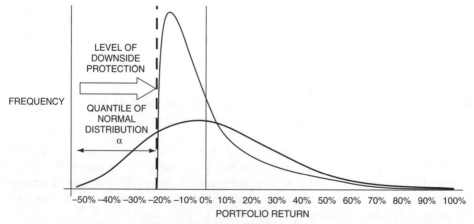

Figure 12.3 CPPI protection strategy with a protection level of 80 per cent, one-year maturity and an expected return of 2.5 per cent

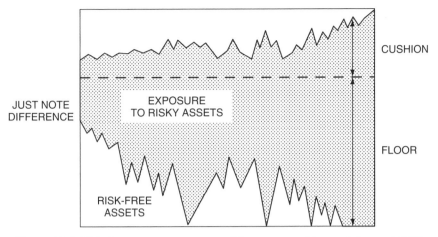

Figure 12.4 Risk-free assets, exposure to risky assets, cushion and floor of CPPI

A CPPI strategy has certain parameters. One of them is *portfolio value*, consisting of underlying value plus reserve account value. Others are the *floor*, whose definition involves the present value of the amount guaranteed at maturity; and *cushion*, expressed as portfolio value minus floor level. The floor, cushion, risk-free assets and exposure to risky assets are mapped into Figure 12.4. It is necessary to appreciate that:

- The CPPI may target a dynamic pattern of portfolio value,
- But the instrument's risk-free assets may be consumed before the market starts to recover.

Another important parameter to a CPPI strategy is the multiplier *m*. This coefficient, when multiplied by the cushion, gives the amount to be invested in risky assets. Still another is the rebalancing trigger, or *threshold*, applied to the variation in cushion value. Beyond this threshold, it is deemed necessary to adjust the asset mix. Two more parameters are:

- *Maximum exposure*, representing the largest proportion of portfolio that can be invested in the underlying, and
- *Minimum exposure*, or minimum proportion of portfolio that can be invested in the underlying.

A CPPI strategy would aim at adjusting the portion of a portfolio's risky assets within a given investment horizon, based on the development of the overall value of asset(s) at a selected wealth protection level (floor). A critical decision is the choice of *confidence level* to ensure wealth protection in each period. This is often taken at 99 per cent, but there is no rule about it. The unprotected investment may be characterized by:

- Expected returns,
- Intrinsic volatility, and
- Value at risk at 99 per cent for one year.

A CPPI strategy does not use options or swaps, and therefore the assets manager does not need to deal with prudential ratio issues involved with derivatives. What, however, he or she must do is to watch carefully the structured product's critical parameters. The following are some of the most important factors:

- Annualized volatility of risky assets,
- Quantile of normal distribution beyond downside protection, and
- Liquidation period, or time step Δ-t.

The parameters of a CCPI strategy require constant vigilance and testing. Because the amount invested in risky assets equals the cushion multiplied by the trading multiple m, a market percentage decrease of $1/m$ of risky assets within the liquidation period would fully eliminate the cushion. The largest historical intraday loss of risky assets can assist in estimating m.

The following example has been provided by one of the banks active in CCPI. On 19 October 1987 the stockmarket crashed. The Dow Jones Industrial Average dropped 508 points or 22.6 per cent in a single trading day. A CPPI strategy using a multiplier of 4.4 would have been safe on that day.

Finally, two types of guarantees are involved with a CPPI product: *legal* and *economic*. Legal guarantees are provided by an institution that is willing and able to assume obligations connected to a CPPI's ability to perform. The legal guarantee is usually exercised by means of appropriately allocating risk capital. With these protections in mind, if this system works well, then the investor:

- Is more or less protected from investment risk,
- But is exposed to counterparty risk associated with the legal guarantor.

Notice that the economic guarantees represent no legal obligation on the part of the manager of a CPPI product. They are connected to investment risk, and are conditioned by the fact that there exists always a *gap risk*, or probability of not achieving indicated returns. In this case the investor is probably carrying much more investment risk than counterparty risk. This is an important element in any decision connected to investments in CPPI.

12.4   FISP versus CPPI: a comparative study

Banks and hedge funds developed the so-called protected investment notes as an alternative to classical investment vehicles. Typically, the sales pitch with FISPs has been that the instrument has low correlation to the equity market (meaning reduced risk for existing portfolios, which is undocumented). Moreover, the vendor says that his product features:

- Anticipated returns considerably higher than with bonds or money market investments,
- A 100 per cent capital protection of the principal ensured any time after the first year, and

■ An unwritten guarantee by the issuing bank that trading of the structured instrument, sold to investors, is available at all times.

It is important to appreciate that all three statements are elastic. For instance, what is said about low correlation with other instruments in the investor's portfolio cannot be made in a flat manner because the vendor does not necessarily know the exact contents of the investor's portfolio. In addition, this statement does not apply to fixed income products with an index or equity in their underlying and, furthermore, the algorithm for anticipated returns is too complex for the typical investor.

Capital protection is provided by only some of the instruments in this class, and even 100 per cent means that the investor loses the interest he or she might have gained over six or seven years. Moreover, from the discussion in Part 3 it will be recalled that there is no price transparency in a secondary market assured by the issuer and/or a market maker.

As far as structured products are concerned, the characteristics of this secondary market are most interesting. 'We trade with an investment bank, within or outside our Group', said a senior private banking executive. This secondary market is almost always with the institution issuing the note, which practically buys back and resells its own produce for a commission. This commission is expressed in the spread, which usually, but not in every case, is:

■ 1.0 per cent for FISPs,
■ 1.5 per cent for commodity structured products,
■ 0.75 per cent for real estate structured products.

The fixing is often done daily, but there are exceptions. Some underlyings have a monthly price-fixing period. Whether the fixing is daily or otherwise, invariably it will be a hedge fund or an investment bank that will decide on the structured instrument's price.

Still, despite these shortfalls, FISPs may be of interest to investors, particularly those who know how to study risk and return in a rigorous manner. The investor must do his or her homework with every structured product considered for investment, keeping in mind that the specific names and characteristics of these products often vary from one issuer to the next, although there are some major classes, as shown in Table 12.1.

The list of structured products presented and described in Table 12.1 is neither exclusive nor all-encompassing. These are some of the instruments whose specific characteristics will be detailed in Chapter 13. New fixed income derivatives come to the market practically everyday. Essentially, Table 12.1 presents some of the main structured products as examples of a larger lot. Some of the fixed interest structured products are hybrids, using as underlying equities and other commodities.

Let us now compare characteristics and marketing/management practices underpinning FISPs (discussed in section 12.2) with those specific to CPPI instruments (presented in section 12.3). How do FISPs and CPPIs compare to one another? As already stated:

■ FISPs are derivative financial instruments.
■ CPPIs do not use derivatives at all; they are based on a trading strategy.

Being derivatives, FISPs depend on an *underlying instrument*. By contrast, the CPPI rests on an *underlying fund*, which is a different notion altogether. We will see why.

The strategy followed with CPPIs is that of investing in a fund that, for instance, may be fixed income, such as that designed to promote investments in an emerging market. The investor is practically holding the underlying fund's notional exposure. His or her income depends on how this fund performs. Put simply,

- Risk and return with FISP depend on the derivative's performance, whereas
- Risk and return with CPPI are a function of the fund manager's performance.

In the case of FISP, for instance, if yield curves move more quickly than predicted by the forward curve, then the investor will receive no income and will end up with a *zero coupon bond*. This zero coupon bond will be redeemed at 100 per cent at maturity because of the capital protection clause, but return on investment is zero.

CPPIs, too, are capital protected at maturity. However, they start by featuring an initial exposure that will probably be carried all the way during the instrument's life cycle, or even be amplified. If a CPPI is 100 per cent capital protected, then the investor ends up holding a zero coupon bond in a way very similar to that of FISP. He or she receives no interest.

In this way, although FISPs and CPPIs are different in their design and in the strategy they follow, as far as the investor is concerned, the net result may be the same. There is no return on investment, although both may return the original capital six or seven years down the line.

Notice that there is also a third alternative known as *Prosper*, which does not feature 100 per cent capital protection. By contrast, this structured product is more likely to pay interest than either FISP or CPPI. In Prosper's case, which resembles the CPPI structure, the division of invested capital between underlying fund and cash, for example, is 80/20 per cent, respectively, and it stays relatively stable. However, capital is at risk.

For reasons explained in the preceding paragraph, contrary to what was said about FISPs and CPPIs, Prosper is not likely to end up as a zero coupon bond, if for no other reason than it is not 100 per cent capital protected. The investor retains exposure to the underlying fund that he or she has bought in the first place, and this fund's performance determines his or her risk and return.

12.5   Borrowing through issuance of derivatives

The aim of this section is to give the FISPs and CPPIs, and financial activities related to them, a more general economic perspective. In the economy as a whole, net lending and net borrowing are calculated as the sum of gross savings and net capital transfers, minus either non-financial investments only, or the sum of non-financial and financial investments. By definition, non-financial investments consist of:

- The sum of gross capital formation and acquisitions,
- Minus disposals of non-producing, non-financial assets.

This is a birdseye view of the way in which the financing of all sorts of companies, and therefore of economic activity, works. Classically, commercial and industrial entities, as well as money-centre institutions, have been going to banks to buy funds through loans. In addition, are they tapping the capital market by issuing bonds.

It is not difficult to appreciate why, in the aftermath of the burst of the stockmarket bubble in 2000, issuance of debt securities shrank most significantly. Companies tried to restructure their balance sheets. Non-monetary financial companies, also known as non-bank banks, followed the same path, albeit with some delay. However, issuance of debt instruments increased among two other classes of borrowers:

- Governments, from 2002 onwards, and
- Credit institutions in 2003 and 2004.

As a report by the European Central Bank (ECB) points out, underlying these developments in Euroland was an increase in annual growth rate of short-term debt securities issuance, from 1.6 per cent in the second quarter of that same year.[4]

At the same time, because of the very low interest rates that prevailed in 2003–2004, the lowest for the last half a century both in Euroland and in the USA, the real costs of debt financing remained very low. Measured as a weighted average of investment-grade bond yields and high-yield (junk) bond yields deflated by inflation expectations for four years ahead, the real cost of market-based debt was also low.

However, as the ECB notes in its study, it is difficult to make a historical comparison because the statistical definition of bank interest rates has changed since the introduction in January 2003 of the new harmonized interest rate statistics of monetary financial institutions (MFI). This new framework for ECB statistics is presented in Table 12.2. The hungriest parties for loans, right after governments, are banks. Even non-banks have surpassed non-financial companies in their need for loaned money and, therefore, for gearing.

Behind these statistics lies the fact that there is a change in the borrowers' pattern, particularly affecting the composition of the borrowing population. This is important inasmuch as borrower patterns can be used to infer market expectations regarding future economic activity, including:

- Interest rates, and
- Inflation.

Moreover, the prices of derivative securities can, up to a point, provide information on the degree of uncertainty associated with market expectations (see the discussion on implied volatility in Chapter 4). This statement should be seen in conjunction with the fact that an estimated 75 per cent of all outstanding derivatives contracts are interest rate derivatives.

To a significant extent, the 75 per cent reference means that structured products are bets on bonds, and interest rate-sensitive securitized instruments at large. They are also a way for banks to borrow money from their clients, masquerading the loan as

Table 12.2 Debt securities issued by Euroland residents[a]

	Amounts outstanding (€ billions)	
	End December 1998	End November 2004
Total economy	6034	9337
of which (% of total)		
Fixed rate long-term debt securities	74	68
Variable rate long-term debt securities	15	20
Short-term debt securities	9	10
Monetary financial institutions	2241	3577
of which (% of total)		
Fixed rate long-term debt securities	72	56
Variable rate long-term debt securities	19	32
Short-term debt securities	8	11
Non-monetary financial corporations	196	740
of which (% of total)		
Fixed rate long-term debt securities	89	56
Variable rate long-term debt securities	7	42
Short-term debt securities	5	1
Non-financial corporations	293	607
of which (% of total)		
Fixed rate long-term debt securities	66	69
Variable rate long-term debt securities	16	13
Short-term debt securities	16	16
Central government	3203	4166
of which (% of total)		
Fixed rate long-term debt securities	75	82
Variable rate long-term debt securities	12	7
Short-term debt securities	10	10
Other general government	102	248
of which (% of total)		
Fixed rate long-term debt securities	89	74
Variable rate long-term debt securities	7	24
Short-term debt securities	4	2

[a] Source: European Central Bank.

FISP. This product defies classical analysis of a bond, the nominal yield of which can be unbundled into three important constituent elements:

- Expected real interest rate required by investors for holding the bond until it matures,
- Compensation for expected inflation rate during the life of the bond, and
- A component part associated with various risk premiums, with credit risk of the issuer at top of the list.

It should also be recalled that with classical bonds, the slope of the yield curve is a good indicator of expectations regarding future economic activity. Steepening of the yield curve is seen as signalling expectation of an accelerating economy; flattening or, even more so, inversion (backwardation) of the yield curve is taken as a signal of expected slowdown in growth.

When the market expects higher nominal growth, the central bank usually reacts by increasing short-term interest rates to contain inflationary tendencies. This is reflected in higher long-term interest rates today, since long-term rates can be viewed as averages of:

■ Expected future short-term rates,
■ A risk premium, and
■ Expected future short-term rates.

If the hypothesis is made that expected real interest rates and risk premiums far ahead in the future are broadly stable, then long-horizon implied forward rates can be interpreted as mainly reflecting expectations for inflation several years from now, after short-term shocks to inflation have abated. Because of this, implied forward overnight rates for very long horizons are looked at as the market's perception of a central bank's credibility.

All these notions from classical economies go out of the window with structured financial instruments used as an alternative to capital market, money market or bank borrowing. The institution selling to its clients FISPs, as well as CPPIs, can design them in a way that masks their real reason for being. What the issuing institution and the bank selling them do is borrow money from:

■ Retail clients, and
■ Institutional investors.

The bank issuing or marketing these structured instruments presents them as if they are there to render a service to the client. In reality, what they do is to offer a great service to the bank by generating cash flow at relatively:

■ Low cost, and
■ Low risk.

Just as important is the fact that the bank designing and marketing the FISPs often, although not always, retains the right to call them in, if the cost of their cash flow proves to be higher than what was foreseen. This is the modern way of cutting the Gordian knot of leveraging:

■ Accumulated debt is typically massaged through derivatives, and turned into assets.
■ Such 'assets' are bought by institutional and retail investors in the form of FISPs.

Not only is this solution an ingenious way to improve cash flow at low cost, but it also plays down uncertainty among market participants with regard to future developments in long-term bond yields. What is reflected in *implied bond market volatility* becomes a concept practically alien to structured products. (As defined by Bloomberg, implied volatility series represent nearby implied volatility on the near-contract generic future, rolled over twenty days before expiry. At that time, a change in the choice of contracts used to obtain the implied volatility is made, from the contract closest to maturity to the next contract.)

12.6   Capital protection notes and bondholders' risk

As mentioned in the Introduction, according to some experts, the concept of capital protection is not necessarily applicable in connection to FISPs. Rather, it addresses equities and currencies. Other experts say that whenever fixed income derivative instruments include a capital protection clause, the notion underpinning it:

- Plays on the probability that interest rates will not rise, or at least they will not increase shortly, and
- Capitalizes on a cultural issue long associated with fixed interest rate products, which now seems in its way to be undone.

In the background of this second bullet point lies the fact that, classically, bond-holders have been much better protected than equity holders in regard to their capital. Recent events, however, including the bankruptcy of Argentina, whose government has been behaving along the model of highway robbers, indicate that bondholders are not necessarily better protected than shareholders.

Here is an industrial example. Owens Corning is the world's biggest manufacturer of fibreglass. The company went into Chapter 11 bankruptcy in 2000, after being hit with more than 460 000 legal claims related to an asbestos product that it sold between 1952 and 1972. Like any other industrial entity, Owens Corning has many creditors:

- Bondholders,
- Trade partners,
- Asbestos claimants, and
- More than forty banks.

In October 2004 the judge overseeing the company's bankruptcy did something that shocked all holders of the company's debt: banks, institutional investors, hedge funds and other distressed debt investors. The judge ruled that the banks would not necessarily be paid back first. Before that decision, banks with loan claims clearly thought that they were senior to bondholders, and bondholders believed that they were senior to equity holders.

There are reasons to believe that cases similar to those of Argentina and Owens Corning will multiply in years to come. These examples are important because they establish a new perspective from which the capital protection of fixed income investors should be seen. Credit risk is being magnified because of:

- Political misconduct and irresponsibility, or
- *Event risk* that lies well beyond the investor's reach.

Some investment bankers suggested that these reasons are what make fixed income structured instruments with a capital protection clause so much more interesting. Indeed, investment bankers do their utmost to promote the appeal of capital protected units. They suggest that such notes assist the investor in participating in the upside potential of an underlying, which may be equity index, currency or other commodity. As we have seen, however, although the name of these instruments implies that there is 'capital protection', what happens is that the amount to be paid depends on:

- The performance of the underlying, and
- A specified level of minimum repayment.

If at the end of the term, the underlying lies above its start value, the investor will benefit from such positive performance, but only up to a specified participation level. There is a cap. By contrast, if the performance of the underlying commodity is negative, repayment will be at the level of the stated capital protection. This has been in the background of the statement made in section 12.4, that both FISPs and CPPIs may become zero coupon bonds.

It should also be noted that throughout this period the investor assumes credit risk associated with the issuer, for which he or she is not adequately compensated. The bank selling the instrument to the investor tells him or her not to worry because 'the issuer is rated AA – or better'. This argument is half-baked.

- AA – is an average credit rating, with considerable probability of default over six or seven years (more on this later), and
- The hedge fund probably issuing the structured product is simply not rated, which greatly increases the investor's credit exposure.

Investors should also appreciate the market risk they assume when selecting a given product structure. Take, as an example the Standard & Poor's (S&P) 500 index as the underlying instrument, with an index reference point at, say, 940; maturity in three years; issued at 100 per cent; 95 per cent capital protection; and a cap at 120 per cent of start value. Under these conditions:

- The minimum repayment will be 95 per cent, and
- The maximum repayment will be 120 per cent, over the three-year life of the product.

Notice, however, that in a way similar to that of all structured products the investor will receive no other interest over the instrument's six-year life cycle. Hence, in the best possible case of 120 per cent, the investor only gets a little better than due interest. In the worst case, he or she is losing 15 per cent (due interest and 5 per cent of capital). In either case, the investor is assuming a rather significant amount of credit risk.

- If during three years the S&P 500 index moves south, the investor will receive just 95 per cent of starting value,
- But he or she will gain nothing from the upside index value to, say, 1400 or beyond, because the cap starts at 1128.

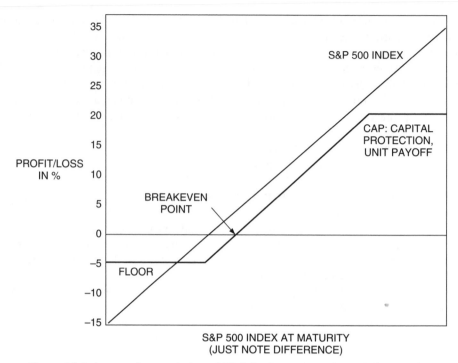

Figure 12.5 A general appreciation of P&L for investments in capital protection units with cap and floor

In other terms, the profit potential from this capital protected structured instrument is limited. If at the end of term the S&P 500 index were to close at a level of 846, therefore 10 per cent below the start value fixed at issue, the investor would receive 95 per cent per capital protection unit that he bought at 100 per cent.

To deliver positive results, some capital protection units also specify a minimum threshold, such as 5 per cent. For instance, the S&P 500 index must increase by at least 5 per cent to see the investor repaid at 100 per cent. Alternatively, there may be other clauses included in the contract, typically favouring the issuer. An appreciation of risk and return under the more generally prevailing conditions is shown in Figure 12.5. As this example demonstrates, much of what is sold as benefits to the investor is theoretical.

Furthermore, also at the downside of the return function is the fact that the amount originally invested is only protected on maturity. Like all other structured products, during their term capital protection instruments may be quoted at levels well below that stipulated by capital protection. Moreover, if capital protection amounts to less than 100 per cent, this means that the underlying must rise by a certain percentage even to reach the breakeven point (see Figure 12.5).

12.7 Structured instruments with underlying credit risk

Section 12.6 made reference to the fact that most structured products, CPPI being an example, are exposed to counterparty risk associated with the issuer or legal guarantor. Credit risk has been discussed to a certain length in Chapter 11, including ways and means for exposure control. Credit risk, however, can also be an underlying for a breed of structured products.

The financial industry has developed some structured instruments where the underlying is indeed credit risk, which is the subject of the present section. These types of notes are linked to an underlying single credit or a basket of credits. Instruments in the class under discussion pay coupons for as long as there are no defaults in the underlying reference entities.

- Credit exposure is created through the *credit default swap* (CDS) market.
- CPPI is part of it, but CDS, in its entirety, is not covered by the present book.

A good way of looking at structured instruments with credit risk as underlying is through the proxy of a risk premium. Economic theory suggests there is a positive correlation between interest rates and risk premium. If interest rates rise, investors tend to move away from riskier investments to safer ones with attractive interest rates. This leads to rising risk premium on issues with lower credit rating.

Inversely, a major fall in interest rates, like the one experienced since the end of 2002, promotes demand for higher interest but lower credit rating instruments. In their search for yield, many investors no longer find the low rate of interest on risk-free investments attractive. This increase in demand for risky debt investments contributes to a significant drop in risk premium.

Another fundamental principle with fixed rate debt instruments is that while risk premiums are influenced by expectations about future interest rate movements, the credit rating component is the dominant one. Junk bonds, for example, feature at the same time:

- High credit risk, and
- A higher interest rate.

Structured derivative products targeting creditworthiness tend to dissociate these two components. They leave aside the interest rate and concentrate on counterparty risk. Hence, one way of looking at the instruments in reference is as 'credit risk only junk bonds'.

One of these structured credit products is known as a *credit range accrual note* (CRAN). This product has a structure similar to the range accrual note in the interest rate world, but instead of referencing Libor it references an individual credit or basket of credits. Usually such notes are 100 per cent principal protected by the issuer. The reference rate being used is accessed through the credit default swap market.

A CRAN accrues a daily coupon for each day the reference credit default swap rate stays within a range defined at issue. If the investor shares the view that credit spreads have stabilized and corporate earnings are improving, which eventually means that spreads could stay range-bound in the future, then he or she reaps a benefit. The question is: How many investors have the know-how necessary to make such bets?

Another credit-linked note pays floating coupon for a period of five years, subject to the underlying. The latter is based on a credit-rated institution not experiencing a credit event throughout the life of the note. Issuers say that such notes often provide a yield enhancement over and above the vanilla bond market. For instance,

- They *may* pay three-month Euribor + 0.50 per cent,
- While similar five-year floating rate notes of the underlying entity pay three-month Euribor + 0.00 per cent.

Investors should always remember, however, that while 50 basis points is a good benefit, the 100 per cent capital protection does not include any guaranteed interest over the life of the note. Hence, credit events can mean that the investor receives no interest at all. This is the thesis discussed in section 12.3, that some structured products are a cheap way of borrowing money.

Many of the aforementioned notes are tailor-made and can reference any underlying credit. Investors can effectively create their own five-year bond, without having to wait for an issuer to come onto the capital market with a bond, and find a bank to underwrite it. However, such notes are only attractive if they offer some significant yield enhancement over the simpler debt instruments, without taking inordinate risk.

Yet another credit product is the *first-to-default basket*. It pays a fixed coupon for a period often set at seven years, subject to the underlying basket of credit not experiencing a credit event throughout the life of the note. In contrast to the preceding example, these notes are not principal protected. They are tailor-made and can reference any underlying basket of credits. Here again, investors can create their own basket, depending on their:

- Risk appetite, and
- Portfolio requirements.

First-to-default baskets work in a manner similar to credit default swaps, but with a critical difference. An investor in this note is essentially selling credit protection against the first reference entity, from the whole basket, that experiences a credit event. The name of the product comes from the fact the investor assumes the *first-to-default risk* on the underlying basket.

On the positive side, the investor may be rewarded with higher yields, as the basket becomes more diversified with lower correlation between the reference entities. The negative is that this is not always feasible, nor is the lack of correlation transparent. Therefore, there exists a higher level of risk exposure.

- If no default occurs on any of the underlying credits,
- Then the note will pay its coupon until maturity and redeem at par.

But this is a big *if*. There are also credit risk-based instruments that address both credit and interest rate risk. In that sense they emulate the junk bond market. For instance, a periodic capped note linked to company X may pay a floating coupon of six-month US $ Libor +2 per cent for a period of five years, subject to a periodic cap of 0.50 per cent at each coupon reset date.

■ Coupons are paid semi-annually, and
■ The cap is in place to prevent any coupon exceeding the previous coupon by more than 0.50 per cent.

An investor who holds this note is essentially betting on his or her belief that neither company X nor the issuer will suffer a credit event during the life of the bond. If company X were to default, then the note would automatically redeem at a price below par, at a level equivalent to the recovery price of the bonds of reference company X at the time, which may be, for instance, 15 per cent of nominal value, or simply zero.

As with any other debt instrument, as long as there are no credit events experienced by the underlying reference credit, the coupons will remain intact. At redemption the investor will receive his or her capital at par. This is again a big *if* and investors going for this type of structured product have to be very careful about the company's rating and the lifespan of the instrument. Even BBB companies that are investment grade have a 3 per cent likelihood of failure over a number of seven years, as documented in Table 12.3.

12.8 Embedded derivatives for the ownership society

Some contracts that are not financial instruments by themselves may have financial instruments embedded in them. An example is a contract to purchase a commodity at a fixed price for delivery at a future date. This type of contract has embedded in it a derivative that is indexed to the price of the commodity. As this example indicates,

■ An embedded derivative is a feature within a contract, and
■ Its presence means that cash flows associated with that feature behave in a way similar to a standalone derivative.

Investors should be aware that, in the general case, contracts that do not entirely meet the definition of a derivative may contain embedded derivatives in implicit or explicit terms. These affect some or all of the cash flows required by the contract. Typically, the instruments in reference are hybrid. Their features:

■ May double the investor's initial rate of return,
■ But also involve significant risks for both counterparties: the seller and the buyer.

Greater risk aside, embedded derivatives also pose fairly complex financial reporting requirements connected to their valuation. According to International Financial Reporting Standards (IFRS), the new reporting standard by the International Accounting Standards Board (IASB), and most particularly IAS 39, whether standalone or embedded, derivatives must be accounted for at fair value on the balance sheet, with changes recognized in the profit and loss (P&L) statement.

Table 12.3 Increasing probabilities of average cumulative default rates over a fifteen-year timespan (in per cent)[a]

	Year 1	Year 2	Year 3	Year 4	Year 5	Year 6	Year 7	Year 8	Year 9	Year 10	Year 11	Year 12	Year 13	Year 14	Year 15
AAA	0.00	0.00	0.07	0.15	0.24	0.43	0.66	1.05	1.21	1.40	1.40	1.40	1.40	1.40	1.40
AA	0.00	0.02	0.12	0.25	0.43	0.66	0.89	1.06	1.17	1.29	1.37	1.48	1.48	1.48	1.48
A	0.06	0.16	0.27	0.44	0.67	0.88	1.12	1.42	1.77	2.17	2.51	2.67	2.81	2.91	3.11
BBB	0.18	0.44	0.72	1.27	1.78	2.38	2.99	3.52	3.94	4.34	4.61	4.70	4.70	4.70	4.70
BB	1.06	3.48	6.12	8.68	10.97	13.24	14.46	15.65	16.81	17.73	18.99	19.39	19.91	19.91	19.91
B	5.20	11.00	15.95	19.40	21.88	23.63	25.14	26.57	27.74	29.02	29.89	30.40	30.65	30.65	30.65
CCC	19.79	26.92	31.63	34.97	40.15	41.61	42.64	43.07	44.20	45.10	45.10	45.10	45.10	45.10	45.10

[a] Courtesy of Standard & Poor's.

IAS 39 further requires that an embedded derivative is separated from its host contract and accounted for as a derivative, when economic risks and characteristics of the embedded derivative itself are not closely related to those of the host contract; when a separate instrument with the same terms as the embedded derivative would meet the definition of a derivative; or the entire instrument is not measured at fair value, with changes in fair value recognized in P&L.

Among embedded derivatives not closely related to their hosts which, therefore, must be separately accounted for, are commodity indexed interest or principal payments; host debt contracts; equity conversion option in debt convertible to ordinary shares from the perspective of the holder; leveraged inflation adjustments to lease payments and commodity indexed interest or principal payments in host debt contracts.

Further examples are currency derivatives in purchase or sale contracts for nonfinancial instruments where the foreign currency is not that of either counterparty to the contract, and is not the currency in which the related good or service is routinely denominated in commercial transactions; or it is not the currency that is commonly used in such contracts in the environment in which the transaction in reference takes place.

All these terms, conditions and exceptions have classically been part of contracts signed between major players in the financial landscape. Typically, banks and industrial corporations employed a golden horde of:

- Financial analysts to study risk and return, and
- Layers able to flash out, and bring to management's attention, embedded legal risk.

Now, these instruments with embedded derivatives and other complex features are becoming investment vehicles for an ownership society, whose members are agnostic about the myriad of risk they may involve. Not only retail investors, but also institutional investors, assume exposure that they are definitely not prepared to handle.

Moreover, an instrument of growing interest to institutional and retail investors seems to be a structured note with fixed or floating rate that contains *embedded options*. Through options new structured instruments can be assembled in virtually any combination designed to provide a customized risk and payoff profile, but the key question is: Does the investor understand risk and return associated with an embedded option?

Embedded options, also known as *embeddos*, are characteristic of tailor-made derivatives increasingly offered to the retail trade. Another class of embedded derivatives is utilizing *swaps*. This is a large family of structured products that usually present significant upside and an even greater downside. The most important among them are:

- *Range floaters*, or notes paying an enhanced coupon while the floating reference trades within a prespecified band. If outside the band, then the investor sacrifices one day's interest for each day the reference is outside the agreed-upon collar.
- *Inverse floaters*: these are notes paying an enhanced coupon as a reference interest rate falls, and a decreased coupon as a reference rate rises, both being based on a formula such as 'x per cent fixed' minus floating. (Inverse floaters sank Orange County; see Chapter 13.)

- *Multiple index floaters*, typically notes paying an enhanced coupon based on the spread between two indexes, which may be similar or different. Spread in a direction opposite to that expected can result in loss of coupons and principal.
- *Leverage floaters*: as the name implies, these are geared notes paying an enhanced coupon based on leverage, with the floating reference coupon magnified by a multiplier formula determining payoff or loss. That formula tends to be fairly complex, and so is the process of finding out where the losses came from.

Inverse floaters are further discussed in Chapter 13. Notice that although only one of these instruments is called 'leveraged', they are all characterized by a significant amount of gearing. This provides greater potential for both gains and losses. Moreover, there are many other variations than the four aforementioned classes. Designers of these instruments also ensure that by embedding derivatives into:

- Convertible bonds,
- Debt instruments with warrants, and
- Structured notes,

and by selling these instruments outright to retail and institutional investors, they eliminate the intermediary's credit risk on the derivatives being traded. In other words, they transfer the risk(s) to the investor.

In conclusion, by and large the structured instruments in reference are quite favourable to the issuer but not necessarily to the investor, as the bankruptcy of Orange County documents.[5] Investors would be well advised to study some of the major investment failures with embedded derivatives that have taken place in the last dozen years, to gain some perspective. People and companies who do not learn from the mistakes of others recorded in economic history are condemned to repeat them.

Notes

1 D.N. Chorafas, *The Management of Bond Investments and Trading of Debt*, Butterworth-Heinemann, London, 2005.
2 D.N. Chorafas, *Alternative Investments and the Mismanagement of Risk*, Macmillan/Palgrave, London, 2003.
3 D.N. Chorafas, *The Management of Bond Investments and Trading of Debt*, Butterworth-Heinemann, London, 2005.
4 European Central Bank, *Monthly Bulletin*, December 2004.
5 D.N. Chorafas, *Managing Derivatives Risk*, Irwin Professional Publishing, Burr Ridge, IL, 1996.

13 Practical examples with fixed income derivatives

13.1 Introduction

To their proponents, structured products offer the investor the opportunity to enjoy higher returns than would be possible with traditional money market instruments; and they do so at short notice. Right? Wrong. This is an absolutely undocumented statement. It says nothing about the amount of assumed risk, and the 'short notice' is typically six years long: too much in living with structured derivatives. Moreover, the investor does not retain anything more than a promissory note by the bank that:

- He or she will get back the capital at the end of the product's life cycle, and
- This will happen only if, in the meantime, the institution giving the guarantee does not go bankrupt.

As an example of imaginary benefits to whose questionable existence investors should be alert, the sellers of structured derivatives say that the buyers can 'successfully' react to short-term market developments, and even create their own specific structure solution geared to their precise needs.

The best way to answer such lightweight arguments is through that joke often heard in Las Vegas, that you stand a good chance of making a small fortune through gambling, provided you start with a big one. Even gambling needs skill, and conveniently the aforementioned sales gimmick forgets that the typical investor does not have the know-how necessary to:

- 'Determine' forex income derivatives transactions, and
- Calculate the risks associated with them which, by any count, is a must.

The only thing the average investor is sure to get from structured products that he or she does not understand is an inordinate amount of exposure. Another frequent but incorrect sales pitch of designers and sellers of structured products is that these are investment instruments that have been 'a key feature of the international finance markets for many years'. Rather than being 'key features', many of them are viewed with suspicion by a large number of investors, bankers and treasurers, who consider them to be:

- Overly complex, and
- Insufficiently transparent.

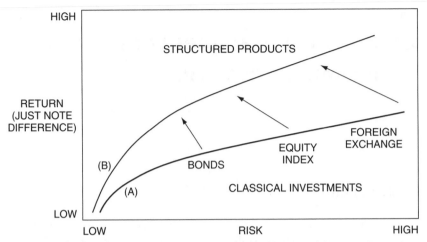

Figure 13.1 This graph is an often used misrepresentation of facts. It shows that a portfolio of structured products has a better risk and reward profile than a classical portfolio, which, usually, is false

Their sellers say that structured derivatives are no more than instruments that can be used as flexible alternatives to the traditional investment classes such as cash, bonds and equities. That is a lie. Untruths also underpin the comparison of risk and return between classical investment (curve A) and investments in structured products (curve B), shown in Figure 13.1, prepared by one of the banks that tried to sell structured products to its clients.

Keywords among most frequently heard sales arguments are: 'better alternative', 'greater flexibility' and 'higher return'. Nowhere is there any statement about the huge amount of risk being assumed not only by private investors, who are viewed by the sellers as being at the low end of the food chain, but also by institutional investors, who should be more careful about what they buy because they administer other people's money (see section 13.5, the case of Orange County).

As with any other commodity, the price of structured instruments can go up, and it can go down. The reader is already aware of the fact that 'capital protection', if there is any, works strictly at end of the term. In between, assuming there is a secondary market, the price of the instrument is volatile. For no reason whatsoever, structured products such as inflation-linked notes, callable reverse floaters and stairway notes (step-ups) are better than time-honoured bonds in wholesale manner.

Yet, this does not mean that they should be discarded altogether. Rather, they should be thoroughly studied, each one on its merits, provided the institutional and private investor fully appreciate the embedded exposure. Every instrument has its own risk profile, both on the upside and on the downside. Figure 13.2 depicts the effects of volatility over a two-year period, taking two structured fixed interest products with secondary market as an example (just note difference).

■ A derivative's downward potential is not always taken into account by institutional investors such as insurance companies and pension funds,
■ Yet, these entities have annuities to meet, and they should not bet other people's money in risky deals in the first place.

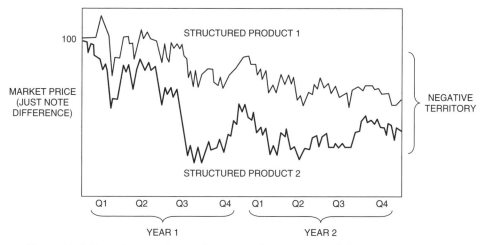

Figure 13.2 Secondary market performance of two structured derivative instruments, bought at 100 per cent at issuance

These remarks are not made to discourage flatly any and every alternative investment. It all depends on the investor's *risk appetite* and other goals, as well as on his or her risk management skills. The most fundamental ingredients in deciding about investing in leveraged structured products, or more generally any derivative financial instrument, are investment horizon, risk appetite, a rigorous analysis of likely returns and in-house availability of high-grade management skills.

13.2   Money rates, money markets and financial instruments

Money is the common denominator of every reference made to risk and return. Therefore, before going into specific issues associated with structured products, it is wise to talk of *money rates*; that is, earnings that an investor would like to lock-up for his or her capital. This provides a background against which to compare different fixed rate structured instruments. A money rate is:

- The cost of an individual capital component, and
- The reward offered by a money market to attract capital.

Different kinds of capital – bonds, preferred stock, common stock and other instruments – have different costs. The difference comes from many factors characterizing such instruments; for instance, the probability of upside and exposure to downside, and investment grade versus non-investment grade.

As far as the relationship between the market needing capital and the investor providing capital is concerned, these various capital factors and components must be combined to form an overall, weighted cost-and-reward equation. Required rates of return differ over time and among markets, not only because of supply and demand of capital, but also for other crucial reasons, market psychology being one of them. If the supply of funds is restricted and the demand is great:

- The cost of capital increases, whether this cost is interest rate on debt or required rate of return on equity, and
- In either case, the money rate can be viewed as the price to be paid for liabilities.

When there is an overcapacity of money in the market, as in the first years of the twenty-first century, the market and/or monetary authorities lower the price to pay for financing outstanding liabilities. To what level? There is no unique answer to this query.

In 1992, the Federal Reserve had to lower the federal funds rate to 3 per cent to reflate the banking system and slow the credit crunch. That figure was about in line with the then prevailing rate of inflation. In the early years of the twenty-first century, the federal funds rate was purposely kept below 2 per cent in the USA, down to 1 per cent at a certain period in 2003/04, and at 2 per cent in Euroland, for the same reasons.

A very low interest rate is most unfavourable to bond investors. Because of inflation, it usually provides a negative return. Investors buy debt instruments for their yield. The same is true with fixed interest structured products (FISPs). There are three types of yield important in evaluating debt securities:

- Current yield,
- Yield to maturity, and
- Yield to call.

Current yield, also known as cash-flow yield, is an often misunderstood measurement. To compute current yield, the security coupon interest is simply divided by its price. This provides a fairly good measure of return if a bond sells at or very close to its par, or face value. The problem is that this is rarely, if ever, the case.

- Usually, current yield understates true return if the security has a low coupon and sells at a discount to its par value.
- Conversely, current yield overstates return if the debt security has a high coupon and sells at a premium to par.

The metric helping to overcome this discrepancy is *yield to maturity*. It provides a better measure of return than current yield, because it takes into account any difference between the price the investor pays for the bond and the par value he or she will receive at maturity, as well as the reinvestment of interest income over time.

A different metric, *yield to call*, measures the return of a debt security selling at a premium to its par value that is redeemable by the issuer before final maturity. Not all debt instruments are bullet bonds. Many corporate debt securities have call features. Therefore, it is important to know the yield to call before one buys a bond priced above its par.

Since the preceding paragraphs have focused on the bonds, it is proper to say a few words in regard to return on equity. Is there substance to the saying at Wall Street that over the longer run return on equity outperforms the return on bonds? Based

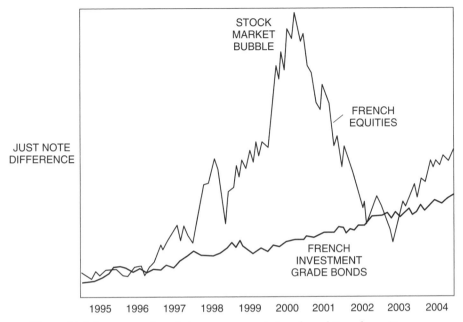

Figure 13.3 Return on French investment grade bonds and French equities over
a ten-year time-frame

on French equity and bond statistics, Figure 13.3 suggests that the answer largely
depends on how long this longer run is.

Besides this, bonds are not a monolithic instrument. Rather, they are a versatile one
that comes in different types and is subject to more than one classification. Bullet, or
straight, and callable bonds are only one type. There are others.

Real bonds are issued by governments (gilts) or corporations. All of them carry
credit risk, with the exact amount depending on the issuer's credit rating. Such bonds
typically offer a fixed income for a period of years. What varies is the price at which
the investor buys the income stream (see the reference to current yield, yield to
maturity and yield to call).

Junk, or *high-income, bonds* are in a class of their own. 'High income' is a misleading qualification, a name invented by marketing people to persuade investors that
they are buying something that has the assurance of a real bond but much higher
yield. That is why serious investment advisors and financial analysts warn individual
investors to educate themselves on the nuts and bolts of:

■ Risk and return associated with debt instruments, and
■ Their many hues of creditworthiness,

before committing themselves to a bond or fixed income structured product.

Under current market conditions, and lack of full know-how of intricate issues
of high finance, in their majority, private investors and even institutional investors
are not able to write down specification for structured products, let alone design
instruments able to protect themselves against adverse movements.

For simple cases, such as hedging a loan against a possible rise in interest rates or currency exchange rates, a bank can be called upon to structure a financial instrument. However, as already seen in Chapter 12, such deals may quickly become very complex and eventually deadly. The reader should keep this reference in mind when going through the following sections, which describe in a fair amount of detail different types of fixed income structured products.

13.3 Inflation-linked notes

As their name implies, these structured products target the investor's protection from a resurgence in inflation. Is this protection real or a fantasy? A sound way of answering is to present a typical question asked by sellers of inflation-linked notes to convince the customer: 'Is the return on your bonds too low?' Unavoidably, in the majority of cases, the answer is 'Yes', and this is followed by another query by the salesperson: 'Does it cover inflation?'

When the investor responds that the real interest margin with classical bonds is too thin, the next query the vendor asks is: 'Are you expecting inflation to rise over the coming years?' rapidly followed by 'Would you like to protect yourself against falling real returns?' Even if the question about the trend in inflation is not answered, the response to the last question is again: 'Yes'. With this, the investor is on the hook.

Two successive 'yes' answers set the stage for the sale of inflation-linked notes which theoretically provide the opportunity of protecting oneself against rising inflation. With these notes, in addition to a (usually low) fixed coupon payment the investor will receive a variable return dependent on a certain index of inflation.

- Again theoretically, it sounds as if this is another floating rate coupon.
- Practically, however, inflation-linked notes are a leveraged instrument (more on this later).

Inflation-linked notes are structured products that capitalize on the fact that nearly every person is concerned about inflation eating up the interest rate of fixed coupon debt instruments, and probably the capital behind it. Therefore, an instrument protecting against inflation seems to be worthwhile to invest in.

To comprehend better what inflation protection means, investors should appreciate that inflation has many causes, one of them being rapid growth in the money supply. A rapid growth in money supply eventually means that too much capital is chasing too few real goods and a limited number of investment opportunities. Figure 13.4, from the Deutsche Bundesbank, gives a perfect view of correlation between core money supply and inflation in Euroland, in the 1981–2004 time-frame.

Beyond money supply and demand for real goods come other factors pushing up inflation. For instance, in 2005 inflation has been strongly influenced by its energy component: the skyrocketing oil prices. A rapid growth in wages also pushes up inflation. This was not the case in 2005 because of lack of pressure from the labour market, but there were other upward risks.

Typically, the outlook for low domestic inflationary pressures is based on the assumption that the price of key commodities such as labour, oil and steel will keep

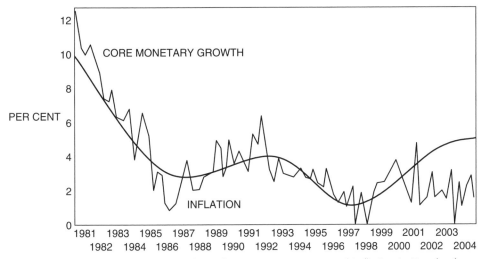

Figure 13.4 Quarterly annualized rate between core money and inflation in Euroland. (*Source*: Deutsche Bundesbank, Monthly Report, January 2005, by permission)

steady or decline. The rapid rise in the price of a commodity that is used in many products, like that of steel shown in Figure 13.5, translates into two results:

- Greater inflation, or
- Lower profit margins for the producers.

Price trends in key commodities are important because, apart from its direct effect on inflation, a rise in oil prices also increases the risk of indirect and second round

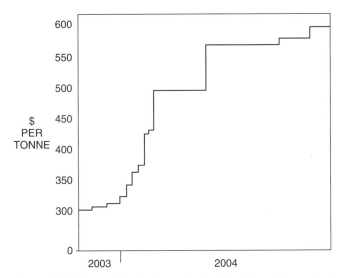

Figure 13.5 The rapid rise in steel price (benchmark hot rolled coil, dollars per tonne)

effects stemming from wage and price-setting behaviour. The 14 June 2004 edition of the *Washington Post* carried a survey focusing on inflation of commodity prices in the Washington, DC, Maryland and Northern Virginia area, over the last twelve months. The figures read:

- Cement up 10 per cent in a year
- Lumber up 20 per cent in six months
- Gasoline costs up 20 per cent in a year
- Steel up 21 per cent in a year
- Wire mesh up 53 per cent in six months
- Metal studs up 150 per cent in six months
- Plywood up 167 per cent in a year.

Inflation-linked notes are supposed to protect the investor's wealth against such spikes. The irony, however, is that these *real* inflationary indices do not enter into the underlying, because issuers choose the easier path of financial leverage and they use rather doubtful overall inflation figures.

In short, no attention is paid to the fact that commodities are one of the best ways to play the longer terms inflation theme. Therefore, inflation-linked notes offered to investors by banks and hedge funds are typically not based on commodities. They are simply another geared financial instrument with an easily marketable name.

Moreover, because, as Chapter 12 has stated, there is no free lunch, the issuer has to protect himself against adversity, given the 'Your money back' guarantee that he offers. To appreciate the way in which inflation-linked notes work, take as an example an instrument whose underlying is US inflation, with:

- Coupon: 1.04 per cent plus a given inflation index,
- A term of five years, coupon distribution annual,
- Issue price: 100 per cent, and
- Capital protection at the end of the term: 100 per cent.

The annual coupon payment the investor will receive from such a structured product consists of the aforementioned fixed component of 1.04 per cent and a variable component which, in this case, is dependent on US inflation over a fixed period. Usually this is calculated using the annual percentage change in the underlying index:

Inflation = CPI for, say, January of current year/
CPI index for January of previous year) − 1

where CPI is the Consumer Price Index. This algorithm means that the exact coupon to be paid is not known until the end of the coupon period. In the event that inflation is negative (a most unlikely event), this is deducted from the fixed component.

If inflation in the current year is equal, or nearly equal to that of previous year, the investor gets a meagre 1.04 per cent interest, which is not appealing at all.

Notice also that if real interest rates rise, which is likely, the inflation-linked note will lose value. The same would be the case in the event that inflation is not rising, but the returns on recently issued normal bonds were. Further, the coupon repayment may fall to 0 per cent in the event of negative inflation. Basically, it is:

- Win–win for the issuer, and
- Lose–lose for the investors, who thought they were buying inflation protection.

Furthermore, as with many products, the amount originally invested is only protected on maturity. During its term, the price of the note may fall well below 100 per cent, and an investor who needs to get back his or her money and must sell this instrument in the secondary market (made by the issuer) will lose a good chunk of the originally invested capital.

A second example is that of a long-maturity, ten-year euro inflation-linked non-callable note, with 100 per cent principal protection. As the issuer sees it, an investor in these notes would be one that has a positive view on the rate of Euroland inflation over the life of the note. The issuer states that:

- If this view is correct,
- Then the investor will receive an enhanced coupon.

To attract buyers, this note pays an annual coupon of 5.00 per cent in year 1. Many investors fail to read the fine print and, therefore, they miss the point that thereafter this inflation-linked note pays a variable annual coupon floored at 0.00 per cent. After year 1, the coupon is conditioned by the year-to-year inflation in Euroland. The status of this note is senior, but unsecured. The algorithm for the coupon after year 1 is:

140 × annual inflation in Euroland

This is payable annually on a 30/360 price period and dates. The redemption price is at par. For each respective coupon period, the annual inflation is computed on the basis of Euroland's CPI, excluding tobacco. The reference index applicable for each day in a given month is:

$$\frac{CPI_n - CPI_{n-1}}{CPI_{n-1}}$$

As an example with the now classical (but inaccurate) level of 2.00 per cent inflation, the interest rate will be 2.80 per cent, which is nothing to crow about. But if inflation drops to 1.40 per cent then the interest rate will be a mere 1.96 per cent, leaving just 58 basis points as real return on these inflation-linked notes.

Here is a third example of an instrument whose stated goal is to achieve an inflation-protected steady total return in euros and 'outperform' the benchmark return of euro CPI + 140 basis points over the medium term. The issuer says that this structured product is attractive,

- As core investment to bond buyers looking at reallocating into a fixed income fund that has a reduced exposure to inflation, and
- To more conservative bond investors, looking to maintain a controlled limit on their interest rate exposure (whatever this 'controlled limit' is supposed to mean).

In terms of mechanics, the issuer and portfolio manager say that they actively invest in a diverse range of inflation-linked bonds, which have the characteristic of protecting the investor from the risk of unexpected inflation. This may be true. The unsubstantiated part of the statement being made is that these inflation-linked bonds can generate an attractive positive level of return during periods of low inflation. The previous case study with US dollars has shown why this is not true.

When the issuer was confronted with this evidence, he answered that, in this case, the portfolio manager adds additional value from translating views on interest rates, sectors and credit spreads into 'appropriate allocation decisions'. This, he stated, is an active investment strategy enabling the portfolio manager to take appropriate and timely decisions:

- Based on the latest market situation, and
- Providing an opportunity to outperform the benchmark within a controlled risk environment.

The whole gamble to convince the unaware investor is based on these three keyphrases an 'active strategy' (which at times backfires), 'outperform' and a 'controlled risk environment', which simply does not exist, but the investor does not know it. Beyond these issues are other exposures connected to market risk and credit risk, which are usually passed over. Yet, credit risk is a real and present danger throughout an investment's time-frame.

13.4   Stairway notes (step-ups)

A stairway note, also known as step-up, is another interest rate instrument. At least theoretically, it offers the investor the possibility to participate in the development of a variable interest rate product, by means of a 'better' coupon payment. A negative of this instrument is that the degree of participating in rising interest rates is subject to an upper ceiling, and there are other risks.

For instance, on the step-up's downside lies the fact that if during a coupon period the short-term interest rate falls by a given percentage, the price of the leveraged instrument falls more rapidly, while the amount originally invested is only protected on maturity. During its term, the price of a stairway note may lie well below par, which will particularly be the case if short-term interest rates rise by more than the coupon period percentage rate. The latter is determined in advance.

The structural characteristics of step-ups are conditioned by the fact that coupon payments are directly dependent on the development of short-term interest rates.

As far as price discovery is concerned, it is not just current interest rates but the interest rate curve as a whole that is relevant, because the value of a note is equal to:

- The sum of coupon payments expected
- Plus the repayment of the original amount, discounted to 'today's' date.

Up to a point, but only up to a point, the steepness of the interest rate curve makes it possible to predict future development of short-term interest rates. However, it is no less true that interest rates can change rapidly and, sometimes, unexpectedly. In general,

- A steep interest rate curve indicates that the market is expecting higher short-term interest rates in the future, and
- Because the coupon payments of stairway notes have a limited upper ceiling in each coupon period, the investor will not be able to participate fully in this rise.

Take the case of a six-month Libor Euribor which stands at 1.20 per cent at the beginning of the term, with the first coupon payment at 2.05 per cent per year. Say that the reference interest rate immediately falls after issue. By contrast, the linked coupon sticks to the level of the preceding coupon, i.e. 2.05 per cent per year.

A different scenario develops when Euribor rises sharply from the second year onwards. In this case, the stairway note cannot participate fully in the rise because of the maximum distribution feature limits to the level of the preceding coupon 'plus'. A frequent example is 0.5 per cent. To the investor, this means a period of underperformance.

Of interest to an investor knowledgeable about controlling derivatives risk would have been an instrument able to duplicate the pattern of central bank tightenings and easings. This would have made the investor a fair player in the interest rate market, without artificial limits on the upside.

Issuers are not ready to develop and market the type of structured product outlined in the preceding paragraph because of the risk that this would represent to them. Instead, they talk vaguely of asset protection from volatility in interest rates, pressing the notion that investors who have large bond portfolios paying fixed interest coupons:

- Are exposed to the interest rates' upward movement, and
- With longer duration on fixed interest bond portfolios, may suffer capital losses.

There is substance to this argument. The counterargument, however, is that, as they currently stand, stairway notes do not answer the challenge of protecting investors' interest from interest rate volatility. While banks and hedge funds do offer a risk and return combination, the matching of interest rate outlooks has too much of a limited perspective on the upside, and it is essentially the upside that will generate profits for the investors.

Some issuers of structured products connected to interest rate volatility suggest that to protect against future losses from rising rates, investors can enter into asset swaps. The idea is that they swap their fixed coupons for floating rate coupons, and this is one way of linking to inflation. As an example, an investor may swap a weighted average coupon of 9.5 per cent on an underlying bond portfolio for a floating coupon paying euro inflation +7 per cent.

- The swap resets each quarter, taking the headline rate of inflation at the time.
- An investor entering into this swap would be one expecting inflation to rise in a growing economy.

Banks make internal interest rate swaps to weed out from their loans book interest rate risk, connected to credits made at fixed interest rates. Regulators accept this practice, and some encourage it, but for internal management information system reasons only, not for regulatory reporting.

Another alternative structured instrument offered to institutional and retail investors is a forward yield curve swap. This approach is often used in assets and liabilities (A&L) management. With such a trade, the counterparty will receive a payment on the swap if the spread is wider than the contractual spread. This type of interest rate swap is often reset and paid quarterly for ten years, so that the counterparty has forty looks at the spread.

As far as this method is concerned, on a marking-to-market basis the counterparty will benefit from an increase in implied volatility on long-dated options on the ten-year swap. Assuming the yield curve maintains its current levels and slope, the counterparty would make a profit of basis points per year as the trade rolls down the curve. However, with this and similar interest rate instruments, the investor is left with the credit exposure to the underlying portfolio.

13.5 Callable reverse floaters

The callable reverse floater, and its sister, the callable range accrual note (see section 13.6), are derivative instruments theoretically providing the investor with the chance of obtaining an attractive return in comparison to traditional bonds. Practically, however, they have embedded into them a great deal of exposure, including the major risk that, under certain circumstances, the investor may lose his or her capital.

To appreciate the statement made in the preceding paragraph, we should look first at the fundamentals of derivative instruments known as callable reverse floaters. A reverse floater structure has the effect of leveraging a movement in interest rates.

- If the floating rate index moves north, then the buyer of the inverse floater will pay less and receive more.
- If, by contrast, there is a downward movement in the floating rate index, then the investor will pay more and receive less.

As an example, let us hypothesize that the pay and receive money flows are equal to one another. Therefore, at inception, one may think that these two components are economically equivalent, which is true only if they are priced correctly. Subsequently, the transaction underpinning the instrument will be based on two swaps, which affect the reverse floater. Moreover, beyond market risk there is credit risk embedded in the instrument, relating to creditworthiness of the counterparty.

Credit risk analysis of the structured product follows about the same thinking as examined with other derivative financial products, but it also features some 'added value'. This comes from the fact that, other things equal, both counterparty risk and market risk are greater because of dealing with leveraged swaps.

- The upside is better gains made possible by gearing.
- On the downside is a likelihood of greater losses, which may become devastating.

At the design phase of a structured product, the analyst can set the leveraged inverse pay flow equal to the floating receive flow. While economic analysis helps to determine the appropriate leverage factor and associated exposure, it should be appreciated that reverse pay and receive flows are not necessarily symmetrical. This has the effect of magnifying the investor's exposure.

Because both callable reverse floaters and accrual notes are highly leveraged instruments, the resulting loss of capital under adverse market conditions can be well beyond the investment being made. This has happened in many cases; for example, in late 1994, the Orange County Fund went bankrupt because of major investments in inverse floaters, which were lucrative up to a point and disastrous thereafter.

The Orange County Fund once had $7.5 billion in real money to invest. A foolish treasurer and his pals leveraged it to nearly $22 billion. Subsequently, after the County's bankruptcy, these same people tried to appear as financial innocents. In testimony before a special California senate panel, Orange County executives said that they were unaware of risks. They knew 'nothing' about reverse floaters and other leveraged investments, yet they bought them in a big way, eventually leading to:

- The county's bankruptcy, and
- Losses of nearly $2 billion.

'I had never owned a share of stock', testified former treasurer Robert Citron, who signed up the County Fund's huge investments in derivative instruments, but said that he relied on the advice of investment houses such as Merrill Lynch.[1] Citron's deputy, Matthew Raabe, said that he did not grasp 'the somewhat bizarre aspects' of high-risk investments that sunk the fund he was managing.

The truth is that the majority of other reverse floater investors do not grasp the depth of the toxic waste assumed by signing up to them. That is why this case study is so important. As a warning to all investors, the reference to the Orange County debacle has come up on several occasions in this book.

The reader should always keep in mind that, most unfortunately, what has happened to the Orange County Fund is not the exception but a case found quite frequently among investors, including the institutional ones. A great deal of the risk comes from the fact that both:

- The interest payable on these instruments, and
- Their market value are dependent on the movements in short-term interest rates such as the three-month Libor.

As shown in section 13.6, with callable range accrual notes, the coupon is only paid for those days on which short-term interest rates lie below a given barrier. Hence, the term 'accrual' is misleading. If short-term interest rates rise above this barrier, no coupon will be paid for the days in question. By contrast, with callable reverse floaters the level of coupon payments for each coupon period is calculated in line with short-term interest rates.

■ The short-term reference interest rate is deducted from a fixed interest rate prescribed at issue.
■ The effect is that coupon payments fall as short-term interest rates rise. Investors beware.

Moreover, with both instruments, reverse floaters and accruals notes, the issuer plays win–win at the holder's expense, because a further feature of both of them is an integrated call provision. This means that the issuer has the right to redeem the note early on fixed dates; and the issuer can redeem them at 100 per cent, even if market conditions mean that these structured products worth much more.

Alternatively, the market price of callable reverse floaters and callable range accrual notes may well fall below the acquisition value paid by the investor. This happens in the event of rising interest rates, as the Orange County Fund found out the hard way. Furthermore, in terms of income, an interest payment will only be made if the reference interest rate remains at a low level.

With this whole bag of tricks behind the structured product, return may end up much smaller than that of a comparable bond investment if interest rates fall further or the interest curve becomes flatter. The upside is limited because the notes can be called by the issuer, at his choosing, at 100 per cent of the nominal value before the end of the term.

Investors in both these structured instruments should understand that by buying them they accept the risk that they will receive no interest for those days on which, for instance, the six-month Euribor closes above the applicable barrier. The coupon payment is not guaranteed in all circumstances, and there is the major risk that if the market moves in the opposite way to the investor's guess, his or her capital goes up in smoke.

What the vendor usually brings to the investor's attention to sell reverse floaters is that the lower the Euribor level, the higher the coupon payment he will receive. Should short-term interest rates remain low or rise only slowly, the vendor says, the reverse floater provides the opportunity to earn higher coupon payments than would be the case, for instance, with a classical fixed-rate six-year bond. Behind this argument, however, are the cutoffs and several risks that are hidden.

The message to retain from this discussion is that stated benefits wane rapidly as short-term interest rates rise more strongly, while the risks are magnified as the instruments' price falls in the event of such a market development. In addition to rising short-term interest rates, rising long-term interest rates or a steeper yield curve also cause the prices of callable reverse floaters to fall, since this indicates that the market is expecting high short-term interest rates in the future.

In conclusion, investors should always bear in mind the risk they are assuming. This is true of all financial instruments, and particularly so with the leveraged ones.

It cannot be repeated too often that people who learn no lessons from past failures, and the stress that other investors have gone through, are most likely to repeat the same errors and see their wealth diminished rather than improved.

13.6 Accrual notes

Accrual notes are another structured interest rate product. Their particularity is that coupons accrue daily as long as the reference index remains within the predefined range. This generates regular cash flows rather than one back-end payment at redemption. The vendors of callable accrual notes say that such an instrument appeals to investors taking the view that rates will either remain stable or rise at a steady pace. A typical reference benchmark is the three or six-month Libor.

A practical example of what investors are offered is a callable US dollar range accrual note that pays a fixed coupon of 7 per cent between years 1 and 7, followed by a revised coupon of 8 per cent between years 8 and 10. This takes place for every day that the six-month Libor sits between the predefined ranges.

The client receives an enhanced coupon as long as Libor stays below the range barrier. The caveat is that the note is callable at 100 per cent every quarterly coupon date. In this way, the issuer limits his exposure at the investor's expense, the latter paying for the fact that the accrual note is principal protected by the issuer at redemption.

Another example is a callable US dollar step-up note, with principal protected by the issuer and callable at 100 per cent every quarterly coupon date. One such structured product pays a fixed coupon of 3.75 per cent in the first year, with step-up by 0.25 per cent each year, and offers the investor a final coupon of 5 per cent in year 5.

Still another example is a five-year US dollar reverse range accrual note with principal protection, callable after three months. The target investor for this instrument is thought to be one who believes that over the next five years the future three-month US dollar Libor rates are unlikely to fall below a predefined range. Should this view be correct, the investor will obtain an enhanced coupon that accrues daily, depending on whether the three-month US dollar Libor fixing on that particular day has fallen below established range boundaries.

As with the previous examples, the latter accrual note is callable by the issuer at par at every quarterly coupon payment date, after the first three months. Therefore, the investor should be prepared to have the notes called on the first possible call date, which severely limits their upside. The coupon is defined by the algorithm:

$$\text{Coupon} \cdot \frac{(c)}{C}$$

where C = number of calendar days from coupon period start date to coupon period end date, and c = number of calendar days from coupon period start date to coupon period end date, where the daily fixing of the three-month US dollar Libor stays within the range.

For calendar days on which three-month US dollar Libor fixing is outside the range, the coupon is 0.00 per cent for that day, which essentially means that the investor earns nothing, and the issuer keeps the capital at no cost. This can happen many times over a five-year maturity. The ranges of three-month Libor are given in Table 13.1.

A British pound example on accrual notes is that of a six-year range accrual product with principal protection. Like the structured instruments in US dollars, the British pound product is callable after three months.

The issuer says that investors in these interest rate notes would be those believing that over the next six years future six-month Libor rates in British pounds are unlikely to exceed a predefined range set presented in Table 13.2. Should this investor's view be correct, he or she will receive a coupon accruing daily at Libor fixing in British pounds on the particular days it has exceeded the range boundaries.

Notice, however, that the note is callable by the issuer at par at every quarterly coupon payment date, after the first three months. Hence, the upside has a cap and the investor should be prepared to have the notes called even on the first possible call date, or thereafter, with redemption at par, no matter what paper gains he or she might have accumulated. The algorithm is:

$$\text{Coupon} \cdot \frac{(b)}{B}$$

where B = actual number of business days from coupon period start date to the coupon period end date, and b = actual number of business days from coupon period start date to coupon period end date, where the daily fixing of six-month Libor in pounds is within the range.

The prospectus for this structured security specifies that the daily fixing of six-month Libor shall be taken at 11.00 a.m. London time, each day from reference page of Telerate. In the event that such a page is unavailable or cancelled, the method of observation will be determined by the calculation agent solely at its discretion, or as set out in the information memorandum.

Apart from this freedom to cherry-pick on the issuer's side, another negative for the investor is the fact that this six-year note has a three-month call option, which makes it win–win for the issuer. The call option is valued at each call date. By giving not less than five business days' prior notice, the issuer has the right, but not the obligation, to call the notes in whole at par. As with the previous case studies, the investor has

Table 13.1 Range boundaries over different time buckets up to five-year maturity

Month 0–6	3-month Libor $\geq$ 2.50%
Month 7–12	3-month Libor $\geq$ 2.75%
Month 13–18	3-month Libor $\geq$ 3.00%
Month 19–24	3-month Libor $\geq$ 3.25%
Month 25–30	3-month Libor $\geq$ 3.50%
Month 31–36	3-month Libor $\geq$ 3.75%
Year 4	3-month Libor $\geq$ 4.00%
Year 5	3-month Libor $\geq$ 4.25%

Table 13.2 Six-year range of interest rates based on Libor for British pounds

Year 1	0.00% < 6-month Libor ≥ 5.25%
Year 2	0.00% < 6-month Libor ≥ 5.50%
Year 3	0.00% < 6-month Libor ≥ 5.75%
Year 4	0.00% < 6-month Libor ≥ 6.00%
Year 5	0.00% < 6-month Libor ≥ 6.00%
Year 6	0.00% < 6-month Libor ≥ 7.75%

no way of benefiting from the note's upside, in case his guess about where interest rates go was the right one.

Euro-denominated accrual notes have precisely the same shortcoming, from the investor's viewpoint. The coupon will not be paid for each day in which a specified three-month (or any other timespan) index trades above a given barrier. In this way, the issuer has at his disposal money at practically zero cost, and:

■ If interest rates fall, and/or
■ If the yield curve associated with this structured product flattens,
■ Then, most probably, the accrual note will be called.

Issuers of accrual notes do not refute these arguments. What they say in response is that investors are 'given a chance'. For instance, the coupons are increasing each year at a gradual predefined pace; and, according to the issuers, investors in these notes who maintain a mildly bearish view on rates over the life of the note are mitigating some of their interest rate risk.

What such vendor arguments forget is that such mitigation provides (to the investor) a very limited perspective, because it is always the issuer who casts the loaded dice, since he retains the right to call in the notes at any time he chooses. Although issuers say that, since this note matures in five years, the step-ups should compensate for short-term spikes in interest rates, the truth is that:

■ If interest rates accelerate at a faster rate than the coupon's step-up on this note,
■ Then the investor will be losing value, because the note is called at par.

There are also other products that the investor may wish to consider. An interest rate product such as a cumulative coupon redemption (CCR) note pays a guaranteed sum of coupon payments during its life, providing an uncompounded, non-annualized rate of return. Coupon payments are fixed for the first year, while subsequent coupons are subject to a variable rate formula.

Issuers say that such instruments are specifically designed for investors who expect rates to stabilize or decrease, because then 'they will be able to capture a total cumulative coupon over a short period'. However,

■ If interest rates rise quickly,
■ Then the risk is that the investor may have to hold the note until maturity before receiving the full sum of coupon payments.

Notice that once the guaranteed sum of coupon payments has been paid, the note is automatically redeemed at par, before the maturity date. If the note is not redeemed early, it will redeem at par at maturity, and a final coupon will be paid, taking the total sum of coupon payments to the assured level. But with so many *ifs* in the way to receiving a reasonable return, investors would be well advised to simulate the likely outcome(s) and judge for themselves about risk and return, before making any commitment to such notes.

13.7 Fixed and variable rate notes

Fixed and variable rate notes are hybrids sold as structured products through which investors can achieve a more attractive return compared with traditional bond investments. That is the same argument made by issuers for any other derivative instrument for retail and institutional investors. For instance, vendors suggest that investors benefit from the fact that:

■ For the first few years investors receive a fixed coupon payment,
■ For the remaining term the amount they receive depends on the price development of an *equity* portfolio.

The string attached to this offer is that in exchange for the opportunity to earn a higher return than is available with a straight bond (a statement that at best is only half-true) the investor must accept the risk that, under certain circumstances, the coupon payment in the remaining years of the term may be very small indeed, or even zero.

The bait offered by the issuer to the investor is that irrespective of market developments, the issuer will repay the initially invested capital at the end of the term. As we have already seen on several occasions, however, even if the capital is repaid at 100 per cent six years down the line,

■ The investor loses the interest he or she would have gained with credit risk-free instruments such as US Treasury Bonds, and
■ At the same time the investor is faced with the (often significant) credit risk associated with the instrument's issuer.

In spite of these shortcomings there are buyers. Fixed and variable rate notes are typically marketed to investors who are looking for a fixed income instrument and consider the companies included in the structured product's basket to be good prospects. Potential buyers are told that such notes offer them the opportunity to profit from high levels of volatility in the equities market. In the majority of cases, however, the risks are not properly explained (more on this later).

Take, as an example, a fixed variable rate note in US dollars based on an underlying consisting of a basket of twenty shares in the technology sector, at 5 per cent rate of participation each. The term is six years, with issue price and repayment both at 100 per cent. The barrier per share is set at 60 per cent of share price on issue date. The coupon is:

- In years 1–3: 2.20 per cent per year, and
- In years 4–6 it follows an algorithm published by the issuer.

Typically, this algorithm conditions coupon payment for years 4–6, depending on the development of the twenty shares contained in the basket. To limit the upside, for each individual share a barrier is prescribed at the beginning of the term. Often, it is set at 60 per cent of equity price at the instrument's issue date.

Stockmarket volatility may have no influence on the (fairly low) coupon payments for the first three years, but it will weight in a significant way over interest payments in years 4–6. As the preceding paragraph explained, the note's coupon is conditioned by the algorithm, established by the issuer, for these latter years of the structured product's life cycle.

Moreover, for *each share* valued at a level below the barrier in the year in question, a deduction of 2 per cent is made from the maximum rate of 10 per cent. With twenty shares in the basket, the probability of deductions is high. The coupon payment is recalculated each year; potential coupon payments for years 4–6 are variable and they have a cap.

Beyond the risks and limitations explained in the preceding paragraphs, there is the fact that fixed and variable rate notes react to movements in interest rates through the effect that these have on equities markets. A proxy to that effect can be used from classical bonds: when interest rates rise, their value falls, and vice versa.

There are linear relationships prevailing with structured products. For instance, if a sufficient number of shares in the basket fall below their respective barriers within the coupon period, then the investor will receive no coupon payment for this period. Moreover, as with nearly all other structured instruments, the capital originally invested is only protected on maturity. During its term, the price of the note may fall well below 100 per cent.

One way of looking at fixed and variable rate structured products is through their similarity to high-yield and high-risk bond funds of the late twentieth century. One of the interesting switches of 1999 engineered by novelty in financial instruments has been that investors have been taking money out of mutual funds that invested in high-risk, high-yield junk bonds after they discovered the amount of exposure that these were assuming on their behalf. This has not happened yet with fixed and variable rate notes, but it is likely to take place. We shall see.

13.8   Bull notes

Also known as bonus notes, a term reflecting their premium, bull notes are hybrids. They are structured products that superficially look just like a traditional fixed income investment. The investor receives a fixed coupon payment throughout the term of the product, and the issuer guarantees 100 per cent repayment on maturity. In reality, however, as their name implies, these notes depend on the bullish performance of an equity index.

When the note matures, the variable index-based component will be paid out in the form of a bonus. However, to receive a high bonus, the investor must depend on a particularly positive market scenario. Should this market scenario not materialize, the bonus offered by the bull note may turn out to be small or even zero.

To explain how this hybrid instrument and its bonus work, take as an example a bull note with Euro Stoxx 50 as underlying. Both the issue price and repayment are 100 per cent. The term is five years, the coupon 1 per cent (only), and bonus on maturity is the sum of quarterly index returns.

- This is limited by a collar, i.e. both upwards and downwards, and
- Payout is subject to *minus* 10 per cent, which goes to the issuer.

Quarterly return limits of the underlying are calculated on the basis of the index level at the beginning of each quarter. Typically, these are: upper: +3 per cent, and lower: −3 per cent. An investor must be really bullish about the stockmarket to make money, in spite of these unfavourable initial conditions and limitations.

The way to look at a structured bull note is that what the investor can expect is to be paid a coupon of 1 per cent, plus something else that is rather stochastic. To gain this stochastic part, the investor hopes to participate in a significant upward movement of the Euro Stoxx 50 index. As far as the structured product is concerned:

- Quarterly performance values of the index are cumulated, in terms of both negative and positive values, and
- These are limited on the upside to the aforementioned +3 per cent per quarter, and on the downside to −3 per cent per quarter.

Remember also that the bonus paid out on maturity is equivalent to the combined sum of the performance values minus the aforementioned haircut of 10 per cent. Once more, it is win–win for the issuer.

As an example, say that in the first quarter after issuance of a bull note, the index rose by 5 per cent. For the purpose of bonus calculation, the investor is credited with the maximum of 2 per cent. Say that in the following quarter the rise is 3 per cent; this does not count towards the bonus.

However, if the index return in the third quarter is −4 per cent, the calculated figure for the investor in this period is −3 per cent. Eventually, all these derived quarterly performance values are added together over the term as a whole, to give a pre-deduction return.

If one hypothesizes that the years in a bull investment have been 'good years' for the stockmarket whose index is targeted by the bull note, then the investor would expect to gain some profit. What is this going to be?

Say, for example, that the underlying index rose by 20 per cent. After deduction of 10 per cent, equivalent to five annual coupon payments, the final bonus for the investor would amount to 10 per cent for the five-year period, or 2 per cent per year.

- The capital that he or she invested would be repaid at 110 per cent,
- But this 10 per cent bonus, or 2 per cent per year, is paid only once for the life of the product. No big deal.

If, for example, the investor had bet directly on the Euro Stoxx 50 index, he would have received a 20 per cent capital bonus, without the credit risk associated with the structured product's issuer. In a way, the meagre return the investor receives with this structured product may be seen as a way of compensating, at least partially, for that credit risk.

Issuers of bull notes are undoubtedly aware of these major shortcomings, which is why they advertise their products as being of interest to investors who are of the view that positive quarterly results and overall stockmarket performance will be the dominant feature of the five years. If, for instance, in this time-frame the Euro Stoxx 50 index increased by 70 per cent, then the 10 per cent haircut the investor suffers will be much less relevant than in the case where the increase was only 20 per cent.

What about the risks incurred by the investor? Some of them, like the credit risk, have been already mentioned, but there is also market risk. If the equity index used as underlying performs rather poorly, the bonus payment at maturity will be either very small or nothing. In other terms, it is always possible that the bull note will underperform a comparable bond investment.

Note

1 *BusinessWeek*, 30 January 1995.

14 Equity-type structured products

14.1 Introduction

Equity derivatives are structured products promoted as a better alternative to directly investing in equities. Their stated goal is to help the investor participate in performance of individual companies quoted in the exchange. The pros say that direct equity investments do not guarantee fixed returns, nor do they provide capital protection, while equity derivatives do. This is a rather loaded statement, which fails to take into account the equity derivatives risks.

To gain perspective, the reader should know that banks and hedge funds have developed a number of structured products as alternatives to direct investment in equities. Table 14.1 lists some of the most important. This is only a sample of what is currently available in the market. New equity-type structured products spring up almost daily, many being designed according to specifications by institutional investors, or even by high net worth individuals.

Several factors influence the price of equity derivatives over the course of their life cycle. Since each type has its own characteristics, design features will be considered in the appropriate sections of Chapter 15, which consists of case studies on equity-type structured products. As with the birdseye view of fixed income derivatives covered in Chapter 12, Table 14.1 does not aim to include all equity derivative instruments. Rather, its goal is to present the reader with a pattern of the most common. The tree of equity derivatives keeps on growing, as Figure 14.1 suggests, with investors' expectations being:

- Positive performance of the underlying, and
- A rising equity market.

However, sideways or negative market developments cannot be ruled out. For absorber certificates, investor expectations centre around recovery of equity markets, while for early repayment certificates the expectation is neutral to slightly positive performance of underlying, which is also true for enhanced yield notes, fixed interest payment and potential share acquisition structured products.

As far as certificates of securitized equities are concerned, investment can be made in a number of different companies, and they can take place in small denominations. Notice however, that, in contrast to an investment fund, this type of certificate constitutes a static investment. No active management takes place. Pre-estimates made about equities behaviour are one reason why the weightings of individual shares in a basket certificate tend to vary.

Table 14.1 A pallet of equity derivatives commonly available in the financial market

Instrument	Characteristics	Underlier	Secondary market
Certificates of securitized equities	Investment in an equity index, or basket of certificates consisting of shares meeting criteria such as country, industry etc. A variety is dynamic certificates with investment in an index or equity basket whose composition is subject to change	Different equity indices and different company stocks	Rather liquid secondary market for purchase and sale, with bid/offer spread of about 1% and fees similar to those for equity investments
Certificates on underlying's performance	Equity investment in the underlying performance, plus possible capital protection at end of term, if a specified barrier is not breached over the term. A variety is equity investment in which the form and level of repayment: cash and/or shares depend on performance of underlying	As above	As above
Absorber certificate	Beyond participation in the underlying, a security buffer that absorbs price losses of the underlier down to a specified level	As above	As above
Early repayment certificate	Bonus in case of early repayment, if the underlying lies above its start value on any of the applicable observation dates. Security buffer that absorbs price losses down to a specified level	As above	As above
Enhanced yield certificate	Early repayment at par on the applicable observation dates, if the underlier is quoted above start value. Fixed periodic distribution during the instrument's life. Capital protection at maturity if applicable knock-out trigger has not been reached over the term	As above	As above
Reverse exchangeable certificates	Fixed interest payment. Repayment in cash or shares dependent on performance of underlier	As above	As above
Potential share acquisition certificate	An option-based product offering the possibility of share acquisition at discount to current market price, but profit potential is limited	As above	As above

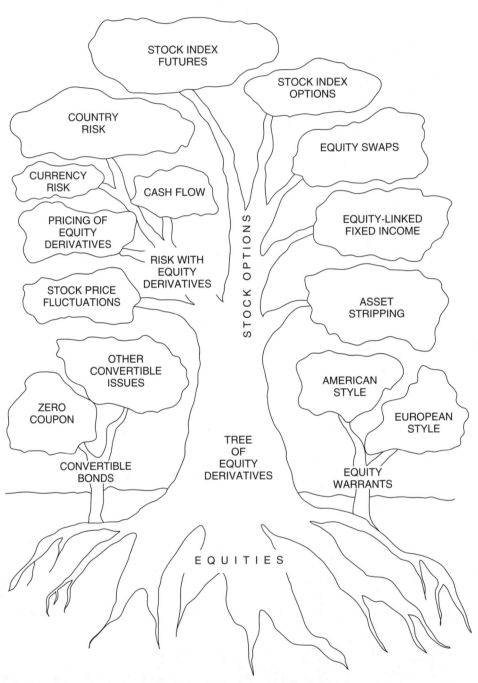

Figure 14.1 The tree of equity derivatives keeps on growing

There is no unique answer concerning capital protection connected to equity-type structured products, but the general trend is rather 'no protection', and reasonably so because of the risk involved in equity markets. Derivatives have the nasty habit of magnifying the underlying's exposure. This contrasts with what has been stated in terms of capital protection in regard to fixed income structured products.

■ Certificates of securitized equities bear the same or greater loss potential as a direct investment in the corresponding equity.
■ With certificates on the underlying's performance, however, capital protection is conditional on the knock-out level not being reached or breached during the term (see Chapter 9 on knock-in and knock-out).
■ With absorber certificates, some capital protection remains in place as long as the underlying does not close below the security buffer on maturity (this, too, is a barrier).

Barriers, knock-out levels, security buffers and other derivatives jargon is nonsense to the typical investor. This is indeed one of the serious problems with all structured products. The investor is asked by the issuer, or by his/her banker, to buy something that he does not really understand. Nor has every investor the risk management skills necessary to come even near to control of exposure in such complex positions in his or her portfolio (see Chapter 11 on risk control).

What has been said about absorber certificates is equally valid for early retirement certificates, while enhanced yield notes feature capital protection if, and only if, the underlying never touches or breaches the specified knock-out value during the term. There is no capital protection similar to that with fixed interest structured products.

Regarding this whole range of equity-type structured products, the vendor typically says to the investor: 'We can offer you a product that is geared to *your* needs and in line with how *you* think the market will develop. This product embodies the specific attributes that are important to *you* in an investment.' This is most evidently an overstatement, and investors who are caught by it are unwise. Still, the growing popularity of equity-type derivatives makes it important for all investors to know about them, their opportunities and their risks.

14.2   Headline risk and the nifty-fifty

Because the underlying of equity derivatives is stocks and indices, upon whose performance the risk and return of the investor from equity-type structure products will depend, it is only reasonable that at the start should come a better appreciation of what can be expected from the equities market.[1] This is the goal of the present section.

Financial analysts and investors look at a number of factors characterizing the behaviour of equities, and the wisdom, or lack of it, of investing in them. These decision factors include dividend growth, price/earning (P/E) ratio, one-year and five-year return on equity (ROE), one-year and five-year ROE adjusted for debt, return on assets (ROA), return on capital (ROC), the equity's volatility (beta) and the company's variability of earnings.

Financial analysts and some investors also examine some negative factors, such as neglect-institutional ownership and neglect-analyst coverage, as well as other criteria such as size, share repurchase, foreign exchange challenges, equity duration and valuation backdrop; essentially a risk premium model. Risk premium estimates are very important because equities are, to so speak, 'living commodities' and, as such, they are exposed to many risks other than the more classical market risk and credit risk. Examples are:

■ Business risk (see Chapter 3)
■ Event risk, such as a leveraged buyout (LBO), and
■ Headline risk, resulting from bad publicity because of management risk[2] or outright fraud.

The aftermath of *headline risk* may be a sharp drop in equity price, as investors react negatively to headline news, and/or widening of credit spread on the entity's bonds, from recent levels. Globalization and widely available communications technology have magnified headline risk; this can hit the investors like a hammer in cases where the underlying of derivative products in their portfolio is that company's equity.

A 2004 example is provided by Fannie Mae. In autumn 2004 regulators uncovered a plethora of accounting manoeuvres at the US government-sponsored mortgage company, allegedly aimed at dressing up its earnings. Subsequently, the firm's financial statements have undergone wholesale restatements. Then, on 15 December 2004, the Securities and Exchange Commission (SEC) ruled that the company's accounting did not comply with generally accepted accounting principles, and advised Fannie to:

■ Restate its financials, and
■ Eliminate hedge accounting.

In addition, the mortgage company disclosed that historical earnings and capital could be subject to a negative adjustment of about $9 billion. According to experts, after the SEC's ruling, Fannie needed to raise more than $12 billion in capital by mid-2005. The financial reporting unreliability of Fannie Mae is particularly damaging, because it comes on the heels of another misbehaving government company, Freddie Mac.

Moreover, OFHEO, the regulatory agency that oversees Fannie Mae and Freddie Mac, required that Fannie should have a 30 per cent excess over minimum capital requirements. At Wall Street, analysts said that the government-sponsored mortgage company needed a combination of:

■ Balance sheet shrinkage, and
■ Capital infusions to meet the terms of its agreement with OFHEO by mid-2005.

The market did not react kindly to such headline news. Another type of headline risk that hit not one entity but whole sectors of the economy in the mid- to late 1990s is that of the 'old, smoke-stack industries'. Table 14.2 shows the market effect on equity prices, which reflects in capitalization, of:

■ Three old industries with relatively medium technology, and
■ Three new economy industries with high technology.

In the go-go 1990s 'new economy' companies and their 'hi tech' were headline news. However, in terms of sales per employee the three new economy firms were not much better off than those of the old economy (with the exception of General Motors). In spite of this, their capitalization had reached for the stars. The difference was made up by market-wide headline news for the hi-tech firms.

During the bubble years of the mid- to late 1990s, the companies whose equities outperformed were the so-called nifty-fifty, mainly high technology and financials. In the summer of 1996, for example, Xerox's shares came close to their historical high. Indeed, adjusted for stock splits, Xerox's shares reached stratospheric levels.

The last time this company's equity had performed a similar feat was a quarter of a century earlier, in June 1972. This, too, was headline news followed by a subsequent slide from the market's grace, which went down in the annals of corporate history. Analysts said that there was a strong link between:

■ The two peaks in the Xerox chart, and
■ The two bull markets that gave them birth.

In other words, Xerox's striking performance in the early 1970s was only partly due to its own merits. Although it had established what appeared at the time an

Table 14.2 The old industries and the new economy

	1996 sales ($ billion)	Sales per employee ($ 000s)	Market capitalization (March 1997) ($ billion)	Market capitalization per employee ($ 000s)
Old industries				
Medium technology				
General Motors	164.0	253	43	66
Ford	147.0	406	38	110
Chrysler	61.4	538	22	193
Total	372.4		103	
New industries				
High technology				
Intel	20.8	424	116	2367
Microsoft	8.7	414	120	5714
Cisco	4.1	410	34	3400
Total	33.6		270	

unchallengeable lead in plain-paper photocopying, that technical leadership was only half the story.

Equally important, if not even more so, in terms of equity valuation was Xerox's membership of the *nifty-fifty*, a loosely defined group of big, glamour stocks that managed to rise to new highs even while the rest of the 1960s bull market collapsed around their ears. For the nifty-fifty, it is good news that headline risk is hitting the other firms quoted in the capital market.

With the noticeable exceptions of companies such as General Electric and Coca-Cola, which manage to sneak into the top list of the market's darlings, every stockmarket bull has its own nifty-fifty. This identification started in the mid-1990s, when the Morgan Stanley Multinational Index (MSMI) put together an ad-hoc list (and index) of 50 big American companies that had been doing particularly well in the preceding months.

The top market performers in that list turned out to be pretty much blue-chips, with Boeing, AT&T, General Electric, Coca-Cola, IBM, Intel, Merck, Microsoft, Oracle, Procter & Gamble and Xerox among them. The major difference between this index and the wider universe of American companies, the Standard & Poor's (S&P) 500, is that the nifty-fifty group has been substantially more exposed to the global marketplace.

Just as important is the fact that most of the nifty-fifty have strong international brands, which is particularly helpful in an era of intensifying worldwide competition. Moreover, the nifty-fifty is famous not just for the way in which its members manage to outperform their peers, but also for the fact that its members can rapidly fall from grace, and not only in a bear market. Xerox is an example.

- After reaching a peak, in 1973/74 its stock crashed in a bear market, and
- While after its 1996 peak, the market continued to rise rapidly, in the late 1990s Xerox's stock tanked because of management problems and the fact that it lost its global market leadership to the Japanese.

These lows in the prices of formerly top performers play against equity-type derivatives that magnify the risk embedded in the underlying. Even if the underlying stock is one of the nifty-fifty, its fortunes can change rapidly. A big part of the appeal of equities in this exclusive group is the belief that its members have established impregnable global market positions in growing industries, and are thus insulated from the ups and downs of the domestic cycle; but when these global positions crumble, so do the corresponding equity-type structured products.

14.3   Equity derivatives defined

Classically, an *equity instrument* has been a contract that provides ownership interest in an entity. Typically, this share of ownership entitles its holder to a pro rata participation in all distributions made to the class of equity holders to which he or she belongs, but it entails a right to receive cash or other financial assets only upon:

- Declaration of a dividend, or
- The issuing entity's liquidation.

Examples include common stock and partnership interests owned. Notice, however, that this definition was valid only until the equity derivatives market took off. Thereafter, it had to be modified because of trading in off-balance sheet assets that do not exactly fall under the original definition of equity.

Trading through continuing *asset unbundling* (or stripping) is a self-feeding cycle and it has certain consequences. The more successful each deal is, the bigger the next deal has to be to continue a pattern of growth and market leadership. This is important inasmuch as unbundling of equity assets has become the basis of work performed by financial engineers, rocket scientists[3] and traders. Three classes of equity derivatives that were originally offered in the over-the-counter (OTC) market help to characterize most trades:

- Equity options on stock indices, baskets or individual stocks,
- Equity-linked fixed income instruments, such as warrant and convertible bonds, and
- Different types of equity swaps, which constitute a flexible and growing class of equity derivatives.

For instance, there are equity derivative swaps allowing the counterparties to speculate on the appreciation or depreciation of an equity as contrasted with that of an index or, alternatively, a basket of equities. With equity derivative swaps maturities typically range from one to five years, but the parties may also agree on transactions that may be structured on shorter or longer terms.

Notice that the three classes identified by the above bullet points were dominant before popularization of equity-type structured products. Institutional investors were the main purchasers of these instruments. An initial source of growth of the market for equity derivatives has been interest in the issuance of Eurobonds with equity-linked elements, either convertible bonds or bonds with detachable warrants. Subsequently, to the aforementioned three classes have been added:

- Different types of equity indices, and
- Instruments with option-like characteristics such as options on futures.

Another change that took place in the late 1990s, and even more so in the first years of the twenty-first century, concerns the population of customers to whom credit derivatives are addressed. While different variations on equity derivatives have long been available to institutional investors and other professionals, only recently have they arrived at individual investor level, presenting themselves as a low-cost way to bet on the stockmarket.

Private investors usually fail to appreciate that these instruments are also huge risk. Unlike short-term options, which expire in three months or less, structured equity products can last for years (more on them in Chapter 15). Because of this longer life cycle, they are subject to fairly significant equity market volatility.

Investors in equity-type structured products should understand that stockmarket volatility can be significant even when it is low by historical standards. In 1999–2004, the average Euroland's equity volatility stood at more than 26 per cent, although it was about 21 per cent in the USA, and this is far from being a worst case.

By and large, equity derivatives for retail investors are a development of year 2001 and beyond, in the aftermath of the stockmarket crash, when many investment banks, commercial banks and hedge funds developed tailor-made products based on equities. These instruments contrasted with the standard features of trading in equity.

Notice too that company stocks and indices are not the only possible underlyings. In fact, equity-linked debt and convertibles warrants are both an alternative, and can be seen as a precursor to equity derivatives. *Equity warrants* have been known in business for many decades, giving the holder the right to purchase a company's stock at a set strike price, within a fixed time-frame.

Sold by the company itself, which puts its equity on the block, such warrants are listed and traded. They are required to issue new equity in exchange for cash, if exercise takes place. Typically, equity warrants are exercised if the investor is in the money.

- Equity warrants are distinguished from call options, because call options do not result in the issuance of new equity.
- If exercise occurs, the effect of a call option is to reallocate an equity holding from the writer to the buyer.

Another class of equity-related derivative instruments is *covered warrants*. These are not issued by the company itself, but are third party transactions. For instance, a bank may sell a warrant backed by the underlying stock, as well as equity warrants or equity options of a company. This type of warrant can be exercised in cash or in underlying shares.

Still another class of equity-type derivatives is the covered *index warrants*. This is a development of the 1980s, with popular index warrants being the S&P 500 in the USA, FTSE 100 in the UK, DAX in Germany, CAC-40 in France and Nikkei 225 in Japan.

Stock index futures are also powerful and versatile derivatives instruments, permitting investors to participate in broad market moves without having to select individual stocks, but also to speculate on short-term market gyrations. Such instruments are thought to:

- Benefit the investor in bull markets without using many funds to purchase stocks, and
- Protect the value of the portfolio in bear markets, at least in theory.

It does not take a high intelligent quotient (IQ) to appreciate that these two bullets express rather contradictory goals, based on half-truths. What such two-way arguments conveniently forget is the amount of risk being assumed due to leveraging. Barings went into bankruptcy because of speculating on the Nikkei 225 index in Osaka, geared up well beyond its financial means to face its commitments.

While, in the most general terms, risk and return are a function of appreciation or depreciation of the chosen stock or market index, depending on which way the investor of speculator bets.[4] This is true all over equity investments, and even more so in connection with equity derivatives.

14.4 Players in equity derivatives

Since the mid- to late 1990s equity derivatives have become an integral part of a fund manager's professional life, as he or she is being judged on results and therefore tries to become increasingly more profitable. Section 14.3 also noted that since 2000/01 the use of equity derivatives has spread to the area of personal finance. With this in mind, users of equity derivatives can be divided into four main classes of investors:

■ *Corporate treasurers*, who want tools to manage or hedge different exposures on their balance sheet,
■ *Insurance companies* and investment funds, which target new products and annuities to sell to their retail clients,
■ *Pension funds*, wanting to have exposure to a certain equity market, without having to go out and buy shares in that market, and
■ *High net worth individuals* and, increasingly, medium net worth private banking clients, lured into equity-type structured products by their bankers or by hedge funds.

Beyond these four classes are the traders who go into equity derivatives transactions not for investment reasons, but for profits to be made from dealing. For clarity of definition, to qualify as a *trade*, in the sense used in this text, a deal must be a transaction designed and executed using financial instruments. Equity derivatives fulfil this definition. The goal of a trade is to profit from an insight or a window in market opportunity.

■ A trade cannot be something that happened by accident or sheer luck, and
■ It cannot be a deal such as a merger, takeover or private placement, even if it is clever and lucrative.

Retail investors are not, and should not, be traders. This being said, since the early years of the twenty-first century, private banking clients have been creeping into what has classically been a largely institutional investment domain. This is promoted by the advent of so-called 'guaranteed return' products (a misnomer), which are heavily marketed to retail investors, particularly to those who have seen their income from cash deposits dwindle as a result of the substantial drop in interest rates in the early years of this century.

All of these players try to capitalize on the fact that most equity derivative products, which are traded OTC or on futures and options exchanges, can be tailored to each client's specific needs. However, as some traders suggest, the drawback of individual structured deals, and a major one for that matter, is that:

■ They are not liquid, and
■ They are difficult to get out of, once you are in.

The counterargument by the pros is that equity derivatives deals are essentially made up of a series of building blocks that can be unwound 'at any time'. But there is little evidence to sustain this argument. More fundamental is the fact that, as a result of the customized nature of instruments offered in this market,

- The more innovative are equity-type structured products,
- The less is their liquidity.

Contrary to custom-made equity-type derivative instruments designed to fit individual needs, products traded on the exchanges tend to be more standardized and they can be attractive to investors who are not allowed to buy financial instruments which:

- Are not listed,
- Cannot be marked-to-market, and
- Have no price-finding mechanism to ensure that liquidity is not obtained through fire sale.

As all investors should appreciate, one important advantage of buying a listed product is that the exchange acts as a central clearing house. This helps to reduce market participants' exposure to credit risk and market risk. By contrast, players in the OTC market:

- May find themselves obliged to trade directly with a counterparty that has an inferior credit rating, and/or
- May discover that their ability to optimize the price of a product they are trading is very limited, because of a lack of options.

An even more pronounced benefit derived from products traded in an established exchange, with lots of players and significant trading volume, is that the price discovery mechanism that they support makes it possible to monitor effectively equity risks associated derivatives, and set limits to exposure. Well-governed credit institutions and assets managers monitor equity derivatives risks through different types of a limits structure:

- Volatility-based market risk limits,
- Currency- and volume-based market liquidity limits,
- Triggers actuating corrective management action for damage control.

Properly studied and established market risk limits involve a total market threshold, first order sublimits and second order sublimits. The responsibility for establishing and monitoring such limits rests with top management, which requires daily reports not just based on a summary value at risk but also, if not primarily, along the frame of reference shown in Table 14.3.

Banks that use high technology go through frequent re-examination of limits associated with equity price risk. They do so on a steady basis, by stock exchange, currency being involved, industry where investments are made and individual equity. This is done at a much greater level of detail with the underlyings of equity-type structured products, down to the level of each family of instruments.

Table 14.3 Controls established for equity derivatives exposure

	Equity derivatives trading	Portfolio derivatives	New issue position(s)	Equity derivatives sold	Equity derivatives secondary market	Infra-structure equities
Evaluation method	Fair value	Fair value	Fair value	Fair value	Lower of cost or market value (LOCOM)	Lower of cost or market value (LOCOM)
Type of limits	Position limits	Position limits	Position limits	According to transaction	According to transaction	Position limits
Product responsibility		1. Department accountable for product 2. Corporate risk management				

14.5 Risks taken with analytics

As far as continental Europe is concerned, the decade of the 1990s has seen a huge surge in direct equity investments and mutual fund shares by private investors. The more affluent the public became, the more it went for equities rather than bonds. Based on statistics by the Deutsche Bundesbank, Figure 14.2 provides an example from Germany in the decade 1992–2001.

After the stockmarket bubble burst in early 2000, when many private as well as institutional investors were burned, their investment advisors at credit institutions suggested that they turn towards alternative investments.[5] A surprising number of high net worth individuals and many institutional investors did so. By contrast, experienced investors understood that:

■ They do not need equity derivatives to participate in the positive performance of an equity or index, and
■ Capital protection with equity-type structured products is conditioned by so many barriers and knock-outs that it is practically an empty promise.

As for promises about receiving an attractive bonus, even if the underlying index has not risen at all, the number of 'ifs' and conditions is so large that 'high returns' is nothing more than a fantasy and marketing gimmick. Such empty promises are the sort of thing making some investors curious to find out more about the different ways in which alternatives to direct equity investments can be sugar-coated to attract buyers.

The vendors of equity derivatives and other similar certificates are aware of the inflated nature of their claims, and therefore they prudently attach to their promotional literature a disclaimer that typically says: 'This document does not constitute

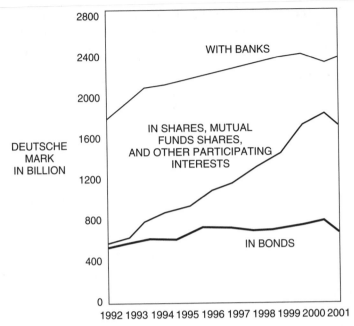

Figure 14.2 Households' financial assets in the German Federal
Republic (year-end data) (*Source*: Deutsche Bundesbank, Monthly
Report, July 2002, by permission)

an issue prospectus as referred to . . . (follows the reference to code of obligations by securities supervisors); it has been compiled to explain the structured product . . .'.

Yes, but explaining is convincing. The disclaimer, most often written in small print, further says that this document has been prepared solely for the information purposes of the recipient. Sometimes it is also stated that any reference to past performance is not necessarily a guide to the future. At least this last statement is true.

Let's face it. In spite of what we think and often say about predicting market trends, the markets are unpredictable. As chaos theory suggests,[6] hundreds of little inputs combine together to lead to a certain event or start a trend. No financial analyst can detect all of these inputs in real-time, and factor them into a model. Infinitesimal as its probability may be, a butterfly batting its wings in Bermuda may contribute to a hurricane hitting Key West.

The same principles of chaos theory also apply in risk control. It is no secret that there is always an equity risk and it is present in all markets. Because with leveraged instruments, as with equity-type structured products, equity risk zooms, investors must embed into their risk and return model a wide margin of error. This margin of error means that:

■ Expected returns would be lower than is implicit in many funds' real return assumptions, and
■ A level of confidence must be established for risk analysis, at the 99 per cent confidence interval, or even better at 99.9 per cent.

Implied market volatility must always be taken into account (see Chapter 4), and this is far from being the same in all industry sectors. An implied volatility series by industry sector reflects the expected standard deviation of percentage stock price changes over a period of up to three months, as implied in the prices of options on stock price indices.

Industry sectors have their own characteristics. In the go-go mid- to late 1990s, the average volatility of developments in technology stock prices was consistently higher than general stockmarket volatility. Between the end of 1991 and 10 May 2000 the historical volatility of the US technology sector was 26 per cent per year, which compared with 14 per cent for the Dow Jones US broad market index and a median of 16 per cent across the principal economic sectors defined by Dow Jones: basic materials, consumer cyclical, consumer non-cyclical, energy, financial, healthcare, industrial, technology, telecommunications and utilities.

In continental European markets the corresponding figures were 24 per cent for the technology sector, 16 per cent for the Dow Jones Euro Stoxx index and 17 per cent for the median. This general pattern of high volatility in technology stocks reflected the higher proportion of new firms in technology, with uncertain business prospects in technology that resulted in higher upward and downward risks to their stock prices.

- All equity investors are in the frontline of such developments, albeit at different levels of market volatility,
- In the general case, the more leveraged the investment portfolio and its instruments, the greater the volatility's impact on the investor.

This is a basic principle applying throughout the knowledge society. Another critical issue connected to risk and return is that of equity research responsibilities and their impact on the market.

Primary agents with responsibility in equity, equity-linked and equity derivative products are research and analysis companies whose activities address individual firms, industry sectors, geographical markets and macroeconomic trends. Opinions expressed by equity analysts and associated equity picks are far from being always objective. The huge penalties paid in April 2004 by some of the best known names at Wall Street document the biases that exist in terms of investment recommendations to institutional and private investors.[7]

- It is simply not possible that all equities quoted in a stock exchange are 'buys' and 'strong buys'.
- While, sometimes, a strong buy may become a buy rating and in some cases a buy may become hold, rarely does a buy become a sell.

Ratings and ratio revisions are always biased on the upside. Typically, investment opinions promote just that: 'investments', but in several cases favoured investments tank. Even when a security is under review with opinion withdrawn, it is likely that it will be restored to good status, with all this means in subsequent risk, because of its inclusion in a basket underlying a leveraged structured product.

Critics say that apart from the bias characterizing investment opinions, the criteria that make a good financial analyst have not been adequately researched. Investment banks and other equity research outfits employing analysts rarely perform the appropriate tests to establish whether the people they employ have an analytical mind. Analytics is a left-brain characteristic. Every person has a decision style pattern distributed in left and right brain, with:

- Analytical and directive capabilities in the left brain, and
- Conceptual and behavioural capabilities in the right brain.

Tests for decision style patterns are no IQ test. The example of eight people shown in Figure 14.3 indicates that these people had the wrong decision styles for stress testing, an activity where conceptual skills dominate, although they had first class analytical skills. Indeed, these eight people were analysts wrongly brought into stress testing.

These criticisms are valid for all equity investments, but because of leverage equity derivatives magnify some of the problems involved with investing. Another case to keep in mind, with negative effects on wealth management, is insider trading. In options markets, in particular, market makers can feel the impact of insider trading quite dramatically.

For example, in March 1994, market makers at the Chicago Board Options Exchange (CBOE) suffered hefty losses on Grumman call options, which gave buyers the right to buy the stock. After the Grumman received a bid from Martin Marietta, Grumman market makers were forced to sell this company's stock to the options holders at below-market prices. Market makers filed a report with the CBOE on this Grumman options imbroglio and threatened to file a lawsuit to recoup the losses of their members.[8]

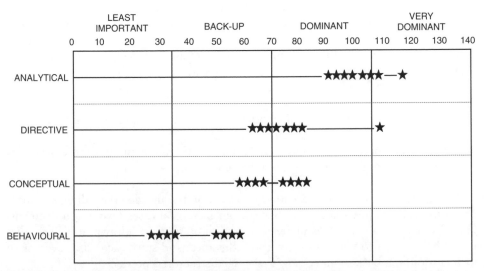

Figure 14.3 Decision style pattern of eight people assigned to stress tests. The all-important conceptual skills are way behind, although analytical skills are strong

14.6 Criteria used for dynamic rotation

This section is a case study on hybrids, which attempt to combine characteristics of equity and debt instruments. It is also a precursor to the discussion on a number of real-life structured products presented in Chapter 15, including a case study on dynamic rotation.

One of the financial instruments addressed to private and institutional investors in the early years of the twenty-first century, when money has been cheap and interest rates of major currencies the lowest in forty-five years, has been based on a selection of stocks that paid a relatively high dividend. Thirty stocks were selected from the universe of 100 different equities that comprise the FTSE Global 100 index. The criteria have been:

- Stocks with the highest dividends, and
- A strategy chosen to maintain the sector diversification of FTSE Global 100.

The issuer of this equity-type structured product underlined in his prospectus that he used a dynamic selection process that allowed for the rotation of the thirty stocks. During the life of the structured instrument, the adopted approach permitted inclusion and exclusion of stocks from the previous year's set.

The retained stocks were ranked according to their dividend yield and divided into three groups: ten stocks with the highest dividend yields weighted at 5 per cent each, ten stocks with next highest dividend yields weighted at 3 per cent each, and the remaining ten stocks weighted at 2 per cent each.

Rebalancing is done, by the issuer, quarterly, with any dividends and option premiums accrued during the previous quarter reinvested into the index constituents. A new selection of the thirty highest yielding stocks has been made annually, as stated, from the 100 stocks comprising the FTSE Global 100 index.

Dynamic rotation is a good idea because nothing guarantees that the higher ranking dividend payers of today will remain so tomorrow. When companies face headwinds, they cut dividends. Damage control, however, requires much more than that. All equities in an investment portfolio must be under steady scrutiny of:

- Quality of management,
- Accuracy of financial reporting,
- Cash flow and earnings, and
- Dividend policy.

In connection to dynamic rotation, important lessons can be learned from the bursting of the late 1990s equities bubble. One of the major failings of investors during the dot-com boom has been that they had become star struck. As internet CEOs turned themselves into celebrities and their company's stock skyrocketed, financial analysts, the media and investors themselves competed to put them on their way to stardom.

- Instead of asking sceptical questions about earnings and cash flow, investors were simply caught by their supposedly innovative strategies, and

■ Many analysts wrote uncritically about the dot-coms and their prospects, failing to question whether 'new' was truly better and whether great company leverage really made sense.

In the minds of those who should have known how to make a critical analysis, companies that stuck with long-held strategies were downgraded and their blueprints were scorned as being behind-the-curve. The media commented that such stodgy firms 'were not thinking outside the box' because they were not changing rapidly enough, and paid dividends instead of reinvesting all of their profits.

Little attention was paid to the fact that not only do companies die, but also those who are the more innovative (a positive characteristic in itself) tend to fall more quickly and in droves. A high death rate hurts investors, even though the very few among the start-ups who succeed may well be on their way to become the next industrial giants. The motor vehicle industry provides an example from the early twentieth century, almost half a century before the computer era:

■ The years 1900–1925 saw 3000 automobile start-ups.
■ Ford, Daimler-Benz and companies that merged into General Motors are among the few surviving today, of the thousands of start-up car firms.

In the post-World War II years these few survivors have been joined by others who learned a lesson from the old start-ups' mistakes, to a global total of not quite two dozen. What are their prospects? Among financial analysts there is increasing speculation that by 2010 the survivors in the global motor vehicle industry will number less than half a dozen, maybe only three or four.

As Gabriella Stern, senior editor of Dow Jones Wires, said in her lecture at the Sixth Trema Forum,[9] with hindsight we realize that it is possible to think 'outside the box' within the framework of a long-standing strategy. At a time when rapid transformation was 'in', clinging to a tried-and-true business roadmap was actually outside the box. Post-1990s:

■ The criteria that we are using for evaluation have changed, and
■ This change ensures that screening on the basis of paid dividends, which are tangible, is a sound approach.

Stern could have added that there is another 'plus' in connection to a sound dividend policy, and it points to risk control. With the exception of companies that sell their assets to maintain a higher dividend, a policy of strong dividends indicates a high likelihood of financial staying power. This reflects on creditworthiness, because a company would pay first its suppliers and its taxes, and then its shareholders.

14.7 Equity derivatives swaps

Structured products based on an equity index and emulating interest on bonds are not a recent discovery. Convertible bonds and warrants were among the earlier financial instruments representing debt and equity at the same time. Equity warrants have been in use for many decades, giving the owner the right to purchase the company's stock at a set price. However:

- Call options do not result in the need to issue new stock.
- In contrast, convertible bonds and warrants require the issuance of new equity.

Covered warrants are not really warrants in a traditional sense; they are third party transactions. For instance, a bank may write a warrant backed by underlying stock or other warrants.

Equity derivative swaps are different instruments altogether. They allow either or both counterparties to bet on appreciation or depreciation of an equity, an index or a basket of equities. Equity derivative swaps are used by institutional and other investors holding equities or indices, to hedge downside exposure.

- They can be structured according to the terms agreed by both parties, and
- Although their maturity can vary, usually it is kept in the one to five-year range.

There are different types of equity swaps, with index call, index put/call, equity/equity, index with embedded option and others. This is part of the universe of swap products that includes interest rate swaps (IRS), currency exchange rate swaps and commodity rate swaps (energy, gold and other physical goods).

The reader should be aware that all swaps have credit risk, because the counterparty in a transaction may be unable or unwilling to perform. It is therefore advisable that investors carefully identify and examine associated risk factors affecting current and future exposure. Swaps also have a good deal of market risk, and equity derivative swaps are no exception to this statement.

Risk evaluation of equity derivative swaps permits one to judge the appropriate level of exposure in a given portfolio or single transaction. The algorithm being used represents the summation of periodic interest payments that may occur only once during the life of the transaction.

Evaluation of assumed risk is crucial. A risk equivalent component can be made more accurate through an adjustment of the risk factor being used to reflect the relevant settlement period of the deal. It can also become more sophisticated by distinguishing between:

- Potential market exposure, and
- The risk resulting by marking-to-market, which means actual exposure.

Institutional investors should be well equipped to perform these risk control functions. Such a statement, however, cannot be made about private investors. Therefore, a sound rule is that:

- If the instrument is complex and damage control is beyond the means characterizing the investor's capabilities and know-how,
- Then he or she should not touch that instrument even with a one-kilometre-long pole.

Investment catacombs are created by failure to have in place a first class system of damage control. An estimated 400 000 Italians, the large part retail clients of local banks, were holding €14.7 billion ($17.65 billion) of Argentina's bonds when that country defaulted in 2001. These unlucky savers had been sold the toxic waste that took care of their savings through branches of banks in which they held their accounts.

Also in Italy, another 100 000 small investors held €1.9 billion ($2.28 billion) of Parmalat's bonds when the hedge fund with a dairy product line on the side failed in December 2003. Still another 30 000 Italian savers were left holding €1.1 billion ($1.3 billion) of Cirio paper when the food processor collapsed in 2003. In short, in just these three incidents of inappropriate sale of highly risky instruments to private investors $21.23 billion of private investors' money went up in smoke.

While the examples given in the last two paragraphs speak of bond investments, which turned sour and left their holders in a mess, stockholders with Parmalat, Cirio and many other firms also lost their fortune. Indeed, equity investors are the first parties in the firing line of a default. Investing is an unforgiving business.

This fact alone should be enough to tell investors that they must avoid leverage and put a limit on their risks.

14.8   The use of embedded barrier options

Options on equity securities are not new. In practice, they include not only common stock and preferred stock, but also American Depository Receipts (ADR) and American Depository Shares (ADS), representing interests in foreign entities. Such options are available on exchange-traded equity securities, unlisted equity securities traded in the NASDAQ and other markets.

- Typically, each option covers 100 shares of the underlying equity, but the number of underlying shares may also be different, as specified in the deal.
- The exercise price of each option must be multiplied by the number of shares underlying the option, to determine the aggregate exercise price and aggregate premium of that option.

Adjustments are made to certain of the standard terms of outstanding stock options when specific events occur, such as a special stock dividend or distribution, stock split, rights offering and recapitalization. Adjustments are not usually made for ordinary cash dividends or distributions. (A cash dividend or distribution will generally be considered 'ordinary' by most issuers, unless it exceeds 10 per cent of the aggregate market value of the outstanding underlying security.)

In general, adjustments are not made for tender offers or exchange offers, whether by the issuer or a third party, and whether for cash, securities (including issuer securities) or other property. Since call holders may seek to capture an impending dividend by exercising, a call writer's chances of being assigned an exercise may increase as the expiration date for a dividend on the underlying security approaches.

Speculators, and some investors, have always been keen on exploiting loopholes in the trading system that permit them to make profits without putting up all of the money. Embedded options assist in this strategy. Like margin trading, buying traded options is a leveraged activity.

- Bankers, investors and speculators can make more money than they would in the underlying shares, if the share price moves in their favour,
- But they can lose a lot if their bet proves wrong and the market moves against their guess.

Investors and speculators can even lose everything by playing with structured products based on equities with a *barrier option*, which is embedded in some structured instruments currently available. As shown in other case studies, this is an option that either comes into existence, or is eliminated, when a market price reaches a predetermined strike level. The primary barriers are:

- *Up and out*, where an option is cancelled out if an index price rises above a certain level, which is up.
- *Down and out*, where an option is cancelled out if an index falls to a certain level, which is down.
- *Up and in*, where an option comes into existence, hence in, if an index reaches a certain level up.
- *Down and in*, where an option comes into being (in) if the index falls below a certain level, hence down.

The types of barrier options described by the first two bullets are known as *knock-outs*. Those described by the second pair of bullets are referred to as *knock-ins*. Neither is a new product. They have been in existence since the late 1960s, but became popular in recent years as their path-dependent feature attracted many traders.

Banks have been buying path-dependent barriers mainly because of gambling. The reason often given, that from their standpoint the fact of losing some traditional economic benefits lowered the premium paid to the seller, simply makes no sense. By contrast, from the standpoint of the seller of the option, although he or she receives less premium income, the seller also assumes a lower degree of risk by:

- Not having to pay appreciation or depreciation when normally required, or
- Having his or her contractual obligation eliminated entirely if a pre-established level (barrier) is breached.

Barrier options may be incorporated into equity derivative swaps, and may also have a different structure to the aforementioned one. An example is the *lookback option*, where the buyer of put or call will receive from the seller the greatest economic value achieved during the life of the option, regardless of the level of expiry.

The name of this instrument comes from the fact that the buyer is able to look back during the life of the transaction and, with the benefit of hindsight, select the point that yields the greatest economic gain. A lookback therefore provides some certainty that the best value has been obtained in a given transaction. (There exist three varieties: American, European and Asian, which are not part of this book.)

While most of the instruments based on barrier options are principally traded among banks, structured products that emulate them are now entering private banking. This is done in connection with *equity exposure* with enhanced yield, in exchange for capital risk. Private investors would be well advised to keep out of them.

For instance, a structured note recently launched by a major commercial bank will pay a fixed coupon of 7 per cent on each anniversary of its launch. At maturity, the capital value of the note is linked to the highest annual value of a basket of twenty international equities, reduced by a fixed amount for each equity that has fallen by more than 25 per cent.

The performance of the basket of shares is calculated at launch and on each of its anniversaries. At maturity, the highest value is taken, but it is reduced to reflect the number of basket members that have closed at or below the 75 per cent barrier of their initial value, on one or more anniversary. Another 10 per cent is deducted for each stock that has touched this down barrier. By contrast,

- If at any of the anniversaries the basket has risen by 20 per cent or more,
- Then capital protection will apply at maturity regardless of the number of equities that breach the barrier.

This is, however, dependent on 'ifs'. A 'best case' scenario would be that the basket rises steadily during the term, and none of the shares in the basket touches the barrier. If so, redemption is at the highest basket value, giving an annualized capital gain in addition to the coupon. Critics say that, under these conditions, the holder would have obtained a better result if he or she had invested directly in equities, rather than buying the structured product.

The reader should also take note of an alternative scenario available with this type of derivative instrument: The basket rises and subsequently falls. Three stocks break the barrier. Accordingly, 30 per cent is deducted from the highest basket value to determine the redemption price. With this option, the risk rises and, not unexpectedly, the investor's returns diminish.

The following case is worse. The basket does not rise sufficiently to trigger capital protection, and while the highest basket value is above par, several equities touch the barrier. The redemption value of the note is 50 per cent of par, with capital loss outweighing income received by the investor. The whole risk and return equation that was sold to the buyer has turned on its head.

Notes

1 D.N. Chorafas, *The Management of Equity Investments*, Butterworth-Heinemann, London, 2005.
2 D.N. Chorafas, *Management Risk. The Bottleneck is at the Top of the Bottle*, Macmillan/Palgrave, London, 2004.
3 D.N. Chorafas, *Rocket Scientists in Banking*, Lafferty Publications, London, 1995.
4 D.N. Chorafas, *The Management of Equity Investments*, Butterworth-Heinemann, London, 2005.

5 D.N. Chorafas, *Alternative Investments and the Mismanagement of Risk*, Macmillan/Palgrave, London, 2003.

6 D.N. Chorafas, *Chaos Theory in the Financial Markets*, Probus, Chicago, 1994.

7 D.N. Chorafas, *Corporate Accountability, with Case Studies in Finance*, Macmillan/Palgrave, London, 2004.

8 *BusinessWeek*, 12 December 1994.

9 *Monte Carlo*, 4–5 June 2004.

15 Practical examples with equity-type derivatives

15.1 Introduction

As explained in Chapter 14, certificates of securitized equities are derivative financial instruments sold by their issuers as structured products. These instruments are complex and they involve a high degree of exposure. Theoretically, they are intended for sale only to investors capable of understanding and assuming the risks involved. Practically, they are sold to everybody.

Therefore, before entering into any transaction involving the purchase of equity-type derivatives, the investor should fully consider the suitability of that transaction to his or her particular circumstances and financial position, including risk appetite. The investor would also be well advised to review independently the specific financial exposure involved in securitized equities, as well as the legal, regulatory, credit, accounting and tax consequences embedded in these instruments.

What the previous paragraphs have stated are 'musts', and they are by no means the issues that a salesperson of equity derivatives would raise in trying to close a deal. Rather, the issuer's or salesperson's questions to the buyer will be: 'Are you an equity investor?' 'Do you expect share prices to rise?' Would you like to profit from the performance of a number of companies with just a modest investment?' All these are queries designed to elicit a 'yes' answer. They can also be traps.

Usually, the buyer will be told that by purchasing a certificate of equity derivatives he or she will be investing in an equity portfolio that is structured in the form of a security, without specifying the exposure this instrument involves or giving a true picture of risk and return. Investors unaware of the risks involved in such instruments will be prone to believe that they represent an alternative to a direct investment in the equity market. The vendor typically says that:

- The structured product's return corresponds to the average return of all underlying listed companies in the portfolio, and
- Because of broad diversification, exposures can be 'enormously reduced' compared with a direct single equity investment.

It would be superfluous to add that such statements are unreliable. With the exception of index-based products, the diversification involved in structured equity derivatives is limited, not broad. What is broad is leveraging, with all this means in terms of assumed risk. Investors should be aware of such facts before deciding to enter into an equity-type derivatives transaction.

Neither are the many products reviewed in this chapter very different from one another. Indeed, rather than thinking of them as different products, as they are usually sold to institutional and private investors, it is advisable to look at them as different *versions* of one and the same product, characterized by:

- An underlying equity, equity basket or index,
- A barrier associated with the index,
- Maturity, several years down the line,
- A security buffer providing a cushioning effect, and
- A cap on the return that the product may offer to the investor on the upside.

In the more general case, certificates on the underlying's performance are leveraged. Moreover, according to the same old 'no free lunch' principle, the issuer must be ahead of the curve in equity investment characterized by an underlying plus possible capital protection at the end of term. Unlike the case with fixed income structured products, this capital protection, whenever it exists, is conditional: *if* a specified barrier is not breached over the term.

There are several types in equities investment in which the form and level of repayment: cash and/or shares depend on performance of the underlying. One of the structured products (studied in section 15.3) goes beyond participation in the underlying. It presents a security buffer that absorbs price losses to a specified level, at a certain cost.

Contrarians are pressing the point that the fact that such risky instruments have reached the private investor's level is largely due to a lack of appropriate legislation, regulation and supervision. New regulation to control effectively derivatives exposure assumed by parties that should be much more careful in their investment choices:

- Private investors,
- Pension funds,
- Mutual funds, and
- Insurance companies,

is an issue that has been made more complex by the fact that, for a long time, hedge funds, whose activities underpin equity derivatives, among other leveraged products, were predominantly *domiciled offshore*, as their managers were looking for:

- Minimum regulatory intervention, and
- Very favourable tax treatment.

More recently, because investors are demanding that there is at least some supervision, and given the light-touch approach by some onshore regulators, new hedge funds have started to consider onshore jurisdictions to govern their operations. No matter where hedge funds are domiciled, however, their managers generally reside in major financial centres and may or may not be registered with local regulatory authorities. (More on hedge funds in section 15.3.)

15.2   Equity index and basket structured notes

Usually index-linked structured notes expose the investor to 100 per cent negative index performance, but only up to a point to positive performance, if there is any; for instance, 80 per cent with a cap. After such a level, Table 15.1 shows this pattern. Notice that for index performance of 0 per cent, after several years the investor receives his or her capital, but no interest. By contrast, if the index moves south, then part of the capital is also lost.

Take index certificates as an example. This index reflects the whole of, or a part of a market, and can serve as a benchmark for other products or for portfolio management reasons. In practice all market indices represent the largest quoted companies in their respective countries, although there are also broad-based indices such as the S&P 500.[1]

- Index certificates have increasingly been issued in an open-end form.
- Within an outlined investment perspective, their certificate is directly dependent on the performance of the index to which the certificate relates.

Contrarians say that the clauses associated with index certificates represent a greater risk for the investor than buying equities. This can be better appreciated by looking at the underlying, which is a basket of equities and consists of a narrow band of stocks relative to the index. For example, the basket is composed of US equities,

- The term is two years,
- Minimum investment is one certificate,
- One certificate is equal to one equity basket, and
- The issue price of one certificate is $1000.

At the time a new basket certificate is designed, the weighting of the underlying listed companies is decided. Together with the relevant share prices, this weighting determines the specific number of shares bought, leading to the fixed number of

Table 15.1   Return profile of an index-based structured instrument

Index performance	Product value
20%	8%
15%	8%
10%	8%
5%	4%
0%	100%
−5%	95%
−10%	90%
−15%	85%
−20%	80%

shares stipulated in the prospectus. These remain unchanged throughout the term of the certificate. Early notes of that type were not capital protected, but because their appeal was limited capital protection has been added subject to a barrier.

The points the vendor will emphasize when contacting the client are that such certificates are suitable for the investor who is expecting a positive performance on the part of underlying shares, and would like to invest in a number of different listed companies simultaneously, which are the underlying quoted companies. The argument is that an underlying basket enables the investor to obtain a degree of diversification, without having to commit a large amount of capital; $1000 is an affordable level.

What is not transparent in this argument is the risk associated with the investment. The choice of companies in the basket may be biased, to fit some of the issuer's objectives, or one or more of these companies could have been subject to event risk over the life of the note. The barrier capitalizes on this likelihood. Other criteria that have influenced this choice are not necessarily those of the investor buying the certificates.

Moreover, such certificates bear the same loss potential as a direct investment in the corresponding shares. The investor is not hedged against any share price losses that may occur. There is also currency exchange risk (see Chapter 16), if certificates are issued in another currency than that in which the shares in the basket are quoted; for instance, dollars for European investors.

These different exposures are evidently known to the issuers of equity derivatives and, therefore, when it comes to designing the structure of a new certificate, among key aspects taken into account are the currency in which the structured product is issued and the nature of the selected underlying. Other criteria, too, may be necessary for a product offering capital protection, such as the knock-out level (more on this later).

Another aspect of the same issue of a basket of equities is that the exposure to any one share may increase or decrease during the term. This changes the weights as one company that has been successful can have a significantly higher weighting relative to the other shares in the basket, leading to risk concentration. There is also the possibility that one of the companies may get into financial difficulties. Even if this happens to be the case, in a typical certificate:

- The share cannot be replaced, and
- It remains part of the certificate through the full term.

To answer this particular concern of investors, issuers have developed a so-called *dynamic certificates* approach, based on a rather complex investment strategy. The latter may involve a great deal of buying and selling during the term. Clients' reluctance to invest in such products also led to other enhancements, one of them offering a potential degree of capital protection. (For a practical example, see section 15.10.)

Even if capital protection is not 100 per cent, it permits the vendor to say to the investor that he can participate fully in the positive development of an equity index or basket of individual shares, and still protect his capital. This is like having one's cake and eating it. But potential investors should appreciate that there is a big 'if'.

If, and only if, the underlying ends the term in negative territory, and has not fallen below a predetermined level (the barrier), the investor can benefit from 100 per cent capital protection on maturity. Otherwise, capital protection is reduced (see Table 15.1) and all interest is forgone. In addition, the instrument's currency and structure of the product can affect the level of capital protection.

Take as an example of underlying the Dow Jones index, with index level at time of issue 10 200 points (start value), knock-out level 70 per cent of start value, term five years, capital protection at 100 per cent of issue price, denomination $1000, issue price $1000, and minimum repayment $1000 if knock-out level is not reached during term. This knock-out level is the barrier that will decide whether the client gets some money back.

In principle, this type of equity certificate allows participation in the positive development of the Dow Jones index at maturity. Notice, however, that this stipulated minimum repayment, which will come into effect at the end of the term, depends on whether or not the knock-out level of 70 per cent was reached *on any single occasion* during the term.

If the knock-out level is not reached at any point during the term, the investor will receive the minimum repayment, irrespective of the actual closing index level. By contrast, if the knock-out level is reached or breached during the term, the capital invested originally is no longer protected, as the investment is wholly exposed to the negative performance of the Dow Jones index.

■ If the Dow Jones index is quoted at, say, 8, 160 or 20 per cent below start value, at the end of the term,
■ Then the investor will accordingly be repaid only $800 of his or her original investment, and will receive neither dividends nor interest.

In other terms, if the knock-out level has been reached during the term and the underlying lies below its start value at the end of the term, the investment will be subject to a loss, with the amount repaid dropping by 1 per cent for each single percentage point the index lies below the start value. At the same time, over the course of the term, the price of the certificate moves in line with the underlying, which is the Dow Jones index, while in exchange for the capital protection the investor has no rights to any dividends that are paid out by the underlying firms.

15.3 Absorber certificates

Like all other structured derivatives products, absorber certificates, also known as airbags, are characterized by the fact that the level of repayment at maturity is calculated in line with the value of the underlying at maturity. The absorber certificate's speciality is that investment is not exposed to capital loss in the event of slightly negative performance. However, the security buffer only absorbs share price losses on maturity, and only at maturity does it take effect. During the term:

■ The absorber certificate behaves just like the underlying index, losing value in the event that the equity index drops, and
■ The security buffer provides no cushioning on the certificate's price, as the price of the underlying may yet change in the remaining term.

By contrast, towards the end of the term the note's behavioural profile changes. If the underlying is trading close to the level at which it was issued, a slight decline in the underlying will no longer lead to a proportional decline in the absorber certificate. The security buffer gains value over time as the probability that the loss threshold will no longer be reached becomes higher.

- If the underlying index is rising,
- Then the certificate will continue to shadow this change almost one-to-one.

Take as an example an absorber certificate whose underlying is the DJ Euro Stoxx 50 index, with index level at the time of issue 2200 points to be used as the start value, and security buffer 20 per cent of index start value. Participation in the underlying is 100 per cent, term is five years and denomination is €1000. The issue price is also €1000.

The investor will suffer the consequences of negative performance if the index falls by more than 20 per cent from its start value, which essentially corresponds to the security buffer. In exchange, he or she will participate in the positive performance of the index upon maturity. For instance, if the Stoxx 50 index were to rise 25 per cent from its start value, the repayment amount would be €1250.

- If, however, the closing value of the index lies below the start value,
- Then, at maturity and only at maturity the investor will receive €1000, the issue price, as long as the index has not lost more than 20 per cent of its value since issue.

In case at the end of the term the underlying index has lost more than 20 per cent of its start value, capital protection no longer applies. For instance, should the index fall by 30 per cent, at 1540 points, then for *every* percentage point the index falls below the security buffer, the investment loses €1 of its value.

As this example demonstrates, the absorption of losses is a very relative issue, since only a limited level of capital protection is being offered. This is explained by the fact that the investor participates 100 per cent in the upside of the underlying. The careful reader will appreciate that this is a different case than of certain bond fixed income structured products where capital is fully protected, albeit only at 100 per cent.

In their way, equity index, basket structured notes, absorber certificates, early repayment certificates (see section 15.4) and other similar structured instruments make a *mini-hedge fund* out of the investor. Not many institutional investors, let alone private individuals, appreciate this fact; and even fewer are ready to face the consequences.

- These mini-hedge funds assume most of a hedge fund's risks,
- But at the same time they reap few or none of the benefits, because they are not offshore and do not have the appropriate legal structure.

The hedge funds' legal structure is most frequently that of private investment partnerships that provide pass through a tax treatment or offshore investment corporation. Part of their attractiveness to high net worth individuals lies in the fact that the master-feeder structure may be used for investors with different tax status, where investors choose appropriate onshore or offshore feeder funds pooled into a master fund (more on tax treatment in the Appendix).

One of the senior investment executives participating in the research leading to this book pointed out that the hedge funds' investor base is that of high net worth individuals, pension funds and other institutional investors. Having said this, he added that high net worth individuals are perfectly entitled to gamble with their money, if they feel like doing so, but he added that this is not necessarily true of pension funds, as they deal with other people's money.

Other cognizant people commented on the fact that this mini-hedge fund syndrome has reached retail investors. Until recently, there have been relatively high minimum investment levels, but these are crumbling as leveraged instruments designed by hedge funds are becoming widely available to the general public via partnership with private banks and other credit institutions through alternative investment vehicles.

To achieve their goal, hedge funds take positions in a wide range of markets as they are free to choose various investment techniques. They also reward themselves lavishly in terms of remuneration. Their incentive structure includes a 1–2 per cent management fee and 15–25 per cent performance fee, with often higher watermarks. This is part of the hidden costs paid by investors.

To summarize, the risks associated with most equity-type structured products, absorber certificates being an example, are that if the underlying remains beneath the loss threshold at the end of the term, the investment will perform negatively. Moreover, the security buffer does not come into play until maturity; over the course of the term the price of an airbag will fall if the underlying falls, even if the loss threshold has not yet been reached.

15.4 Early repayment certificates

Also known as bonus certificate, an early repayment structured equity product offers the possibility of making a return if the underlying closes above its start value on one of the annual observation dates. This contrasts to other structured products, where the investor must wait until maturity. The issuer also gains from an interim decision since this certificate can be redeemed early.

The level of repayment of an early retirement certificate depends on the number of investment years that have elapsed. The structured product comes with a security buffer, which offers capital protection on the initial investment at maturity, provided the price of the underlying does not fall below a predetermined level. If it does, the investor will start to incur losses.

Over the course of the term, the price of an early repayment certificate is influenced mainly by the performance of the underlying index. If the index rises, the price of the certificate will also rise, but it will do so less than proportionately, for two reasons:

- The return on an early repayment certificate is capped on the upside, and
- There is always the possibility that the underlying will fall back below its start value before the next observation date.

Should the underlying share, basket of equities or index fall during the term of the certificate, the security buffer only offers partial protection. The extent to which this structured equity product reflects negative performance of the underlying depends on the:

- Remaining time to maturity, and
- Distance from the security buffer.

Both of these factors affect the probability of whether the underlying index will be quoted at a level below the security buffer on maturity. Notice that only the level of the underlying at maturity is of importance for this type of certificate. Even if the security buffer is breached at some point during the term, there is a possibility that the underlying will rebound before maturity, which will mean that capital protection is retained. This is, however, a chance event.

Take, as an example, the Dow Jones index at 9900. This is both the start and strike value. The security buffer is 25 per cent below start value, repayment bonus 10 per cent for each investment year that passes, observation dates for the possibility of early repayment are annual, denomination is $1000, and issue price also $1000.

If the Dow Jones index closes at or above start value on one of the annual observation dates, the certificate is repaid immediately. With repayment, the investor will obtain the maximum return of 10 per cent for each investment year that has elapsed.

If the Dow Jones index closes below the start value of 9900 points, on each of the annual observation dates, the investor will be repaid $1000 of issue price at maturity, so long as the Dow Jones has not fallen more than 25 per cent below its start value, which corresponds to the security buffer. Investors should nevertheless appreciate that even a 100 per cent repayment of initial capital is a very limited return potential, for two reasons:

- With a 10 per cent cap on returns for every year, investors participate very partially in the good years of the stockmarket, and
- While a 100 per cent capital return, if the security buffer is not breached (in bad years), looks good, the holder still loses the interest that he or she would have made with bonds.

Observation dates for early repayment are very important because these derivatives certificates have no annual distributions. The performance is annually aggregated and credited in a single amount at the end of the term, or in the event of early repayment. There are, also, some varieties of this structured product offering regular coupons.

The downside is that, if the underlying to an early repayment certificate rises very strongly in any one investment year, this structured product would not outperform a direct investment in the underlying index, because the return is capped on the upside. Further, as already stated, a major risk is that if the Dow Jones index closes at a level that is more than 25 per cent below start value, the investor suffers a loss.

- One percentage point is deducted from the issue price,
- For every percentage point the index closes below the 75 per cent mark.

With this, and most other equity derivatives structured products, the reader should pay particular attention to the effect of the barrier. The common characteristic of these products is that the level at which the security buffer is set is determined when the derivative instrument is designed and issued. Typically, the barrier depends on a number of factors:

- The term,
- The currency of issue,
- The interest rate level(s),
- The underlying basket or index, and
- The basket's or index's volatility.

In principle, the greater the volatility of the underlying, the more interesting the product can be from a risk and return perspective. For this reason, the potential payment of an early repayment certificate will likely be set at a higher level with a security buffer and carefully studied barrier (by the issuer). Notice also that current level of volatility is mainly interesting at the time of issue. If market volatility increases during the term, this will be compensated by price differentials affecting the value of the instrument.

15.5   Enhanced yield certificates

Enhanced yield certificates are another structured product through which banks are offering to their clients an alternative to direct investment in equities. Such certificates offer a fixed annual coupon payment and 100 per cent capital protection, if the underlying index does not fall below a barrier identifying the knock-out, and determined at the time of issue.

A characteristic of the enhanced yield certificate is that it may be repaid at 100 per cent before maturity if the index is quoted at a higher level than when the certificate is issued. Another important factor connected to this instrument, of which investors should take notice, is that it does not participate in positive performance of the stock index.

Take, as an example, a certificate whose underlying is the DJ Euro Stoxx 50 index, with start value (index level at time of issue) 2510, knock-out level 50 per cent of index level at issue (hence 1.255), coupon 4.50 per cent per annum, annual observation dates, term equal to four years, and denomination €1000. Issue price is also €1000.

The investor will receive an annual coupon of 4.50 per cent, irrespective of performance of the index. However, if the DJ Euro Stoxx 50 closes above its start value on one of the annual observation dates, then the enhanced yield certificate will immediately be repaid at 100 per cent plus the coupon that becomes due at that time.

- If the barrier was not reached at any point during the term, the investor's capital is 100 per cent protected,
- But if the knock-out level has been reached, the originally invested capital is no longer protected.

In this case, the investment is fully exposed to the fall in the STOXX 50 index. In compensation, as already stated, the investor has received a 4.5 per cent coupon. As for the capital, the level of repayment at the end of the term depends on whether or not the knock-out level was reached at any point during the term.

The risk that investors assume with this so-called enhanced yield structured product is that if the knock-out level is reached during the term, and the index is below its start value at the end of the term, the amount repaid will be less than 100 per cent of the original capital. It will also drop by 1 per cent for each single percentage point the index lies below start value, which is a loss function similar to practically all equity-type structured products studied so far.

In conclusion, while the 4.50 per cent return looks good at a time when interest rates have been at rock-bottom, as in 2001–2004, investors would have been able to obtain a better return with a direct investment in equities. Notice also that in the case where the enhanced yield certificate is subject to early repayment, the investor has no right to any future coupon payments.

15.6   Reverse exchangeable certificates

Like enhanced yield certificates, structured products known as reverse exchangeable are equity based and offer a fixed coupon. In the early years of the twenty-first century this has been typically higher than the low level of interest available with bonds or money market instruments at the time of issue, but this difference did not necessarily compensate for the risk assumed by investors.

As with all investments, reverse exchangeable certificates are subject to market volatility and the issuer designs them in a way that protects his or her interests. The buyer receives a coupon payment, but in exchange when the market goes north the profit potential is quite limited.

- If the underlying share price rallies strongly,
- Then the fixed coupon only accounts for small participation in the upside.

One of the risks the investor faces with so-called enhanced yield certificates is that of receiving equity despite the instrument's bond-like characteristics, and the fact the coupon that it offers does not compensate for an upside in the equities price. Moreover, the risk and return profile of this certificate may be varied by shifting the exercise price. In terms of other design characteristics:

- The higher the exercise price at issue, in comparison to the current share price of underlying equity, the higher the coupon payment will be.
- By contrast, the more defensively, or lower, the exercise price is set, the smaller the fixed coupon payable to the investor.

As the term of the instrument progresses, this risk and return pattern is maintained by the price movement of the reverse exchangeable certificate. If share price is far below exercise price, then the investor is confronted with a significant increase in equity risk.

Take as an example CISCO registered shares as the underlying, with a share price of $23.50 at the time of issue (April 2004). The strike price was $23.50, the coupon 6.00 per cent per annum, term three years, denomination $1000, number of shares per certificate three, and issue price $1000.

Let us start with the hypothesis that at the beginning of the term the investor purchases a reverse exchangeable certificate at $1000. He or she will receive a fixed annual coupon payment of 6.00 per cent for the entire term. In contrast to a bond, however, the performance of the underlying CISCO share until maturity has an effect on the repayment amount:

- If CISCO closes above the strike price of $23.50 at maturity, the investor will be credited with the full amount he paid for the certificate ($1000). Hence the coupon repayment of 6.00 per cent per annum will offer a good return.
- If, however, the CISCO share closes below the exercise price on maturity, the investor will receive an amount part in register shares, but below the price at which the certificate was purchased. The share price on the fixed closing day is the crucial factor in this calculation. (In April 2005, a year after issue, CISCO's share price hovered around $17.50.)

Suppose that the term has been one year. CISCO shares purchased in mid-April 2004 at $23.50, were worth $17.50 in mid-April 2005, and this is the value of shares that the investor will receive. For the investor the transaction represents a net loss of capital of over 25 per cent.

This example helps in appreciating the effect of clauses associated with equity-type structured products on the investor's capital. The effect of a barrier can be added to this. If the investor had bought equity structured notes (see section 15.2) with CISCO as the underlying, then the knock-out point would have been reached since $17.50 per share is well under the 20 per cent margin below the start value of $23.50. In this case, even with capital protection, the investor would have received at maturity 74.6 per cent of his or her original capital.

In conclusion, although reverse exchangeable certificates pay interest, this should not lead investors to confuse them with bonds. Regular distributions of a payout do not make a bond, like a priest's robe does not make a priest. Moreover, the investor's capital loss is a distinct possibility, while his or her maximum profit is limited. In the event that the underlying rises strongly, the certificate's performance will disappoint the investor when compared with direct equity holdings.

15.7 Potential share acquisition certificates

Take potential share acquisition certificates as another example. This is a structured product sold as an alternative to direct equity investment. Issuers promoting this instrument say that it is suitable for investors who believe that a particular share will either move sideways or rise slightly, because it allows the holder to acquire a given equity at a lower price than is currently available on the stock exchange.

Yes, but if the equity market moves north a major rise in value would not benefit the investor because of the cap. With potential share acquisition certificates, the investor has to accept that he may not participate fully if the underlying share price rallies. This practically means that:

- The return on this certificate is limited,
- But there is a negative impact if the shares fall.

Some issuers say that potential share acquisition certificates are suitable if the investor is looking for a short-term equity holding or, alternatively, if market volatility is high, because a lower certificate issue price increases the potential return. This is a doubtful statement that conveniently forgets about the downside: For a given amount of capital, this type of certificate increases the investor's exposure to market whims.

One of the issuers of potential share acquisition certificates I spoke to emphasized that these structured products behave as if they were an option, and they can be issued with different exercise prices on the same underlying share. What this argument forgets is that the risk and return profile of the certificate is far from being clear to the typical investor, and it can be altered depending on how aggressively the exercise price is contrasted to the current share price.

Take as an example of a fairly classical potential share acquisition certificate, one with Vodafone registered shares as the underlying; share price at time of issue is 122 pence (£1.22), exercise price of the certificate also 122 pence, certificate price 110 pence, a discount of 10 per cent, term ten months, and maximum return 10 per cent or 12 per cent per annum.

Within the perspective of the certificate, the investor acquires Vodafone shares at 110 pence, instead of the actual price of 122 pence. Hence, the return consists of the difference between the acquisition price of 110 pence and the exercise price of 122 pence, with net gain equating to the higher possible return of 10 per cent. This happens if, on maturity, Vodafone shares close above the exercise price.

If, however, the underlying is valued below the exercise price on maturity, then the investor loses money. He or she will be delivered a Vodafone share for each certificate purchased, but in this case the effective acquisition price for the delivered share is below the certificate's price of the 110 pence. Return is negative because the share price has fallen below the acquisition price.

For the investor there is also a twist. The certificate's return is added to the share price at issue, but the dividends have to be deducted because, unlike a direct equity investment, the potential share acquisition certificate has no claim to dividend payments. By contrast, for a direct equity investment the return obtained is a combination of share price gain and dividends received.

Aware that this difference may hold back investors from purchasing this type of certificate, some issuers have designed an alternative allowing the investor to double his or her profit if the share price rises (more on this later). Critics say that the lack of dividend for an equity-looking investment is not the only downside.

Potential share acquisition certificates offer no capital protection and have the same risk profile as a direct investment in equities. However, in the event of physical delivery of the underlying, the loss potential is limited to the price paid for the certificate and the price of the underlying at the end of the term. At the same time, the maximum profit is also limited. These certificates may therefore *underperform* the direct equity investment in the event that stockmarket prices move north.

One of the alternatives to which reference has been made in the preceding paragraphs is for practical purposes an equity option certificate, which up to a certain level of share price could earn twice the return of a direct investment at maturity. In exchange, the investor accepts that he or she will not enjoy unlimited participation (beyond the aforementioned level) in any price rise of the underlying equity.

As another example, take the case of a certificate with SAP registered shares as underlying. Share price at time of issue is €130. The price of the certificate is also €130, as is the strike price. That is the point where double profit participation might kick in. The cap level of the certificate is €143. Double profit margin ends at this cap level. The term is one year.

If the SAP registered share is quoted in the stockmarket either at or above the cap level on maturity, the investor will receive the maximum possible repayment, defined as:

$$\text{Repayment amount} = 2 \times \text{Cap amount} - \text{Strike price}$$

If the SAP registered share lies between the exercise price and the cap level on maturity, the investor will receive the underlying share. In addition, he or she will be paid the difference between the closing price and the exercise price of the share. If the market price of the SAP registered share lies below the exercise price on maturity, the investor will receive a share for each purchased equity option certificate.

Investors should appreciate that equity option certificates offer no capital protection. In that sense, they have the same risk profile as a direct equity investment. Also, because with potential share acquisition certificates the maximum profit is limited, their performance in the event of a bull market will be poorer than that of a direct equity investment.

Moreover, the often advertised doubling of equity gain is only realized on maturity, and it only concerns a very limited price margin. During its term, the certificate's price will not reflect this two-fold increase in the event that the underlying has risen. If physical delivery of shares takes place, the investor may suffer a loss because of the difference between the certificate's price and the price of the underlying on maturity.

15.8 EUR complete participation securities

A three-year EUR complete participation security, known as COMPS, which is the subject of this section, is linked to a basket of European equities. This is a cashback equity basket, and the reader should notice that this investment is not principal protected. COMPS are notes issued by a major broker that enable the holder to participate directly in both the:

- Upside, and
- Downside of the underlying.

The underlying of COMPS is a basket of equity indices and/or shares. Return on the notes is linked to the value of this basket of European equities. The issuer says that an investor in these notes would be one who understands, and is willing to accept, the risks involved in an investment linked to a basket of equities; also, one who believes that the value of the reference basket will appreciate over the life of the notes.

In a particular issue, the basket of European equities underlying the instrument includes twenty-five names, each with a weight of 4 per cent. On maturity date, each COMPS unit will redeem an amount defined by the following algorithm:

$$\text{EUR [Invested capital} \cdot (1 - 3 \cdot \text{AMF})] \cdot (X_v/X_p)$$

where X_p = value of the reference basket on the pricing date, X_v = value of the reference basket on the valuation date, and AMF = actual management fee, in this case equal to 0.75 per cent.

Among the subjects that investors should keep in mind in relation to this instrument is the existence of reference basket rebalancing risk. The equities comprising the reference basket may change substantially over the life of the structured product. It is possible that some of the initial constituent securities will increase substantially in value before maturity date, but value-wise the rebalanced reference basket might not perform better.

There is also credit risk associated with this structured product because the value of the notes will be negatively affected by any decline in the creditworthiness of the issuer. Moreover, there may be a compound effect as a fall in creditworthiness can affect the trading value of the notes. There is also liquidity risk.

At the same time, while the issuer states that it intends to provide a secondary market in the notes under ordinary conditions, there can be no assurance as to the prices that would be indicated. Nor is it certain that a secondary market will be liquid, or that the issuer will offer to purchase the notes. An illiquid market may have an adverse impact on the price at which the notes may be sold. Hence, before maturity, their price will be affected by many factors including, but not limited to:

- Remaining time to maturity date,
- Outstanding principal amount of the notes,
- Performance of the reference index,
- Prevailing interest rates, and
- Credit spreads.

Furthermore, because the notes are denominated in euros, any investor from outside Euroland also faces foreign exchange risk. A non-euro investor will be subject to fluctuations in exchange rates that could have an adverse effect on risk and return, upon conversion into local currency received at maturity of the notes.

This is not all. The promotional literature released by the issuer brings the investor's attention to the fact that the issuing entity may enter into other transactions with respect to the reference basket and/or undertake activities that may be perceived as a conflict of interest. For instance, the issuer may buy or sell obligations linked to the reference index for its own account, for other business reasons or in connection with hedging of obligations under the notes. Investors should be fully aware of these possibilities, which may affect both the credit of the issuer and the value of the structured product.

15.9   US dollar non-interest-bearing note linked to equity

This is a different example to the one in section 15.8. It regards a three-year US dollar non-interest-bearing note linked to a tailored equity basket. The issue features a 101.5 per cent minimum redemption at maturity. The non-interest-bearing characteristic of the note raises the query: Who, as an investor, would put their money into this security? The issuer answers this by saying that an investor in this note would be one who believes the value of the reference basket will rise over the next three years. What the note offers the investor is participation in the upside of the reference basket.

■ Minimum redemption at maturity is 101.5 per cent (meaning an interest of 0.5 per cent per year).
■ Maximum redemption at maturity may be 133 per cent of the principal amount, or roughly 11 per cent per year.

Most evidently, this maximum is a hypothetical amount stated by the issuer. The reference basket of equities includes ten stocks of well-known US companies, bearing equal weight. Rollover return per year is given by the algorithm:

$$\max\left(0, \frac{1}{10}\sum_{i=1}^{10}\left(\frac{x_{i,j}}{x_{i,0}} - 1\right)\right)$$

where $X_{i,j}$ = price of stock i in the reference basket in year j, on the anniversary of the pricing date, and $X_{i,0}$ = price of stock i on the pricing date.

The return on each stock in the reference basket is capped at 11 per cent for each $j = 1, 2, 3$. The sum of rolled over returns consists of rolled over return in year 1, plus rolled over return in year 2, plus rolled over return in year 3.

One way of looking at this equity structured product is that it resembles investment in a growth stock that pays no dividend. The downside is the 11 per cent cap applied every year, without compensation for losses in case the stockmarket goes south. If in one of the three years of the derivative instrument's life cycle there is a strong bull market and the underlying equity rises by 35 per cent, the investor's gains will be capped at 11 per cent. Red ink, however, is not capped.

15.10   The strategy of pruning the basket and reallocating securities

One of the equity-type structured products seen in this chapter features a strategy of dynamic reallocation of securities, done by the issuer or asset manager mid-term. The pros look at this as a dynamic approach designed to profit from pruning weak underlyings and reallocating securities in the portfolio.

Take as an example one of the instruments examined in the research that led to this book. This structured product was originally linked to twenty-four equities, as underlyings. The issuer endowed this instrument with a mechanism to rebalance the underlying portfolio of shares according to the following strategy:

- During the first ten months, at the end of every two months, the two stocks recording the worst performance since inception are excluded from the portfolio.
- From then on, the four lowest performing shares among the remaining fourteen will compose the core portfolio, the composition of which also changes annually, over the five-year investment, to reflect the changing performance of the fourteen stocks.

Final redemption value of the note will depend on the value of the core portfolio at maturity, and on the conditional capital protection that can be activated at the end of years 3 and 4. If at either of these dates the core portfolio performance is positive, then a minimum redemption amount of 100 per cent of capital initially invested is set, regardless of any subsequent fall in core portfolio.

As the reader will appreciate, this capital protection is conditional and therefore the investor may lose some or all of the capital that he or she invests. The instrument's issuing bank suggests that such structured notes are suitable for clients seeking yield enhancement, but at the same time accepting the consequent equity market risk to their capital.

Advantages of this structured instrument are a relatively high fixed annual coupon and participation in the performance of the core portfolio with no cap or averaging. Disadvantages include the fact that capital invested is *not protected* at maturity, unless the conditional capital protection feature has been activated. Moreover, investors do not receive the dividend yield of the stocks that constitute the underlying. These go to the issuer to compensate for the risk that he is taking.

Note

1 D.N. Chorafas, *The Management of Equity Investments*, Butterworth-Heinemann, London, 2005.

16 Currency exchange structured products

16.1 Introduction

The majority of now classical fixed income instruments are offered and traded in the capital market, but indexed inflation notes and floating rate notes, among other structured products, are traded in the money market. The same is true of certificates of deposit, money market claims and Treasury Bills (by definition). As this example demonstrates, capital market and money market overlap at least in some of the transactions being performed.

Common wisdom has it that the capital market addresses itself to equities. Not only are equities pre-eminent capital market instruments, but they are also at the origin of the capital market.[1] At the same time, however, the capital market handles debt instruments, and since the last two decades of the twentieth century it has proved itself most cost-effective in raising capital in competition to bank loans.

As Figure 16.1 shows, up to a point, but only up to a point, capital market and money market overlap. In general, short-dated instruments are traded in the money market and longer dated ones are traded in the capital market. This, however, is not always the case, with many financial products falling into a grey area of exceptions.

Currency exchange rate (forex) trades are not part of the markets discussed in the preceding paragraphs. For any practical purpose, the foreign exchange market is one on its own. Bob Keen, a director of Merrill Lynch, and several other experts correctly believe that forex is really two markets rather than one:

- A spot market, which is the original landscape of foreign exchange trades, and
- A forward market, which is part of the money market even for longer dated transactions, for instance up to five years.

The reason for this dichotomy is that foreign exchange forwards are part of the interest rate market, which itself belongs to the money market. Also, as practised in the thirteenth to seventeenth centuries by the Bardi, Peruzzi and the Medicis, bills of exchange were part of what was the money market of its time.

Based on these concepts, Figure 16.1 suggests that the capital market, money market and forex market are both distinct from one another and overlap two-by-two. Failure to appreciate this overlap means that some people are under the illusion that these are distinct and unrelated markets. Neither concept is correct. The truth is that, depending on the product that is traded, they are both distinct and interconnected.

The foreign exchange market, and its derivative instruments, are the theme of this chapter. For instance, a *quanto*, also known as guaranteed exchange rate contract,

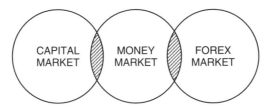

Figure 16.1 The capital market, money
market and forex market are both distinct and
interconnected, depending on the instrument
being traded

is a forward currency exchange derivative incorporated into an underlying equity
option, or equity swap. The quanto allows investors to lock in a known currency
exchange flow, for instance hedging forex risk. Instruments such as this essentially
make the private investor a player in macromarkets, where he or she has neither the
training nor the experience needed to win.

Foreign currency forward and option contracts are traded on a global scale in connection with servicing the needs of business, industry and private individuals, as well
as for proprietary trading. As with other derivative instruments, currency-related
exposure to market risk is influenced by various factors, including:

- Macroeconomics affecting the global economy, as well as the economy sustaining
  each currency, and
- Political and speculatory reasons, which are beefing up and putting down a
  currency's exchange rate.

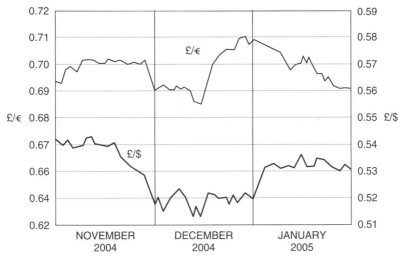

Figure 16.2 Exchange rate volatility characterizing major currencies over
a three-month period. (*Source*: European Central Bank, Monthly Bulletin,
February 2005)

Today, daily average turnover in foreign exchange trades stands at US $1.9 trillion, or $475 trillion annually. Of this, the spot market turnover on a daily basis is $620, or about one-third of the total.[2] But of all this, only 3–5 per cent represents the requirements of global commerce. Much of the balance is speculative, which means that there is a great deal of volatility in currency exchange.

The volatility in currency exchange rates occurs both daily and in the medium and longer term. Based on statistics by the European Central Bank, Figure 16.2 shows, as an example, the British pound to euro, and the pound to US dollar exchange rate over a three-month period (1 November 2004 to 31 January 2005).

16.2 Currency transactions and economic exposure

Credit institutions, other financial entities, manufacturing companies, merchandising firms and other businesses, particularly those with international operations or with significant import and export activity, face currency and exchange risk and try to hedge them. For an American company, for example, the value of the dollar, which rose significantly in 2001/02 and tanked in 2003/04, can affect financial results in a big way.

To appreciate this reference, the reader must remember that an American manufacturing company's functional currency for its international subsidiaries is the US dollar. When the dollar strengthens against other currencies, particularly in trade-weighted terms, sales made in those currencies translate into lower revenue in dollars. By contrast, when the US dollar weakens, sales made in local currencies translate into higher dollar revenue.

This, however, is no one-way street because, correspondingly, labour costs, materials costs and other expenses incurred in non-US dollar currencies increase when the dollar strengthens. Hence, changes in exchange rates may positively or negatively affect:

- Sales as expressed in US dollars,
- Operating expenses,
- Gross margins, and
- Overall results of business operations.

For this reason, companies engage in hedging programmes involving derivative financial instruments. These are aimed at limiting, in part, the impact of currency volatility. For instance, US companies hedge their non-US dollar net monetary assets through the issue, or purchase, of forward exchange contracts.

But not everything is linear in terms of hedging results. As an example, in its 1996 Annual Report Compaq noted that for certain markets, particularly in Latin America, it was determined that ongoing hedging of non-US dollar net monetary assets is not cost-effective. Instead, management attempted to minimize currency exposure risk through working capital management.

A similar statement about foreign exchange risk is valid in terms of investments in the global market: banks, institutional investors, manufacturing and merchandising firms, and high net worth individuals have an increasingly internationalized portfolio, whose value is significantly affected through forex volatility, which impacts their assets abroad.

Fluctuation in currency exchange is visible in terms of net worth because practically every investor has a base *currency* against which investments in other currencies are judged, whether these concern financial instruments, such as equities and bonds, real estate or other holdings. Notice that of equities and bonds, the latter are more affected by currency volatility than the former, which have a volatility of their own. This relationship between values is shown in Figure 16.3.

In other words, in a globalized economy, with several major currencies and a myriad of minor currencies, there is always economic exposure due to currency

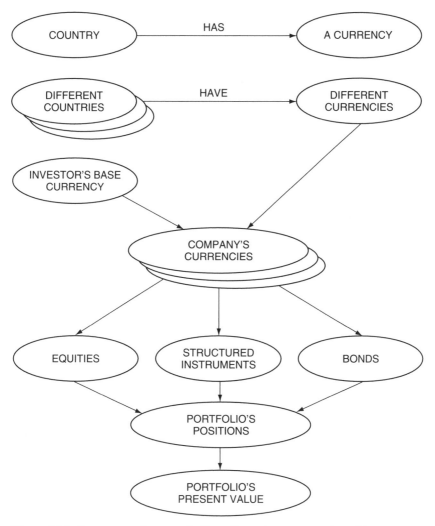

Figure 16.3 Currency exchange volatility affects the present value of investments

volatility. This is true not only of portfolio positions but also of transactions. Forex exposure also reflects past management decisions.

- Cash flows from abroad often represent investments made decades in the past, and
- Translation risk is connected to the volatility of the value of assets and liabilities in foreign currencies, and their characteristic pattern.

Research and development (R&D) and production costs, for instance, may be in one country and currency, while a large chunk of current sales income may come from other countries and currencies because of well-established local sales operations and/or export trade. This example points to *translation exposure*, with risk of losses or lesser profits than those projected, in the aftermath of consolidating the accounts of the parent firm and its foreign subsidiaries.

Notice that economic exposure may be direct or indirect. The former relates to current and future sales in foreign market(s). The latter reflects competitiveness in the home country in terms of costs relative to conditions prevailing in other rival producers. For instance, for the USA this will mean producers in trading partner countries such as the UK, Germany, France, Italy, Japan, Korea and China.

- A country's higher currency exchange rates threaten to damage its recovery and reduce the incentive to invest in the local economy, and
- The size of central bank intervention in supporting or dumping a currency is often a drop in the foreign exchange market's ocean, unless several central banks co-operate towards the same end.

In all of the foregoing examples we have been practically speaking of transnational trade, which means that a company incurring costs is one country and earning money in another may be unable to compete on a level ground. It is, however, appropriate to take note of two other factors that enter into the algorithm of a company's competitiveness in the global economy:

- The effect of speculation in forex rates, and
- The quality of corporate governance, which can tip the scales.

The statement was made in the Introduction that, day in, day out, only 3–5 per cent of foreign exchange transactions represent currency requirements of international trade. To a large extent, the balance represents financial investments and speculative transactions. It follows that speculative moves can affect the profitability of companies that have nothing to do with them.

With regard to overall corporate governance, currency exchange factors are not the only ones creating economic exposure. Others are productivity costs, strikes, labour skills, quality problems, infrastructural reasons and, most evidently, the board's and CEO's ability to run the firm.

Changes in economic exposure can happen not only in the short term. If and when budgetary and other imbalances remain, these constitute a longer term menace to competitiveness. Moreover, economic exposure, portfolio positions exposure, transaction exposure and currency translations exposure correlate. The risks feeding on them:

- Become current,
- Affect the bottom line, and
- Show up in consolidated profit and loss statements.

Productivity issues, cost problems, labour skills and quality assurance are not the subject of this book. Therefore, from this point onwards the treatment of economic exposure will be limited to the issue of currency transactions, the way in which forex volatility affects one's portfolio, and the role that derivatives and other tools may play in righting or upsetting the balances in currency exposure.

16.3   Exchange rate volatility and risk control

Currency risk is measured in the form of position per currency. Typically, on a daily basis banks exercise risk management in foreign exchange by allocating limits to trading lines. In the general case, the treasury (or international operations division) delegates the limits and also exerts an influence by means of directives.

Notice, however, that it is usually that same department that, by and large, assumes forex positions and tries to control currency exchange risk. This is lop-sided in terms of risk control. The risk controller should *always* be a unit independent from the operating departments. At branches and in foreign operations, it is the responsibility of the parties receiving the limits to operate within them. Normally,

- Transactions in foreign currencies are executed by trading lines and interest-related deals, and
- Both at the centre and in the periphery middle rates are often used when foreign currency profits and losses are calculated.

In the case of trading lines, profit is usually computed by the net present value (NPV) method. This is also popular with other business lines, except in the case of interest rate business where the discounted squaring result is often used.

The job of risk controllers in currency exchange operations is different. Since the early 1970s, when the regime of floating exchange rates was established, exchange rate volatility, and most specifically currency risk, have had to be watched most closely. Another necessity is to follow up correlations between interest rates and exchange rates. Real-time information technology and modelling approaches can be of help.

A sound way to face currency risk is to maintain in real-time[4] a breakdown of assets and liabilities by main currency. This helps in following a policy on limits as well as on hedging transactions used to manage foreign currency risk. Table 16.1 presents, as an example, an analysis of assets and liabilities to be detailed by main currency.

Risk controllers should monitor all limits and other criteria used in keeping forex risk under lock and key. As a matter of relatively common practice, non-trading lines do not receive limits. Therefore, they have to close their foreign currency positions on

Table 16.1 Risk position needed to manage foreign currency risk at a financial institution: breakdown of assets and liabilities with US dollars as base currency

	US $	£	€	Yen	CHF	Other currencies
Assets						
Cash and balances with central banks						
Due from banks						
Cash collateral on securities borrowed						
Reverse repurchase agreements						
Trading portfolio assets						
Positive replacement values						
Loans, net of allowance for credit losses						
Financial investments						
Accrued income and prepaid expenses						
Investments in associates						
Property and equipment						
Goodwill and other intangible assets						
Other assets						
Total assets						
Liabilities						
Due to banks						
Cash collateral on securities lent						
Repurchase agreements						
Trading portfolio liabilities						
Negative replacement values						
Due to customers						
Accrued expenses and deferred income						
Debt issued						
Other liabilities						
Minority interests						
Shareholders' equity						
Total liabilities						

a daily basis. In several countries, daily closing of forex books is a requirement imposed by bank supervisors.

Positions from other businesses in foreign currencies, such as commissions or fund transfers, are closed through internal transactions with the currency's trading line. As far as risk control is concerned, a good practice is to convert cash flows in foreign currencies into base currency.

Apart from the base currency, Table 16.1 shows four other currencies that belong to the major trading partners of the form that follows this model, as it has lumped together other forex exposures under the heading 'other currencies'. The level of detail should be decided by the company's currency exposure profile by country and currency. For instance in 2002, seven of the world's ten worst performing currencies against the dollar, which itself had fallen, were in Latin America.

- Argentina's peso lost 73 per cent,
- Venezuela's bolivar lost 48 per cent,
- Uruguay's peso lost 47 per cent,
- Brazil's real lost 32 per cent,
- Colombia's peso lost 19 per cent,
- Mexico's peso lost 10 per cent, and
- Chile's peso lost 9.5 per cent.

As far as these countries are concerned, except for Argentina, which defaulted, currency devaluations resulted in increases in foreign debts and soaring costs of imports. Companies trading in these countries have also suffered. For example, at the end of 2003, Peter Brabeck, Nestlé's chief executive, pointed out that his company's volume of sales in Brazil (excluding water) rose by 10 per cent in 1998–2002 but, because of currency deterioration, revenues in Swiss francs were down by 30 per cent.[5]

The expectations of market participants regarding future exchange rate of a given currency can be measured by the mean (expected value) of estimated risk-neutral probability density function. For instance, as shown in Figure 16.4, in 2003 the markets' assessment of the balance of risks between a much stronger and a much weaker dollar (described by the skewness of these density functions) was weighted noticeably towards the latter (statistics by the Bank for International Settlements, BIS).

Economists, financial analysts and traders have available tools for a factual and documented study of exchange rate volatility and its impact. Mathematically speaking, a risk-neutral probability density function is estimated using indicative quotes of a market maker on three derivatives contracts:

- At-the-money implied volatility,
- Risk reversal, and
- The strangle.

The calculation is based on weekly averages of daily estimated density functions, for the weeks ending on indicated dates. The maturity of the options is fairly constant and equal to one month. A study in late 2003 showed that this pattern has been particularly pronounced in the dollar/euro exchange rate. Such expectations, however, started to change in early 2004. Between February and mid-May 2004, option prices suggested that the attitude towards the dollar had become less negative:

- The previous skewness tended to disappear, and
- The market assigned approximately equal likelihood to a substantial strengthening or weakening of the dollar.

The BIS 74th Annual Report notes that, according to market participants, broad exchange rate movements took place against the background of two noteworthy developments in forex conditions. One was the fact that the volume of trading generally rose sharply, continuing a trend that had started in early 2001. This was driven by a greater activity generated by leveraged entities, such as macro-hedge funds.

The second factor was that in contrast to the other main market segments, in 2003 the yen/dollar market was characterized by both a decline in activity and a lower level

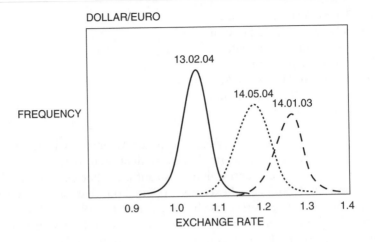

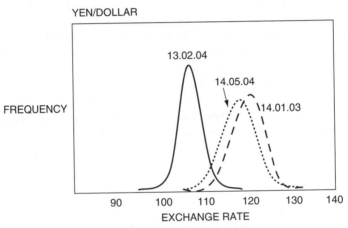

Figure 16.4 Risk-neutral probability density functions of the
US dollar against the euro and yen. (*Source*: Bank for
International Settlements, by permission)

of liquidity. According to experts, both changes seemed to be associated with the
two-way risk introduced into that market by systematic official intervention. This
was one of the cases where central banks seem to have had their way.

16.4 Mismatch risk and carry trades

There used to be a time when banks, manufacturing firms, merchandising companies,
institutional investors and private individuals invested their equity capital in the currency of their country of origin: dollars, pounds, yen, German marks or Swiss francs.
The first to take a leave from such a policy were money centre banks, which created
a basket of currencies for reference reasons. Infrastructural assets held abroad, such
as real estate, were another exception to the base currency rule.

A further exception with money centre banks, and increasingly also with other banks and institutional investors such as pension funds, is foreign currency assets that have turned sour, such as defaulted foreign currency securities or claims that have become valueless. While the policy on what to do with these valueless assets varies from one entity to another, a usual approach is:

■ To have them refinanced with provisions in the same currency as that of the claim, and
■ To abstain from using third party liabilities in that foreign currency.

In this context, there is, in currency terms, the possibility of *mismatch* between assets and liabilities. This is always present in cross-border financial operations, even if its existence is not properly appreciated by every party. In a way, mismatch risks with currencies resembles mismatch risk with interest rates, and it should be recalled that mismatch risk with interest rates brought down in flames the American Savings and Loans (S&L, thrifts, building societies) in the late 1980s to early 1990s.

An example involving currency mismatch risk can help in demonstrating what it involves. Before the introduction of the euro, the assets of Luxembourg banks were in Belgian francs, because of the monetary union between Belgium and Luxembourg. Essentially, the two countries shared the same currency. However,

■ At the end of 1996 Luxembourg was the only country in the European Union (EU) qualifying under the Maastricht criteria.
■ Belgium did not qualify because of very high public debt relative to its gross national product (GNP), and budgetary overruns.

Therefore, there was a discrete possibility that while Luxembourg entered the first nucleus of the currencies merging into the euro, Belgium would be left out. In the end, Belgium, along with Italy and Greece (which faced similar problems), was squeezed into the euro, but if this had not happened the Belgian francs of Luxembourg banks would have been refinanced in euros, while those of Belgian banks would not have qualified.

Under this fairly realistic scenario of currency mismatch, the Belgian francs of Belgian banks had to be devalued; a devaluation induced by the fact that if Belgium had stayed outside the European monetary union the Belgian franc would have dropped in value in connection to the euro. Worse still, those Luxembourg banks that had given their clients a guarantee of 1:1 conversion between the Belgian franc and Luxembourg franc (the large majority) would have faced other penalties resulting from:

■ The mismatch risk in terms of currency exchange, and
■ The solutions they had to provide to their clients, to satisfy their claims.

At the time, experts suggested that this would have proved very expensive for Luxembourg banks. The message that this example conveys is that currency risk goes well beyond the usual interpretation that it is related only to foreign exchange operations. Structured forex products, such as those covered in the next sections, can create problems akin to the example of mismatch risk shown.

A different example that could end up with a roughly similar pattern of mismatches is that of *carry trades*. Its practice rests on the fact that fluctuations in currency exchange rate present business opportunities. A strategy used to capitalize on forex volatility is to:

- Take up short-term loans at low interest rates, and
- Invest in higher remunerated longer term securities.

For instance, compared with the near-zero interest rate of the Japanese yen that prevailed in the 1990s and early years of the twenty-first century, Western government debt, corporate debt, emerging markets debt and junk bonds are more highly remunerated. As a trading strategy, carry trade aims to take advantage of the interest rate differential between two currency areas. In this case, investors and speculators:

- Fund themselves in the currency with the lower interest rate,
- Sell this currency against a higher yielding one, and
- Invest the proceeds at the higher interest rate.

Through this type of money market and currency exchange transactions they are earning a *carry*. This strategy can be profitable under certain conditions. One of them is zero or very low currency exchange risk. This means that the higher yielding currency does not depreciate against the lower yielding one, which can happen.

Because changes in currency exchange rates are fairly unpredictable, carry trades involve a significant exposure to the institutions, investors and speculators undertaking them. They can also be damaging to the economy as a whole, particularly so when their volume rises. An upward movement of yields and risk premiums in individual market segments can be magnified by a sudden unwinding of carry trade positions. When this happens, it generates tension in a given market, which could spill over globally.

There are also other risks, apart from the effects of forex volatility, currency mismatches and carry trade speculations. While routine changes in currency exchange rate play a key role in forex risk, there are also reversals in leading trends to which the management of a bank, institutional investor, or other entity, must be on alert. Reversals in currency rates affect both portfolio positions and transaction profits and losses related to:

- Balance of settled and unsettled receivables and payables in other currencies,
- Positions purposely kept open by the bank in other currencies, betting on a projected trend,
- Foreign currency futures and options (per currency) including accrued foreign currency exposure, and
- Currency exchange structured products sold to clients, which continue to be served by the bank.

Accrued foreign currency exposure includes the discounted future fixed margin from balanced assets in the interest business, discounted squaring results from the interest business, NPV per currency from trading lines, commitments made from underwriting structured derivative products and other factors. All of these positions must be effectively managed in terms of risk.

16.5   Forex rates and structured instruments

Take as an example the case of an American investor offered by his bank a euro/US dollar structured product. Depending on the euro/dollar exchange rate at maturity, the investor is told that he might achieve returns of up to 6 per cent per year. What he does not know is that there is a downside both for the bank, as issuer, and for himself; and this risk has to be managed.

Typically, the expectation behind the investment briefly described in the preceding paragraph is that the euro will appreciate in value relative to the dollar. Nothing, however, precludes that it is not the euro but the dollar that strengthens. Indeed, at maturity, one of the following three scenarios may materialize.

If the euro has appreciated over the six-month period and the euro/dollar exchange rate at the end of the term is either at or above a given upper exercise price, the investor will receive the original amount invested as well as a return corresponding to the euro's appreciation, minus a haircut and subject to a limit.

Alternatively, if at maturity the exchange rate lies between the lower and upper exercise prices the investor will receive the original amount invested as well as an interest payment. In the example presented in Figure 16.5, this is expected to be

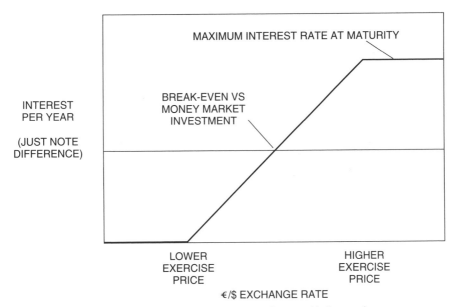

Figure 16.5 A payoff diagram at maturity of a euro/dollar exchange rate structured derivative

between 0 and 3 per cent per year, calculated on a linear basis in line with the exchange rate.

The third alternative is that the euro weakens against the dollar over the target period of the investment, and is valued at the end of the term at less than the lower exercise price. In such a case, the investor will be repaid the amount originally invested provided the structured instrument specified that the capital is 100 per cent protected. Short of this, he or she may get nothing.

With this particular alternative outcome, the investor is taking two risks. One is credit exposure: the bank giving the guarantee may file for protection from creditors. The other is market risk. The market rate the investor may obtain with a credit risk-free instrument, such as US Treasury Bills, stands a good chance of being higher than the average 1.5 per cent rate that this structured product pays, and it will always be higher than the 0 per cent rate that depends on guesses over forex rates, where:

■ The investor has nothing to say, and
■ The experts are usually wrong about future expectations.

The banker selling a forex structured product to the investor may present some good reasons why the euro has no other way to go but 'up'. However, in early 2005 no lesser authority than Dr Paul Volcker, the respected former Federal Reserve chairman, said that there was a 75 per cent chance that the dollar may go to the abyss. (Volcker, of course, mentioned some conditions associated with this crack, but the vendor of the structured product would not necessarily explain them to the investor.)

Volcker's conditions were hypotheses that might never materialize. Or, if they happened they might be overrun by other events such as the euro's woes in March 2005. In late March 2005 in Wall Street, analysts were of the opinion that a French 'no' vote to the European Union Constitution would be a stab in the heart to the euro. That 'no' was seen as the kind of political act that could serve as a catalyst in:

■ Causing a currency to fall, and
■ Sinking the euro/dollar investor in red ink.

This concern for the euro coincided with another event that has been a longer term worry: the decision by European finance ministers, and confirmation by heads of state in the week of 21 March 2005, to ease limits on budget deficits for the twelve countries participating in the euro, essentially killing Europe's Stability Pact. This set the stage for greater deficits in major European economies such as Germany, France and Italy as those countries explore ways to stimulate their sluggish economies.

Taking the two events together, financial analysts were concerned that the two events could eventually put pressure on the euro by casting doubt over Europe's fiscal restraint. In a similar manner, the widening US budget deficit has been weighting most negatively on the dollar, a reason why the banker had told the investor that making money with the euro/dollar structured product was a 'sure thing'.

Indeed, by the end of March 2005 several experts were of the opinion that with the developing politicoeconomic chaos in Euroland, we had reached the point where the euro being an obvious alternative to the dollar was nowhere near as clear as it was two to three years earlier. That did not mean that the dollar bear market will end soon. Rather, it meant that the euro became:

- Bruised, and
- Less attractive than it used to be.

Neither did what happened in the week of 21 March 2005 mean that all of Europe was doing badly. By some measures Finland is the world's most competitive country, with Denmark and Ireland close behind. Germany is the world's biggest exporter, but unemployment in Germany is at 10.6 per cent, with more than 5.2 million people out of work, and this situation is worse for the young and those near retirement age. The economic conditions in France and Italy are not much better.

For instance, Italy's competitiveness problems are deep-rooted, not just in strict economic terms, but all over, from R&D spending to red tape. In 2003, Italian spending on R&D as a share of gross domestic product (GDP) was barely half the EU average. In the same year the mean number of workers per enterprise was just over four, the second lowest figure in the EU. All three major Euroland countries: Italy, France and Germany:

- Underinvest in R&D,
- Have overly regulated labour markets,
- Feature hire-and-fire rules, and
- Promote high minimum wages, which make them less competitive in the global market.

The average investor does not have the information in these four bullet points, and does not necessarily appreciate that excessive interference to 'protect people in work' penalizes those who are out of work. The evidence is widespread, yet this has seldom been as clear as in Europe over the past five years, in spite of the euro's temporary strength.

Another ill-advised and ill-fated Euroland effort to protect services from competition has been spectacularly wrong-headed. Services now account for 70 per cent of Euroland's GDP and for all of net job growth in the 2000–2005 time-frame. An official French report in autumn 2004 suggested that opening France's services sector to as much competition as America's could generate over three million new jobs, and France has another 500 000 jobs vacant. They cannot be filled because its workforce lacks the appropriate skills.

An investor properly exposed to these facts would be in error to bet the euro against the dollar in the medium to longer term. Quoting Andrew Carnegie: 'Don't begin any new departure without first testing fully upon a small scale'. The testing ground of a new departure, such as investing in currency exchange structured products, is the fundamental underpinning a currency, such as the notions presented by the foregoing text.

As with fixed income structured instruments (see Chapters 12 and 13) and equity-type derivatives (Chapters 14 and 15), investors should understand that a structured product has risks, even if it features capital protection. The issuer gives no certainty of a fixed interest rate or other return. In this particular case of euro/dollar, the exact interest payment at maturity:

■ Will depend on the exchange rate at that time, and
■ In the worst case scenario will amount to zero.

Worse, in terms of potential losses, is a structured instrument without capital protection, because it can result in capital loss in the aftermath of possible changes in currency exchange that went against the issuer's and investor's guesses. The risks that have been outlined make a mockery of the structured product's seller's arguments to the investor, which usually go like this: 'As you are indirectly participating in the currency markets you can achieve higher potential returns than with a traditional money market investment', or, 'Buying structured derivatives can help you to achieve a better exchange rate, in the event that this is converted into the second currency on maturity' (see sections 16.6 and 16.7).

Typical investors do not need these 'conversions'. What they need is to get their money back and, with it, a fair return. Profiting from forex conversions is a far-fetched idea, particularly so for people and companies who have no way of steadily and analytically managing currency rate risk.

16.6   Dual currency structured products

One of the instruments frequently offered by private banks to retail investors is dual currency structured notes. As will be shown in this section, these have an interesting particularity which, in itself, defines risk and reward. Take as an example a British pound/euro dual currency product that permits the investor to receive supposedly enhanced yield over fixed deposits, in return for accepting the risk that the issuer may repay the pound sum invested in the alternative currency at a predetermined exchange rate.

Part of the marketing effort surrounding this type of structured product is that it can be custom-made. Typically, the principal currency is that of the original investment. The client often chooses the alternative currency. As in roulette, essentially the private investor plays against the bank, and there is no capital protection.

■ The investor will be repaid in the alternative currency, euros in this case, *if* at expiry the pound/euro exchange rate is higher than the predetermined strike rate.
■ This 'if' suggests that the pound/euro dual currency is a barrier product, with the effect that if the movement in exchange rate is adverse to the investor's hypothesis, such adversity will lead to loss of capital.

Currency structured notes are typically short-term instruments, of up to one month, appealing to investors who think that they are experts in forex, and some-how expect slight fluctuations or a stable exchange rate. Given the exposure embedded in this structured product, investors must be greatly interested in, and closely follow, exchange rate price movements. They should also be prepared to accept higher risks.

Another example of a currency exchange structured product is the dollar-denominated twelve-month euro/US dollar reset binary range note, linked to the euro/US dollar forex rate (similar to the example in section 16.5). An investor in this note, which offers principal protection, would typically believe that over the coming year the euro will move within a range against the US dollar. The note is dollar denominated.

- Its reset future allows the buyer to continue earning a coupon in future interest periods,
- But this happens only in the event that in earlier interest periods the coupon has been zero owing to the range being breached.

In connection to the instrument in the background of this case study, the first range for the first observation period is determined by the exchange rate of dollars per €1 ± 0.045. When this product was issued, the spot reference for the first observation period was 1.3400. The range for the first observation period was set to be from 1.3850 to 1.2950.

The range reset dates are: trade date plus three months 10:00 hours; trade plus six months 10:00 hours; and trade plus nine months 10:00 hours, all at New York time. The rule of the game is that:

- If the reference index has not traded outside the range at any time in the previous range observation period, the coupon will be 1.575 per cent in the specified quarter,
- Otherwise it will be zero.

In this and similar cases, calculation of the return on this sort of structured note is linked to the value of the euro relative to the value of the US dollar. Each exchange rate range usually has a three-month duration. If, during any such period, the euro/dollar trades outside the exchange range applicable to such period, no coupon will be payable on the notes in respect to the period in reference.

It is possible that, if the euro/dollar trades outside all of the exchange rate ranges applicable during the term of the notes, no coupon will be payable on the notes at all. This sort of structured product involves a high degree of risk which, with non-capital protected notes, is practically without limitation. Exposures assumed by the investor include principal and interest rate. Moreover,

- The principal market is currency exchange.
- There is also credit risk associated with the issuer, and
- There is political risk as well as country risk in the case of currencies other than dollar, euro, pound and yen.

A longer term example with currency exchange structured products is three-year range accrual note with 6 per cent coupon, for instance linked to the euro/US dollar, dollar denominated with principal protection. Such notes pay semi-annually a maximum coupon of 6 per cent per annum on the invested principal amount, which is, however, calculated on a daily basis. The principal amount invested will be repaid at maturity. Typically, investors buying these notes believe (or, rather, guess) that the euro/dollar exchange rate will remain within a range over the next three years, which is an absolutely undocumented assumption.

What investors do not appreciate is that investment return is defined through an algorithm most favourable to the issuer. Each day the reference rate falls inside the fixing range, the coupon accumulates at 6 per cent per annum, paid semi-annually. By contrast, for each day that the reference rate does not fix inside the fixing range, no coupon is accumulated. Therefore, this note is win–win for the bank. Total coupon payment is:

$(n/N) \cdot 6$ per cent per annum

where N = total number of business days between trade date and valuation date, and n = number of business days that the reference rate fixes inside the fixing range.

Investors should appreciate that a variety of market factors may affect the outcome. Sensitivity analyses presented in the issuer's prospectus do not reflect all possible loss scenarios, because there is no certainty that the parameters and assumptions used in these projections can be duplicated with actual trades. Most often, they cannot.

Historical exchange rates, interest rates or other reference rates or prices that are used are not necessarily indicative of future exchange rates, interest rates, or other reference rates or prices. This means that future risks are being assumed by the investor on matters that are way beyond his or her control. The same is true with other similar structured instruments in the currency exchange rate domain.

16.7   A US dollar/Asian currency basket and a forex benchmark fund

One of the major credit institutions offers its private banking clients a structured product based on an Asian currency basket, with the view that within the next two years China will revalue its currency, the renminbi (RMB). According to the issuer, the best way to gain exposure to China's revaluation is through a basket of mainly Asian currencies because, once a revaluation happens, other Asian countries will be more willing to tolerate their currencies appreciating against the US dollar. The currencies in reference are shown in Table 16.2.

- The note consists of a basket of eight Asia-Pacific currencies versus the US dollar.
- If the basket appreciates against the dollar, investors have geared participation in this positive performance with no cap.
- If the basket depreciates against the US dollar, investors' principal will be 98 per cent capital protected, with no interest paid in either case.

The currencies in this basket are weighted. These weights have been chosen to reflect the countries that would benefit from trade linkages with China. This

Table 16.2 Currencies in this structured instrument

Australian dollar
Indian rupee
Indonesian rupiah
Japanese yen
Korean won
Singapore dollar
Taiwan dollar
Thai baht

structured note provides uncapped, geared exposure to the basket and might out-perform in a rising market if, and only if, the basket as a whole rises against the US dollar.

The downside of this structured instrument, and a major one for that matter, is that the basket of currencies needs to appreciate by at least 1.52 per cent to ensure that investors receive back 100 per cent of the capital invested, and forget about prof-its. Moreover, any individual currency's strong performance against the US dollar could be offset by other currencies in the basket with negative performance. The hypothesis that a rising renminbi will carry along all boats is no more than a tenta-tive statement.

Another example of an instrument offered to institutional and retail investors involving Asian currencies is an eighteen-month US dollar-denominated Asian cur-rency basket note, with 97 per cent principal protection. An investor in this currency exchange product would be someone who thinks that an Asian currency basket can provide an enhanced return over the coming eighteen months. This note has a payout formula linked to the extent of this appreciation.

- The maximum potential return on the note is unlimited, but there may also be no return.
- A minimum of 97 per cent of principal amount invested will be repaid at maturity by the issuer, barring credit risk.

Basically, the instrument consists of a portfolio of five Asian currency positions against the US dollar. In contrast to the previous case, these five Asian currencies have equal weights. The reference index represents the value of the basket. Investment return on this note is linked to the appreciation of this reference index.

Like nearly all derivative financial products, this structured instrument involves credit risk connected to the issuer's ability to face up to his or her obligations. Not only the case of bankruptcy, but also changes in the issuer's credit rating may affect the trading value of the notes. As a holder of the notes, the investor will be an unse-cured creditor of the issuer. However, given that the investor's return depends on performance of the Asian currency basket over the term of these notes, an improve-ment in the issuer's credit ratings will not reduce the market risks related to the notes.

To the untrained eye, currency speculation may look like a game that has only an upside, but this is far from being true. Not only structured products, but also parts in forex benchmark funds have been sold to institutional and private investors without them understanding the risks they are taking. To beef up their forex skills and guess 'the right way',

- Some investors have bought models supposed to foretell movements in currency exchange, and
- Others invest in benchmark funds blindfolded, betting 'for' or 'against' the dollar or any currency whose fundamentals fall in their knowledge gap (see section 16.6).

Figure 16.6 maps the fortunes of such a forex benchmark fund in which major investors had put their money. Over a period of nearly two years, in the early 1990s, its net asset value tanked right after launch, and with one exception it stayed well under water. Then it zoomed to 1.12. Attracted by greed, many new investors joined, buying parts at high price. Five months later, the fund's net asset value had fallen to –11.

Rabbi Arthur Hertzberg has good advice to would-be forex speculators. As he related in an interview with *EIR*, some twenty-five or thirty years ago, when he was getting old enough to think seriously about making provisions for old age, a Wall Street financier and man of moral principles who helped him on financial matters gave him this advice: 'I will let you put half on Wall Street, and I will invest it for you. But, remember, you can lose it, as well as make money on it. The other half, you're going to put into bonds, you're going to put it into the safest possible kind of investment, so that if everything else goes to hell, you will still be able to eat'.[6]

In the interview to *EIR*, Rabbi Hertzberg said that he has followed that principle and found it rewarding. He also added that, 'Everything else is speculative'. If investing in stocks is speculative, think of throwing money at leveraged currency

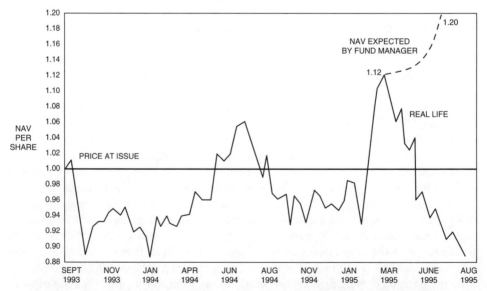

Figure 16.6 Forex benchmark fund: net asset value (NAV) per share (US dollars)

exchange instruments and other structured products, about whose market behaviour one knows nothing.

16.8 Conclusion

Structured products involve major risks. Many of these risks are unknown to the investor in terms of their frequency and magnitude. Quite often, these risks are also unknown to the issuer. The greater exposure lies not in the high frequency of the distribution but in its tails, and this is the domain of stress tests.

The concept underpinning stress testing was introduced in Chapter 4. Stress tests go beyond normal tests targeting events that happen at the long leg of a risk and return distribution. These are typically low-frequency but high-impact (LF/HI) events that can wipe out portfolio positions and turn a fortune into dust.

Institutional investors should definitely acquire skills in stress testing and undertake tightened inspection of their portfolio positions regularly. No investment is immune to tail events and the high risk associated with them. Even private investors can acquire stress test skills, through appropriate training.[7] All investors should appreciate that what they are really testing is the future of *their* fortune.

Another matter on which institutional and private investors should keep their eyes wide open is management risk, and its aftermath. This is best exemplified by the long list of *Spitzer investigations* (named after Eliot Spitzer, the New York State attorney general), that took place in the first years of the twenty-first century and brought to light a long list of scams.

It is fairly safe to assume that the public reaction to the investigations into the business behaviour of many players – bankers, insurers, brokers and even customers – revealed an awful lack of ethics. This lack of ethics might have been much less damaging to the public if the investment business had not been:

- A very special function in our economic and social system, and
- One of the pillars sustaining the edifice of the ownership society.

Many of the activities discovered by the Spitzer investigations were nearly criminal and would have been prosecuted in any other business sector as well. But this case is worse in banking, insurance and the investment business at large, because all activity relies on trust, and when trust is destroyed, nothing can go any more.

Sound, factual and well-documented investment advice is not only a professional responsibility, it is also a matter of *virtue* on behalf of the person who gives it; and as, the Ancient Greek philosopher Socrates said, virtue is knowledge that cannot be taught.

For their part, investors should be prepared to live with uncertainty, because nothing is 'sure' in financial and business life. A Wall Street adage expresses this concept in a nutshell: 'What is most expected to happen is least likely to take place. The unexpected has a better chance.'

When the financial markets operate in an environment of trust, institutions and people improve their knowledge about the value of *their* assets and what might threaten them. The buying of an investment product, whether or not structured, should be closely tied to a risk assessment exercise.

Banks often conduct such tests. The point is that their results must be fully shared with the prospective client. In this way, banks and other financial companies would act as crucial providers not only of products and services, but also of knowledge and training to their clients. Moral hazard can cut both ways and some people become more reckless when their risk exposure is supposedly covered through what has become known as 'capital protection'.

While risk assessment is a 'must', the additional effects of comprehension of the uncertainty associated with risk and return (including exposure at the tails of the risk distribution) are important for both ex ante activities, such as efficient prevention, and ex post activities, such as speedier and better focused damage control. As people and organizations learn more about their exposure, they often change their behaviour and become more risk averse.

As for the reader who had the luck to make some money with one or two currency exchange structured products, he or she should heed the advice that Darius, the king of kings, gave to Alexander, his challenger and successor, in the third century BC: 'I advise you not to challenge fate, because it is a fickle companion and might just turn its back on you at any moment'.[8]

Notes

1 D.N. Chorafas, *The Management of Equity Investments*, Butterworth-Heinemann, London, 2005.
2 These figures come from BIS reports, and they are valid as of April 2004.
3 D.N. Chorafas, *The Real-time Enterprise*, Auerbach, New York, 2005.
4 *Economist*, 13 December 2003.
5 *EIR*, 11 February 2005.
6 D.N. Chorafas, *Stress Testing. Risk Management Strategies for Extreme Events*, Euromoney, London, 2003.
7 V.M. Manfredi, *Alexander. The Sands of Ammon*, Pan/Macmillan, London, 2001.

Appendix Derivatives as a tax haven

A.1 Introduction

Every jurisdiction has its own tax policies and rates, as well as procedures and means of enriching the government's coffers. While there is a myriad of taxes, only two of them are of interest in this appendix, because they are the only ones that may be applicable to transactions involving derivative instruments and structured products:

- Wealth tax, and
- Income tax.

Moreover, because derivatives deals are increasingly used as means for tax evasion, this appendix will look at how people and companies try to engineer what they call 'tax optimization' through derivative financial instruments and their alter-ego, the offshores.

A.2 Wealth tax

In contrast to real property such as land and buildings, the ownership of financial instruments usually leaves no footprint regarding a person's or a company's wealth. This is an important consideration as far as taxes are concerned. Invented by socialist governments to appease the 'have-nots', wealth tax has been one of those measures that proved to be ineffective and counterproductive, but it is still practised in many jurisdictions.

If governments have taxation, investors have their own adage, which says: 'Money is like hearts. It goes where it is appreciated.' Some jurisdictions have taken note of it. Indeed, the majority of wealthy countries cut their top tax rates by an average of 2.4 percentage points between 2000 and 2005 because of growing concern about disincentives of overtaxing personal income and wealth.

While a system of checks and balances is of crucial importance in fighting tax evasion, too much tax kills the tax receipts. Therefore, the more clear-eyed governments are now questioning whether imposing large tax burdens on high earners, and beyond that taxing them on their wealth, actually boost revenues.

Belatedly, 'tax and tax' politicians are findings out that there are some core principles about the relationship between taxes, incentives and economic performance.

For the majority of the population, higher marginal taxes reduce work incentives; and they also have the adverse effect of driving high net worth individuals to tax havens.

In Sweden, most of the richer people who care to take proper tax advice usually find ways to get around the wealth tax, often by taking on loans or adjusting their portfolios of equities at the right moment. As a result, it is usually the less wealthy or mediocre tax optimizers who are caught in the wealth tax trap. 'We must tax the poor, they are the more numerous', said André Tardieu, a French socialist prime minister in the early 1930s.

It is interesting to note that this wealth tax experience has not been rewarding for the Swedish government. Plenty of evidence suggests that it has been a highly inefficient proposition, since it does not produce much income for the government's coffers. In 2002 it contributed only SKr 6.5 billion ($8 billion). This compares poorly to more than SKr 500 billion that Swedes are thought to have stashed offshore, away from their government's eyes.

Recent news from Sweden suggests that even its socialist 'tax the rich' government is considering abolishing the wealth tax. In the words of the country's prime minister, 'It's neither fair nor efficient. It brings in some money but it probably erodes the overall tax base substantially'.[1] Governments are expected to be aware that their miscalculations in regard to taxation carry a heavy price.

The Swedish prime minister also admitted that wealth tax also causes some peculiar distortions. For example, shares on the A-list of the Stockholm Stock Exchange have to be declared for wealth tax purposes, but shares on the O-list (generally smaller companies) do not usually have to be declared. However, although the wealth tax is inefficient, it is not easy for a socialist government to scrap it because it has been advertised too long as a 'just tax' and the socialist party's voters believe that it is a way to:

- Punish the rich, and
- Assist in wealth redistribution, whatever this might mean.

Still, tax and tax socialist policies that are sometimes implemented, or at least maintained, even by centre-right governments, are so persistent and biting that they should not be taken lightly. To be appropriately informed, investors should consult their own financial, accounting and tax advisors about the risks associated with investments in structured instruments, as well as:

- The appropriate tools to analyse their risk and return,
- Their suitability in each investor's particular circumstances, and
- Their impact on the investor's wealth, as well as on other taxes.

The irony is that because no private investor has yet become wealthy by betting on structured derivative products – and this is unlikely to happen in the foreseeable future – there is not much risk that structured financial instruments, single-handedly, would make a person subject to wealth tax. On the contrary, derivatives have been used on many occasions, and quite successfully, as a way to minimize income tax.

A.3 Derivatives, offshores and private individuals

In the USA, the Internal Revenue Service (IRS) is concerned about the growth of foreign trusts that mainly consist of several layer firms. The strategy behind these trusts is that one is distributing income to the next, thereby reducing taxes to a bare minimum. There is also an expanding horizon of tax havens, such as the greater Caribbean region, which amounts to 20 per cent of an estimated $7.0 trillion in offshore assets.

No wonder offshores are now targeted by the Group of Ten (G10) as engaging in 'harmful tax practices'; harmful, that is, to the countries of G10 which see part of their citizens' wealth behind a screen and their taxes drained away. Unless these tax havens agree to revamp their current tax systems, the G10 nations are threatening to hit them with sweeping sanctions:

- From disallowing the large tax write-offs that offshore companies typically take for business costs,
- To ending double taxation agreements, by which companies avoid paying taxes at home if they pay them at the offshore address.

Financial institutions and other companies are, however, inventive. The heydays of the offshores are now past, not so much because of G10 restrictions as for the fact that financial institutions have found out that the use of a derivative instrument can waive certain tax provisions, particularly those provisions that might have a major tax impact if a traditional investment formula were used. For example:

- Taxation of derivative transactions depends on their particular legal form and on the underlying to which they relate.
- Withholding tax obligation is triggered upon the payment of interest, but swap payments escape this tax clause, thereby opening a floodgate of tax avoidance.

Profits from deals with payments made under swap agreements are typically computed by reference to a notional principal amount. As such, they are not regarded as 'interest' for tax purposes, because no underlying loan exists between the counterparties. Even though certain swap payments may have some characteristics of annual receipts, authorities do not necessarily regard them as such.

A similar argument is valid about regular swap receipts and payments that relate to interest on trade borrowings. In computing trading profits, the interest on trade borrowing is tax deductible. Other derivative instruments, too, fall into this class, whose tax characteristics lie in a twilight zone between what is and is not taxable.

For instance, profit derived from the use of financial derivatives in the ordinary course of banking trade tends to be regarded for tax purposes as being part of trading profits. Different jurisdictions, however, do not have a homogeneous approach to this issue. Moreover, permitted accounting treatment plays an important role in determining:

- The recognition of such profits, and
- The timing of this recognition for taxation reasons.

In the specific case of income from structured instruments, amounts due to be paid to an investor are described on a gross basis, without calculating tax liability. Typically, the issuer makes no deduction for any tax, duty or other charge unless required to do so by law. It is then up to the investor to declare profits and losses from structured products.

At the same time, however, investors should be warned that tax treatment of profit and loss from structured products can be complex. Therefore, to avoid getting into trouble with tax authorities, investors should obtain professional tax advice appropriate to their own circumstances before investing in derivatives. They should also keep in mind that, in the general case, taxation may be altered during the term of a structured product.

Investors should also be aware that there exist alternatives that may be better than taking on derivatives risk. According to a book review in *BusinessWeek*, in *The New Logic of Money and Power in Hollywood* (Random House, 2005), Edward Jay Epstein digs into Hollywood financial schemes to find that Arnold Schwarzenegger 'lent' his services to *Terminator 3*. His pay of $29.25 million went not to him personally, but to the actor's company, Oak Productions Inc., a stratagem that allowed Schwarzenegger to avoid certain tax liabilities.[2]

A.4   Companies have been masters in using derivatives and offshores

Reports released in mid-February 2003 to the US Senate Finance Committee document that Enron, and other big companies, have consistently escaped US taxes through financial manoeuvres so complex that the IRS has been unable to understand them. Many of these twisted affairs were derivatives based. Experts spent nearly a year going over Enron's tax returns to work out what was happening.

From the accounts of knowledgeable people privy to the findings of these investigations, American companies have also found a good way to avoid taxes by exploiting differences in the rules governing the two sets of books that all companies must keep:

- One of the two books is for shareholders,
- The other is for the IRS.

Differences between what are known as *book accounting* and *tax accounting* can be used to make a good chunk of taxes disappear. This usually involves costly derivative transactions that create risks for shareholders, and most of these risks are not disclosed. Current laws, the experts add, are ineffective at stopping the use of such transactions, the only purpose of which is to avoid paying taxes.

These and other findings were revealed in the February 2003 report to the US Senate Finance Committee, which contained disclosures on corporate tax avoidance, as well as details on outrageous executive compensation through options and other gimmicks. In the specific case of Enron, the aforementioned report painted a shocking picture of:

- Its tax avoidance strategies,
- Its structured transactions, and
- Its huge executive compensation.

Enron, of course, is not alone. These practices have by now become widespread, involving many other companies that out-complex the IRS. More and more evidence suggests that, accustomed to handling classical accounting misrepresentations and double books, the IRS just cannot handle the inherent complexity of some of the derivatives transactions with a major impact on taxes.

Offshores, too, have contributed to a greater complexity of tax declarations. For instance, Enron created 881 offshore subsidiaries, 692 of them in the Cayman Islands, as part of its strategy to avoid taxes. After the company's December 2001 bankruptcy, the new management of Enron co-operated with tax authorities and the US Senate study,

- Turning over internal documents, and
- Helping tax lawyers, accountants and economists, on the joint committee staff, to understand the transactions.

Evidence available some time after the bankruptcy had indicated that Enron did not pay taxes in four of the five years before its collapse. More recently, however, the company has hinted that it might have paid some tax in those four years, because of a levy known as the 'corporate alternative minimum tax'. If it did so, that would raise fresh questions about:

- The reliability of reports to shareholders, and
- Whether the Securities and Exchange Commission (SEC) is adequately policing rules on disclosing material information contained in official financial statements.

Moreover, the case of offshores took a new twist when, in January 2003, Wall Street became nervous about big companies registered in tax havens. The reason was the aftereffects connected to president George W. Bush's plan to eliminate taxes that investors pay on stock dividends. Buried in the fine print is a condition that would strike a blow against corporate tax shelters by forcing companies to choose between:

- Slashing their own tax bills, and
- Ensuring dividend relief for their investors.

For instance, a company that did not pay corporate income taxes, thanks to credits, shelters, derivative instruments and so on, would find that the eligibility of its shareholders for dividend tax relief is very limited. Theoretically, this could push CEOs and CFOs to trim their reliance on tax breaks. Practically, it could make investors dump the equities of companies that persist in patronizing tax havens.

'This is a big deal', says one congressional tax expert, 'dramatically changing the economics of these tax preferences'. Behind this reference lies the fact that such a move would undermine corporate tax avoidance. The stakes are high. According to one estimate, among large companies, in 1998 book earnings exceeded taxable income by $287 billion.[3]

A.5   Shifting the 'Risk with No Return' to the household sector

Today, many companies, both financial and industrial, make a big chunk of their earnings by gambling through derivative financial instruments. Because derivative products are traded, for the most part, outside of official exchanges, in the form of bilateral deals between two counterparties, nobody really knows the actual dimension of toxic waste in the banks' trading books – including the financial institutions who own them.

Banks aside, a substantial amount of betting through derivatives is done by hedge funds, which are not subject to any kind of regulation or supervision. Then, hedge funds and banks working in unison shift part of this risk to the household sector, as we will see in this section. How deep is the derivatives abyss? According to the Bank for International Settlements (BIS):

- In early 2005 the outstanding volume of over-the-counter derivatives alone amounted to $248 trillion, while the annual turnover of exchange-traded derivatives is close to $900 trillion.
- If so, because exchange traded derivatives account for about 22 percent of the total, annually traded derivatives stand at more than $4 quadrillion, with about $3.18 quadrillion over the counter (OTC).

This means that the financial world is sitting on a balloon with $4 quadrillion of hot air, and part of this hot air is pumped into the savings and investment accounts of households, through structured financial instruments (see Chapter 9 to 16). With derivatives becoming the tool of megaspeculation, all this trading is a waste:

- It's like burning wood to sell the ashes, and
- At the same time unloading all of the risk but giving none of the profits on the households.

Quoting from the BIS 75th Annual Report: 'Recent structural trends point to a shift of risk bearing away from financial institutions and markets, and towards the household sector. Some of this shift is voluntary. Greater access to diverse financing tools has increased household debt relative to income...'. These trends, BIS suggests, raise the question of whether this shift might affect the risk-bearing capacity of the economy, pointing out that:

- 'Households are the ultimate bearers of all economic enterprises', and
- 'The overall level of financial risk is not independent of the financial structure, institutional features or the distribution of risk-bearing.'

The overall level of financial risk is spread to the households with no real return to the risk-takers; which means the households and private banking clients. Table A.1 documents the statement just made. It tells the story of how clients are being cheated of the returns they should have had by means of structured financial products (For the complete case study, see D.N. Chorafas *IFRS, Fair Value and Corporate Governance: The Impact on Budgets, Balance Sheet and Management Accounts*, Butterworth-Heinemann, 2006).

Table A.1 Shifting the 'Risk with No Return' to the household sector

Structured Financial Instrument	Market Values				Return on Structured Instruments			
	Start Value at Beginning of Term	Current Value (12.7.05)	Difference in Points	Difference in %	When Bought	On 12.7.05	Investor Gain/Loss	Final Difference to Investor Disfavour
'SMI Certificate' Zurich Stock Exchange	5693	6323	Up 630	+11.1	100	101–102	1%	−10.1%
'Nikkei Certificate' Tokyo Stock Exchange	11 × 488	11 × 623	Up 135	+1.0	100	96–97	−4%	−5%

There has been as well a 10% Bonus Coupon Note which has no index for direct comparison. The bank who sold the "alternative investment" says that over the elapsed year, its overall performance was 6.80%. What the investor got was 1.37% – a difference of 5.43% to his disfavor.

A.6   Cynics look at the private banking client as a cash cow

The case study in section A.5 should have been enough to convey the message that private banking clients should be double careful about what they buy, particularly when structured instruments are concerned. A thorough risk and return evaluation should take place not only prior to making the commitment, but also on yearly basis, or more frequently, to make sure if there is return for risk being assumed.

The asymmetrical nature of risk and return, exemplified by the three structured products, is by no means the investor's only worry. Private banking clients should also be watching out for all sorts of tricks *some* of the banks are in the habit of pulling. The main body of this book has given several examples from real life, but I kept the best one on account management irregularities and illegalities for the end.

This is the case of one of the better known international banks which, through a letter dated July 27, 2005 summarily informed its private banking client about a size-able charge to his account for 'custody fees', without bothering to detail over which period these fees were applied or the services to which they correspond. This July 2005 mail made reference to a confirmation letter of five years earlier (30 June 2000). Such letter, however, concerned a company account not a private one.

In fact, the international bank in reference had written as well other letters dated February 15, 2000, and March 10, 2000, to the representative of the *company* which owned the account. All of them were stating that:

'We are pleased to advise you that we should be able to do away with custodian, coupon and dividend income collection fees. As you see this is highly competitive in the banking environment in which we operate.'

In none of the letters officially written by the bank was mentioned a US $5 million limit for this clause to be effective. What was said in the paragraph preceding the above confirmation, was a statement about the company's intention, not a minimum requirement implied on the bank's behalf.

To make matters more complex, the person who wrote the July 27, 2005 letter for the bank was a lawyer and compliance officer. It is curious having to explain to a lawyer that the argument about a minimum account level will not stand up in court due to lack of evidence. Moreover, there is no excuse that a bank (particularly a major institution like the one subject of this case study) and its highly paid executives, do not know the difference between:

- A legal entity and its representative, and
- A physical entity which several years down the line had the misfortune of becoming its private banking client.

There have been absolutely no conditions outlined regarding a minimum amount balance in the second case, or even fees. No document of that sort was addressed to the owner of the personal private banking account at the bank. This is plain mismanagement on the bank's behalf.

The confusion in the head of private banking executives between two different entities and accounts, and resulting predatory charges, was by no means the only legal reason for re-crediting these charges. There has been as well the fact that the company account itself was solicited by a senior executive of the bank in reference, and opened on the specific condition there will be no charges – a pledge for which the executive gave his word of honor.

Evidence to this has been provided over a multi-year period. It lies in the fact that when charges were made, these charges were indeed reversed. Such reversal of charges has happened over five years, thereby creating *a pattern of full circumstantial evidence*, including:

- Safekeeping fees, and
- Charges of commission for collection of dividends.

Illegal, irrelevant and abusive charges are by no means a specialty of *this* bank. Based on its examination of publicly available information, *The Economist* recently published a very interesting article on what goes on behind the customer's back, when credit institutions engage in a desperate attempt to boost profits.

The article concerns a highly controversial deal around Banca Populare Italiana (BPI) and its efforts to take over Banca Antoniana Popolare Veneta – a much bigger entity. To beautify its balance sheet and P&L, in the fourth quarter of 2004 BPI charged customer accounts with unusual entries, amounting to Euro 30 million in increased 'expenses'.

Astonished customers, *The Economist* says, suffered charges ranging from €30 to €125, for items such as 'urgent commissions', 'post and telephone expenses', and 'extraordinary commissions'. Their bank statements have been subject to creative accounting on the bank's behalf. Not surprisingly,

- Many asked for reimbursement, and
- Some raised the matter with the judicial authorities.[4]

In the case of the bank which is the main theme of this section, in mid-August 2005 the client informed its chairman and its CEO (the latter through registered letter with receipt) not only about the facts just described, but as well that his account has been mismanaged in a financial accounting sense; a case bordering on fraud. Whether this was a failure of omission or commission is irrelevant. What is relevant is that money has been missing from the account for over a month.

Specifically this concerned an important credit of dividends paid on June 9, 2005 and credited in the client's account on July 11, a month later, only *after* the client specifically complained to the bank that credit for the dividend was missing from the account.

Everything told, the inefficiency of Private Banking at this major credit institution makes a legend, and the successive failures to meet commitments and honor promises have been one long deception. This damned way of handling private banking accounts is, to say the least, cynical – a word characterizing the acts of cynics. There is practically no limit to what cynics might do.

In ancient Greece, Diogenes and his followers were called *cynics* because, according to their theories, nothing that is 'natural' can be judged obscene, and so they did everything in public. Just like dogs.[5]

Notes

1 *Financial Times*, 29/30 November 2003.
2 *BusinessWeek*, 28 March 2005.
3 *BusinessWeek*, 20 January 2003.
4 *The Economist*, August 13 2005.
5 Valerio Massimo Manfredi. *Alexander* Pan Books, Macmillan, Londan, 2001

Index